SANCTIFY THEM IN THE TRUTH

*To the people who gather to worship God
at Aldersgate United Methodist Church,
Chapel Hill, North Carolina*

SANCTIFY THEM IN THE TRUTH

Holiness Exemplified

❧

STANLEY HAUERWAS

ABINGDON PRESS
NASHVILLE

SANCTIFY THEM IN THE TRUTH

Published in Great Britain by T&T Clark Ltd
59 George Street, Edinburgh EH2 2LQ, Scotland

This edition published under license from T&T Clark Ltd by Abingdon Press.

Library of Congress Cataloging-in-Publication Data

Hauerwas, Stanley, 1940–
  Sanctify them in the truth : holiness exemplified / Stanley Hauerwas.
    p.   cm.
  ISBN 0-687-08223-4 (pbk.)
  1. Truth (Christian theology).   2. Sanctification.   3. Holiness.
  I. Title.
  BT50.H36   1998
  230'.76—dc21   98-44290
                                                                CIP

Typeset by Waverley Typesetters, Galashiels
Printed and bound in Great Britain by Page Bros, Norwich

Contents

Acknowledgments   ix

Preface   xi

Introduction   1

Part I

THE TASK OF THEOLOGICAL ETHICS: TRUTHFUL SPEECH

1   On Doctrine and Ethics   19

2   The Truth about God: The Decalogue as Condition
    for Truthful Speech   37

3   'Salvation even in Sin': Learning to Speak Truthfully
    about Ourselves   61

Part II

THE TRUTH ABOUT SANCTIFICATION: HOLINESS EXEMPLIFIED

4   The Sanctified Body: Why Perfection Does Not Require
    a 'Self'   77

5   Going Forward by Looking Back: Agency Reconsidered   93

6   Gay Friendship: A Thought Experiment in Catholic Moral
    Theology   105

7   Characterizing Perfection: Second Thoughts on Character
    and Sanctification   123

8   Timeful Friends: Living with the Handicapped   143

9   In Defense of Cultural Christianity: Reflections on
    Going to Church   157

Part III

SPEAKING TRUTHFULLY IN, FOR, AND AGAINST THE WORLD

10 The Non-Violent Terrorist: In Defense of Christian
    Fanaticism   177

11 No Enemy, No Christianity: Preaching between 'Worlds'   191

12 Christians in the Hands of Flaccid Secularists: Theology
    and 'Moral Inquiry' in the Modern University   201

13 Christian Schooling or Making Students Dysfunctional   219

14 For Dappled Things   227

Part IV

SERMONIC ILLUSTRATIONS

15 Practice Preaching   235

16 Reformation Is Sin   241

17 The Cruelty of Peace   245

18 Living on Dishonest Wealth   249

19 God's Grandeur   253

20 On Not Holding On or Witnessing the Resurrection   259

Index   263

Acknowledgments

The author and publisher are grateful to the following for permission to reprint:

Cambridge University Press, publishers of *The Cambridge Companion to Christian Doctrine*, edited by Golin Gunton, 1997, for 'On Doctrine and Ethics.'

New Zeitschrift für Systematische Theologie und Religionsphilosophie for 'The Truth about God: The Decalogue as Condition for Truthful Speech,' reprinted from vol. 40 (1998): 17–39.

The Pilgrim Press, publishers of *Christian Ethics: Problems and Prospects*, edited by Lisa Cahill and James Childress, 1996, for 'Going Forward by Looking Back: Agency Reconsidered.'

Irish Theological Quarterly for 'Gay Friendship: A Thought Experiment in Catholic Moral Theology,' there published as 'Virtue, Description, and Friendship,' reprinted from vol. 62/2–3 (1996–97): 170–84.

Kingswood Books, publishers of *Wesleyan Theology Today: Bicentennial Theological Consultation*, edited by Theodore Runyan, 1985, for 'Characterizing Perfection: Second Thoughts on Character and Sanctification.'

The Journal of Preachers for 'Practice Preaching,' reprinted from vol. XVIII/1 (Advent 1994): 21–24; for 'Living on Dishonest Wealth,' reprinted from vol. XX/1 (Advent 1996): 15–17; for 'On Not Holding On or Witnessing the Resurrection,' there published as 'The Resurrection and the Jesus Seminar: A Sermon with Commentary.' from vol. XXI, 3 (Easter 1998): 25–29.

Preface

I am grateful to be able to dedicate this book to the people who constitute the Body of Christ at Aldersgate United Methodist Church in Chapel Hill, North Carolina. I am even more grateful that these same people, along with our Pastor, the Reverend Susan Allred, have been such a sustaining community for my wife, Paula Gilbert, and myself. Anyone reading this book will understand why dedicating the book to Aldersgate requires no further explanation.

This is the second time I have dedicated a book to a church. *The Peaceable Kingdom* was dedicated to Broadway United Methodist Church in South Bend, Indiana. I seem condemned not only to be a Methodist but to be a member of churches whose names I do not like. I would like a name like 'Saint James by the Sea' or even 'Holy Family.' Instead, I get Broadway, which was named after the street it faced, and Aldersgate, a name that has served as a pietistic distortion for the reading of Methodist history. The last thing I desire is to have my heart 'strangely warmed,' particularly among Methodists. However, I take it as a sign of the material character of God's good care to make me come to terms with being stuck in churches in which not only do I have to learn to live but with whom I fall hopelessly in love.

There are, though, limits. Aldersgate is in Chapel Hill, North Carolina. Most of the congregation support the basketball team called (for no apparent reason) the 'Tar Heels.' They even say they like the faded baby blue color called 'Carolina blue.' Paula and I are Duke basketball fans which means we are the subject of much derision. It is a great thing that God has made us a church in spite of this great division.

Of course, the Gospel is about how strangers can be made friends. For reasons completely inexplicable, those people called Scots have claimed me as a friend. I have been honored to be made a Doctor of Divinity by the University of Edinburgh. I will give the Gifford Lectures at St Andrews in 2000–2001. This book is the result of being asked to be the *Scottish Journal of Theology* lecturer in 1997 at the University of Aberdeen. My only explanation is that the Scots, like Texans, have long been ruled by a foreign power, which may not only create certain sympathies but also provide common skills for survival. Whatever the explanation, I am indeed grateful to the Scots kind enough to take my work seriously even if that means helping me see where I may be mistaken.

I am particularly grateful to Morag and Iain Torrance for their wonderful hospitality while I was in Aberdeen. I am indebted to Iain not only for making the lectures possible but also for helping me conceive the book. He made the suggestion that 'Gay Friendship' should be included not only because it extends the analysis of agency but also because it exemplifies a kind of casuistry made possible by a people committed to being holy. I am, of course, also grateful to the Department of Divinity with Religious Studies, and in particular David Fergusson, at Aberdeen for being such wonderful conversation partners during my stay with them.

While I was in Aberdeen, Iain gave me a copy of John Buchan's fine novel *Witch Wood*. In one of the explanatory notes to that novel, we are told that one of Buchan's favorite quotations was from the seventeenth-century Quaker, Isaac Pennington:

> All truth is shadow except the last truth. But all truth is substantial in its own place, though it be but a shadow in another place. And the shadow is a true shadow, as the substance is true substance.[1]

In a book entitled *Sanctify Them in the Truth* such a truth is important to remember, since it is surely our God's power to be present in Jesus that makes possible our ability to be, as well as to speak, the truth to one another in different places and times.

I am, as usual, in debt to many for helping me make this book a reality. Jim Fodor in particular must be mentioned, along with my Dean, Greg Jones. I am wonderfully supported by graduate students – David Cloutier, Chris Huebner, Kelly Johnson, Joel Shuman, David Stubbs, Laura Yordy – who make me think better than I could do on my own. The onerous work of indexing fell on Abraham Nussbaum, the son of students I taught as undergraduates at Notre Dame (am I getting old or what?). How extraordinary that Christianity, even in America, can produce people like Abraham. What a gift. Sarah Freedman serves as Secretary to the Faculty at the Divinity School at Duke. How she does that God only knows. I know, however, how much she does for me. Without her this book could not and would not exist. I thank God not only for her intelligence but for her wacky sense of humor.

By the time this book is published, Paula and I will be grandparents. For that and much else we thank Laura and Adam. How wonderful our God is to make us a people of hope who need not fear being surprised.

---

[1] John Buchan, *Witch Wood*, edited with an Introduction by James C. G. Greig (Oxford: Oxford University Press, 1993), 313.

Introduction

The 'Rough Ground' of Theology

The invitation to give the *Scottish Journal of Theology Lectures* indicated that I was free to lecture on any subject I wished. In a polite yet unequivocal manner, however, it was suggested that many people in Scotland (and, perhaps, elsewhere) would be quite pleased if I used this occasion to make my theological views explicit. It was observed that readers of my work sense what I do has been and continues to be shaped by strong theological judgements and decisions and such readers would welcome a more candid statement by me of my theological position. In effect, I think I was being told that in Scotland I should feel free to do some 'real' theology.

To be free to do theology in our current academic and social worlds is a wonderful permission and gift. The loss of theology's status as a knowledge deserving of recognition in the current academy has often meant that, if theology is done at all, it must be disguised as history, cultural criticism, ethics, or, may God forgive us, sociology. The problem with such disguises is that, unfortunately, the disguise very quickly becomes the reality, which means that theology gets left behind. As much as I have tried surreptitiously to do theology under the cover of ethics, I suspect at least some, particularly in Scotland, have worried that I have subverted the theological task.

So the invitation for me to do theology 'straight up,' so to speak, should be something I particularly welcome. Yet I am by no means sure those who wish me to do theology in a more straightforward manner will be happy with what they find in this book. To be given the permission to do theology is, at least for me, a frightening task. I am not sure I know how to do theology 'straight,' which means I may well disappoint those who think that if pushed, I will know how to 'pay up' theologically. It is not that I am just unsure how to do theology, but that even if I knew how, I am not sure I would want to do it. At least I am not sure I want to do theology the way many who bear the title 'theologian' do. I certainly have learned and continue to learn from those who do theology in a more systematic fashion than my work takes, but I continue to worry that such theology in our time cannot

I

avoid giving the impression that Christianity is a set of ideas that need to be made consistent with one another.

Of course it is true that 'all *loci* of theology are interconnected as nodes of an intricate web,'[1] which rightly requires theologians – in a manner not unlike that of spiders – to explore, repair, as well as, perhaps, discover new connections. Theology is always a matter of finding the interconnections in a manner that helps our lives not to be distorted by overemphasis on one aspect of the faith. For example, the recovery of the significance of the doctrine of the Trinity in contemporary theology was not only necessary to distinguish the God we worship from the god of the deists, but that recovery had the happy effect of forcing Christians to reassess our relation to the people of Israel. At the very least, the doctrine of the Trinity has been the church's attempt to make clear that the God we know in Jesus Christ is not different from the God that called Israel to be God's promised people.[2]

That theology works like a web helps us understand why the work of theology is never done. Webs, after all, are fragile. They must constantly be redone. Theology can become a fascinating game in which the various *loci* are reconfigured by making one *locus* determinative for all the others. This kind of theology has been turned into an art form in Germany, in which every theologian is expected to produce something called 'doctrine.' Theology so produced can be quite impressive. It can give one a sense of 'completeness,' but such 'completeness' can be quite deceptive. Too often, I fear, this mode of theology provides answers to questions no one is asking.

Indeed, one of the aspects of Barth's theology that has always attracted me is the unfinished character of the *Church Dogmatics*. By 'unfinished' I do not mean that he did not live to complete volume four; but even if he had been able to accomplish that task, everything would have yet remained to be done. Each volume of the *Dogmatics* exemplifies how any attempt to treat one aspect of Christian doctrine

---

[1] Robert Jenson, 'The Church and the Sacraments,' in Colin Gunton (ed.), *The Cambridge Companion to Christian Doctrine* (Cambridge: Cambridge University Press, 1997), 207. Since I have an essay in Gunton's book, it may seem disingenuous for me to say that I regard this book as one of the most helpful for introducing the basics of Christian theology, but I certainly think that to be the case. My essay, 'On Doctrine and Ethics,' now stands as this book's first essay. For a systematic presentation I much admire, see Jenson's *Systematic Theology*, Vol. 1 (New York: Oxford University Press, 1997).

[2] For an extraordinary account of these matters, see Bruce Marshall's article, 'Christ and the Cultures: the Jewish people and Christian Theology,' in *The Cambridge Companion to Christian Doctrine*, 81–100. Also of note is R. Kendall Soulen's, *The God of Israel and Christian Theology* (Minneapolis: Fortress Press, 1996). While I am deeply appreciative of Soulen's book, I am more sympathetic with Marshall's account of how the Trinity helps Christians understand the God's calling of Israel as well as the continuing importance of the Jews for Christian theology. For a wonderful exploration of these issues, see Scott Bader-Saye, *Aristotle or Abraham: Church, Israel, and the Politics of Election* (PhD dissertation: Duke University, 1997).

2

requires all the others in a manner demanding that you return to the beginning and start all over again – which is particularly challenging once you recognize, as Barth did, that there is no one beginning or place to start, since Christian theology always finds itself *in medias res*. The massiveness of the *Dogmatics* witnesses to Barth's confidence that the truthfulness of the Christian faith does not depend on theologians 'getting it right.'[3]

Yet the appeal to Barth as an exemplary theologian raises the thorny question of why, given the opportunity finally to 'do' some theology, I continue to be coy. (At least I suspect that what I have done in this book will frustrate some who would like my theological views to be more explicit.) Even though the essays in the first part of the book may appear to be more strictly theological than some of my past work, the chapters of this book still look like the same strange mixture of theology, ethics, social criticism, sermonic asides and illustrations, and polemics which readers have become accustomed to expect from my pen. Why do I seem to resist just doing some good old-fashioned theology?

There are no doubt many reasons for why I have learned to write (and, of course, to think) the ways I have over the years. Trying to find time to write in a busy schedule no doubt explains something of the character of my work. That I often write in response to specific occasions and challenges may be another reason my work appears occasionalistic, devoid of anything resembling a 'center.'[4] Moreover, I am an academic theologian, which means that I must constantly respond to the challenges of doing theology within the constraints of a contemporary university. No matter how critical I may be of such constraints, it nonetheless remains true that even arguments meant to clear the ground for theology have the ironic result that one never gets around to doing theology.

Without denying any of these explanations, I hope that one of the ordinary reasons I do not ever seem to get around to doing 'real' theology is that I am a very simple believer. That way of putting the matter is not quite right. The truth is that I simply believe, or at least I believe I should want to believe, what the church believes. Believing thus means I never get over being surprised by what wonderful things the church affirms that at best I only dimly 'understand.' Therefore, I

---

[3] This does not mean, of course, that Barth thought the question of the truthfulness of Christian claims unimportant. For example, see George Hunsinger's account of Barth's understanding of truth in his *How To Read Karl Barth: The Shape of His Theology* (New York: Oxford University Press, 1991).

[4] I have made no attempt to hide the occasional nature of these essays. As will be apparent, some were written as *Festschrift* articles, others for particular occasions and conferences, and some 'because I wanted to.' Knowing I was to do the *Scottish Journal of Theology Lectures*, however, enabled me to write the different essays with some sense of how they might contribute to the general argument of the book. The four lectures that I delivered in Aberdeen were 'The Truth About God,' 'Salvation Even in Sin,' 'The Sanctified Body,' and 'The Non-violent Terrorist.'

do not assume that my task as a theologian is to make what the church believes somehow more truthful than the truth inherent in the fact that this is what the church believes. One of the reasons, moreover, why I resist those who urge me to 'pull it all together' is that attempts to do so impose false unity on the wonderful anarchy of life called church.[5]

Such a declaration invites, particularly in our time, counter-declarations that it is by no means clear what the church believes, which church is doing the believing, or why the church should believe now what was believed 'back then.' These are not unimportant questions and I have no wish to silence them. But if you begin theological work with such questions you seldom get around to the work that is theology. Theology becomes instead a discussion of methodological considerations about how to do theology, if you should ever get around to doing any. This way of approaching theology, or better of evading theology's challenge, has been turned into an art form in the United States.[6]

I do not presume, therefore, that I can or do represent anything so grand as a theological position or method. But there is a kind of 'method to my madness' in the way I do theology. That 'method,' I suspect, is one of the reasons why I frustrate those who want me to be more 'theological.' Indeed, I should like to think that, at least in some ways, this book does what those who were kind enough to invite me to give the *Scottish Journal of Theology Lectures* suggested I do – that is, make more candid my theological convictions. Yet my theological convictions mean that my theological method cannot help but appear haphazard to these expectant readers when contrasted to those who believe that theology has no claim to truth unless displayed as a system of ideas.

In John 17, Jesus prays that those that follow him be sanctified in the truth. 'Sanctification' and 'truth' are seldom paired in contemporary philosophy or theology. It is as if we think it possible to determine in

---

[5] One of the reasons I am so fond of the work of Aquinas, Barth, and von Balthasar is because the very character of their work defies any attempt to summarize what they 'think.' The complex relationship between piety and thought, I think, is one of the reasons theologians should never aspire to 'pull it all together.' For example, the debates about the fatherhood of God in recent theology look quite different in a Protestant context in contrast to the Catholic and Orthodox. If you lose the practice, as it has been lost in Protestantism, of praying to Mary as the mother of God, then the suggestion that mother is as appropriate an appellation for God as father at least initially seems to make sense. I think a very interesting book could be written showing how the reductive tendencies in Protestant theology can be correlated with the loss of the theological significance of Mary not only in our theology but more importantly in Protestant piety. Of course, many Catholics will immediately point out that the emphasis on Mary has had some deleterious results both in theology and piety. But misuse is but a testimony to significance. I am not suggesting, of course, that we learn to call God father through Mary. That is learned from the one who is the Son of God.

[6] Method becomes the dominant way to do theology once it is assumed that positive theological claims are expressions of a prior content. For a diagnosis of the deleterious distinction between form and content, see Garrett Green, 'Kant as Christian Apologist: The Failure of Accommodationist Theology,' *Pro Ecclesia* 4/3 (Summer 1995), 301–17.

the abstract that what we believe as Christians is true as an issue separable from how we believe that which we believe. The heart of the position I develop in this book, and hopefully in one way or another in all my work, is that such accounts of the Christian faith cannot help but distort the very character of what we believe.

The power of the view of Christian belief I am trying to counter is apparent just to the extent that we continue to speak of 'Christian beliefs or belief.' Of course Christians believe such things as God created the world, that God called Abraham, worked through the prophets, chose Mary, and raised Jesus from the dead. Indeed, it would be quite strange to say that one 'believes,' for instance, in the resurrection and yet assume that some further decision or attitude needs to be taken in relation to such a belief. Even stranger would be the notion that believing any of these things as true could be abstracted from the kind of life commensurate with holding such beliefs. For example, what could it possibly mean to 'believe' that Jesus has been raised from the dead if a people do not exist who continue to 'eat and drink' with their Lord?[7]

Accordingly, I try to do theology in a manner that exposes the politics, the material conditions, of Christian speech. I cannot nor do I wish to deny that this generates the strange kind of mixture I indicated above. You will not find in this book, or anywhere in my work for that matter, a discussion of two natures of Christ as if the problem of Christ's two natures were just 'given' – that is, given as a 'problem' for theologians to solve or as a landscape where any ambitious theologian will take a 'stand.' The absence of that kind of discussion does not mean that I do not believe that Jesus Christ was at once very God and very man.[8]

I assume Nicaea and Chalcedon as normative boundaries for Christian reflection on the Trinity and Incarnation. The creeds are not meant, however, to still the mind from further reflection on the mystery of God's salvation, but rather to spur the imagination. Yet I think it is

[7] Bruce Marshall rightly argues that beliefs which identify Jesus and the Triune God cannot be held as true except by engagement in worship and prayer in the name of the Trinity. As he puts it, holding such beliefs as true 'changes your life and unless it changes your life, you are holding true some other beliefs.' 'What is Truth,' *Pro Ecclesia* 4/4 (Winter 1995), 423. Marshall's article provides as close a definitive account of how 'truth' works in Christian theology as I know.

[8] David Fergusson raises the question of whether I have provided a sufficient account of the 'once and for all' character of Christ's work. He observes that Christ is present and active in church and world, 'but this presence and activity are dependent upon what is already accomplished in his life, death, and resurrection.' 'Another Way of Reading Stanley Hauerwas?' *Scottish Journal of Theology* 50, 2 (1997), 245. Fergusson fears I do not allow for the 'already.' I hope that is not the case, but I acknowledge it is a danger, since I refuse to separate Christological and soteriological reflection. Put differently I have always thought attempts to develop a 'doctrine of the atonement' subsequent to Christology to be a mistake. That is why I have thought Barth was right to refuse to distinguish between the person and work of Christ. I believe that in Christ's resurrection the very character of the universe was changed, but I assume that that change changes us. As Jenson puts it in his *Systematic Theology*, 'Philip Melanchthon's maxim that to know God is to know his benefits can hold only where the identity of the

a theological mistake for theologians to draw on the formulas of the past in the attempt to show the intelligibility or coherence of Christian beliefs on the assumption that Christians at one time 'got it right.' The problem lies not in the creeds but in the attempt to turn them into 'thought' in the interest of securing the 'truth' of what Christians, then and now, allegedly believe.[9] Such a transformation is often an indication that our lives as Christians are no longer characterized by the risks that have required, and must continue to require, Christians to confess that in this man Jesus God is to be found.

I confess one of the other reasons why the way I do theology does not seem to conform to what theology is supposed to be is due to my concern for an audience. I fear that too often contemporary theology is produced in such a way that it can be read only by other theologians. This may be quite fortunate, given the kind of work that currently passes for theology today. Yet if theology is a servant ministry in and for the church, I do not think the alienation of theology from the church's common life, which is so prevalent today, can be a matter of indifference. Theologians do not have the gifts of poets, but we must nonetheless use our skills to help the church produce adequate speakers of the faith.[10] At the very least, that means theologians must attend a church and attend to how that church makes them responsible to other churches, as well as to the church through time.

Some may find this an odd position for me to adopt, given my unrelenting criticism of mainstream Protestantism in America. Yet I do not think Christian theology abstracted from the people who gather to worship God in the name of Jesus is possible. I am, moreover,

---

God to be known is antecedently secure. In modern context, it is plainly false and has been a disaster for the church' (51). That is why I refuse to isolate crucifixion in the interest of a 'doctrine' of the atonement from resurrection. To be saved is to be sanctified. While Fergusson may be right that I have not put these matters rightly, I am unconvinced that a different account of the 'already' would, as he suggests, entail a more positive view of liberalism.

[9] For an extraordinarily imaginative Christological proposal, see James McClendon's proposal of a 'two-narrative' Christology in his *Systematic Theology: Doctrine* II (Nashville: Abingdon, 1994), 274–79.

[10] By this I do not mean everyone in the church must be an intellectual, but rather that the speech of the baptized is not inconsistent with the language that is used in baptism. Part of our difficulty, particularly in mainstream Protestantism in America, is the loss of knowing how to speak the faith even in Baptism. It is as if we need to 'explain' the 'symbolic' significance of being baptized into Jesus' death and resurrection as if there is something else going on that is 'deeper' than Jesus' death and resurrection. I take it that one of the roles of the creeds is to help all Christians as a community to be adequate speakers. I put the matter that way because I never forget there are some in the community, who sometimes are called the mentally handicapped, who may not be speakers as we usually understand what it means to 'speak.' This is why it is all the more important that we recognize that to be adequate speakers, we must depend on one another for help. That, I assume, is one of the important tasks for those called to be bishops.

convinced that where such a people gather, God cannot be kept away. As I hope the essays in this book display, a surprising amount of life that may prove a ready resource for Christian faithfulness remains even in the churches of mainstream Protestantism. Our theological task is to help Christians discover that practices as common as praying for the sick during our common worship have implications that are as wonderful as they may be frightening. I do not assume that such a theological task will best be done by theologians, but I at least want to try.

If the way I do theology is in any sense new, and I certainly do not desire to do anything unique, it is my conviction that theologically we have to get back to the rough ground.[11] I quite simply mean that theologians must attempt to help those of us who worship God make the connections that such worship requires but also makes possible. The stories we will need to tell in order to make such connections will require that we defy current academic specializations, particularly those that presently dominate theological curricula. In the process, however, I am convinced that we will discover in the sheer determination of people to be faithful worshipers of Jesus Christ resources we had not imagined, that will enrich theology as well as attract others to it. That determination, that fidelity, provides resources that theology as such has never imagined.

But there is a problem with trying to do theology in the manner exemplified in this book. Can it, or should it be reproduced by others? Do I represent a method for others to use? Recently a student who is doing her PhD with me was told by another graduate student: 'Hauerwas will never be able to establish a school because after he is gone it will never hold together. The only reason the contradictions in his position are not more apparent than they are is because they are part of the same body.' An extraordinarily astute remark that is all the more important given the account of the body I develop in this book. Of course, I hope it is not the case that the way I try to do theology is filled with contradictions, but I know that if what I have been trying to do is even close to being right, then everything yet remains to be done. And because everything remains to be done, of course, I hope the work will be shared and continued.

I think of my work as a massive call for help. I would not expect those who read me to copy what I do, but rather to be intrigued sufficiently to try to do it better. I do not write to encourage anyone ever to think that they 'have gotten Hauerwas.' How could that possibly do anyone any good? I write to make those who read me work at least as hard as I have worked. For it is only through such work that one discovers why theology is at once a continuing frustration and a joyful

---

[11] See, for example, Joseph Dunne's attempt to display what may be called returning (in Wittgenstein's phrase) 'to the rough ground' in Dunne's *Back To The Rough Ground: 'Phronesis' and 'Techne' in Modern Philosophy and in Aristotle* (Notre Dame: University of Notre Dame Press, 1993).

activity. Theologians cannot help but be frustrated because we know we will never get it 'right;' but what a joy it is to be called to the task of theology, since we know that the truth of that which is the 'subject' of our endeavors does not depend on our getting it 'right.'

On Genre and Bricklaying: What This Book Is About

The above account is as close as I will perhaps ever get to discussing my 'theological method.' This description of my 'method,' moreover, can be read as an elaborate justification for yet one more book of seemingly disconnected essays from Hauerwas. A number of years ago, I was told by a dean of a rather important divinity school that I was wasting my 'talent' by writing frivolous essays and books. He was particularly disdainful of *Resident Aliens*.[12] He told me it was high time to take the time to write the 'big book' in Christian ethics. I responded that, after Wittgenstein, I simply had no idea what it would mean to write the 'big book' in Christian ethics. Such a book might be quite impressive, even secure some academic status, but how such a book could avoid giving the erroneous impression that Christian ethics is a subject in itself is beyond me. In other words, to write the kind of book he thought I should write would, for me, underwrite an account of Christian theology that I have continuously and vigorously tried to defeat.

That I cannot write the 'big book' does not mean, however, that I write without purpose or that the various emphases characteristic of my work are not interconnected. This is not the place for me to defend that claim, let alone try to give an overview of my work. I am not even sure if I am the one best situated to provide such an account or such a defense. But I do not think the essays I have written over the years, or the way I have brought them together in different books, or the relation between the books are at all 'disconnected.' I have not written thinking thoughts such as: 'Now that I have made my doctrine of God clear I must now proceed to my Christology.' I have rather moved from one essay to another trying to use what I had learned in the process of writing it to force me to say what I was not yet sure how to say.

[12] I am and will continue to be in debt to Will Willimon, the co-author of *Resident Aliens*, for helping me write for a larger audience. The distinction between 'serious' and 'popular' that bedevils all contemporary work is a terrible judgement on our culture. That Shakespeare is now considered 'literature' and not entertainment is surely a sign that something has gone wrong. I do not pretend that my attempts to write for a general readership have the same character as, for example, the essays in this book. Writing more popularly means that references that set context are often abridged, but that does not mean that such writing by definition must be simplistic. I am particularly proud of *Lord, Teach Us* (Nashville: Abingdon, 1996) which Willimon (with Scott Bader-Saye) and I wrote on the Lord's Prayer. I often think my 'best' work, by which I mean my most honest theological reflection, is to be found in books like *Lord, Teach Us*, my sermons, and my prayers.

In a sense, I am a theologian who still works like a bricklayer. You can only lay one brick at a time. Moreover, each brick you lay is different. Though bricks look quite uniform, and they often are, there are always variations that force the bricklayer to cut head joints in a manner necessary for the bond to be true. In other words, you have to adjust how you lay the next brick because of what happened when you laid the previous brick and, at the same time, in anticipation of the one to come. Moreover, bricklayers may work from a blueprint, but the way the brick must be laid often means the relation between what is originally drawn and what results defies easy comparison.

That much of my work is done in the form of essays is, therefore, not accidental. Composing essays is something like doing theology one brick at a time. Just as laying bricks requires as well as allows for exploration and experimentation, so does the writing of essays. Having to work in such an experimental yet conscientious fashion seems to me to be particularly appropriate, given the ecclesial challenges before us. Such work can only be done in communion. Thus my obvious dependence on Robert Jenson, James McClendon, Nicholas Lash, John Howard Yoder, John Milbank, Jean Elshtain, Greg Jones, David Burrell, Nancey Murphy, Eugene Rogers, James Fodor – and I mention but a few – whose work is done so well and is far beyond my competency or talent; I cannot nor do I need to do again what they have done. I should like to think that everything I have written could, like most papers in research science, have been jointly authored.[13]

That I try to write in a manner that exposes the community that makes my writing possible is but a reflection, or at least I hope it is a reflection, of what I write about. *Sanctify Them in the Truth* is certainly a book about the church. But then I am sure for many that is what all my books seem to be about. Yet I think *Sanctify Them in the Truth* makes it clearer than I have been able to do in the past why an adequate account of sanctification requires ecclesial practices for the shaping of the body. Accordingly, some may prefer to begin to read this book by beginning with the second part, 'The Truth about Sanctification: Holiness Exemplified,' because these essays are the heart of this book.

Sanctification is, to be sure, a quaint notion. Few contemporary Christians think they are going on to perfection. We are more likely to be willing to confess our sin than claim we have been made more than we otherwise could be through God's good work. That such is the case is quite reasonable given most Christians' images of sanctification – images that make any claim of holiness almost indistinguishable from claims of individual self-righteousness. Thus there is the challenge to offer an account of holiness that avoids the individualistic and pietistic

---

[13] I do not think that the moral significance of scientific papers, which are almost always jointly authored, is sufficiently appreciated by those in the 'humanities.' For a wonderful novel that involves the moral issues surrounding joint authorship in science, see Carl Djerassi, *Cantor's Dilemma* (New York: Penguin Books, 1989).

displays (and pietism may be responsible for the overdetermined emphasis on the individual) that grip so many Christian imaginations. I have tried to develop such an account in 'The truth about Sanctification' by offering some criticism of my earlier views as well as developing an alternative way to understand, by drawing on a renewed understanding of the body, the holiness of the whole church.

'Characterizing Perfection: Second Thoughts on Character and Sanctification,' a paper I wrote some years ago, may seem to exemplify the kind of individualistic views of sanctification I am criticizing. I have included it because I think it helps maintain the balance I am attempting between a Catholic and pietistic account of the holiness of the church. The holiness of the church can only be but a reflection of God's holiness and, thus, is not an invitation for a narcissistic fascination with my peculiar status. Yet there is surely a rightful place for self-examination made possible by the wisdom of Christian practice.[14] William Law's *Serious Call to a Devout and Holy Life* is surely a fascinating example of what such self-examination might look like, given its setting as part of a life of prayer. I would not pretend, however, that in some ways this paper may be in tension with what I am trying to do in 'The Sanctified Body' as well as the chapter on agency.

In many ways Chapter Eight, 'Timeful Friends: Living With the Handicapped' is the crucial chapter in the book, drawing as it does on the work of Jean Vanier. How God shapes that body called 'handicapped' through baptism is surely paradigmatic for any account of sanctification. That the holiness that is 'of God' is constituted through the vulnerability of the presence of the other, particularly the other called handicapped, unquestionably is one of the defining marks of the church. Moreover, such presence is made possible by a community which has been shaped by the diversity of gifts required to live out the Decalogue.

This section of the book also serves as a response to the oft-made claim that the kind of church for which I am an advocate does not exist. For me the church exists no matter how accommodated it may be. Holiness exists even in our unfaithfulness. One of my tasks is to develop the skills to help us see that as Christians we continue to be surrounded by extraordinary riches, not the least being worship, through which we can discover a God who has made us more than we

---

[14] Of course, part of the difficulty is the very notion of self-examination. Can we or should we ever trust ourselves with such a task? I think the answer is clearly 'no.' The process described by William Law, moreover, is not self-generated but rather dependant on the skills derived from the wisdom of a community. Yet I believe the problem of self-examination remains in Protestantism because we lack any meaningful penitential practice. The development of penance I describe in 'On Doctrine and Ethics' is intelligible given the presumption that the church that comes to Eucharist is a reconciled and holy community. That Protestantism lost the means to have our sins named by the church puts not only an intolerable burden on the individual but becomes an invitation to self-deception.

can 'will' or imagine on our own. The problem is not that the church does not exist, but that we too often lack the vision to see the miracle that is the church. The problem is the blindness of our sight. To see truthfully we must be sanctified.

Sanctification is often characterized in 'moral' terms. That it is so is certainly appropriate, but insufficient for the kind of sanctification Jesus indicates is ours in John 17. The sanctification that characterizes those who are made disciples of Jesus through the work of the Spirit is that which makes it possible for us to see the world, which includes ourselves, in the truth that is Christ. To receive such a gifted truthfulness shatters our easy distinctions between that which is 'spiritual' and that which is 'ethical,' between worship and ethics.

From a Wesleyan perspective, to be made holy, to be made capable of accepting forgiveness for our sins so that we might worthily worship God, is not just 'personal holiness.' As Augustine argued in *The City of God*, nothing is more important for a society than to worship God justly.[15] Without such worship terrible sacrifices will be made to false gods. Contrary to the modern presumption that as enlightened people we are beyond sacrifice, few societies are more intent on sacrifice than those we call modern.[16] Societies that think they have left sacrifice behind end up basing their existence on the sacrifice of the poor in the name of human progress. Christians believe that we are the alternative to such sacrificial systems because we have been given the gift of offering our 'sacrifice of thanksgiving' to the One who alone is worthy to receive such praise. That is what makes us a holy people, a people set apart, so that the world might know there is an alternative to murder.

That I teach 'ethics' through the liturgy I hope is a working out of my Methodist 'perfectionism.'[17] I have staked my work and life on the presumption that if, in some small way, I can help the church recover liturgical integrity, questions about the relation between worship, evangelism, and ethics will no longer be asked. Of course, it may still be useful to distinguish between worship, evangelism, and ethics as subjects of study, but hopefully such distinctions will be seen as part of the church's ministry reflected in a diversity of gifts. Such gifts, however, cannot become separate disciplines or realms if they are to be of service.[18]

---

[15] Augustine, *The City of God*, trans. David Knowles (Harmondsworth, England: Penguin Books, 1972), 280 (19, 23).

[16] For an extraordinary account of the current sacrificial system we call America, see Gil Bailie, *Violence Unveiled: Humanity at the Crossroads* (New York: Crossroad Books, 1995). Bailie's analysis draws on the remarkable work of René Girard.

[17] For an account of the way I teach Christian ethics at Duke Divinity School, see my *In Good Company: The Church as Polis* (Notre Dame: University of Notre Dame, 1995), 153–68.

[18] For a fuller argument, see my 'Worship, Evangelism, Ethics: On Eliminating the "and",' in E. Byron Anderson and Bruce T. Morrill (eds.), *Liturgy and the Moral Life: Humanity at Full Stretch Before God* (honoring Don Saliers), (Collegeville MN: Liturgical Press, 1998).

I owe the reader some explanation for why Chapter Six, 'Gay Friendship: A Thought Experiment in Catholic Moral Theology,' has been included in this book and, in particular, in the section on sanctification. I have included the essay because not only does it continue the themes of bodily agency (and friendship), but more important, I hope the essay exemplifies the kind of reflection that a sanctified people not only makes possible but requires. I situate the essay within current discussions in Roman Catholic moral theology not just because I wanted to work within the most 'conservative' position available but more importantly because most of what and how Catholics think about these matters I think is true. In particular, Catholic moral theology, drawing on the practices of the Christian tradition shaped by holy living and dying, has refused to develop sexual ethics abstracted from singleness and marriage.[19]

I hope any reader will take seriously the subtitle of this chapter – 'A Thought Experiment' – because that is exactly what it is. This essay is my attempt to avoid the generalizations used by those who take 'sides' by offering an account of how the church can remain committed to the practices of singleness and marriage while providing an alternative to Christians who are gay. I do not pretend I am successful nor that I have even begun to deal adequately with the complexity of the question raised. Rather, all I have tried to do is provide a disciplined discussion of how Christians might think about how faithful and sexual relations between gay Christians might be understood. I suspect that what I have done will convince no one who has already made up their mind that nothing is wrong with sexual acts between consenting gay adults or those who assume such acts are always wrong. I only ask that both sides keep in mind that the issue is what contributes to the upbuilding of God's church.

The essays in the first section of this book may seem quite distant from those in 'The Truth about Sanctification,' but I hope the reader will discover that not to be the case. In the essays on 'The Task of Theological Ethics' I attempt to unsettle some of the received ways of thinking about theology and ethics in order that the kind of work I do in the second part may not be dismissed as 'sociology.' By 'received ways of thinking about theology and ethics' I mean, in particular, the assumption that there is something called theology and something called ethics that can be distinguished in a manner that suggests they are separable activities. 'On Doctrine and Ethics' is an attempt to locate the source not only of the possibility but of the undesirability of that assumption. While I have no wish to deny that some

[19] For two important but very different articles that share this presumption, see Gilbert Meilaender, 'The First of Institutions,' *Pro Ecclesia* VI/4 (Fall 1997), 444–55; and David McCarthy Matzko, 'Homosexuality and the Practices of Marriage,' *Modern Theology* 13/3 (July 1997), 371–98. The future of reflections on this issue depends on the discussion of the differences between these two articles.

kinds of rough and ready distinctions between theology and ethics may be both possible and useful for Christians, I argue strenuously against all attempts to make ethics the 'upshot' of theological beliefs.

The next two essays may seem uncharacteristic in relation to my past work to the extent that they can be characterized as 'theology proper.' For example, I usually avoid the distinction between nature and grace, which I discuss extensively in 'The Truth about God,' because I distrust how that distinction is used to reify the distinction between theology and ethics. Yet I have never assumed theology can avoid the concept of nature just to the extent that nature names God's gracious desire to have all that is exist. As Thomas makes clear, our nature even prior to the fall is graced so that we might be friends with God.[20]

There is, however, another reason why I have avoided the distinction between nature and grace. Grace too readily becomes a way to provide a generalized account of God's alleged relation to us that renders God's call of Israel – as well as the life, death, and resurrection of Jesus – secondary. When this happens, and much of Protestant liberal theology is a prime example, salvation becomes a reality available without historic mediation.[21] Christianity becomes 'religion' and salvation is displayed primarily through the therapeutic categories characteristic of liberal social orders. Appeals to Jesus in such schemes are used to confirm truths about the human condition that lack any Christological justification.

My strategy, therefore, in 'The Truth about God' is to 'historicize' the distinction between nature and grace and at the same time provide an account of salvation that is determinatively moral. Yet the moral, given the very content of the Decalogue, cannot be divorced from

---

[20] Eugene Rogers nicely puts the matter when he notes that in Thomas '"merit" turns out to name the way in which God grants that our leaning upon grace truly befits and in that sense belongs to us. We merit God's favor when we lean upon God's power, and it becomes connatural to us, by grace, to do so. That is, God does not violate human nature by grace, but incorporates our nature into the divine plan for us.' 'Good Works and Assurance of Salvation in Three Traditions: *Fides Praevisa*, the Practical Syllogism, and Merit,' *Scottish Journal of Theology* 50, 2 (1997), 152. As Rogers observes, the integrity of nature that God respects is no integrity of human self-sufficiency, but rather the integrity of nature consists in its grace-relatedness.

[21] *Wilderness Wanderings: Probings in Twentieth Century Theology and Philosophy* (Boulder: Westview Press, 1997) is my attempt to counter these extraordinarily powerful modes of thought. Their power is apparent because most of the time they remain 'unthought,' that is, we are in their grip so thoroughly that they think through us even when we are trying to avoid them. I do not pretend to presume what I have written in the past or even now is as free as I would like of those habits that tempt us to present Christianity as ahistorical truth. Again Jenson in *Systematic Theology* has it right when he observes that the God we know from the Bible is not eternal if by eternal we mean immune to time. 'The biblical God cannot be the object of knowledge that secures us against historical contingency' (200).

truthful worship of the One True God. I acknowledge that much work remains to be done to explicate the Christological presumptions that shape how the Decalogue is understood, but I at least believe that what I am trying to do in this essay, as well as in 'Salvation even in Sin,' provides a way to help us know better what it means for Christians to speak truthfully about God and ourselves.

The essays in Part Three, 'Speaking Truthfully, In, For, and Against the World,' are more polemical in tone. The first essay, 'The Non-violent Terrorist,' is an attempt to defeat any presumption that my refusal to provide the conditions for truth on a priori grounds cannot avoid relativism. No one can or should try to avoid believing what they believe is true. The interesting questions are what practices in fact constitute us and how we might better know the ways in which they force us to be truthful. In 'The Non-violent Terrorist' I explore how the obligation of Christians to be God's witnesses forces us to engage others in a manner that cannot help but be disconcerting to us and them. The martial imagery that dominates this and the next chapter may seem odd, given my pacifism, but I hope these essays suggest how truthfulness and nonviolence are not only inseparable but cannot help but expose the violence that grips our lives.

The last three essays in this part deal with 'academic' issues. The university, and in particular, the Christian university is at least pledged to be truthful. I presume these essays are exploratory in nature because we simply lack the knowledge necessary to have any idea what a Christian university might look like. In the meantime, however, I think it important that we quit acting as if we know what universities are or what they are supposed to be doing. That I am a citizen as well as a lover of universities should be clear from these essays. My criticism of some of the forms the contemporary university takes, and in particular the subversion of theology in and by some of those in universities, is but a reflection of that love. I have included 'For Dappled Things,' not only because it shows how a theologian can address a secular audience, but also because I hope it exemplifies – contrary to oft-made criticism – that I have a deep appreciation for the goodness of God's creation to which, of course, universities often in spite of themselves witness.

The last section of the book is the most important, but also the most easily ignored. I strongly believe that the proof is in the pudding. The pudding for me is that, occasionally, I am asked to preach. I, therefore, conclude this book with one essay on preaching, accompanied by some sermonic illustrations. Each of the sermons is meant to illumine the more discursive essays in this book. Yet as the last sermon in the book suggests, I cannot try to 'hold on' by telling the reader what they are reading. It is hard to remember that what I have written is not all that important, even though what I have attempted to write about is everything.

A Thank You

I did not intend to be Stanley Hauerwas. I have trouble identifying with the person 'out there' bearing that name. I realize something called 'Stanley Hauerwas' has become rather well 'known.' But that notoriety (and I continue to think for a theologian to be famous means a mistake has been made) I do not recognize as me. Yet I also must acknowledge that my willingness to stake out strong positions entails that I be willing to take responsibility not only for what but how I write. That I expect people to read so much is, of course, asking a great deal. Even more sobering is the fact that there are those who not only read what I write, but also engage with it seriously, and get in various kinds of trouble as a result. They may well have gotten in trouble without my influence, but nonetheless that there are such people cannot help but, as they say, 'concentrate the mind.' This is not finally just another set of ideas.

It is therefore not inappropriate at the end of this 'Introduction' for me to express my thanks to the hearty souls who have persisted in being my readers over the years. In agreement, but also and especially in disagreement, these readers have made me think harder and I hope better than I could have ever done on my own. For what more could anyone ask? It is a wonderful thing indeed to be claimed by God's people; for otherwise it would be hard to know what it would mean to be claimed by God.

PART I

THE TASK OF
THEOLOGICAL ETHICS:
TRUTHFUL SPEECH

I

On Doctrine and Ethics

Problematizing the Relation between Doctrine and Ethics

Strange as it may seem, [the] general conception of ethics coincides exactly with the conception of sin. So we have every reason to treat it with circumspection. We do take up the question of the good and we try to answer it. But there can be no more trying to escape the grace of God. On the contrary, we have to try to prevent this escape. When we speak of ethics, the term cannot include anything more than this confirmation of the truth of the grace of God as it is addressed to man. If dogmatics, if the doctrine of God, is ethics, this means necessarily and decisively that it is the attestation of that *divine* ethics, the attestation of the good of the command issued to Jesus Christ and fulfilled by Him. There can be no question of any other good in addition to this.[1]

Any account of the relation between Christian doctrine and ethics must take account of this passage from Karl Barth. By 'take account' I mean at the very least we need to understand Barth's claim that the general conception of ethics coincides with the conception of sin. What is entailed by 'the general conception of ethics' and why would such a conception seem so theologically problematic? What developments in theology and ethics would have led Barth to make such an exaggerated assertion? After all, is not one of the defining marks of being Christian, particularly in modernity, that Christians still believe they ought to be morally good? In fact most people, including most Christian people, assume that if Christianity is not about morality it is not about anything.

As a result many Christians remain relatively indifferent about 'doctrinal matters,' but assume that one cannot make any compromises when it comes to moral questions. For liberal Christians one can be a Christian without being too concerned with questions, for example, about the Trinity, but you cannot remain indifferent to 'justice issues.' Conservative Christians often claim to care a great deal about doctrine, particularly doctrines about the Bible, but they assume that doctrines

---

[1] Karl Barth, *Church Dogmatics* II/2, trans. G. W. Bromiley et al. (Edinburgh: T&T Clark, 1957), 518.

about the Bible are necessary to reinforce their prior established views about personal and sexual misconduct. For both, 'ethics' has become the justification for being Christian. Yet from Barth's standpoint both liberal and conservative Christians, Catholic and Protestant, mistakenly have assumed that a distinction can be drawn between doctrine and ethics. However, from Barth's perspective something has already gone wrong if Christians have to ask what the relation or relations might be between doctrine and ethics. To assume that a 'relation' between doctrine and ethics needs to be explicated unjustifiably presumes that something called 'ethics' exists prior to or independent from 'doctrine.' Yet it is exactly that assumption which has shaped Christian practice and reflection about ethics in modernity. For example, most Christians now assume that a word like 'justice' is about ethics, but a word like 'creation' is what you say if you are being theological. The burden of this essay is to provide a narrative which explains how the disjunction between doctrine and ethics arose and why, as Barth claims, such a division cannot be justified theologically.

Yet surely, it may be asked, you are not saying that Christian ethics does not exist. After all, there is even a discipline called Christian ethics that is widely taught in colleges, universities, and seminaries. That such a discipline exists cannot be denied, but its existence may be an indication that something has gone wrong in basic Christian practices that makes such a discipline necessary.[2] Once there was no Christian ethics simply because Christians could not distinguish between their beliefs and their behavior. They assumed that their lives exemplified (or at least should exemplify) their doctrines in a manner that made a division between life and doctrine impossible.

It is important that this point not be misunderstood. As I will indicate below, Christians of different times and in different ways have distinguished theology and ethics, life from doctrine, if only to emphasize various aspects of faith or underscore certain qualities of character. There is, moreover, always the danger that because such analytical distinctions can be made that the Christian reality itself can be so divided. As we shall see, the task of the theologian is not to deny that for certain limited purposes ethics can be distinguished from theology, but to reject their supposed ontological and practical independence.

Unfortunately the provisional nature of the distinction between theology and ethics is too often forgotten, leading some to presume

---

[2] See, for example, my 'Why Christian Ethics is a Bad Idea,' in Hilary Regan and Rod Horsfield (eds.), *Beyond Mere Health: Theology and Medicine* (Adelaide: Australian Theological Forum, 1996), 64–79. For a much deeper challenge to any account of ethics as a self-generating enterprise, see John Milbank's chapter 'Can Morality Be Christian?' in his *The World Made Strange* (Oxford: Basil Blackwell, 1997), 219–32. Milbank has a subsequent article that develops his argument called 'The Midwinter Sacrifice,' *Studies in Christian Ethics* 10/2 (1997), 13–38.

that histories of Christian ethics in distinction from Christian theology can be written. Such histories cannot help but distort the character of Christian discourse. At least it cannot help but distort the character of Christian discourse that we find in Scripture and Christian theology through most of Christian history.

For example, too often it is assumed that 'biblical ethics' is to be found in materials in the Bible that look like 'ethics' to us. The Ten Commandments or the Sermon on the Mount are assumed to be prime candidates for ethics. This creates the problem of whether they must be taken literally, since at least some of the commandments, particularly in the Sermon on the Mount, seem impossible, or at least impractical, to follow. These assumed practical difficulties in following the 'ethics of the Bible' are often given quite sophisticated theological expression in terms shaped by the Protestant Reformation. For instance, the Bible is commonly read as an exemplification of the tension between law and Gospel. From such a perspective the central questions with which Christian ethics deals are how to understand the relation between creation and redemption or why justification precedes sanctification.

That we now think, for example, that there is a 'problem' for understanding the relation between Paul's discussion of justification in Romans 5:1–11 and the 'moral' instruction he gives in Romans 12–14, says more about us than it does about Paul. Our assumption that Romans 5 is theology and that the later chapters of Romans constitute ethics is not a distinction Paul would recognize. There is nothing in Romans that indicates or suggests Romans 5 is more significant than or foundational to Romans 12. That we now think one of the tasks of Christian ethics is to provide some account of this 'problem' in Paul is but an indication that the Pauline text is being read through the polemics of the Reformation.

Of course it can be argued that we have learned much since Paul's day, or at least we face different challenges, and that we rightly ought to subject Paul's work to our own peculiarly modern questions concerning the relation of theology to ethics. The difficulty with such a response is that it fails to appreciate that the question of the relation between doctrine and ethics is not just a 'conceptual' matter but an institutional, or more accurately, an ecclesial issue. That Christians must begin to ask what relation might pertain between their theological convictions and their ethical practices indicates changes in the character of the church as well as the church's relation to the world.

For example, Paul saw no tension between his account of justification and the admonitions in Romans 12 because he assumed the church was the subject of God's imperatives. As Richard Hays points out, because Paul thought God was forming a covenant people, 'the primary sphere of moral concern is not the character of the individual, but the corporate obedience of the church. Paul's formulation in Romans 12:1–2 encapsulates the vision: "Present your bodies (*somata*, plural) as a

SANCTIFY THEM IN THE TRUTH

living sacrifice (*thysian*, singular), holy and well-pleasing to God. And do not be conformed to this age, but be transformed by the renewing of your mind . . . ." The community, in its corporate life, is called to embody an alternative order that stands as a sign of God's redemptive purposes in the world.'³ That we now think we must ask the question of the relation between doctrine and ethics indicates that we inhabit a quite different set of ecclesial practices than those assumed by Paul.

Which is a reminder that questions about the relations between doctrine and ethics are not simply a matter of the relation between 'ideas,' but rather a reflection of the ever-changing practices of the church.⁴ Hence, the development of 'doctrine,' which was at least in part determined by the church's response to heresy, can look quite different if and when the boundaries between church and the world have become blurred. If, for example, Christians are no longer distinguishable from the world by how they use their possessions, questions concerning the two natures of Christ may assume quite a different character, as questions of 'belief' now become the defining mark of the Christian rather than our willingness to share our possessions as part of our discipleship.⁵

I am not suggesting that questions about the two natures of Christ are unimportant. Rather, I am noting that only when such issues become 'doctrine' is one then led to ask what such doctrines have to do with how Christians are to live. What seem at first glance to be theological questions involving conceptual relations between ideas can in fact hide what are actually issues concerning the nature of the church. Barth's suggestion that any general conception of ethics is equivalent to sin is, therefore, a claim with implications about the church's relation to the

³ Richard Hays, 'Ecclesiology and Ethics in 1 Corinthians,' *Ex Auditu* 10 (1994), 33. I continue to think there is a tension in Hays' work on New Testament ethics and his presentation of the content of such as ethic. For if he is right, as I think he is about community, cross, and new creation as themes central to the New Testament understanding of Christian existence, then I do not think you have from a Christian perspective the politics necessary to produce questions such as: 'What is the relation between the New Testament and Ethics?' In other words I find Hays' material account much more substantive than the methodology that sometimes frames that account. See Hays, *The Moral Vision of the New Testament* (San Franciso: Harper, 1996).

⁴ One of Troeltsch's insights was how 'doctrine' often reflected prior assumptions about the church. Even though I find his typology (i.e., church, sect and mysticism) problematic, at least it rightly emphasizes how our theologies reflect prior assumptions about the church's relation to the world. See Ernst Troeltsch, *The Social Teachings of the Christian Churches*, trans. Olive Wyon and introduced by James Luther Adams (Louisville KY: Westminster/John Knox Press, 1992).

⁵ James McClendon observes, 'Is it not worth considering, finally, how different might have been the history of Christianity if after the accession of the Emperor Constantine the church's leaders had met at Nicaea, not to anathematize each other's inadequate christological metaphysics, but to devise a strategy by which the church might remain the church in light of the fateful political shift – to secure Christian social ethics before refining Christian dogma?' *Ethics*, Vol. 1 (Nashville: Abingdon, 1986), 42.

world that is not immediately apparent. In order to understand better what is at stake in Barth's claim I must first provide the story that constitutes the background to Barth's insistence that doctrine is ethics.

How Christians Have Thought about Being Christian: Some Historical Considerations

I observed above that the notion of Christian ethics is a modern invention. At one time Christian ethics did not exist. That does not mean that Christians did not think about how best to live their lives as Christians. There are obvious examples of such reflection in the New Testament as well as in the Church Fathers. That may well put the matter too lamely just to the extent that the New Testament and the early Christian theologians thought about little else than how Christians were to live their lives. For the ancients, pagan and Christian, to be schooled in philosophy or theology meant to submit one's life to a master in order to gain the virtues necessary to be a philosopher or a Christian.[6] Ethics, in such a context, was not some 'aspect' of life, but rather inclusive of all that constituted a person's life.[7]

That we do not find explicit treatises on Christian ethics in Scripture or in the work of the Patristic writers does not mean they were unconcerned with giving direction to the church. They simply did not distinguish between theology and pastoral direction as we now do. Tertullian's *On Patience* may well have been the first treatise by a Christian on what we think of as a specifically moral topic, but there is no indication that he would have understood this treatise to be anything substantially different from his other theological and pastoral work.[8]

---

[6] Robert Wilken provides a very helpful account of how such schools worked in his 'Alexandria: A School for Training in Virtue,' in Patrick Henry (ed.), *Schools of Thought in the Christian Tradition* (Philadelphia: Fortress Press, 1984), 15–30. This understanding of the relation of theology to moral formation was not peculiar to Christianity but characteristic of all serious study in the ancient world. For example, Pierre Hadot observes that for the ancients philosophy, even in its most theoretical and systematic form, was 'written not so much to inform the reader of a doctrinal content but to form him to make him traverse a certain itinerary in the course of which he will make spiritual progress . . . For the Platonist, for example, even mathematics is used to train the soul to raise itself from the sensible to the intelligible.' *Philosophy as a Way of Life* (Oxford: Basil Blackwell, 1995), 64.

[7] For example, Aristotle thought how a person laughed not unimportant for morality. See his *Nicomachean Ethics*, trans. Martin Ostwald (Indianapolis: Bobbs Merrill, 1962), 1128a33–35.

[8] Tertullian, 'On Patience,' in Philip Schaff (ed.), *The Ante-Nicene Fathers* (Grand Rapids: Eerdmans, 1989), 707–17. For a further discussion of Tertullian's account of patience as well as that of Cyprian, Augustine, and Aquinas, see my 'Practicing Patience: How Christians Should be Sick,' in *Beyond Mere Health*. Robert Wilken rightly directs attention to the importance of the lives of the saints for Christian reflection on the moral life in his *Remembering the Christian Past* (Grand Rapids: Eerdmans, 1995), 121–44.

Augustine probably did more to shape what would later be thought of as Christian ethics, than any of the early Church Fathers. In his *On the Morals of the Catholic Church*, he suggested that the fourfold division of the virtues familiar to pagan philosophers could rightly be understood only as forms of love whose object is God. Thus 'temperance is love keeping itself entire and incorrupt for God; fortitude is love bearing everything readily for the sake of God; justice is love serving God only, and therefore ruling well all else, as subject to man; prudence is love making a right distinction between what helps it towards God and what might hinder it.'[9]

Augustine's conflict with the Pelagians resulted in a particularly rich set of treatises dealing with topics such as grace and free will, but also marriage and concupiscence.[10] Equally important is Augustine's *The City of God* in which he narrates all of human history as a conflict between the earthly and heavenly cities.[11] The earthly city knows not God and is thus characterized by order secured only through violence. In contrast, the heavenly city worships the one true God, making possible the collection of 'a society of aliens, speaking all languages. She takes no account of any difference in customs, laws, and institutions, by which earthly peace is achieved and preserved – not that she annuls or abolishes any of those, rather, she maintains them and follows them, provided that no hindrance is presented thereby to the religion which teaches that the one supreme and true God is to be worshiped.'[12] How properly to understand the relation between the two cities becomes the central issue for the development of what comes to be called Christian social ethics. Of course Augustine would have found the modern distinction between personal and social ethics at the very least questionable and more likely theologically a mistake.

The Church Fathers and Augustine did much to shape the way Christians think about Christian living, but equally, if not more

---

[9] Augustine, 'On the Morals of the Catholic Church,' in Waldo Beach and H. Richard Niebuhr (eds.), *Christian Ethics: Sources of the Living Tradition* (New York: The Ronald Press, 1955), 115. It would be hard to underestimate the significance of the Beach and Niebuhr anthology for the creation of Christian ethics as a discipline. Their anthology, which in many ways remains unsurpassed, made it seem apparent that for all its diversity something called Christian ethics is a distinctive subject running through Christian history. Their selections range from the *Didache*, to Clement of Alexandria, the ethics of monasticism, Martin Luther, Calvin, Wesley, Edwards, Kierkegaard, and Rauschenbusch. It would be carping to criticize whom they chose to include as it is impossible to include everyone who might have a claim to have done 'ethics.' More important is the impression the volume gives, which may even be contrary to some aspects of Beach's and Niebuhr's own views; namely, that ethics is a subject that can be 'abstracted' from ecclesial and theological practices.

[10] These treatises can be found in the *Nicene and post-Nicene Fathers of the Christian Church: Saint Augustine's Anti-Pelagian Works*, Vol. 5, trans. Benjamin Warfield, edited by Philip Schaff (Grand Rapids: Eerdmans, 1956).

[11] Augustine, *The City of God*, trans. Henry Bettenson and introduced by David Knowles (New York: Penguin Books, 1972).

[12] Ibid. 877–78.

important, is the development of the penitential tradition. In 1 Corinthians 5 Paul had insisted that the Corinthians were to 'root out the evil-doer from the community,' but the question remained whether such an evil doer should be received back into the community after due repentance. This was an issue that was not resolved until the Council of Nicaea in 325. That Council, which is primarily known for maintaining the full divinity of Christ against the Arians, also set a policy for the readmission of excommunicates after appropriate periods of penance. This was particularly significant since often the sin they had committed had been apostasy during times of persecution. Other major sins involved idolatry, adultery, and homicide – all of which required public penance which was not only quite onerous but available only once in a person's life.[13]

A major development occurred in this tradition largely by accident. Drawing on the monastic practice of spiritual direction of one monk by another, there developed in Ireland the practice of private confession to a priest with forgiveness of sins offered after appropriate penance. This practice resulted in the development of books called Penitentials that were meant as aids to confessors so that the appropriate penance would be given for the corresponding sin. These books differed markedly from one another, indicating different Christian practices at different times and places. Their organization was *quite* varied with little or no attempt at theological rationale. For example, *The Penitential of Theodore* stipulated the following with regard to avarice:

> 1. If any layman carries off a monk from the monastery by stealth, he shall either enter a monastery to serve God or subject himself to human servitude.
> 2. Money stolen or robbed from churches is to be restored fourfold; from secular persons, twofold.[14]

These books were carried by Irish missionaries across Europe and soon became the rule throughout Christendom. Though they were not explicitly theological, they depended on the continuing presumption that the church through baptism was to be a holy community. They were no doubt open to great misuse, but they also became the way the church grappled with the complexity of Christian behavior *through* the development of casuistry, that is, close attention to particular cases. From these beginnings there developed as part of the church's theological mission a special task called moral theology. Under the guidance of Pope Gregory VII the church's practice concerning moral questions was made more uniform through canon law and the

---

[13] I am indebted to John Mahoney's *The Making of Moral Theology: A Study of the Roman Catholic Tradition* (Oxford: Clarendon Press, 1987) and John A. Gallagher's *Time Past, Time Future: an Historical Study of Catholic Moral Theology* (New York: Paulist Press, 1990) for their accounts of the penitential tradition.

[14] Gallagher, *Time Past, Time Future*, 7.

development of *Summae Confessorum*. The latter were pastoral handbooks that gave theological order to the penitentials so that priests might be given guidance in the administration of what had become the sacrament of penance.

Thus a clear tradition was established in the Penitentials, in canon law, and in the *Summae Confessorum* in which ethics was distinguished from theology and doctrine. There was, moreover, specialist training for each of these tasks, as canon lawyers, moral theologians, and theologians were given distinctive training for their different roles. However, these diverse tasks were, in fact, one insofar as their intelligibility depended on the practices of the church. Ethics was not something done in distinction from theology, since both theology and moral theology presumed baptism, penance, preaching and Eucharist as essential for the corporate life of the church.

Perhaps nowhere is this inseparable unity between the ethical and the theological dimensions of Christian living better exemplified than in the great *Summa Theologiae* of Thomas Aquinas. Though often characterized as a defender of 'natural theology,' Aquinas' *Summa* is first and foremost a work in Christian theology. The structure of Aquinas' *Summa Contra Gentiles*, as well as the *Summa Theologiae*, draws upon the image of God as artist, such that all created realities are depicted as exiting and returning to God.[15] In other words, Aquinas' great works evince a three-part structure. The story of creation begins in divine freedom; then Aquinas treats how all creation, and in particular that part of creation called human, returns to God; finally, in the third part he provides an account of the means of creation's return to God through Christ and the sacraments. The *Summa*, rather than being an argument for the independence of ethics, as it is sometimes characterized, is concerned to place the Christian's journey to God squarely within the doctrine of God.

Indeed, it has been argued that one of Aquinas' main purposes in writing the *Summa* was for the sake of the second part, which treats moral matters more specifically and directly. Aquinas thought the manuals far too haphazard in their presentation of the Christian moral life.[16] He therefore sought to place the discussion of morality in the context of a consideration of human nature and the virtues appropriate

---

[15] As Aquinas says in *Contra Gentiles*, 'All creatures are compared to God as artifact to artist. Whence the whole of nature is like a certain artifact of the divine art. It is not, however, opposed to the nature of an artifact that the artist should work in a different way on his product even after he has given it its first form. Nor therefore is it against nature that God should work otherwise in natural things than the customary course of nature operates' (3, 10). Quoted in Thomas Hibbs, *Dialect and Narrative in Aquinas: An Interpretation of the Summa Contra Gentiles* (Notre Dame: University of Notre Dame Press, 1995).

[16] Leonard Boyle, OP, *The Setting of the Summa Theologiae of St. Thomas* (Toronto: Pontifical Institute of Medieval Studies, 1981).

to our nature as creatures whose destiny was nothing less than to be friends with God. Drawing deeply on Aristotle's account of the virtues, Aquinas nonetheless argued that even the so-called natural virtues must be formed by charity if they are to be capable of directing us to God.

Aquinas' intentions, however, were subverted as it was not long before the *secunda pars*, the second part, was abstracted from its context in the *Summa* and used as if it stood on its own.[17] This kind of anthologizing in part accounts for the presumption by later commentators that law, and in particular natural law, stands at the center of Aquinas' account. Yet Aquinas' understanding of the moral life is one that assumes the primacy of the virtues for the shape of the Christian life. Aquinas' work was either misunderstood or ignored through subsequent centuries, even to the point that he was used to support positions almost diametrically opposed to his own views.

The developments of the late Middle Ages are not unimportant, but in many ways they are now lost due to the profound effect the Reformation had for shaping how Protestant and Catholic alike began to think about the Christian life. It is not as if Luther and Calvin in their own work mark an entirely new way for thinking about the Christian life, but certainly the forces they unleashed changed everything. Neither Luther or Calvin distinguished between theology and ethics. Certainly Luther stressed the 'external' character of our justification, yet in *The Freedom of a Christian* he equally maintained that 'a Christian, like Christ his head, is filled and made rich by faith and should be content with this form of God which he has obtained by faith; only he should increase this faith until it is made perfect. For this faith is his life, his righteousness, and his salvation: it saves him and makes him acceptable, and bestows upon him all things that are Christ's.'[18]

Yet the polemical terms of the Reformation could not help but reshape how ethics was conceived in relation to theology. Faith, not works, determines the Christian's relationship to God. Moreover works became associated with 'ethics,' particularly as ethics was alleged to be the way sinners attempt to secure their standing before God as a means of avoiding complete dependence on God's grace. So for Protestants the Christian life is now characterized in such a way that there always exists a tension between law and grace. The law is needed, but we can

---

[17] For an extraordinary account of why Aquinas' *Summa* must be read as a whole as well as evaluated as a whole, see Alasdair MacIntyre, *Three Rival Versions of Moral Enquiry: Encyclopedia, Genealogy, and Tradition* (Notre Dame: University of Notre Dame Press, 1990), 133–37. MacIntyre argues, rightly I think, that integral to Aquinas' understanding of becoming a person of virtue, particularly the virtues of faith, hope, and love, is a recognition of our disobedience (400).

[18] Martin Luther, *The Freedom of the Christian*, in John Dillenberger (ed.), *Martin Luther: Selections from his Writings* (Garden City NY: Anchor Books, 1961), 75.

never attain salvation through the law and the works of the law. A similar tension constitutes the Lutheran understanding of the Christian's relation to what is now known as the 'orders of creation,' i.e., marriage, the legal order, the state. Christians are called to love their neighbor through submission to such orders, recognizing that such service is not and cannot be that promised in the order of redemption.[19]

Calvin, and in particular later developments in Calvinism, was not as determined by the polemical context of the Lutheran reformation. However, justification by faith is no less central for Calvin, who equally insists that 'actual holiness of life is not separated from free imputation of righteousness.'[20] Accordingly, Calvinists stressed the importance of the sanctification of the Christian and the Christian community. Christians were expected to examine their lives daily so they might grow into holiness. This theme was retained in the Anglican tradition and was given particularly strong emphasis in the Wesleyan revival in England as well as other forms of Pietism.

Certainly the Protestant Reformation changed the language for how Christians understood 'ethics,' but far more important were changes in the ways Christians related to their world. In earlier centuries, the Christian understanding of life could be articulated in the language of natural law, but it was assumed that natural law was only intelligible as part of divine law as mediated by the church. What was lost after the Reformation was exactly this understanding of the church as the indispensable context in which order might be given to the Christian life. For example, with the loss of the rite of penance in Protestantism casuistry as an activity of moral theologians was lost. Such a loss did not seem to be a problem as long as it was assumed that everyone 'knew' what it meant to be Christian. However, as it became less and less clear among Protestants what it 'means' to be Christian there have increasingly been attempts to 'do' ethics. The difficulty is that no consensus about what ethics is or how it should be done existed. As a result, theologians often turned to philosophy for resources in their search for an ethic – resources that ironically helped create the problem of how to relate theology and ethics because now it was assumed that

---

[19] Luther maintains that Christians must bear the 'secular' sword even though they have no need for it for their own life, since the sword is 'quite useful and profitable for the whole world and for your neighbor. Therefore, should you see that there is a lack of hangmen, beadles, judges, lords, or princes, and find that you are qualified, you should offer your services and seek the place, that necessary government may by no means be despised and become inefficient or perish. For the world cannot and dare not dispense with it.' *Secular Authority: To What Extent It Should be obeyed*, in *Martin Luther: Selections from his Writings*, 374–75. The contrast between Lutheran and Calvinist positions about such matters is frequently overdrawn. See, for example, Quentin Skinner, *The Foundations of Modern Political Thought*, II (Cambridge: Cambridge University Press, 1978), 189–238.

[20] John Calvin, *Institutes of the Christian Religion*, ed. John MacNeill and trans. Ford Lewis Battles (Philadelphia: The Westminster Press, 1960), Chapter III, 1.

'ethics' is an autonomous discipline that is no longer dependent on religious conviction.

How Ethics Became a Problem in Modernity

The birth of modernity is coincident with the beginnings of 'ethics' understood as a distinguishable sphere or realm of human life. Faced with the knowledge of the diversity of moral convictions, modern people think of themselves as haunted by the problem of relativism. If our 'ethics' are relative to time and place, what if anything prevents our moral opinions from being 'conventional' and if they are conventional some assume they must also be 'arbitrary.' But if our morality is conventional how can we ever expect to secure agreements between people who disagree? Is it our fate to be perpetually at war with one another? 'Ethics' becomes that quest to secure a rational basis for morality so we can be confident that our moral convictions are not arbitrary.

The great name associated with this quest is Immanuel Kant. Kant sought to secure knowledge and morality from the skepticism which the Enlightenment, by its attempt to free all thought from its indebtedness to the past, had produced. Kant also wanted thought to be free from the past; thus his famous declaration – 'Enlightenment is man's release from his self-incurred tutelage. Tutelage is man's inability to make use of his understanding without direction from another. Self-incurred is this tutelage when its cause lies not in lack of reason but in lack of resolution and courage to use it without direction from another.'[21]

Kant's commitment to this Enlightenment ideal was his response to the breakdown of the Christian world. If ethics depended on or was derived from religious belief, then there seemed to be no way to avoid the continuing conflict between Catholics and Protestants as heirs of the Reformation.[22] Accordingly, Kant sought to ground ethics in reason itself, since, in Kant's words, 'It is there I discover that what I do can only be unconditionally good to the extent I can will what I have done as a universal law.'[23] Kant called this principle the 'Categorical

---

[21] Immanuel Kant, *Foundations of the Metaphysics of Morals and What is Enlightenment?*, trans. Lewis White Beck (New York: Liberal Arts Press, 1959), 85. The quote comes from the first paragraph of 'What is Enlightenment?'.

[22] It should never be forgotten that one of Kant's last projects was his *On Perpetual Peace* in which he sought to provide an account for how nations determined by republican principles based in his ethics had a better chance of maintaining a world free of war. The oft-made claim that liberalism, and in particular the liberal nation state, arose in response to the wars between Catholics and Protestants is simply wrong. William Cavanaugh notes that: 'The rise of a centralized bureaucratic state preceded these wars and was based on the fifteenth-century assertion of civil dominance of the church in France.' See his 'A Fire Strong Enough to Consume the House: The Wars of Religion and the Rise of the State,' *Modern Theology* 11/4 (October 1995), 397–420.

[23] Kant, *Foundations*, 18.

Imperative' because it has the form: 'Act only according to that maxim by which you can at the same time will that it should become a universal law.'[24]

Only an ethics based on such an imperative can be autonomous, that is, free of all religious and anthropological presuppositions. Only by acting on the basis of such an imperative can an agent be free. Such an ethic is based on reason alone and can therefore be distinguished from religion, politics, and etiquette. Yet Kant did not understand his attempt to make ethics independent of religion to be an anti-religious project but rather one that made faith possible. Indeed in many ways Kant becomes the greatest representative of Protestant liberalism; that is, Protestant liberal theology after Kant is but a series of footnotes to his work.[25]

For example, Protestant theologians, no longer sure of the metaphysical status of Christian claims, sought to secure the ongoing meaningfulness of Christian convictions by anchoring them in anthropological generalizations and/or turning them into ethics. No longer convinced that Jesus is the resurrected Messiah, his significance is now said to be found in his proclamation of the Kingdom of God. The Kingdom is the outworking in human history of the fatherhood of God and the brotherhood of man.[26] Theology, at least Protestant liberal theology, became ethics, but the ethics it became was distinctively Kant's ethics dressed in religious language.

Such a generalization must be qualified in the light of Friedrich Schleiermacher's theology and philosophy. Schleiermacher was part of the romantic revolt against the rationalism of Kant, but it was a revolt that sought to stay within the presuppositions of the Enlightenment. Schleiermacher's great work, *The Christian Faith*, has no section devoted to ethics.[27] Yet Karl Barth rightly argues that Schleiermacher's work was motivated by the ethical project of drawing people into the movement of education, the exaltation of life, which he understood at bottom to be religious and, thus, Christian. Barth goes so far as to suggest that 'Schleiermacher's entire philosophy of religion, and therefore his entire teaching of the nature of religion and Christianity

---

[24] Ibid. 39.

[25] The liberal presuppositions that shape Kant's religious views are nicely exemplified in his observation that 'in the appearance of the God-Man (on earth), it is not that in him which strikes the sense and can be known through experience, but rather the archetype, lying in our reason, that we attribute to him (since, so far as his example can be known, he is found to conform thereto), which is really the object of saving faith, and such a faith does not differ from the principle of a course of life well-pleasing to God.' Immanuel Kant, *Religion Within the Limits of Reason Alone*, trans. with an introduction by Theodore Green (New York: Harper Torchbooks, 1960), 109–10.

[26] Though this position is associated with Ritschl and Harnack, it perhaps found its most powerful expression in the American social gospel movement.

[27] Friedrich Schleiermacher, *The Christian Faith*, trans. H. R. MacIntosh and J. S. Stewart (Edinburgh: T&T Clark, 1960).

was something secondary, auxiliary to the consolidation of this true concern of his, the ethical one. The fact that, in academic theory, he ranked theology below ethics, is but an expression of this state of affairs.'[28]

Schleiermacher sought to support Christian theology through the development of a philosophical theology which could demonstrate that the existence of the church was necessary for the development of humanity. This philosophical project was ethical just to the extent that ethics is understood to express those principles of history by which reason permeates nature and gives it form. In short, ethics is the study of how nature comes to consciousness. The most determinative form of such consciousness Schleiermacher identifies with the 'feeling of absolute dependence.' Thus he begins *The Christian Faith* with a long prolegomenon to establish the proposition: that 'the totality of finite being exists only in dependence upon the Infinite is the complete description of that basis of every religious feeling which is here to be set forth.'[29]

Christian theology and ethics for Schleiermacher are descriptive disciplines inasmuch as their task is to set forth the ideas and behavior of Christian communities in different times and places. Though Schleiermacher often lectured on philosophical and Christian ethics, unfortunately he never published his ethics. From his lectures and posthumous writings we know that Schleiermacher was critical of what he considered the formalism and legalism of Kant's ethics. As a great Plato scholar, he reintroduced the language of virtue and the highest good, though he identified the latter with the rational content of life as a whole. His account of the Christian life was that of 'a continuum between the beginnings of one's desire for communion with God and the culmination of that desire in absolute blessedness.'[30]

More important, however, than Schleiermacher's explicit view about ethics was his conception of the dogmatic task as a civilizing and thus ethical task. The crucial institution for such a task in civilizing for Schleiermacher was the university, and in particular, the University of Berlin.[31] Theology could be part of the university, according to Schleiermacher, insofar as it meets, like medicine and the law, human

---

[28] Karl Barth, *Protestant Thought: From Rousseau to Ritschl*, trans. Brian Cozens (New York: Harper & Bros, 1959), 317.

[29] Schleiermacher, *The Christian Faith*, 142.

[30] Friedrich Schleiermacher, *Introduction to Christian Ethics*, trans. and with introduction by John Shelley (Nashville: Abingdon Press, 1989), 27 of Shelley's introduction.

[31] For a wonderful account of the significance of the University of Berlin, as well as Schleiermacher's decisive role in its shaping, see Hans Frei's *Types of Christian Theology*, eds. George Hunsinger and William Placher (New Haven: Yale University Press, 1992), 95–132.

needs indispensable for the state.[32] Since the state needs religion, theology is justified for the training of clergy who are thus seen as servants of the state. The theology that is so justified is now the name of a cluster of disciplines (scripture, church history, dogmatics, and practical theology), that are understood to be descriptive in character. Accordingly, theology is no longer understood to be practical knowledge necessary for the acquisition of wisdom, but a 'science' for the training of semi-public officials.

This reconstrual of the tasks of theology shaped and continues to shape the curricula not only in Germany but in universities and seminaries around the world and, in particular, in the United States. Of course the division of the curriculum into scripture, church history, dogmatics, and practical disciplines in these different contexts does not mean that theology was or is necessarily understood in Schleiermacher's terms. But the curriculum so structured did and continues to create the 'problem' of what relation there might be between theology and ethics. In other words, it is unclear exactly where 'ethics' should be located. Is its proper place in 'dogmatics' or in the 'practical disciplines?' The rise and importance of Christian ethics as a discipline in the United States (associated with such people as Reinhold and H. Richard Niebuhr, Paul Ramsey, and James Gustafson) has not resolved this fundamental issue. If anything, it has only deepened and further obscured the issue. Indeed the institutional shape of the theological curriculum, particularly in Protestant seminaries, and increasingly in Catholic institutions that have at least in America imitated the Protestants, has resulted in intellectual developments that distort the character of theological discourse. The assumption, for example, that students should take 'systematic theology' before they take ethics invites the presumption that theology is in some sense more basic than ethics. In such a context theology begins to look like a 'metaphysics' on which one must get straight before you can turn to questions of ethics. Yet as I have indicated above, through most of Christian history Christians have *not* thought it possible to distinguish so easily between what they believe and what they do. At stake is the question of whether theology is first and foremost a discipline of the church or the university.

Thus the significance of Karl Barth's challenge quoted at the beginning of this essay. For Barth, indisputably the greatest Protestant theologian of this century, there can be no ethics that is not from beginning to end theological. Indeed, ethics is theological through and through because for Barth theology is more than simply one discipline among others. Theology rather is the exposition of how God's Word as found in Jesus

---

[32] Edward Farley provides an extremely helpful account of the importance of Schleiermacher's views on these matters in *Theologia: The Fragmentation and Unity of Theological Education* (Philadelphia: Fortress Press, 1983), 73–98. Schleiermacher's position concerning the university was quite similar to Kant's. Schleiermacher, in spite of his criticism of Kant, continued to presuppose the basic structure of Kant's position.

Christ provides not only its own ground but the ground for all that we know and do. Barth, therefore, rejects Schleiermacher's attempt to make theology part of a 'larger essential context, of a larger scientific problem-context,' by returning theology to its proper role as servant to the church's proclamation of Jesus Christ.[33] For Barth dogmatics cannot have access to a higher or better source of knowledge than that which is found in the church's proclamation that the God Christians worship is Triune.

Barth, thus, begins his *Dogmatics* with the doctrine of the Trinity since it is from that doctrine 'we actually gather who the God is who reveals Himself and therefore we let it find expression as the interpretation of revelation.'[34] For Barth 'ethics' is but an integral part of the dogmatic task and, therefore, cannot be treated as an independent subject. Barth's explicit reflections on ethics occurs in several places in his multi-volume *Church Dogmatics*,[35] but it would be a mistake to assume that Barth's ethics is to be found only in those sections explicitly devoted to ethics. As John Webster argues, Barth's *Dogmatics* is:

> a moral ontology – an extensive account of the situation in which human agents act. Barth's ethics has, therefore, a very particular character, both materially and formally. It is primarily devoted to the task of describing the 'space' which agents occupy, and gives only low priority to the description of their character and to the analysis of quandary situations in which they find themselves. Barth's ethics tends to assume that moral problems are resolvable by correct theological description of moral space. And such description involves much more than describing the moral consciousnesses of agents. A Christianly successful moral ontology must be a depiction of the world of human action as it is enclosed and governed by the creative, redemptive, and sanctifying work of God in Christ, present in the power of the Holy Spirit.[36]

The 'ethics' that animates Barth's project is thus quite different than that of Schleiermacher. Barth does not seek to make the church a servant of a civilizing project and thus a supplement for what is a prior

---

[33] Karl Barth, *Church Dogmatics* I/1, trans. G. T. Thomson (Edinburgh: T&T Clark, 1960), 39.

[34] Barth, *Church Dogmatics* I/1, 358.

[35] Barth's first treatment of ethics is to be found in *Church Dogmatics* II/2 as part of his exposition of the doctrine of election. His special ethics is in *Church Dogmatics* III/4, that is, the last volume in his doctrine of creation. The ethics volume that was meant to climax his account of the doctrine of reconciliation was not completed but in it Barth was explicating the Christian life in terms of baptism with the Holy Spirit and water. *Church Dogmatics* IV/4, trans. G. W. Bromiley (Edinburgh: T&T Clark, 1969). Further lecture fragments of Barth's last reflections about the Christian life can be found in his *The Christian Life*, trans. Geoffrey Bromiley (Grand Rapids: Eerdmans, 1981). In this last volume Barth builds his reflections around the Lord's Prayer.

[36] John Webster, *Barth's Ethics of Reconciliation* (Cambridge: Cambridge University Press, 1995), 1–2. For another excellent secondary source on Barth's ethics, see Nigel Biggar, *The Hastening that Waits: Karl Barth's Ethics* (Oxford: Clarendon Press, 1993).

conception of ethics. Rather, just as Israel 'annexed' the land of Palestine, so Christians must appropriate 'ethics' as a secular, Enlightenment subject-matter.[37] For example, notions such as 'the good' or the 'Categorical Imperative' are far too abstract to give the guidance that can come only from the concreteness of God's command as found in Jesus Christ.[38]

Barth provides extensive discussions of such matters as suicide, euthanasia, marriage and singleness, the ethics of war, the Christian calling to serve the neighbor, but denies that casuistry can ever predetermine 'God's concrete specific command here and now in this particular way, of making a corresponding decision in this particular way, and of summoning others to such a concrete and specific decision.'[39] Accordingly Barth's ethics is often criticized for being too 'occasionalistic,' since he denies that we can ever predetermine what we should do prior to God's command. While Barth may be vulnerable to such criticism, what should not be lost is that Barth in his *Dogmatics* has sought to do nothing less than displace human self-consciousness as the legitimating notion for the creation of ethics independent of God's revelation in Christ. By doing so he has returned theology to the presumption that there can be no 'ethics' separate from theology, particularly when theology is understood as an activity of the church.

Theology and Ethics after Barth

By ending the last section with Barth I do not suggest that Barth's position has won the day. In fact, Barth remains a minority voice among those Christians presently doing theology and ethics. Barth is particularly unwelcome among those who seek to develop practical or applied ethics in such areas as medicine, business, and the professions in general. Those working in such areas assume that the particularity of Christian convictions must be suppressed in the interest of developing an ethic for 'anyone.' Many working in these fields originally had theological training, but they now have come to assume that at most consideration of Christian doctrine is a methodological afterthought to the real business of ethics.

Those trained to do theology 'proper,' however, seldom stray into 'ethics' as part of their job description. Too often theologians spend their time writing prolegomena, that is, essays on theological method meant to show how theology should be done in case anyone ever got around to doing any. Those who do try to do theology too often assume that their primary task is to construct a systematic presentation of theological *loci* and their interrelations. Ethics is what is done *after*

---

[37] Barth, *Church Dogmatics* II/2, 518.
[38] Barth, *Church Dogmatics* II/2, 665–69.
[39] Barth, *Church Dogmatics* IV/4, 9.

one has accomplished these more primary tasks or ethics becomes the responsibility of those who teach courses in ethics.

Happily there are some exceptions to this state of affairs that are signs of hope. For example, James McClendon begins his projected three-volume *Systematic Theology* with *Ethics*, to be followed by *Doctrine*, and then by a last volume dealing with philosophical questions raised within our cultural context.[40] McClendon does not think that by beginning with ethics he is delaying the theological task, but rather he begins with ethics in order to remind us that theology gains its intelligibility through the practices of the church. Therefore, McClendon commences his project with ethics not because he assumes that Christian theology can be reduced to ethics, but to reclaim theology's task in the shaping of the Christian life. Accordingly, his *Ethics*, like Barth's, requires discussion of baptism and forgiveness, cross and resurrection, but also is built around the display of lives like Jonathan and Sarah Edwards, Dietrich Bonhoeffer, and Dorothy Day, lives which were shaped by and in turn shape our understanding of Christian doctrine.[41]

What McClendon helps us see is that what we need, if we are better to understand the nature of our existence as Christians, are not fuller, more nuanced accounts of the relation of doctrine *and* ethics. For such accounts too often simply reproduce the presuppositions that created the 'and' which divides theology and ethics into separate realms, the conjunction against which we must now struggle. Rather what is needed are Christian speakers for whom doctrine is speech that does work. Rowan Williams, a theologian and bishop, offers us another fine indication of what a truly ethical-theological discourse might look like in an address before the Wales and Chester Judges' Circuit on 'Administering Justice.'[42] At first glance, this would not appear to be a particularly promising context for the display of doctrine, yet Williams begins with justice and ends with the Trinity.

Williams observes that justice means giving to each their due, but that requires that we must reflect back to others what they truly are. 'Doing justice' begins in our effort to respond to the reality of one another, which demands that we see one another as God sees us. We only see one another, therefore, when we look towards God, so justice is impossible without the vision of God. Which leads Williams to

[40] James McClendon, *Systematic Theology*, Vol. I, *Ethics* (Nashville: Abingdon Press, 1986). McClendon's second volume, *Doctrine*, was published in 1994 from Abingdon.

[41] Also to be noted is the work of Gregory Jones who argues in his *Transformed Judgment: Toward a Trinitarian Account of the Moral Life* (Notre Dame: University of Notre Dame Press, 1990) that 'the moral life, when understood in terms of Christian life, receives its shape and pattern from God's Trinity. The vocation of the moral life is to learn to see and act rightly by participating in the mystery of the Triune God' (120). Jones has developed this position further in his *Embodying Forgiveness* (Grand Rapids: Eerdmans, 1995).

[42] This address is in Rowan Williams, *Open to Judgement* (London: Darton, Longman & Todd, 1994).

observe that the administration of justice, as is increasingly evident in our times:

> . . . becomes harder and harder, the more we cease to take it for granted that God is to be honored. Ultimately, all that can be said by the Christian about justice rests on the doctrine of God, not simply as the God whose truthful love is directed towards us, but as the God whose very life is 'justice,' in the sense that Father, Son and Holy Spirit reflect back to each other perfectly and fully the reality that each one is, 'give glory' to each other . . . . So the Uxbridge Magistrates' Court and its local equivalents point us towards the contemplation of the Holy Trinity, and that contemplation, with all that it says about truth and reciprocity, grounds, for the Christian, the vision of a just society. Administering justice is a ministry of the truth of God's life to our imaginations, whether we know it or not.[43]

Both Williams and McClendon exemplify the rediscovery that Christians have little reason to disjoin doctrine from ethics. To speak truthfully and intelligibly of one will always require speaking of the other. And if, with Williams, Christians learn to speak to the magistrate as if Jews and Trinity matter, then the church may indeed have some interesting times ahead. Indeed, one might argue that precisely because Christians in modernity have presumed that ethics can safely be treated apart from theology (if only to provide a non-particularistic, tradition-independent ethic suitable for 'anyone') that their attempts to speak truthfully and convincingly to magistrates and other civil officials have proved so ineffectual. That is, the persuasive power of Christian discourse rests upon the indissoluble unity of the theological and the ethical aspects of Christian faith, not their separation.[44]

---

[43] Ibid. 245–46.

[44] I am indebted to Professors Scott Saye, Jim Fodor, and Greg Jones for their suggestions and criticisms of this essay.

2

The Truth about God:
The Decalogue as
Condition for Truthful Speech

God and Morality

I am too much the Barthian to admit I found God in England. Better to say that God found me. Being found by God feels odd anywhere, I suppose, but especially so in England – in Oxford, no less. Even stranger still, it occurred during a meeting of the English Society for the Study of Christian Ethics, which is surely the last place most of us would expect God to show up. So perhaps an explanation is in order.

I had come to England to do a paper at the Society for the Study of Christian Ethics. Immediately following the Society's meeting a conference was convened on Karl Barth, for which I had also prepared a paper.[1] God's discovery of me happened during the transition between these conferences. I was walking – to supper, I think – with that able expositor of Barth's theology, Nigel Biggar. As we were walking together Nigel observed, rather astutely, that for all my insistence that Christian ethics be Christian, in spite of my repeated and tiresome emphasis on the unavoidable reality of the church for how we think about the nature of the moral life, God was nonetheless curiously missing from my work.[2]

My response to Nigel's remark was, of course, defensive and I proceeded to show why he had to be wrong. But afterwards, the more I thought about it, the more it occurred to me that he might be right. In spite of everything I was trying to do to sustain the integrity of Christian speech, despite my repeated attempts to reclaim the Christian qualifier for how we think about the character of the Christian life, when all is said and done, I may have done nothing more than reproduce Durkheim, albeit with an ecclesiological twist.[3] Even if I have shown the difference

---

[1] The year was 1986 and the conference on Barth was a commemoration of the centenary of his birth. The papers from the conference were published in Nigel Biggar (ed.), *Reckoning with Barth: Essays in Commemoration of the Centenary of Karl Barth's Birth* (London: Mowbray, 1988).

[2] I leave to the reader to assess how my work may or may not have changed since 1986, but I certainly have not forgotten Biggar's observation.

[3] I mention Durkheim because he, along with Feuerbach, provided such a compelling account of the social and moral significance of 'religion.' Durkheim and Feuerbach both sought to give an account of the persistence of religion, insisting that if it was not

that Christian convictions may or should make for how our lives are shaped, such a project does not in itself entail that the god in view be the God we worship as Father, Son and Holy Spirit. That failure, however, may not be peculiar to me alone but may be the fate of theology in modernity.

I have always hoped that my work might exhibit Cardinal Suhard's claim: 'To be a witness does not consist in engaging in propaganda nor even in stirring people up, but in being a living mystery. It means to live in such a way that one's life would not make sense if God did not exist.'[4] Over the years I have tried to write about Christian ethics in a manner that would render Christian life unintelligible if God – in particular, the God of Jesus Christ – did not exist. What I may have succeeded in doing, however, is reproduce the modern presumption that even if something called god does exist, we cannot know such a god. And if perchance we could somehow come to know that god, we certainly could not talk about that god as one capable of saving us.

Of course, part of my difficulty is that I learned how to do theology by reading Karl Barth. I assume that theology's task is not to make God intelligible to 'modern man,' whoever that may be, but rather to make ourselves intelligible to God. The appropriately phrased theological question is never 'Does God exist?'[5] but 'Do we exist?' This observation is but a reminder that 'existence' is not a given into which God must then be situated or otherwise accommodated. Rather, existence itself is an analogical term that can be properly displayed only as

---

grounded in real human needs religion would not continue to survive. As Karen Fields puts it in the 'Introduction' to her translation of *The Elementary Forms of Religious Life* (New York: Free Press, 1995), Durkheim concluded that the idea of the soul 'was needed to solve a problem that the daytime course of social life forced human reason to confront: the indisputable reality that there is death, yet communities live on, and there is birth: "In sum, belief in the immortality of souls is the only way man is able to comprehend a fact that cannot fail to attract his attention: the perpetuity of the group's life." Socially, he argued, it stood for that collective life: individualized, it stood for the social part of every human being, the human (as distinct from the animal) part. It is at once a discrete being and an ethereal substance, at once individualized par excellence and yet social' (xxiii–xxix).

For a compelling account of Feuerbach that frees his account of too easily defeated 'projection' theories of religion, see Van A. Harvey, *Feuerbach and the Interpretation of Religion* (Cambridge: Cambridge University Press, 1995). The problem is, quite simply, that much of modern Christian theology tries to justify theological claims on grounds not unlike that provided by Durkheim and Feuerbach in spite of the fact that the latter understood their accounts in no way entailed that God – at least the God Christians have traditionally worshipped – exists. Equally problematic have been Christian theologians, Barth being the great exception, on the category of religion.

   [4] This quotation comes from Cardinal Suhard, in *Growth or Decline* (Notre Dame: Fides Press, 1951). It appears on the Revd Michael Baxter's (CSC) announcement of his ordination as a presbyter.

   [5] Accordingly, all attempts to correlate God with some aspect of human experience are, I assume, doomed to failure. For if god names such a correlated experience, I see no reason how or why one would be led to worship such a god.

God's free gift. Such a position is not, of course, peculiar to Karl Barth but is increasingly recognized to be the heart of Aquinas' account of God's relation to God's creation.[6]

I am not suggesting that the differences between Barth and Aquinas are negligible or even non-existent, but rather that at least on the question of our knowledge of God there are striking parallels.[7] Eugene Rogers, for one, has called attention to Barth's admission that 'the world which has always been around [the Gentiles], has always been God's work and as such God's witness to himself. Objectively the Gentiles have always had the opportunity of knowing God, his invisible being, his eternal power and godhead. And again, objectively speaking, they have always known him. In all that they have known otherwise, God as the Creator of all things has always been objectively speaking the proper and real object of their knowledge, exactly in the same sense as undoubtedly the Jews in their law were objectively dealing with God's revelation.'[8] Rogers observes that such a claim may even go beyond what Aquinas would say, just to the extent that Barth does not distinguish God's essence from God's effects. Indeed, Barth's recourse to dialectic frequently forces him to take back claims like those made above.[9]

Yet if such claims are withdrawn, then assertions about the self-validating character of God's revelation can become, as John Milbank observes, but a variant of liberal Protestantism. 'A revealed word of

---

[6] The work of David Burrell has long been helping us recover this view of Aquinas. See especially his *Aquinas: God and Action* (London: Routledge & Kegan Paul, 1979). Burrell notes that Aquinas looked to philosophy for appropriate intellectual therapy not as an explanatory framework. Accordingly, Aquinas' strategy, as he says in the *Summa*, is to show 'the ways in which God does not exist' by ruling 'out from him everything inappropriate, such as compositeness, change and the like' (14). It is precisely this point, I take it, that leads John Milbank to consider Aquinas among those who understood that 'only theology overcomes metaphysics.' For Aquinas speaks of God creating Being as such and not just beings and, thus, 'conceives the divine *esse* as incomprehensibly other than the *ens commune* of creatures, because it uniquely coincides with his essence, or his infinite "whatever he is."' The *Word Made Strange: Theology, Language, Culture* (Oxford: Basil Blackwell, 1997), 41. Milbank's comment comes in his quite appreciative critique of the work of Jean-Luc Marion.

[7] No one has developed the similarity between Aquinas and Barth more carefully than Eugene Rogers. See his *Thomas Aquinas and Karl Barth: Sacred Doctrine and the Natural Knowledge of God* (Notre Dame: University of Notre Dame Press, 1995). By comparing what Aquinas and Barth say in their respective commentaries on Romans, Rogers is able to show that for each 'concrete nature is shot through with grace' (7).

[8] Ibid. 7–8. This quote from Barth comes from his *A Shorter Commentary on Romans* (Richmond, Va.: John Knox Press, 1959), 28.

[9] For the most thorough treatment of Barth's understanding of the dialectic, see Bruce McCormack, *Karl Barth's Critically Realistic Dialectical Theology: Its Genesis and Development. 1909–1936* (Oxford: Clarendon Press, 1995). McCormack notes that Barth's insistence on the Bible as the rule of faith, at least in his book on Calvin, did not mean that God was excluded from speaking in nature and history. Like Calvin, Barth assumed that there was 'natural revelation,' but such revelation was 'actualized' by the lens of Scripture which, of course, requires the action of the Holy Spirit.

God which speaks only of itself, which does not really penetrate the realm of human symbolic constructions without getting tainted and distorted, must continue to be without impact upon the world, and therefore remains locked in a category of the specifically religious, just as much as the liberal Protestant notion of "religious experience."[10] As a result, we lose the means to counter Durkheimian-like accounts of our faith in a God who is both the beginning and end of our existence.[11]

God must matter, but how God matters cannot be shown, as Eugene Rogers puts it, by beginning from the bottom up.[12] Aquinas' so-called 'proofs' for God's existence, for example, have all too often been mistakenly construed as an attempt to begin from the bottom up. Yet Aquinas, insofar as he was shaped by Aristotle's account of demonstration, knows that one can only begin such proofs with Christ. As Rogers has it, 'The paradigm of demonstration is the "demonstration of the Father"' by Jesus Christ, 'who, as a human being, is the "demonstration" [via] stretched out for us into God' (ST I, proemium to q. 2). According to the philosophy of science implicit in the Summa, it is

[10] John Milbank, Theology and Social Theory: Beyond Secular Reason (Oxford: Basil Blackwell, 1990), 101. Milbank does not explicitly associate Barth with this criticism, but I think it safe to say that such a characterization is meant to suggest a Barth-like position. Of course, while such a position is Barth-like it may not, as I have already suggested, be Barth.

[11] There is a fascinating parallel to these developments in Catholicism which is nicely brought out by Fergus Kerr, 'French Theology: Yves Congar and Henri de Lubac' in David Ford (ed.), The Modern Theologians: An Introduction to Christian Theology in the Twentieth Century (2nd edn), (Oxford: Basil Blackwell, 1997), 105–17. Henri de Lubac rightly noted in his Surnaturel that the grace/nature dualism in Catholic theology, though intended to protect nature against Lutheranism and grace against Enlightenment humanism, became itself the creator of deism and atheism. Thus, the anticlerical laicism of the Third Republic was simply the mirror image of a supernaturalist religion that was either the empty shell of cultic practice or a retreat into a spirituality of private interiority (109). According to Kerr, the 'central thesis of Surnaturel, positively put, is that in the whole Catholic tradition until the sixteenth century the idea of humanity as the image of God had prevailed. Neither in patristic nor in medieval theology, and certainly not in Thomas Aquinas, was the hypothesis entertained of a purely natural destiny for human being, something less than the supernatural and eschatological vision of God. There is only this world, the world in which our nature has been created for a supernatural destiny. Historically, there never was a graceless nature, or a world outside the Christian dispensation' (113). For a wonderful account of the Catholic discussion of nature/grace within the politics after the French Revolution as well as how that discussion is necessary for understanding Rahner, see R. R. Reno, The Ordinary Transformed: Karl Rahner and the Christian Vision of Transcendence (Grand Rapids: Eerdmans, 1995). In Immortal Longings (London: SPCK, 1997) Kerr responds quite positively to Reno's attempt to read Rahner in a manner that makes him not so susceptible to criticism of Rahner's transcendentalism in Theology After Wittgenstein.

[12] For a helpful discussion of the ways in which the descriptions 'from above' and 'from below' are on the one hand misleading and obfuscatory yet on the other necessary in theology, particularly in Christology, see Nicholas Lash, 'Up and Down in Christology,' in Stephen Sykes and Derek Holmes (eds.), New Studies in Theology, Vol. 1 (London: Duckworth, 1980), 31–46.

other scientific disciplines that mimic *that*. The scientific character of other, Aristotelian and christoform demonstrations comes from the top down; 'to call Aristotelian and christoform arguments both "demonstrations" and both "scientific" is not equivocal, according to sacred doctrine, just because Aristotelian demonstrations too participate in the Logos by analogy.'[13]

The so-called 'Five Ways,' therefore, do not represent for Aquinas the paradigm of demonstration. On the contrary, Aquinas' theological appropriation of the Five Ways saves them, as Rogers has effectively argued, from not counting as demonstrations at all.[14] 'The appropriation saves the Five Ways by taking them up into the realm of *revelabilia*, in which, through God-bestowed faith, they are joined with the first truth they cannot otherwise reach. The Five Ways are caused to assert the unGod-forsakenness of nature under conditions short of the will's assent to God. They are caused to assert the unGod-forsakenness of nature

---

[13] Eugene Rogers, 'Thomas and Barth in convergence on Romans 1?' *Modern Theology* 12, 1 (January 1996), 66. Rogers argues that Aquinas and Barth understood themselves to be commentators on Scripture, which is why any comparison of these two theologians must first turn to their scriptural commentaries. Rogers maintains that 'Barth and Thomas want to affirm that what God primarily reveals is God's own self in Jesus Christ. For Barth Jesus Christ is the primary form of the threefold Word of God, incarnate, written, and preached. For Thomas Jesus Christ must also be the real, light-giving aspect of the Revelation in order to ground the new *scientia* of sacred doctrine as other revelations grant to other Aristotelian disciplines the first principles that give them rise. According to the *Summa's* account of "proceeding from first principles," sacred doctrine is not a deficient science for proceeding from Revelation: it is rather for that reason a proper science; indeed, it is science *par excellence* . . . For both Barth and Thomas scripture is the place from which one mounts arguments, for Barth as the second form of the Word of God, for Thomas as the propositional form of the first principles to which sacred doctrine must attend and return in order to exercise its scientific character. And for both Barth and Thomas the scripture witnesses, whether as the Word's secondary form, or as *scientia's* propositional aspect, to Jesus Christ as the argument that trumps or absorbs all others' (80).

[14] For similar accounts of Aquinas' 'method', see Thomas Hibbs, *Dialectic and Narrative in Aquinas: An Interpretation of the Summa contra Gentiles* (Notre Dame: University of Notre Dame Press, 1995) and Robert Barron, *Thomas Aquinas: Spiritual Master* (New York: Crossroad Books, 1996). As Barron observes, what is crucial is the tag line with which Aquinas concludes his 'proofs': 'and this (the first mover) all understand to be God.' From this Barron infers, correctly I think, that Aquinas' proofs are part and parcel of the same spiritual dynamic of the tenth book of Augustine's *Confessions*, where 'the saint interrogates nature, all the beauty and splendor of finite creation, in search of God. The "sea and the deeps . . . the things that creep . . . the winds that blow . . . the heavens, the sun, the moon and the stars" join in unison and deny their divinity: "we are not the God whom you seek." In other words, God, the ultimate good of one's life, cannot be discovered in anything that is merely finite, anything that can be found "in the world." In the more sober language of Aquinas, the soul is urged to look for God, neither in himself (no self-movement) nor in the things of the world, no matter how impressive (no infinite regress of moved movers), but rather only in that power that is fundamentally transcendent, only in the "unmoved mover." There is something implied in this proof that is great comfort to sinners. Thomas shows that whatever is in motion is in fact always and inevitably moved by God' (67–68).

even in conditions of a will's dissent from God. In so doing they save Paul's usage: they save *cognitio subtracta*. And in so doing they claim the world for the realm of *revelabilia*. The point is not that Aristotle is outside the realm of *revelata*; he is led by the hand into the world of *revelabilia*.'[15] In short, Aquinas' 'method,' the 'proofs,' help us see that if God is indeed the kind of God found in Jesus Christ, then we should not be surprised that the world looks the way it does. That is to say, any account of the way things are requires a first cause and a last end.[16] As Aquinas puts it in his commentary on the Gospel of John, 'creatures were not sufficient to lead to a knowledge of the Creator . . . Thus it was necessary that the Creator himself come into the world in the flesh, and be known through himself. And this is what the Apostle says: "Since

---

[15] Rogers, 'Thomas and Barth in Convergence on Roman's 1?', 66–67. The phrase, *cognitio subtracta*, is Rogers' invented technical term employed as a convenient device to summarize Thomas's views on Rom. 1:18, in particular, the Pauline phrase, 'they detained the truth in unrighteousness.' *Cognitio subtracta* is an appropriate description of such knowledge 'since it results from subtracting from or insulting the power and *scientia* that God possesses, on which it should depend' (64). In short, *cognitio Dei subtracta* is 'a cognition of God without the ramifications or the full coherence that faith requires.' The fact that such knowledge does not exhibit the full coherence of faith, however, does not invalidate its status as a preamble to faith. On the contrary, 'preambles are "pre-" not because they are foundational (in the sense of logically prior or more generally accessible), but because they are serviceable (in the sense of standing at sacred doctrine's disposal)' (64). Such knowledge may therefore be taken up into faith, become faith. The implication, then, is that this knowledge, incomplete as it is, should not be despised but rather respected inasmuch as it is precisely by this means that defective human intellects are more easily remedied by the 'leading by the hand' (*manuductio*), moving the unregenerate from the realm of revelata into the world of *revelabilia* (66).

Rogers, in words almost identical to Kerr's (see Note 10 above), notes that 'Thomas inter*defines* nature and grace. That is because we cannot understand properly functioning nature apart from grace, and we cannot recognize nature, either as it concretely subsists in the faithful or as it concretely subsists in the unfaithful, without knowing what its *end* is, a purpose that God graciously *bestows* upon it elevating it. This much any Barthian should grant: we ought to define nature in terms of grace because it takes Jesus Christ to tell us what nature is' (70).

[16] Burrell puts the matter as follows: 'if created existence is God's proper effect, then it must bear his likeness. And Aquinas affirms as much. In the context of God's perfection, he asks whether creatures can be said to resemble God. After rejecting any thought of a specific or even generic likeness, he does admit a sort of likeness. Creatures find themselves reflecting the creator "by an analogical similarity like that holding between all things because they have existence in common. And this is how things receiving existence from God resemble him: for precisely as things possessing existence they resemble the primary and universal source of all existence" (1.4.3). So if we could know what it was for anything to exist, we would have a proximate lead to what God was like. Then we would be in possession of one of his proper traces, like Friday's footprints' (*Aquinas: God and Action*, 51). Burrell observes that this can only be taken as a joke, since even if we assert that something exists we cannot know what it is to exist. Thus, we cannot speak of creatures resembling God in any way that would allow us to know, from creatures and from a creaturely point of view, what God is like. What we discover in our understanding of God, therefore, is our limits, which, given God, is precisely what we should expect.

in the wisdom of God the world did not know God by its wisdom, it pleased God to save those who believe by the foolishness of our preaching."[17]

By this point you may well be asking, 'But what does this have to do with morality?' That the question carries with it a certain obviousness and urgency is itself suggestive. Put bluntly, I think it underscores the fact that the various attempts by theologians in modernity to 'do' ethics from the 'bottom up' has, understandably, amounted to nothing less than an apologetic strategy which is bound to fail. Such accounts of morality are destined to run aground precisely because they confirm modernity's presumption that God is, at best, something 'added on' to the moral life. Hence, the challenge most central to modern theology is: how can we show that God matters without such a display appearing as a form of special pleading? I want to propose that one of the ways we might begin to mount such a display is to attend to what might be characterized as the grammar of the Decalogue. In particular I hope to show that those who would ground a natural morality on the basis of the so-called second table of the commandments are making a profound mistake. As creatures of a gracious God we should not be surprised to discover that learning to be truthful is an activity that leads us to acknowledge the one true God or that the worship of such a God requires we be truthful. That truthfulness and worship of God are inseparable is what I hope to show. The truth is finally known in the showing.

In order to provide such a 'showing,' I propose to look at Aquinas' and Luther's accounts of the Decalogue. I have chosen these two central figures primarily because I find their construals so persuasive. Moreover, I think it a useful ecumenical exercise to indicate, this side of modernity, just how much there is that unites, rather than divides, Aquinas and Luther. Furthermore, each provides important emphases for the argument I want to make. Aquinas' account of the Decalogue as natural law conforms exactly to Rogers' depiction of the Five Ways; that is, they are Aquinas' way of showing what our lives should look like as people created for friendship with God. Luther, as might be expected, provides a quite extraordinary account of how the last nine commandments depend on, and in that sense are an elaboration of, the first. This precludes any view of the commandments as some necessary minimum designed to preserve us from moral anarchy and thereby insure our survival. On the contrary, they entail positive duties the following of which constitutes a life of human flourishing.

---

[17] Quoted in Barron (48). Iain Torrance directed my attention to this wonderful quote from Athanasius that I think also expresses Aquinas' views, 'It would be more godly and true to signify God from the Son and call him Father, than to name God from his works and call him Unoriginate.' I read this in Thomas F. Torrance's, *The Trinitarian Faith: The Evangelical Theology of the Ancient Catholic Church* (Edinburgh: T&T Clark, 1988), 49.

Aquinas' and Luther's accounts of the Decalogue help us see how any attempt to tell the truth about God is unavoidably connected with our ability to speak the truth about the world. Truth about the way things are, accordingly, cannot be isolated from the kind of people capable of acknowledging the way things are. For the way things are, the God who creates the way the world is, is revealed by a people trained to be truthful. Holiness and truth are inseparable, which means that no metaphysics is or can be sufficient if a community has lost the skill to recognize lies. Such a skill, moreover, requires constant attention since truth at one time or in one context can so quickly become the lie.

Before turning to Thomas and Luther on the Decalogue, let me put as clearly as I can what I am trying to do. My main objective is to avoid the abstract relation between nature (natural law) and grace (revealed law) which so dominates theological thinking in modernity, especially as that gets played out in what is commonly known as 'theological ethics' or 'moral theology.' By concretely situating the relationship between nature and grace within the ethical practices of everyday Christian life (the content and shape of which are stipulated in the Decalogue), I want to show that the proper way to construe human knowledge of God is neither from 'the bottom up' nor from 'the top down' (insofar as this strategy merely reproduces the epistemological dualisms upon which modernity founders) but is according to the mutual interpenetration of grace and nature as exhibited in the inescapably analogical and historically ordered uses of language by which God's relation to God's creation is articulated. Because human language and reasoning work by virtue of their participation by analogy in the divine Logos, rather than by human conceptions derived independently of and antecedent to any revealed knowledge of God (although temporally and humanly considered they no doubt appear to be antecedent to and independent of any revealed knowledge of God), 'nature' is never abandoned by God and in that sense devoid of grace. The fact that this judgement concerning nature's ineluctably 'grace-full' character can only be determined retrospectively in no way compromises its verity. In short, my argument is that apart from grace we are not even in a position to recognize nature (i.e., name it as such) let alone properly understand it; that is to say, without knowing its true end in Christ, 'nature' is largely unintelligible.

Of course, such a claim begs for the 'we' to be named. Who is this 'we' that is not in a position to recognize nature apart from grace. The 'we' may be considered to be human beings *per se* who are in principle capable of such recognition, but who in fact may not exist. More likely is the 'we' that finds itself in a tradition or engaged by a tradition which is shaped by years of inquiry. Such traditions may well testify to the way of life found in the Decalogue. Finally the 'we' names a person in such a tradition who may be more or less than the possibilities offered within their tradition. The crucial point is that the recognition of our 'nature' as creatures is possible only to the extent we discover we are constituted by a *telos* not of our own making.[18]

That nature's *telos* is in Christ means that both the beginning and end of human existence cannot be other than in a God whose creation encompasses both nature and human nature. In other words, the true character of nature/human nature only comes to light when set within the purview of God's 'grace-full' dominion. God's rule or lordship over creation, however, is not exercised externally or 'at a distance' but comes close in Jesus Christ. Indeed, God's 'grace-full' dominion is embodied most preeminently in human form: the fleshly person of Jesus of Nazareth, the prolongation of whose earthly life finds embodiment in the church. This does not mean that God's dominion is limited or confined to the church; only that its 'origin,' its most concentrated expression, is there displayed. All of which is to say that a true and proper understanding of nature cannot be had apart from a true and proper understanding of the politics of God's rule. Any discussion of natural law which excludes or omits its ecclesial dimension is therefore bound to be distorted. The converse is also true: any understanding of ecclesiology which occludes its 'natural' dimension is likewise skewed. In short, because the God who exercises 'grace-full' dominion over creation (nature/human nature) is the same God who has revealed himself in Jesus Christ, it follows that such a self-disclosure entails the eschatological necessity (though perhaps not the temporal permanence) of the church.

That politics and nature are so intimately conjoined is perfectly consonant with the character of God's dominion as expressed in the Decalogue. In this regard, it is clearly correct to speak of the Decalogue as God's 'natural law,' insofar as the Ten Commandments reveal what our lives should look like as people created for friendship with God. But the expression 'natural law' does not entail a knowledge which could be had anterior to or separable from an understanding of the politics of God's law. Because politics and nature are indissolubly joined, because grace and nature cohere, it would be a mistake to assume that a correct understanding of one could be had without the other. As both Aquinas and Luther argue, the last nine commandments in the Decalogue depend upon, and in that sense are an elaboration of, the first. This means that our understanding of the natural cannot be separated from the political any more than the theological can be separated from the ethical/ecclesial.[19]

---

[18] I am indebted to L. Gregory Jones for helping me clarify these matters.

[19] I am indebted to Dr James Fodor for these last three paragraphs. He has helped me better to see, as well as to say, what I have been struggling to see and say in this paper. Aquinas' and Luther's accounts of the Decalogue do not explicitly place the law within the covenant with Israel. Any full accomplishment requires such

Aquinas and Luther on the Decalogue

The assumption that the Decalogue represents a minimum or baseline morality has dominated interpretations of the Decalogue in modernity. In spite of all our heated and often rancorous disagreements, many assume that we can at least still agree on one or two fundamental, inviolable moral precepts: for example, that stealing, lying, and perhaps adultery, are wrong. My suspicion, however, is that such a consensus about the purported intention and moral content of the Decalogue is usually entertained by those who have never read Exodus 20. And even among those who have taken the pains to read Exodus 20, concentration is commonly focused on the Decalogue's so-called 'moral precepts,' the assumption being that these can be safely and relatively easily separated off from the first three commandments. Alan Donagan, for one, contends that despite the fact that Christian moralists frequently find themselves divided over the sense in which 'the universal part of the Mosaic law is written in the hearts of all men,' they all nonetheless agree upon the common morality which the Decalogue advocates. 'The stricter opinion was that the bulk of the Ten Commandments are written in every heart, in the sense that nobody can be ignorant of them except through some wilful misuse of his mind, and that consequently, ignorance of the law is always culpable.'[20] Donagan notes that while anthropological knowledge of

---

a display. For a particularly suggestive account, see James McClendon's reflections on the Decalogue in his *Systematic Theology*, Vol. I, *Ethics* (Nashville: Abingdon Press, 1986), 177–84. He notes that the two positive commandments – remember the Sabbath day, and honor your father and mother – can be said to provide cultural and biological time that exemplifies the rhythm of memory and hope which characterizes Israel's life. So each of the commandments (except perhaps the first and the last) has its place in connection to practices that make Israel's existence possible through time. For example, it only makes sense to honor fathers and mothers if there are mothers and fathers. The prohibition against adultery requires the practice of marriage. So all the commandments are ordered to one another through the story 'in which these practices (of worship, art, the rhythm of time, kinship, and the rest) arise and take their place – to the story of Israel, and behind that, as Genesis 1–11 shows, to the story of all the earth – and to the role of YHWH in each of these stories. In these human ways, out of these drives and needs, the practices did arise, but they arose already subject to abuse or corruption. Confronting this crisis of human and institutional corruptions, the establishment of the community of Israel represents a redemptive move by God ('You shall be to me a kingdom of priests') designed to free Israel and finally all of us from our missing of the way, and to do so through this community, via this story, by means of these particular laws (183–84). Obviously the Decalogue requires narration within God's covenant with Israel. The Decalogue, so to speak, provides the practices that give form to God's promise to make Israel a holy people – not the least implication means that Israel must take the time to be holy.

[20] Alan Donagan, *The Theory of Morality* (Chicago: University of Chicago Press, 1977), 5. Donagan's position in *The Theory of Morality* has always struck me as odd – he wants to identify and defend something called the Hebrew-Christian moral tradition yet give what is essentially a Kantian account of morality. How one can be a 'little-bit historical' and Kantian at the same time is not clear.

the great variety of human mores has made this severe opinion more or less incredible, such evidence has not 'touched the less strict opinion that certain common conceptions underlying the Torah are accessible to everybody.'[21] Donagan is thus pleased to congratulate the Jewish and Christian traditions for advocating a common morality that in no way requires us to be religious; that is, to live a Jewish or Christian life.

The presumption that the so-called moral precepts of the Decalogue could be separated from our obligation to worship God would, I think, strike the Church Fathers as distinctly odd. Augustine, for example, notes that 'The beginning of freedom is to be free from crimes . . . such as murder, adultery, fornication, theft, sacrilege and so forth. When once one is without these crimes (and every Christian should be without them), one begins to lift up one's head toward freedom. But this is only the beginning of freedom, not perfect freedom. . . .'[22] The commandments cannot be separated, viewed in isolation from one another, and in particular, from the first commandment.

Aquinas

Aquinas' account of the Decalogue presumes the necessary interrelation of the commandments. For example, in the first article dealing with the precepts of the Old Law, Aquinas asks whether the Old Law contains but one precept. He has, of course, to account for Romans 13:9, a text which seems to suggest that all the commandments are contained in the command to love our neighbors as ourselves. While conceding the necessity of the diversity of the precepts of the Old Law, Aquinas nonetheless notes that they are all one in respect to their relationship to the one end, which is charity. According to Aquinas, every law – especially the Decalogue – 'aims at establishing friendship, either between man and man, or between man and God. Wherefore the whole Law is comprised in this one commandment, *Thou shalt love thy neighbor as thyself*, as expressing the end of all commandments: because love of one's neighbor includes love of God, when we love our neighbor for God's sake. Hence the Apostle put this commandment in place of the two which are about the love of God and of one's neighbor, and of which Our Lord said (Matt. 22:40): *On these two commandments dependeth the whole Law and the prophets.*'[23]

[21] Ibid. 5.

[22] Quoted by Reinhard Hütter, '"God's Law" in *Veritatis Splendor: Sic Et Non*,' forthcoming in *Ecumenical Ventures in Ethics: Protestants Engage John Paul II's Moral Encyclicals* (Grand Rapids: Eerdmans, 1997). I am indebted to Professor Hütter not only for his analysis of *Veritatis Splendor*, but for the perspective he provides in general on these issues.

[23] Thomas Aquinas. *Summa Theologiae*, I–II, 99, 1. ad. 2. Translated by the Fathers of the English Dominican Province (Westminster, Maryland: Christian Classics, 1981). All references to the *Summa* (ST) will appear in the text.

I am aware that Aquinas has often been interpreted as a 'natural law' thinker, which allegedly means the so-called moral precepts of the Decalogue can be defended on grounds of reason alone.[24] There is no question that Aquinas thought that the Decalogue contained the moral precepts that are discoverable in human community unaided by revelation, but he thought that the commands to have no other gods, not to take the name of God in vain, as well as to worship God, were all moral commands (ST I-II, 99. 3). Aquinas observes, for example, that the time and manner of worshipping God is a matter of ceremonial law and wisdom, but that we are morally obligated to worship God is rightly understood as what we owe God and therefore is a moral precept (ST I-II, 100, 3, ad, 1 and 2). As Aquinas puts it: 'Worship is merely a declaration of faith: wherefore the precepts about worship should not be reckoned as distinct from those about faith. Nevertheless precepts should be given about worship rather than about faith, because the precept about faith is presupposed to the precepts of the decalogue, as is also the precept of charity. For just as the first general principles of the natural law are self-evident to a subject having natural reason, and need no promulgation; so also to believe in God is a first and self-evident principle to a subject possessed of faith: *for he that cometh to God, must believe that He is* (Heb. 11:6). Hence it needs no other promulgation than the infusion of faith' (ST I-II, 100, 4, ad, 1).

The precepts of the Decalogue are therefore rightly ordered, since we need first to be rightly related to God in order that we might thus be related to one another. Aquinas assumes that this ordering is neces-

---

[24] Given present constraints, I simply cannot enter into the more general questions surrounding Aquinas' account of natural law and the relation of his account of natural law to the virtues. Clearly it is the virtues that are the primary way Aquinas thinks about the nature of the moral life, but it was simply not part of his world to assume that one must choose between law and/or virtue for displaying the nature of the Christian life. For example, in answer to the question whether or not the old law contains moral precepts, Aquinas responds: 'The Old Law contained some moral precepts; as is evident from Exod. 20:13, 15: *Thou shalt not kill, Thou shalt not steal.* This was reasonable: because just as the principal intention of human law is to create friendship between man and man; so the chief intention of the Divine law is to establish man in friendship with God. Now likeness is the reason of love according to Eccles. 19:2: (cf. 9:45): *You shall be holy, for I am holy.* But the goodness of man is virtue, which *makes its possessor good.* (*Ethic.* 2, 6). Therefore it was necessary for the Old Law to include precepts about acts of virtue: and these are the moral precepts of the law' (ST I–II, 99, 2). Herbert McCabe has it right, I think, when he suggests, 'You cannot fit the virtues into a legal structure without reducing them to dispositions to follow rules. You can, however, fit law and obedience to law into a comfortable, though minor, niche in the project of growing up in the rich and variegated "life of virtue."' See his 'Manuals and Rulebooks,' in John Wilkins (ed.), *Considering Veritatis Splendor* (Cleveland: Pilgrim Press, 1994), 66. For an account of the natural law and in particular its relation to the old and new law, see Pamela Hall, *Narrative and the Natural Law: An Interpretation of Thomistic Ethics* (Notre Dame: University of Notre Dame Press, 1994). In particular see her account of how the narrative of Scripture contains for Thomas a history of what happens to human beings when they thwart the teleology of their natures (100–106).

sary because he thinks of the Decalogue as a law of dominion. Just as human law directs man in his relation to human community, 'so the precepts of the Divine law direct man in his relations to a community or commonwealth of men under God. Now in order that any man may dwell aright in a community, two things are required: the first is that he behave well to the head of the community: the other is that he behave well to those who are his fellows and partners in the community. It is therefore necessary that the Divine law should contain in the first place precepts ordering man in his relations to God: and in the second place, other precepts ordering man in his relations to other men who are his neighbors and live with him under God' (ST I-II, 100, 5). Aquinas acknowledges that even though our neighbor is better known by way of the senses than God, 'nevertheless the love of God is the reason for the love of our neighbor. Hence the precepts ordaining man to God demanded precedence of the others' (ST I-II, 100, 6, ad, 2).

For Aquinas the Decalogue is nothing less than the precepts of charity.[25] A person cannot fulfil the precepts unless all things are referred to God. Therefore, to honor one's father and mother must be done from charity, 'not in virtue of the precept, *Honor thy father and mother*, but in virtue of the precept, *Thou shalt love the Lord thy God with thy whole heart*' (ST I-II, 100, 4, ad, 2). The first commandment is therefore the necessary presumption of all the commandments, since it is, as I indicated earlier, the purpose of the law to make us friends with God. Of course, such friendship is finally the gift of the Holy Spirit without which even the New Law cannot justify. Aquinas appeals to Augustine's *The Spirit and the Letter* to explain this, for there Augustine rightly speaks of the relationship of letter and spirit. The letter denotes any writing which is external to man, which includes even the 'moral precepts such as are contained in the Gospel. Wherefore the letter, even of the Gospel would kill, unless there were the inward presence of the healing grace of faith' (ST I-II, 106).

Luther

At first blush, Luther might be viewed as a most unlikely ally of Aquinas, but he too understands the purpose of the Ten Commandments in a way quite similar to Aquinas.[26] Luther goes so far as to praise the

---

[25] Of course, Aquinas also thought the precepts of the Decalogue were also the precepts of justice. See, for example, his treatment of the Decalogue in ST II-II, 122, 1-6.

[26] In his 'Treatise on Good Works', Luther asks – given the harsh reality of our sin – why God does not help everyone that needs help, since he is able and knows how to help? In reply, Luther says, 'Yes, he [God] can do it: but he does not want to do it alone. He wants us to work with him. He does us the honor of wanting to effect his work with us and through us. And if we are not willing to accept such honor, he will, after all do the work alone, and help the poor.' 'The Treatise on Good Works', in James Atkinson (ed.), *Luther's Works: The Christian in Society*, Vol. 44 (Philadelphia: Fortress Press, 1973), 52. Luther wrote the 'Treatise on Good Works', which consists

Decalogue for providing a complete guide for the moral life. Curiously, though perhaps not surprisingly if read in context, Luther's general polemic against the law never comes up in his treatment of the Ten Commandments. As George Lindbeck points out, Luther never calls the Decalogue 'law' but 'instruction or teaching (*doctrina*) of the type which can variously be termed *praeceptum Gebot*, and *mandatum*.'[27] Indeed, Luther claims that anyone who knows the Ten Commandments perfectly knows the entire Scripture and is therefore qualified to sit in judgement on all doctrines, estates, persons, laws, and everything else in the world.[28] According to Luther, we have in the Ten Commandments 'a summary of divine teaching as to what we are to do in order that our whole life may please God. They are the true fountain and channel from which all that is to qualify as good works must spring and flow. Apart from the Ten Commandments no deed or conduct can be good or pleasing to God, however great or valuable it may be in the eyes of the world.'[29]

For Luther, the Decalogue is 'inscribed in the hearts of men' as the abiding structure of human existence issued from the Creator's hand.

---

entirely of his reflections on the Decalogue, in 1520. Even though I can discern no difference between his account in the Treatise and the later treatment of the Decalogue in the 'Large Catechism,' I will primarily use the latter. I do so partly to avoid the criticism that the Treatise is early, thereby implying that what Luther says there about the Decalogue cannot be viewed as reflective of his mature position. No such assumption can be made about the 'Large Catechism.' I am using *Getting into Luther's Large Catechism*, introduced by F. Samuel Janzow (St Louis: Concordia Publishing House, 1978).

Hütter argues, in the article cited above, that in contrast to Aquinas and Luther *Veritatis Splendor* is dominated by a far too univocal account of 'law.' Hütter notes that sin and grace do not qualify sufficiently the encyclical's notion of law, obscuring the way the law is always first and foremost encountered by the sinner, that is, by the human being who does not live in communion with, but rather stands in opposition to, God.

[27] George Lindbeck, 'Martin Luther and the Rabbinic Mind,' in Peter Ochs (ed.), *Understanding the Rabbinic Mind: Essays on the Hermeneutic of Max Kadushin*, (Atlanta: Scholars Press, 1990), 151. I am indebted to Reinhard Hütter for calling my attention to Lindbeck's article.

[28] Lindbeck, 152.

[29] *Large Catechism*, 78–79. Though Luther's well-known attack on Aristotle has meant that his 'ethics' has been interpreted as antithetical to virtue language, the truth is that Luther's work is shot through with appeals to virtue. For example, Luther comments, 'I should think that we would have our hands full trying to keep these commandments and to practice gentleness, patience and love toward enemies, chastity, kindness, and so on, together with everything else connected with these virtues. In the eyes of the world, however, works of this kind do not count for much and make little impression. For they lack novelty and pomp and are not bound to special times, places, rites, and ceremonies. They are rather the common, everyday domestic duties that one neighbor can render another: for this reason they are given no recognition' (79). Unlike Aquinas, Luther provides no systematic account of the virtues; nevertheless, like Aquinas, he simply assumed that law and virtue were complementary.

Likewise, Luther maintains, as does Aquinas, that the commandments have been obscured by sin so that now we must rely on God's outward proclamation of the commandments.[30] Nevertheless, the 'external' character of the Decalogue does not in any way render its commandments any less an indicator of what it means to be a Christian.

Like Aquinas, Luther thinks that the first commandment is the key to all the others because 'if the heart is in a right relationship with God and this commandment is kept, then all the other commandments will follow of themselves.'[31] The first commandment 'illumines' all the others and shares its splendor with them. 'For example, in the Second Commandment we are told to fear God and not misuse His name by cursing, lying, deceiving, or other kinds of wickedness and rascality: instead, we are to use it properly and worthily, addressing God in the prayer, praise, and thanksgiving that flow from the love and truth created in the image of the First Commandment. Such fear, love, and trust in Him should drive us and draw us not to despise His Word, but learn it, hear it gladly, keep it holy, and honor it.'[32]

This holds true also of those commandments that involve our relation to our neighbor. Everything 'stems from the force of the First Commandment' so we are to obey father and mother not just for their own sake but for God. This means, according to Luther, that we are not to give inordinate respect to those in authority, but rather such authority is limited to what God expects of us.[33] That all the commandments must be seen in the light of the first commandment, moreover, means that it is not enough to refrain from doing our neighbor any harm, injury, or violence. 'On the contrary, you are to do good to all, helping them and promoting their interests however and whenever you can, purely out of love to God and in order to please Him in the confidence that He will richly repay it all. You see, then, how the First Commandment is the fountainhead and source of what flows through all the rest: to it they all again return as to the source upon which they all depend, for here in this First Commandment the end and the beginning are firmly looped and linked together.'[34]

---

[30] Lindbeck suggests that Luther emphasized more than most in the natural law tradition the need for outward proclamation (152). Such a generalization would certainly not be true of Aquinas.

[31] *Large Catechism*, 36. Berd Wannenwetsch has suggested to me that Luther began later to emphasize the centrality of the third commandment for understanding the interrelating of the commandments. He suggests Luther did so exactly because he understood that without the Sabbath we lacked the material means to locate concretely the sin that grips our lives.

[32] *Large Catechism*, 81-82.

[33] *Large Catechism*, 82.

[34] *Large Catechism*, 82. This view of the commandments as requiring what might be described as positive duties is usually associated with Calvin rather than Luther, but there can be no doubt that Luther was as insistent on this point as Calvin. Indeed, the often emphasized contrast drawn between Luther and Calvin on the role of the law

Such a view of the positive duties entailed by the commandments indicates why Luther, in commenting on the fifth commandment, maintains that God rightly calls all persons 'murderers who fail to give counsel and aid to those who are in need and in peril of body and life.'[35] He supports this view by appealing to Matthew 25:42–43. Luther calls those thieves 'who turn the open public market into a wrecker's yard and robbers' den' by daily taking advantage of the poor by raising prices simply because they can.[36] To raise prices when there is no reason to do so indicates that those who engage in such practices do not put their trust in God. According to Luther, they will bear the burden of being punished by their wealth.

Like Aquinas, Luther presumes that the Decalogue is given in a sequence through which we learn that the commandments are interconnected to the single goal of rightly worshipping the one God. Also, like Aquinas, Luther assumes the God of the first commandment is the same God we find in Jesus Christ. That the God of Jesus Christ is the God of the Decalogue is corroborated by Luther's comments on the command not to bear false witness. He begins by noting that without faith 'no one is able to do this work. In fact, all works are entirely comprised in faith. Therefore, apart from faith all works are dead, no matter how wonderful they look or what splendid names they have. For just as nobody does the work of this commandment unless he is firm and unshaken in the confidence of divine favor, so also he does no work of any of the other commandments without this same faith. Consequently, on the basis of this commandment, anyone may very easily try and find out whether he is doing good works or not. We now see how Almighty God has not only set our Lord Jesus Christ before us that we should believe in him with such confidence, but we also see that in Christ God holds before us an example of the same confidence and of the same good works. God does this so that we believe in him, follow him, and abide in him forever, as he says in John 14:6. 'I am the way, and the truth, and the life': the way, in which we follow him: the truth, that we believe in him: the life, that we live in him forever.'[37]

Aquinas and Luther understood the interrelation of the commands of the Decalogue as practices capable of making us a people truthful before God and one another. To refrain from bearing false witness

---

cannot help but appear, in the light of what Luther actually says on the subject, but the result of later polemics. See, for example, David Steinmetz's account of Luther and Calvin on the first commandment in his *Calvin In Context* (New York: Oxford University Press, 1995), 53–63. That said, Calvin's account of the Decalogue in the *Institutes of the Christian Religion* in many ways remains unsurpassed. Indeed, I had originally planned to compare Calvin to Aquinas, but given the stereotypes of Luther I thought it might be more interesting to use him rather than Calvin on this point.

[35] *Large Catechism*, 59.
[36] *Large Catechism*, 66.
[37] 'Treatise on Good Works,' 113.

does not insure we can be trusted to be faithful in marriage, but such forebearance at least puts us on the path necessary for our acknowledgment (worship of) God who alone can be trusted to be truthful. Accordingly, for Aquinas and Luther the Decalogue gives form to our lives that we may be adequate to be a people with the skills to be truthful with one another and even with God.

How the Law Reveals God: The Necessity of the Church

To this point I have tried to do no more than suggest that Aquinas and Luther are in fundamental agreement concerning their respective displays of the interrelation between the commandments of the Decalogue. I have taken the time to bring these two monumental Christian theologians into conversation because their accounts are, from a modern point of view, quite extraordinary. Neither is concerned in the least with questions that bedevil us – for example, whether we should obey the law because God has commanded it or because the law in itself is good and thus ought to be obeyed.[38] Such a way of putting the matter is, of course, designed to disqualify or make redundant any 'thick' theological account of the moral life. At the very least, it puts any such account in a severe bind. For if what it means to be moral can be justified without appeals to God, then, it seems, God is not especially germane to a description of the moral life. But if morality is not only inadequate but unintelligible without reference to God, then it appears, on modern accounts at least, that we are left with this bizarre but pressing conundrum: Is it possible for God to command that which is immoral?[39]

This unhappy alternative in many ways simply reproduces the questions with which I began this paper. By starting from the 'bottom up,' by trying to show the intelligibility of morality in itself, we cannot

[38] It is important to note that these types of questions are not strictly confined to, nor are they the exclusive product of, modernity but are generated by a more general nominalist outlook. In this regard, see Alasdair MacIntyre's helpful discussion of William of Occam, 'Which God Ought We to Obey and Why?' *Faith and Philosophy*, Vol. 3 No. 4 (October 1986), 361. For an account of Occam's influence in this respect, see Frederick Bauerschmidt, *Juliana of Norwich and the Mystical Body Politic of Christ* (PhD dissertation, Duke University, Durham NC, 1996), 64–80. Bauerschmidt provides a compelling account of how Julian represents an alternative to Occam.

[39] Aquinas does consider whether, for example, the Israelite despoiling of the Egyptians should be viewed as theft or whether Abraham's consenting to slay his son Isaac murder. In the former case, he argues that it was not theft because the Egyptian property came to Israel by 'the sentence of God' and, in the latter, that Abraham did not consent to murder because his own son was to be slain by God. Accordingly, Aquinas maintains that the precepts of the Decalogue are unchangeable, but in their application to individual actions – whether this or that be murder, theft, or adultery – they admit of change; 'sometimes by Divine authority alone, namely, in such matters as are exclusively of Divine institution, as marriage and the like; sometimes also by human authority, namely in such matters as are subject to human jurisdiction; for in this respect men stand in the place of God: and yet not in all respects' (ST I-II, 100, 8, ad, 3).

help but give an account of a world in which God does not finally matter. As a result we lack any response to Durkheim-like construals for our faith. But if we begin from the 'top down,' that is, with God the Commander, then the God who commands risks appearing as arbitrary or at best external to God's own creation. As I tried to suggest above, such an alternative in matters involving our knowledge of God is the result of ahistorical accounts of nature and grace. Hence, the usual questions about 'God and Morality' are necessarily distorted whenever we suppose that we can think about what appears on one side of the 'and' in isolation from what appears on the other.

As I have tried to show, Aquinas and Luther assumed – albeit in quite distinct but I think compatible ways – that the nine precepts that follow the first in the Decalogue are but a commentary on the first and great commandment. Of course, it is good for us to know, for example, that stealing is wrong. However, in order to comprehend in the 'full sense' this prohibition against stealing, we must have some intimation of the fact that everything that is, is God's. Likewise, it is good for us to speak the truth, but without acknowledging the One who is the truth, it is hard to imagine how any human speech could be truthful and trustworthy. Moreover, in order for us to know what it means not to steal or not to tell a lie, we must understand why it is that none of the commandments can stand on their own and why it is that their vital interconnection is necessary for the formation of a community of people capable of friendship with one another and with God.

I am all too well aware that Aquinas' and Luther's exposition of the Decalogue can only appear in modernity as a 'top down' strategy. But such a judgement is neither necessary nor final. Herbert McCabe, for one, has provided an account of the Decalogue that is not only consistent with that of Aquinas and Luther, but also counters any suggestion that their descriptions are intelligible only on the supposition that one already believes that 'God exists.' McCabe notes that Aquinas clearly thought that the Decalogue was promulgated to us through our capacity to reason. But reason names the process of discovery to which we as a community have come in order to live well together. Such discoveries McCabe compares to a county council's decision to pass laws and put up signs such as '30' or 'Dangerous Bend' on curvy roads. Even if we were all wonderful and careful drivers – in short, virtuous people – such signs are still justified, if only for reasons of predictability and information.[40]

---

[40] Herbert McCabe, *What Is Ethics All About?* (Washington, DC: Corpus Books, 1969), 46–56. I regard this book as one of the genuinely great books written in ethics over the past fifty years. That it has been overlooked and ignored says much more about our context than it does about the importance and profundity of McCabe's book. The superiority of McCabe's approach is that while it concedes that the Decalogue is promulgated to us through our capacity to reason, it in no way implies that reason is a fixed, ahistorical feature of humans or that reason somehow lies 'outside' or is separable

Aquinas, too, did think that the 'county council' had spoken – to extend McCabe's image. In other words, Aquinas 'thought that God, as the inventor of mankind, the one who made the decisions about what sort of institution mankind should be, had as a matter of fact issued the basic laws of mankind as well. He thought that the ten commandments were a matter of God telling us the natural law. Now in a queer way I think Aquinas was right about this, though it would be better put the other way round. It is not God who reveals to us the ten commandments, but the ten commandments that reveal God to us.'[41] This is a startling but I think appropriate suggestion, as long as we remember that the God thus revealed is the same God who has created us to be friends with one another. And if we are so created, then we should not be surprised to discover that the world has a purpose and that human friendship means that we cannot lie to or steal from one another.

Alasdair MacIntyre has also argued McCabe's and Aquinas' point, albeit in a more thoroughgoing, historicized manner. In one sense it is readily apparent that any attempt to define or understand key evaluative terms – like justice or the good – independent of any knowledge of God or of God's commands, and which then proceeds to apply those terms to God, would be to treat God as a finite being. In short, invoking 'a standard of truth or goodness, established independently of our knowledge of God's revealed Word and will,[42] is and must be an appeal to something external to that Word and will.' This means that 'if something external to the Word of God were necessary to establish that Word as good, then it too would be greater than the Word of God,'[43] which of course is theologically unacceptable. What this assumption overlooks, however, is that independent and antecedently derived evaluative concepts (like justice) can, and indeed must, be used in an

---

from the jurisdiction of God's 'grace-full' dominion. Reason names not so much an invariant property of human beings but a process of discerning to which we as a community have come in order to live well together. I am again indebted to Jim Fodor for this formulation.

Pamela Hall describes this aspect of Aquinas' account of natural law as the narrative nature of our knowledge of natural law. 'The natural law (as both knowledge of human nature and what conduces to the flourishing of human nature) is discovered progressively over time and through a process of reasoning engaged with the material of experience. We learn the natural law, not by deduction, but by reflection upon our own and our predecessors' desires, choices, mistakes, and successes' *Narrative and the Natural Law*, (94).

[41] McCabe, *What is Ethics All About?*, 57.

[42] MacIntyre, 'Which God Ought We to Obey and Why,' 366. I had originally entitled this essay 'Which God? Whose Morality?,' obviously playing off MacIntyre's *Whose Justice? Which Rationality?* but I was urged to abandon that title because it had become trite. Be that as it may, my indebtedness to MacIntyre should be obvious just to the extent the position I try to develop here owes much to his work.

[43] Ibid. 366.

analogical and historically ordered way. It is at least logically possible, therefore, that divine claims might be evaluated by standards acquired and elaborated independent of knowledge of God, but it does not follow that God is thereby judged by a standard external to God. Such would be the case only if we restrict our attention to that preliminary moment; that is to say, the initial historical situation in which we first acquired our evaluative concepts. 'But if we progress beyond [that initial stage], something we are able to do rationally only because and insofar as we first assented to the divine claims because we judged them to be just (and, of course, true), then we discover, as our analogically and historically ordered concept of justice develops, that the standard by which we judged God is itself a work of God, and that the judgments which we made earlier were made in obedience to the divine commands, even although we did not and could not have recognized this at that earlier stage. God, it turns out, cannot be truly judged of by something external to his Word, but that is because natural justice recognized by natural reason is itself divinely uttered and authorized.'[44]

All of which is to say that it makes *all* the difference which God commands and whose morality is commanded. Neither can be divorced from the other. Whenever such a divorce is attempted, either for apologetic or political purposes, the very character of Christian existence and self-understanding becomes distorted. Indeed, only a community

---

[44] Ibid. 370. For an attempt to spell out MacIntyre's suggestion as an alternative to divine command theories of ethics, see Charles Pinches' and Hauerwas' chapter, 'Is Obedience a Virtue?' in *Christians Among the Virtues: Conversations with Ancient and Modern Ethics* (Notre Dame: University of Notre Dame Press, 1997), 129–45. This way of understanding the significance of the law has crucial implications for getting right the connections between act descriptions and the virtues. Bernd Wannenwetsch, for example, argues that moral judgements are always inseparably tied to the task of description. So even the apodictic phrases of the Decalogue must be heard in a community that has learned to understand in the right way moral notions such as murder. 'You shall not kill' presupposes an extended casuistry that is formed by a community's memory. Wannenwetsch rightly observes that such descriptive considerations remind us that the struggle for morality is always a struggle for language. This serves as a reminder that moral notions are not just 'declared' but rather are shaped by the linguistic conventions of a community and that these conventions are inextricably correlated to practices. There are, accordingly, no such things as 'isolated actions,' since any action derives its intelligibility from being part of recognizable types of conduct represented and passed on through narratives that shape the community's identity. Wannenwetsch thus concludes: 'We do not *first* have the principle of sacredness of life and then refrain from abortion. Rather, our capacity and will to refrain has to do with whether we have experienced ourselves as children accepted and loved; whether we are taken seriously as persons in our formative social relations; whether we have been introduced to the world of biblical narratives that shape our patterns of perception both emotionally and intellectually. Little, perhaps, has been so important over the centuries for the attitude of Christians toward abortion as the liturgical tradition of Advent and Christmas.' Bernd Wannenwetsch, '"Intrinsically Evil Acts" or: Why Abortion and Euthanasia Cannot be Justified,' in Reinhard Hütter and Theodor Dieter (eds.), *Ecumenical Ventures in Ethics: Protestants Engage in John Paul II's Moral Encyclicals* (Grand Rapids: Eerdmans, 1997), 208.

that has properly learned to honor mothers and fathers, to share rather than steal, to speak truthfully and to respect what rightfully belongs to one another, and, equally important, to recognize through all these lessons what constitutes idolatry – only a community so formed is capable of, and more important, desires to worship the one true God truly.[45]

The natural question, of course, is where does such a community exist? As we have already seen, this is not a question peculiar to modernity. Aquinas, no less than his contemporary counterparts, understood the Decalogue to involve questions of dominion. He rightly assumed that the Decalogue is the law for all people, but he also knew that only those that had been given the gift of the Holy Spirit had the opportunity to live out the interrelation of the commands necessary to be a holy people. The church, then, becomes the politics – the dominion – that makes the exhibition of the morality God desires for all people a material reality. To be part of such a politics is to be provided with the means to live the way God created and intended all humans to live.[46] Christians therefore should not be surprised to discover that people who are not Christians find themselves attracted to the church not so much by our beliefs, nor necessarily always by how we live, but by the God whom we worship and who by his Spirit is pleased to dwell within and among us. Of course we hope through such attraction they will discover why our beliefs are the way we live.

That our natural knowledge of God cannot be divorced from a way of life which the church embodies, does not undercut, delimit or otherwise diminish God's jurisdiction of grace. After all, some might argue, if God's dominion is all-encompassing, if nature is never God-forsaken but shot through with grace, then surely knowledge of God (natural law) is accessible to all apart from and anterior to the giving of the revealed law (the Decalogue). Such a view, however, not only shifts the focus of God's rule away from its verbal, active character ('dominion' first of all names an activity) to a nominal and spatially limited domain, but it also confuses the retrospective character of all human knowledge, including our natural knowledge of God, with the specific, gracious, and historically contingent avenues through which

---

[45] Reinhold Niebuhr and Paul Tillich made idolatry the besetting sin of the human condition. Such accounts, however, isolated the first commandment from the other nine. Accordingly, idolatry was depicted as a loyalty to a finite good in a manner that ignores how such a good must always be bounded by the infinite. As a result, such accounts of idolatry could not provide the basis for the discriminating judgements necessary to characterize the kind of lives capable of making all we do and do not do prayer. A God that only makes everything that is finite – thus justifying the attitude of humility – is too transcendent to be found in the commandments and/or the flesh of Jesus.

[46] For a wonderful account of how a truthful church cannot help but be subversive, see Walter Brueggemann, 'Truth-Telling as Subversive Obedience,' *Journal for Preachers* XX/2 (Lent 1997), 2–9.

that knowledge is given. The result is doubly distorting. First, it makes it appear that grace can be separated off from nature, given their apparent spatial coordinates and descriptions. To be sure, speaking of nature and grace in terms of their respective domains or spheres may not necessarily imply that they are mutually exclusive; they may in fact overlap and interpenetrate in a number of ways. Nonetheless, describing God's rule in predominantly spatial terms (e.g., jurisdiction, domain, sphere, realm) tends to fracture and dismember the one activity of God's grace. Little wonder, then, that many contemporary understandings of the relation between nature and grace are also afflicted with dichotomies and dualisms. Second, confusing the historically contingent and temporally particular channels through which knowledge of God's grace has come to us with the retrospective character of all human knowing effectively cuts the historical nerve that runs through the center of God's 'grace-full' activity. Again, this makes ahistorical accounts of the relation of grace and nature appear not only plausible but sufficient. Depriving human knowledge of its inescapable historical dimensions, however, fails to do justice to natural human reason even on its own terms.

That the church is that body chosen by God to display the Decalogue does not mean that everything about how Christians live is or should be in discontinuity with how those who are not Christians live. Indeed, we should expect to find continuities. Christians of all people are committed to discovering analogies – positive and negative – between what God has made possible for us who live as the church and what God has made possible for those who live otherwise. It may even be the case that Christians will discover in those who are not Christians how we might live more faithfully and truly. That God has given to the church the gift of the Spirit does not insure that the church rightly obeys and embodies the commandments. What the gift of the Spirit insures, rather, is that the church is a politics that will surely be appropriately judged if it fails to live true to God.[47] Without such a politics the Decalogue cannot help but appear as an isolated and arbitrary set of injunctions devoid of any rationality. But if the dominion of God is of the sort that takes up the life of the church (and with it the world) into God's very life, then surely any attempt to divorce God and morality, theology and ethics, is a mistake. But I do not wish to conclude by dwelling on mistakes but by pointing to hopeful signs of renewal and recovery which include, even though they are by no means limited to, the re-appropriation of Aquinas and Luther on the Decalogue. Accordingly, I can do no better than to close with an observation by John Milbank:

[47] I think this is also true of the Jews. I am sure, from a Christian theological perspective, that this is true of the Jews. However, I am rather hesitant to make the claim, since it is inappropriate for Christians to make pronouncements about what Jews should or should not think.

[Although] Luther fails to see that faith is from the outset received and enacted charity or a *habitus*, he nonetheless and in a remarkable fashion shows how every good work is itself nothing but faith or confidence. The confident man, believing in plenitude, does not steal, and does not need lies to protect himself. The confident man, trusting in God, is like the good husband who never needs to impress his wife with an exceptional work nor needs a manual of instruction for marriage, but out of his confidence *improvises* exactly good and always non-identical good works all the time . . . The Christian good man is simply for Luther an artist in being, trusting the perfect maker of all things. Essentially his message is that of Augustine: without the virtue of worship there can be no other virtue, for worship gives everything back up to God, hangs onto nothing and so *disallows* any finite accumulation which will always engender conflict. Confident worship also knows that in offering it receives back, so here the temporal world is not denied, but its temporality is restored as gift and thereby rendered eternal. Only the vision and hope of heaven makes us socially and politically just on earth – and how is it, one wonders, that we have ever come to think otherwise?[48]

[48] John Milbank, *The Word Made Strange*, 230–31.

3

'Salvation even in Sin': Learning to Speak Truthfully about Ourselves

Now, what about truth as a duty in our Christian societies? As everybody knows, Christianity is a confession. This means that Christianity belongs to a very special type of religion – those which impose obligations of truth on the practitioners. Such obligations in Christianity are numerous. For instance, there is the obligation to hold as truth a set of propositions that constitute dogma, the obligation to hold certain books as permanent source of truth, and obligations to accept the decisions of certain authorities in matters of truth. But Christianity requires another form of truth obligation. Everyone in Christianity has the duty to explore who he is, what is happening within himself, the faults he may have committed, the temptations to which he is exposed. Moreover, everyone is obliged to tell these things to other people, and thus to bear witness against himself.

Michel Foucault[1]

The Trouble with Sin

Just as Milton struggled not to let the devil become the hero in *Paradise Lost*, so any theologian who takes up the subject of sin must wrestle with the temptation of making sin more interesting than God. This is particularly a problem in our time, given the widespread habit of using the word 'God' as a generalized concept to name all that which remains inexplicable. Not surprisingly, in such a time many people are often more ready to believe themselves sinners than creatures of a gracious God. At least they are more ready to believe they are sinners than they are to believe in a God who not only is the beginning and end of all that is but who has refused to abandon us to our sins.

---

[1] Michel Foucault, *Ethics: Subjectivity and Truth* I, ed. Paul Rabinow (New York: New Press, 1997), 178. The trick is to see all the interconnections between these obligations, which while separable, are finally one and the same. A friend, Janine Fodor, observed on reading this quote, 'And Foucault thought Christianity was a problem!' which nicely indicates my difference from Foucault: he thought bearing witness against oneself is a problem for Christianity; whereas I regard this as one of Christianity's distinctive assets.

That Christ Jesus came into the world to save sinners may be a trustworthy saying (1 Tim. 1:15) but it can also be deeply misleading. Claiming oneself a sinner in our time often invites undisciplined speculation about one's status as sinner to insure, if for no other reason, that one needs saving. If you were shaped as I was, in the revival tents of the American South, you could come to believe that your profoundest religious obligation was to be a sinner worthy of God's salvation. Indeed I have sometimes thought the high point of most revival meetings was the colorful account the preacher must give of everyone's past sins of which, of course, they are now 'free.' Such accounts may not have been good theology, but they were certainly great entertainment.

It is hard to dwell in tents for the whole of one's life. This is true even in the American South. For some of us, learning to live in solid buildings (the kind of structures that usually constitute universities) required us to reject the moralistic and individualistic understanding of sins depicted in the tents and, correlatively, the moralistic and individualistic understanding of salvation that went along with it. Theologically we were reschooled to say that the problem is not sins, but sin. The problem is not our drinking, our sexual immorality, our cheating, our lying. Those are just the forms sin can take. Sin is the problem, not our sins. The only problem with 'sin rather than our sins' is that we are left quite unsure what it means for us to be saved, much less be made holy. As a result, we lose the ability to tell the truth about our lives.

Interestingly enough, what those of us who left the tents behind failed to understand – and I need to be clear that I think the tents should have been left behind – was that the substitution of sin for sins reproduced the same structure of the revival. In fact, the accounts of sin developed by liberal Protestant theologians ironically mirrored the Protestant revival just to the extent that they accepted the presumption that we can have surer knowledge of sin, that we can speak more truthfully about our sin, than we can speak of God. As a result, sin and salvation, while often described as 'social,' remained fundamentally individualistic. The 'social' becomes a substitute for our need of the good company necessary for us to have our sin recognized and from which we hopefully can be saved.

I will try to provide an alternative to such liberal accounts of sin by offering a different account of Paul's understanding of sin. By 'Paul's account of sin' I mean how Paul exemplifies the actual naming of sins that draws on the concrete practices of the community of the baptized. Such an account, I believe, God has given us so that we might have a way of speaking truthfully with one another. Before I offer such an account, however, I need to substantiate a little more fully the claims I have made about the problematic role of sin in recent theology.

Sin and the Human Condition: Why They Are Not the Same

In *Christian Theology: An Introduction to its Traditions and Tasks*, a book designed to introduce students to the major motifs of Christian theology, Robert Williams' article on 'Sin and Evil' is not only a model of clarity but also an exemplification of the liberal account of sin I criticized above.[2] Williams begins by noting that the doctrine of sin (and evil) occupies an anomalous position in Christian doctrine.[3] There is, for example, no officially stated orthodox doctrine of sin comparable to what Williams characterizes as the 'soteriological doctrines of Trinity and Christology' (168). Williams observes, however, that certain views of sin, such as that of the Manichees and Pelagians, are clearly incompatible with the Christian faith. Augustine's role in combating both of these heresies has not resulted in his account of original sin being adopted as doctrine by the church, but Williams rightly suggests that Augustine's thought on these matters is so influential that his views have semi-official standing. After Augustine no one doubts that the concepts of sin and salvation are systematically related, such that the one cannot be formulated without the other.

That sin and salvation are so linked, however, creates as many theological problems as it solves. When the relation between sin and salvation, for example, is worked out in general anthropological terms, too often the account of sin controls the correlative understanding of Christ's person and work. Williams indicates this was not a problem for Augustine because his account of sin took shape through his reflection on Scripture. The 'Fall' names for Augustine the disobedience of our first parents whose story becomes, through Christ, the story of all our lives. Augustine's reading was, of course, shaped by Paul's claim: 'By one man's disobedience many were made sinners, so by one man's obedience many will be made righteous' (Rom. 5:19).[4]

Williams argues, however, that Augustine's way of displaying sin through scriptural narration is no longer a possibility for us because we can no longer believe in the literal interpretation of Genesis 2–3 as

---

[2] Robert R. Williams, 'Sin and Evil,' in Peter Hodgson and Robert King (eds.), *Christian Theology: An Introduction To Its Traditions and Tasks* (London: SPCK, 1982), 168–95. All references to this article will appear in the text.

[3] I will not try to distinguish sin from evil in this article. They are obviously not the same, but naming the difference between them is a complex matter that cannot be determined in principle.

[4] Williams characterizes Paul's account as an 'anthropological theory of evil' (172) in contrast (I think) to the view that evil is to be found in supernatural powers and demons that have invaded creation and the human soul. Why Williams assumes these are different accounts of sin I am not sure. Even more puzzling is why he would prefer 'the Pauline' account. I suppose it is because he thinks Paul's view is 'anthropological.' Such a view of Paul is a fantasy necessary for Protestant liberals to still think they are being 'biblical.' How, for example, such a view could be consistent with Paul's account of how the Spirit overcomes sin is not considered.

'actual history' (181).[5] Moreover, according to Williams, the classic doctrine of original sin has the further disadvantage of being in contradiction to the two central convictions of modernity: (1) the essential goodness of the human, and (2) the presumption of human freedom and autonomy. Williams observes that even defenders of the classic doctrine, such as Reinhold Niebuhr, make the doctrine appear self-contradictory. On the one hand, sin is not regarded as belonging to essential human nature and therefore not something for which we can be responsible. On the other hand, sin is inherited corruption and, thus, inevitable.

Williams indicates that one theological response to the difficulties associated with the classic doctrine of sin is that of Robert Bellarmine in the sixteenth century and Karl Barth and Karl Rahner in the twentieth. According to Williams, they offer a revision of the classic doctrine which 'logically derives human solidarity in sin from human solidarity in redemption through Christ. In effect, the doctrine of sin becomes a postulate derived from redemption and may be defined as a privation of redemptive grace' (184). From Williams' perspective, this position has the advantage of making clear that the Christian account of sin is primarily soteriological rather than punitive.

Williams argues, however, that this proposed revision, which is an 'important corrective,' creates more problems than it solves. In his words, 'it runs the risk of becoming an abstract fideism. Fideism is present in the attempt to derive the meaning of sin entirely from soteriology and Christology, for if the meaning of sin is entirely generated out of the symbols and concepts of soteriology, no real insight is obtained into sin and evil as aspects of human experience. It was precisely its genuine existential and phenomenological insights into the human experience of evil that made the Augustinian tradition so persuasive and powerful. Augustine's and Aquinas' discussion of concupiscence, for example, provide brilliant insight into the human condition' (184).[6]

[5] I confess I am dumbfounded by the notion that Augustine read anything 'literally,' but for purposes of argument I will let Williams' characterization stand. However, I cannot refrain from observing that the self-assuredness that characterizes such judgements often prevents serious intellectual work. For example, think of the work required to defend philosophically Williams' easy appeal to 'actual history.' I assume the story of our existence we learn through Scripture is as close to 'actual history' as we will ever get.

[6] I am indebted to Professor Steve Long for calling my attention to Williams' article as well as his astute criticism of Williams' position. For example, in an as yet unpublished manuscript, Long notes that Williams must assume that no insight into human experience is obtained from Christology, since putatively something will be lost if sin is bounded by soteriological themes rather than by an account of the human condition. Yet Williams provides no defense for why anyone should think that to be the case. You know you are in the world of Protestant liberalism just to the extent that calling soteriology a 'symbol' is assumed to be unproblematic, as Williams apparently assumes.

According to Williams, Christians must remain committed to an anthropological account of sin so as to avoid the difficulties associated with Augustine's 'classic formulation of the doctrine of sin.' This means that theology must acknowledge that evil – disease and death for instance – preceded the emergence of humankind, making any theory of a historical fall out of the question. Evil permeates human existence to the extent we are constituted by a fundamental ontological insecurity that arises from the nature of freedom itself. 'Freedom is the capacity for self-transcendence; as such it requires that humanity not coincide completely with itself, but rather choose itself in the face of its possibilities. Precisely because freedom has no given nature, it is inevitably accompanied by and gives expression to *Angst*, or constitutive anxiety. Freedom and anxiety are the specifically human way of being fallible, which is to say, vulnerable and susceptible to sin and evil' (186).[7]

Williams draws on traditional Christian characterizations of sin in order to suggest how these accounts remain in continuity with the classical doctrine. Sin is still a matter of unbelief just to the extent that sin is a turning away from the transcendent by failing to acknowledge our dependency. Unbelief gives rise to pride as our refusal to be properly

---

In her *Theories of Culture: A New Agenda for Theology* (Minneapolis: Fortress Press, 1997), Kathryn Tanner argues that the Christian belief in 'the universality of sin and in the capacity of all persons, however sinful, to be saved by the free grace of Jesus Christ' means any strong social difference between Christians and non-Christians cannot be justified (100–101). My problem with such accounts of sin and grace is the complete lack of specification. God does not and cannot be found in God's own creation. Thus Tanner observes, 'Even in Christ the human never approximates the divine but remains distinct and unmixed, no third thing approaching the divine by way of the alternative of properties. The word can be identified with a particular human being, Jesus Christ. But his Christian disciples follow after him at a distance. And the Incarnate Word is only at best indirectly identifiable with even those human words of the Bible that Christians believe effectively witness to him' (26). I fear 'Incarnate Word' becomes but a way to say that 'now you see and now you do not.' Humility is a Christian virtue but one disciplined by a cross that is unmistakably the cross of Christ. That we follow Christ at a distance I take as a given, particularly in liberal cultures. The problem is whether we believe we ought to follow Christ at all.

In fairness to Tanner she may be making the quite orthodox claim that we can become disciples of Christ because Christ's work alone makes it possible for us to be disciples. As Paul Ramsey was fond of observing, Jesus had no one to imitate so his work makes it possible for us to follow him exactly because we do not have to do again what he did. But what one finds missing in any accounts like that of Tanner is specification of what Jesus made possible. The Christian affirmation is not that God can be found in Jesus, but that God is found in Jesus, which means God's 'otherness' is all the more frightening because God is among us.

[7] Williams rightly credits Immanuel Kant's description of 'radical evil' in *Religion Within the Limits of Reason Alone* as one of the first to give an account of sin as inexplicable but unavoidably present. Williams denies, however, that his account of sin makes (as he suggests Niebuhr's account of sin makes) the human condition the equivalent of sin. Yet Niebuhr was equally insistent that the inevitability of sin did not entail its necessity. It is hard to see Williams' or Niebuhr's denials as anything more than assertions.

dependent results in an inordinate desire to insure our own existence. Unbelief and pride lead to avarice and idolatry because, from Williams' perspective, the refusal to live in communion with and dependence on the transcendent means the self is drawn to an inordinate desire for finite goods (189).

According to Williams, the advantage of this account of sin is that there is no need to posit a fall. 'Rather, the starting point is the onto-logical *imperfection* of creation manifest in the instability and ethical-religious immaturity of humankind. Human beings as initially created are not perfect, but they are perfectible. The ethical-religious perfection of humankind is capable of being actualized only in a temporal-historical career. Such ethical perfection cannot be ready-made even by God, for growth in maturity of freedom requires purposive action carried out over a period of time. Under the conditions of ethical-religious imma-turity, sin is virtually inescapable' (191). Redemption can, therefore, be understood as the 'completion of the creation of humankind' (192).

I confess I am always puzzled by accounts of sin like those Williams provides. Whom, I wonder, are people like Williams (and Schleier-macher and Reinhold Niebuhr) writing to and for? Do they think that those who are not part of the Jewish and Christian traditions will be more inclined to understand their lives as sinful than do those who believe themselves created and redeemed by God? Secular intellectuals, when they are thinking hard, have no more use for sin than they do for God.[8] That humans do terrible things to themselves and one another is undeniable, but why call such behavior sin? James Gustafson, given his theological presuppositions, I think rightly no longer talks of sin but rather of the 'human fault.'[9]

Why, in other words, is talk of Christ considered 'fideistic' but not talk of sin? That many who are otherwise not connected to Christianity

---

[8] Martha Nussbaum, for example, in her review of *Whose Justice? Which Rationality?*, criticized Alasdair MacIntyre for taking sin seriously. According to Nussbaum, the concept of sin simply has no purchase in philosophical discourse. Indeed she accuses MacIntyre of introducing sin to underwrite an authoritarian account of reason. While I think she is certainly wrong about MacIntyre's account of rationality, I do wonder if MacIntyre's account of sin in *Whose Justice? Which Rationality?* does not at least muddy the rather strict distinction MacIntyre maintains between philosophy and theology. Nussbaum's review appeared as 'Recoiling from Reason,' *New York Review of Books* 36 (7 December 1989), 38. MacIntyre's discussion of sin in *Whose Justice? Which Rationality?* (Notre Dame: University of Notre Dame Press, 1988) can be found in his chapters on Augustine and Aquinas. MacIntyre notes that the crucial difference between Aquinas and Aristotle is that for Aquinas 'the single most important experience of human beings in relation to the divine law, whether in the form in which reason apprehends its precepts as the natural law or as revealed directly by God in the Ten Commandments, is that of disobedience to it, a disobedience ineradicable by even the best moral education in accordance with reason' (181). He goes on to observe that the only remedy for such disobedience for Aquinas is grace.

[9] James Gustafson, *Ethics from a Theocentric Perspective* I (Chicago: University of Chicago Press, 1981), 293–306.

may describe certain kinds of behavior as sinful testifies not to the universality of sin but to the lingering influence of Christian habits. Such habits may well possess some potential for helping the recovery of more disciplined forms of Christian speech, but I see no reason to think they should tempt us to believe that sin, from a secular point of view, is any less a problematic theological notion than God.

The abstractness of Williams-like accounts of sin cannot help but reinforce the general assumption in modernity that Christianity is primarily a matter of having the right kind of attitudes. If unbelief is refusal to acknowledge our finitude, what could it possibly mean to know that we believe other than to have some general sense that when all is said and done I guess I am really a finite being destined to die? It is not by accident that humility becomes the primary virtue recommended by liberal Protestant theologians. The difficulty is not that humility is a virtue required of Christians but that humility recommended as a general attitude toward death looks suspiciously like Stoic *apatheia*.

The only humility Christians are to nourish is that determined by the cross of Christ. Given Williams' account of sin, however, I cannot understand how it could have happened that some people thought it expedient to kill Jesus. One can only think of Jesus' crucifixion as 'an unfortunate but avoidable failure in communication' if one believes that the remedy for sin is merely better training in the techniques of conflict resolution. Given the way Williams has structured his account of sin, it is hard to see how any resulting Christology can avoid depicting Christ as a great gnostic teacher whose life and words illumine the human condition. As Williams would have it, Christ represents a truth that can be known irrespective of what Jesus may have said or done. The gnostic temptation, which I think is always just around the corner in Christianity, is indicated just to the extent that Israel and the law are not part of the narrative necessary to name sin and redemption. God's promise to Abraham, the giving of the law through Moses, David's kingship, the prophets, John the Baptist, and Jesus' teachings and miracles are displaced in Williams' account, or at least given a secondary role, in favor of something called history.[10] Yet history so understood is not of flesh and blood but a ghostly presence that haunts our lives.

A difficulty seldom noticed about accounts like that of Williams is how such views divorce salvation from ethics. Better put, when sin is mapped over a generalized anthropology the politics necessary for the

---

[10] For my extended critique of the displacement of the narrative of Israel and the church by the notion of history, see *Wilderness Wanderings: Probing 20th-Century Theology and Philosophy* (Boulder: Westview Press, 1997). See also John Howard Yoder, *For the Nations: essays evangelical and public* (Grand Rapids: Eerdmans, 1997). Yoder says, 'History is a process in which specific events can be identified as links in a chain leading from God's past to a common future' (202).

naming of sins is lost. As a result, salvation becomes 'something other' than how our lives are conducted in everyday interactions. The Protestant character of such proposals is manifest by how such accounts of sin render unintelligible the ancient and current practice of confession, penance, and reconciliation. That salvation must be mediated by a community in and through time is simply unimaginable for those who would make the truth about Christ a truth accessible to anyone.

These are harsh criticisms and I need to be fair. For in truth Williams only reproduces in liberal Protestant guise the structure of accounts of sin and atonement often assumed to be orthodox. Satisfaction theories of the atonement have been used to underwrite pretentious, universalistic accounts of salvation that make unnecessary the actual existence of a reconciled people. It is as if the crucifixion covered our overdraft in God's universal bank making all humanity solvent again. Williams (and Reinhold Niebuhr) offer a spectacularly more sophisticated version of what is taught in tent revivals.

John Milbank observes that such an approach seems to say to people that they must accept the basic 'datum' that God became incarnate and, in addition, that his death made atonement for our sins. Put in such an 'extrinsic' fashion, according to Milbank, two objections are provoked: (1) by what process does one arrive at the conclusion that God is incarnate or that a single death is universally efficacious? and (2) what difference does the mere *fact* of God's identifying with us make to our lives or how can the event of the atonement be uniquely transformative? 'To collapse both objections into a single more positive question: how can incarnation and atonement be communicated to us *not* as mere facts, but as characterizable modes of being which *intrinsically* demand these appellations?'[11]

From Milbank's perspective it is pointless to approach incarnation and atonement as revealed propositions. To find out what Christ's person and work was like we must attend to the Gospel narrative. Such 'attention' must be done by a community that has the ability to read the Gospels in confirmation of what makes that community what it is – namely as the story of the '(re)foundation of a new city, a new kind of human community, Israel-become-the-church.'[12] Milbank

[11] John Milbank, *The Word Made Strange: Theology, Language, Culture* (Oxford: Basil Blackwell, 1997), 148.
[12] Ibid. 150. While I am in fundamental sympathy with Milbank's approach, I am not quite willing to say, as he does, that Christological and atonement doctrines are theoretically secondary to definitions of the character of the new universal community of the church (148). Of course everything turns on what Milbank means by 'theoretically secondary' and I am not sure how to read that phrase. Moreover, he argues quite powerfully that his approach to Christology through ecclesiology actually allows for a full retrieval of the Chalcedonian position (156). I suppose my concern is that Milbank's way of working should not just allow for such a retrieval but that it should require just such a retrieval.

68

accordingly represents an alternative to both Williams as well to Williams' alleged more orthodox alternatives.[13] It is an alternative that I will try to explore by attending to Paul's understanding of the relation between sin, stealing, and learning to speak truthfully.

Speaking the Truth, Stealing, and Sin

> So then, putting away falsehood, let each of us speak the truth with our neighbor, for we are all members of one another. Be angry yet do not sin; do not let the sun go down on your anger and do not make room for the devil. Those who steal must stop stealing. Rather, let them do honest work with their own hands, so as to have something to share with those in need. Let no evil talk come out of your mouths, but only what is good for building up as fits the occasion, that it may impart grace to those who hear. Do not grieve the Holy Spirit of God in whom you were sealed for the day of redemption. Put away from you all bitterness and wrath and anger and wrangling and slander together with all malice, and be kind to one another, tenderhearted, forgiving one another, as God in Christ forgave you. Therefore, be imitators of God, as beloved children, and walk in love as Christ loved us and gave himself for us as a fragrant offering and sacrifice to God. (Ephesians 4:25–5:2)

Stephen Fowl observes that this passage offers a series of sharp injunctions about the way Christians ought to use words.[14] That is no doubt true, but one of the other remarkable aspects of the passage is the connection that Paul makes between speaking truthfully and stealing. Why are these peculiar forms of behavior linked in this passage? Why do we get this rather odd list of warnings about anger, wrangling,

---

Milbank observes that Jesus figures in the New Testament as a new Moses, that is, as the founder of a new or renewed law and community. 'It is for this reason that he cannot be given any particular content: for the founder of a new practice cannot be described in terms of that practice, unless that practice is already in existence, which is contradictory. This is why Jesus is presented not simply as the source of the Church, but as arriving simultaneously with the Church. The waters of baptism, the fire of the Holy Spirit, Mary's consent to the incarnation, all in a historical sense "precede" Jesus, although Jesus (through a kind of retroactive causality) makes them operative' (152). To which I can only say: 'I think that is right, but how it can be affirmed as right without diminishing Jesus in the flesh remains to be seen.'

[13] Milbank wonderfully observes that 'the universality of the Church transcends the universality of enlightenment in so far as it is not content with mere mutual toleration and non-interference with the liberties of others. It seeks additional work of freedom which is none other than perfect social harmony, a perfect consensus in which every natural and cultural difference finds its agreed place within the successions of space and time. In this context it is correct to say that the Church is a "community of virtue" which desires to train its members towards certain ends, rather than a "community of rights" founded upon liberal indifference' (154).

[14] Stephen Fowl, *Engaging Scripture: An Essay on Theological Interpretation* (Oxford: Basil Blackwell, forthcoming). As will become apparent, I am in Fowl's debt for much of what follows and, in particular, for making me aware of the extraordinary character of this passage in Ephesians. I will not attempt to provide page references, since I am using Fowl's typescript.

slander and admonitions to be tenderhearted and forgiving? No doubt such a list is determined, at least in part, by what is going on in the church at Ephesus. Obviously some people in the church are stealing, but why does Paul bring it up in the context of a passage having to do with speaking truthfully to one another?

To answer that question, we need to remember that earlier in his letter Paul reminded the Ephesians that once they were dead in their transgressions and sins (Eph. 2:1–2). But through the work of God in Christ they have been saved by grace. So saved they have become God's peace. Once they were excluded from citizenship in Israel, but now they have been brought near through the blood of Christ. 'For he himself is our peace, who has made the two one and has destroyed the barrier, the dividing wall of hostility, but abolishing in his flesh the law with its commandments and regulations. His purpose was to create in himself one new man out of the two, thus making peace, and in this one body to reconcile both of them to God through the cross, by which he put to death their hostility ... Consequently you are no longer foreigners and aliens, but fellow citizens with God's people and members of God's household, built on the foundation of the apostles and prophets, with Christ Jesus himself as the chief cornerstone. In him the whole building is joined together and rises to become a holy temple in the Lord' (Eph. 2:14–22).

Just as we are only able to name as well as identify violence by discovering the practises of peace in which we are imbedded, so we are only able to name, identify, and see the connection between our sins by the practises that constitute a community made possible by Jesus' resurrection from the dead.[15]

As James McClendon puts it,

> Not even the knowledge of sin is our very own contribution to salvific understanding; sin is not a (negative) human achievement to be painted with Faustian pride. Rather authentic knowledge of my sin, clear awareness that I am a sinner, comes only when and as I am saved from it. Only when the strong light of grace penetrates our lives do we see clearly the long shadow cast by past sin; only then, the crannies of corporate or societal corruption; only then, the menace of a future outside the coming rule of God.[16]

[15] I tried to develop this point about violence in *Dispatches From the Front: Theological Engagements with the Secular* (Durham: Duke University Press, 1994), 116–35. I use the language of 'try' to indicate my frustration that I have yet to find a way to put this issue that others will find convincing. The graphic nature of violence seizes our imaginations so we think we know what it is quite apart from whether or not we know peace. As a result, we assume that the burden of proof is always on those who refuse to take up violence in the name of order. Yet the very logic of the just war position, at least in the Christian context, assumes the burden of proof works the other way round. God's peace is deeper and more profound than our violence. Accordingly, those who would use violence purposively bear the burden of proof.

[16] James W. McClendon, Jr, *Systematic Theology*, Vol. II, *Doctrine* (Nashville: Abingdon, 1994), 122.

That Paul, therefore, addresses questions of stealing as part of a general admonition for Christians to speak truthfully to one another is not surprising. As Stephen Fowl notes, these are not demands addressed to isolated individuals, but rather reminders, both positive and negative, of the practices necessary for the common life of the church. 'It is not hard to see that lying (v. 25), allowing one's anger to lead one into temptation (vv. 26–27), stealing (v. 28), destructive speech (v. 29), grieving the Spirit (v. 30), along with bitterness, rage, wrath, quarreling, blaspheming and the like (v. 31) and the inability to forgive one another (v. 32) are all potentially mortal wounds to the common life of the church. Such practices stand in sharp opposition to the life of *agapē* commended by Paul and exemplified by Christ (5:1–2). Given that Paul's aim in this passage is maintaining the common life of the church as a faithful testimony to the work of God, it is no more odd for him to address the issue of Christians stealing (particularly from each other) than it is for him to emphasize truth telling.'[17]

For Christians, therefore, the ability to name, recognize, and remember the connection between our sins is a theological achievement.[18]

---

[17] Fowl, *Engaging Scripture*. Fowl develops the connection between truth-speaking and stealing by showing how they are positive and negative witnesses to God's generosity. Fowl quotes Luther, who in his *Treatise on Good Works* maintained that stealing covers 'every kind of sharp practice which men perpetrate against each other in matters of worldly goods. For instance, greed, usury, overcharging, counterfeit goods, short measure, short weight and who could give an account of all the smart, novel and sharp-witted tricks which daily increase in every trade.' Fowl observes that such practices but manifest the fear there will not be enough. Lying is fueled by the same presumption that people do not have the time to learn how to speak truthfully to one another. Christians do not believe we are constituted ontologically or politically in a world that is a zero-sum game.

[18] In her novel *The Towers of Trebizond* (New York: Farrar, Straus & Cudahy, 1956), Rose Macaulay places her heroine, who is currently having an affair with someone else's husband, in the ruins of a Byzantine church in Tebizond. She discovers a Greek inscription 'which was about saving me from my sins, and I hesitated to say this prayer, as I did not really want to be saved from my sins, not for the time being, it would make things too difficult and too sad. I was getting into a stage when I was not quite sure what sin was, I was in a fog, it makes a confused sort of twilight in which everything is blurred, and the next thing you know you might be stealing or anything, because right and wrong have become things you do not look at, you are afraid to, and it seems you live in a blur. Then comes the time when you wake suddenly up, and the fog breaks, and right and wrong loom through it, sharp and clear like peaks or rock, and you are on the wrong peak and know that, unless you can manage to leave it now, you may be marooned there for life and ever after. Then, as you don't leave it, the mist swirls round again, and hides the other peak, and you turn your back on it and try to forget it and succeed. Another thing you learn about sin, it is not one deed more than another, though the Church may call some of them mortal and others not, but even the worst ones are only . . . a chain, not things by themselves, and adultery, say, is chained with stealing sweets when you are a child, or taking another child's toys, or the largest piece of cake, or letting someone else be thought to have broken something you have broken yourself, or breaking promises and telling secrets, it is all one thing and you are tied up with that chain till you break it, and the Church calls it not being in a state of grace' (150). Only Augustine in the *Confessions* may have said it better. I am in the Revd James Burtchaell's debt for reminding me of Macaulay's wonderful novel.

What the world calls wrong, immoral or, in some cases even praise-worthy, Christians call sin. We do so, not because we are trying to parade our righteousness, but because we know that the lives we hold in common stand before God. Nothing is more indicative for what it means for the church to be holy, God's very temple, than the privilege we have been given to confess our sins to one another. Knowing our sins as sins and, furthermore, admitting to one another and before God (out loud) that we are sinners – that unlikely act constitutes whether in faith we can hope to make progress toward holiness. We are not just 'saved even in sin,' but because of our sin.[19]

Such a view is anything but fideistic. That Christians are required to be a community capable of speaking the truth to one another means that they must also be able to speak truthfully to those who are not Christian. Yet truthfulness remains a task not a result. To claim Christian convictions as true does not mean that Christians have answers before the questions have been formulated or asked. The truth is that often Christians will not know what to say as times and places change. Moreover, the obligation of Christians to be witnesses means we cannot safeguard ourselves from new challenges.[20] The temptation is always to seek safety in past achievements in the hope that the courage that made those achievements possible will not be required of us. That is why the confession of sin is so critical to being a truthful community. Christians do not claim that we are superior to others, only that by having the skill to confess our sins we at least have been given the means to discover our lies.

The seemingly paradoxical claim that we discover our sins in righteousness is not paradoxical at all. Learning not to steal is insufficient to make us righteous, but learning to live through work

[19] The phrase 'salvation even in sin' I stole from Shusaku Endo in a response he gave to a paper by Michael Gallagher, 'For These The Least of My Brethren: The Concern of Shusaku Endo.' Gallagher's paper and Endo's response can be found in the *Journal of The Association of Teachers of Japanese* 27, 1, 75–87. Gallagher's paper and Endo's response issued from the events surrounding Endo's reception of an honorary degree awarded by John Carroll University. Endo's phrase comes as part of his reflection on what it means to be a Christian writer and in particular on the work of Greene and Mauriac. He says, 'I learned from these two writers that there exists a possibility of *salvation even in sin*. The art of Christian writers in the twentieth century, not only of Greene and Mauriac, is similar to that of magicians. Put a woman in the box and cover her with a cloth. Take off the cover and she has changed into a pigeon and flies away! For Greene and Mauriac, sin includes the possibility of salvation . . . I have a firm belief that has been growing stronger with age. It is that Christianity is not a single sound responding to another single sound. Human hearts make a variety of sounds. True religion is the orchestra which puts these different sounds together and responds to all of them. This is the reason I put my trust in Christianity' (87).
[20] The truth is that often Christians will find through witness that those to whom we witness are speaking more truthfully than the church is able to speak.

may help us discern how to be truthful. The law is the way to righteousness, but through the law we are able to discover our sins. In Romans 7:7–12 Paul says,

> Is the law sin? Certainly not! Indeed I would not have known what sin was except through the law. For I would not have known what coveting really was if the law had not said, 'Do not covet.' But sin, seizing the opportunity afforded by the commandment, produced in me every kind of covetous desire. For apart from the law, sin is dead. Once I was alive apart from law; but when the commandment came, sin sprang to life and I died. I found that the very commandment that was intended to bring life actually brought death. For sin, seizing the opportunity afforded by the commandment put me to death. So then, the law is holy, and the commandment is holy, righteous, and good.

Too many theologians, particularly since the Reformation, have spent much time and inordinate amounts of paper trying to explain how such passages are or are not consistent with what is alleged the 'Pauline conception of grace.' Grace, it seems, cannot come in the form of law. Such views of grace and its relationship to the law usually result in an account of sin that looks very much like that provided by Williams.

I should like to think the account I have tried to provide helps us see why all such attempts to 'explain' Paul's view of law and gospel cannot help but fail. Paul simply means what he says. What he says, moreover, is not an invitation to develop a general anthropology that will enable the 'truth' of his perspective to be available to anyone. Rather, what he says about the law to be intelligible requires the existence of a people who are part of a community constituted by practises – practises named by the Decalogue – that make the law serve the purpose of worshiping of God. It must never be forgotten, therefore, that the confession of our sins, which the law makes possible, is intrinsic to the sacrifice constitutive of worship.[21]

James McClendon observes that such a view of sin 'gives no reason to impute mortal sin to members of the human race who have not received Jesus' graceful invitation, his "gospel of the kingdom" (Mark 1:14f). One cannot reject what one has not been offered!'[22] No inference should be drawn, however, that God has abandoned or is not present to those who have not heard the Gospel. We have all been created to desire the right worship of God. From this perspective 'original sin' is the way Christians name our solidarity with all of God's creation. Rather than being a condemnation, 'original sin' is the hopeful affirmation that when Christians faithfully witness to the Gospel through word

---

[21] See, for example, Gregory Jones' account of forgiveness as intrinsic to baptism, eucharist, reconciliation, prayer and healing in his *Embodying Forgiveness: A Theological Analysis* (Grand Rapids: Eerdmans, 1995), 163–204.

[22] McClendon, *Systematic Theology: Doctrine*, 131.

and sacrament those that receive that witness have the means to locate their lives within that witness.[23]

To be able so to locate one's life means, however, being put on the way to perfection through the discovery that, though sinners, we have nonetheless been made righteous. Salvation, then, is best understood not as being accepted no matter what we have done, but rather as our material embodiment in the habits and practices of a people that makes possible a way of life that is otherwise impossible. That is why we are not saved in spite of our sin, but we are saved precisely through practices of confession, forgiveness and reconciliation, which make Christian happiness possible. For what greater joy is there but the knowledge that there is 'salvation even in sin.'

---

[23] It is in this context that Christian attempts to develop an account of the natural law should be understood. For example, Pamela Hall rightly characterizes Thomas' understanding of natural law this way: 'the narrative of Scripture contains for Thomas a history of what happens to human beings when they (try to) thwart the teleology of their own natures. Sin, while an offense against God, is also an injury to the creature sinning. And relearning the natural law requires, Thomas indicates in his explanation of the Old Law and the Jews, coming to terms with the authority of this teleology in achieving one's good and the good of one's community. This meant in part, after the Fall, acknowledging one's inability to do the good one knows; acknowledging one's sinfulness, one then must have recourse to the help of God in revelation and grace. The Jews were taught, Thomas narrates, their own insufficiency and need for God by their inability to keep the natural law. In this regard, the natural law has for Thomas an inescapable theological dimension. We are ordered to union with God, but we cannot attain God, even according to our natural capacities, without divine assistance.' *Narrative and the Natural Law: An Interpretation of Thomistic Ethics* (Notre Dame: University of Notre Dame Press, 1994), 102.

PART II

꧁ꕥ꧂

THE TRUTH ABOUT SANCTIFICATION: HOLINESS EXEMPLIFIED

4

The Sanctified Body:
Why Perfection Does Not
Require a 'Self'

The Problem with Holiness

I am an evangelical Catholic. Which is but a way to say that I am a
Methodist. Methodism is a movement that by accident became a church,
or at least claims to be a church, in America. Wesley charged his
followers to cover the world. We have done that, but as a friend
observes, like Sherwin-Williams paint we are only a fourth of an inch
deep. A strange result for a holiness movement meant to renew an
established church. Yet at least on some readings Wesley represented a
peculiar combination of Catholic and perfectionist theological
convictions.[1] As one wag once put it, 'If Wesley had not been Wesley
he would have been Ignatius Loyola' or, more seriously, there is Albert
Outler's often made claim that the true character of Methodism is to
be an 'evangelical order' with 'a catholic Church.'[2]

I have always found this peculiar combination, even though it may
not represent the 'historical Wesley,' theologically attractive and

---

[1] I do not mean to suggest that sanctification and holiness are not equally central to
Catholic practice and theology. The crucial issue is where such holiness is to be found.
Geoffrey Wainwright helpfully notes that Catholic teaching serves to give the believer
an assurance concerning the church's proclamation of the Gospel, while the Methodist
tends to point to the assurance of the Spirit manifest in the individual believer (*Methodists
in Dialogue* (Nashville: Kingswood Books, 1995), 20). Wainwright quotes from the
1986 Nairobi Report of the Methodist–Roman Catholic Joint Commission that rightly
suggests that Methodists 'might ask whether the Church, like individuals, might by the
working of the Holy Spirit receive as a gift from God in its living, preaching and mission,
an assurance concerning its grasp of the fundamental doctrines of the faith such as to
exclude all doubt, and whether the teaching ministry of the Church has a special and
divinely guided part to play in this' (21). That question asks Methodists to develop an
adequate ecclesiology that given our beginnings has always been absent.

[2] Wainwright uses Outler's quote in a sympathetic way throughout his book. As
Wainwright observes 'if one were to reflect more fully than John Wesley did on the
theological implications for ecclesiology of (his) view of the appropriation of salvation,
it would put Wesley rather on the "Catholic" side in the debates concerning the
instrumentality of the Church, in which some contemporary ecumenists have located
"the basic difference" between Roman Catholics and Protestants' (104). That seems
exactly right.

promising. Yet one must also acknowledge that the position is inherently unstable, particularly in modernity. It will be the burden of my argument that recent developments, which some call postmodernism, offer some extremely helpful ways for a display of holiness without a loss of the Catholic character of the church. The loss of the 'self' and the increasing appreciation of the significance of the body, and in particular the body's permeability, can help us rediscover holiness not as an individual achievement but as the work of the Holy Spirit building up the body of Christ.

Yet I first need to suggest why an evangelical Catholicism has been so hard to sustain theologically as well as in the actual practice of the church in modernity.[3] To do so I am going to make generalizations about Catholicism as well as Protestant practice that would require much qualification if they were to reflect the complexity of each. I think it worthwhile to risk being accused of over-generalization in the interest of making clear the challenge I see before us. By 'us' I mean those who think any intelligible account of Christianity requires Christians to lead lives of holiness that make clear the church is integral to that project and not just a means to that end.

Part of the great genius of Catholicism was its ability to sustain Christianity as a way of life for peasants. To so put the matter will seem to many, both Catholic and Protestant, to put Catholicism in a negative light. Yet I mean such a characterization to be nothing but positive. First of all I do not think there is anything wrong with being a 'peasant,' that is, someone who works everyday at those crafts necessary for us to eat, have shelter, sustain the having of children, and allow us to carry on the basic practices necessary to sustain communities. Peasants may not be 'intellectuals,' but they have knowledge habituated in their bodies that must be passed on from one generation to another. Peasants are often suspicious of intellectuals because they rightly worry about 'ideas' that come from people who do not work with their hands.

Christian peasants usually do not think they are called to be holy. It is enough that they pray, obey, and pay. Peasants, however, are usually more than willing to acknowledge the importance of holiness – venerating people, sacraments, and relics that are clearly 'different.'[4] Peasants

---

[3] Pietism and holiness while often connected historically are not only distinguishable, but can be antithetical. That is particularly the case when the emphasis of pietism on the individual's experience undercuts any account of the importance of discipline as a form of discipleship. One of the ironies of American Methodism is how the revivalistic enthusiasm of the nineteenth century served to render impotent Wesley's understanding of these matters.

[4] One of the striking themes of Caroline Walker Bynum's remarkable book, *The Resurrection of the Body in Western Christianity, 200–1336* (New York: Columbia University Press, 1995) is how the 'common piety' of 'common Christians' acted as a check on the theological temptation toward a 'spiritualization of the body.' As she puts it, 'something very deep in third- and fourth-century assumptions was unwilling to jettison material continuity in return for philosophical consistency' (68). At least part of that 'something' was the veneration of relics of the saints whose bodies had already

also know that those with authority over them, particularly those with ecclesiastical authority, may be anything but holy. Yet they understand that the salvation offered by the church is not dependent on her ecclesial representatives, but rather is to be found in sacrament and saints.

No doubt 'peasant Catholicism' was and is open to great perversions. Yet it is equally the case that one of the great virtues of such a Christianity is its capacity to be practised by people who are poor. Such a Christianity is not a set of beliefs or doctrines you believe in order to be a Christian, but rather Christianity is to have one's body shaped, one's habits determined, in a manner that the worship of God is unavoidable. Of course beliefs and doctrines matter, but it is not the peasant's task to ensure they are rightly maintained. That is the task of the church located in the office of the bishop assisted by the theologian.

Whatever the limits and virtues this kind of Catholicism represented, it no longer seems to be an alternative for Protestants or Catholics who live in the so called 'developed societies.' For in such societies no one any longer believes, in spite of evidence to the contrary, they are peasants.[5] We believe our lives are the outcome of choices we have made. Such a world seems, moreover, to be the kind of context which the pietist longed for. No longer is anyone made to be a Christian, but one only becomes a Christian through experience and voluntary commitment.

This view of the importance of individual commitment is often thought to be the great achievement of the Protestant Reformation. After all is this not what the priesthood of believers is supposed to

---

become relics through martyrdom and holiness while they were alive and so continued to be such after death. The Protestant rejection of such veneration as idolatry as well as the Enlightenment's characterization of such practices as superstition or magic most charitably can be described as superficial.

In her book, *Christ's Body: Identity, Culture and Society in Late Medieval Writings* (London: Routledge, 1993), Sarah Beckwith describes how Christ's body became the site for contestation in a manner that calls into question our assumed divisions between pre- and post-Reformation history.

[5] Bankers, lawyers, university professors, and other 'professionals' have difficulty thinking of themselves as peasants. They certainly do not work with their hands. Yet in many ways they are much more at the mercy of those that rule than the traditional peasant. Perhaps their perilous state is the reason they are so convinced they are in control of their destinies, that is, that they are not peasants. Of course that is why professionals are less free than peasants. Peasants know there are masters and accordingly develop modes of resistance. Professionals think they are the masters which, of course, makes them completely incapable of defending themselves. Professionals present a peculiar challenge to the church because they assume the church has no right to tell them what to believe or do. They assume what they know as a banker or lawyer or university professor gives them a critical perspective on Christianity. Too often they think they get to make up the kind of Christianity they like. It would be a step in the right direction if such people could see that at least in terms of their ability to control their lives they are not distinguishable from peasants. If such a recognition of their situation were possible, they might be able to develop peasant skills of resistance and survival – skills of hope that hopefully are drawn from practices provided by the church.

mean? The answer is, of course, 'no' if by the priesthood of believers you mean, as many American Christians seem to assume, that you can have an unmediated relation to God in which you are your own priest. Luther and Calvin would have been stunned by the suggestion that the church is a collection of individuals in which each person gets to determine their relation to God. Yet such individualistic presumptions have become the hallmark of Protestantism, particularly in America. Even more surprising, such individualism is underwritten by holiness traditions on the assumption that sanctification names our effort to lead a Christian life.

In such a context the emphasis on sanctification is not only Pelagian, but also often confuses middle-class moralism with 'being Christian.' Whatever the possibility Methodism may have represented for there to be a church that was at once evangelical and Catholic, it has been lost in the interest of being a church in which 'anyone is welcome.' Honesty compels me to acknowledge, of course, that there was never any great effort by American Methodists to embody Wesley's peculiar under-standing of the church as a disciplined community. But whatever sense might have existed of that option is now submerged in debates about what techniques might provide for 'church growth.'

If we have any hope of reclaiming the church as a disciplined body of disciples I believe some analogue to peasant Catholicism will be required. In other words we need to recover the discipline of the body that at least offers an alternative to the endemic individualism and rationalism of modernity – an individualism and rationalism that has too often been thought necessary or at least confused with a concern with holiness. As a way to recover what holiness might look like as a discipline of the body I am going to discuss two quite different texts – Dale Martin's *The Corinthian Body* and Arthur Frank's, *The Wounded Story Teller: Body, Illness, and Ethics.*[6] Though these books treat quite different subject-matters, I hope to show they exhibit quite similar views of the body made possible by recent challenges to modernist notions of the self and, accordingly, can help us think better what a recovery by Christians of the sanctification of the body might look like.

The Permeable Body in Paul

Martin takes as his task nothing less than freeing Paul from our modernist reading habits exemplified by Cartesian soul/body dualism. Note the way I put the matter, that is, Martin does not claim he is telling us what Paul 'really' meant by the 'body,' but rather he is trying to prepare us for being better readers of Paul by providing us with

---

[6] Dale Martin, *The Corinthian Body* (New Haven: Yale University Press, 1995), Arthur Frank, *The Wounded Storyteller: Body, Illness, and Ethics* (Chicago: University of Chicago Press, 1995). References to Martin and Frank will appear in the text.

conceptual skills to make us better readers. Of course he also thinks in the process we will better understand what Paul 'meant,' for example in 1 Corinthians 12, but by that he means he expects us after having read his book to be able to make better sense of the many things Paul says about the body. In other words Martin refuses to acknowledge a 'text' which must be interpreted by an autonomous agent in the hope of discovering 'what the text really meant.'

The dualism between 'text' and 'interpreter' is but one form the body/soul dualism takes that his book is meant to challenge. Descartes gave the definitive expression to this dualism by associating body with matter, nature, in an attempt to show the body can be explained in mechanistic terms. The soul in contrast to the body was identified as 'mind,' non-matter, the supernatural, and the spiritual (6). Martin does not attribute the power and ubiquity of the body/soul dualism in modernity to Descartes, but rather Descartes provides for him one of the most compelling intellectual justifications of this dualism – a dualism Martin thinks disastrous for our understanding of Paul.

Drawing on ancient philosophical and, in particular, medical sources, Martin challenges our presumption that the ancients shared a Cartesian view of body/soul. Prior to modernity the soul, while certainly different from the body, was not conceived in the Cartesian sense as 'non-matter.' Of course there was a wide variety of ways the soul and the body were understood in the ancient world, but Martin convincingly argues that however the soul was distinguished from body the former was assumed to take up space, to consist in stuff. Accordingly our common distinctions between the inner and outer, the individual and the social body, were unknown or understood quite differently. For example it was assumed by many in the ancient world that the individual human body was but an instance of the social body (37).

Martin does not provide this background in order to convince us that Paul was influenced by this or that ancient thinker, but rather to help us understand that the various passages in Paul about the body, which initially may seem quite odd or at least unconnected, are not only interconnected but also make a great deal of sense. For example, Martin suggests that in 1 Corinthians 15:12–24 Paul meant that the resurrection of Christ necessarily entails the future resurrection of Christians. Paul assumes that Christian bodies have no integral individuality to them; so due to their existence 'in Christ' through baptism they must experience the resurrection. 'To deny the resurrection of their bodies is to deny the resurrection of Christ; to deny the resurrection of Christ is to render any future hope void. The Christian body has no meaning apart from its participation in the body of Christ' (131).[7]

---

[7] Martin rightly points out this is why Paul sees no difficulty with the practice of baptism for the dead in 1 Corinthians 15:24–25. Such a suggestion makes particularly embarrassing reading given more orthodox Christian polemics against the Church of the Latter Day Saints.

This perspective provides the background of Martin's main thesis that Paul, as well as most Corinthian Christians, saw the body as a dangerously permeable entity threatened by pollution. Against Paul there were at Corinth those who were better off as well as being of a higher status who stressed the hierarchical arrangement of the body without being overly concerned about the body's boundaries or pollution (xv). What is crucial for Martin's case is the recognition that the battle over hierarchy is a battle over the body. That some have become sick and have even died as the result of their behavior at the Lord's supper is what should be expected. Martin observes that Paul's advice to the better off at Corinth 'flew in the face of the accepted practice and common sense of the upper class of Greco-Roman society. Paul's instructions represent a direct challenge to upper-class ideology and required that the higher-status Corinthians adjust both their expectations and their behavior to accommodate the needs of those of lower status' (74–75). This is not a surprising conclusion, but what Martin has helped us see is that Paul assumes those upper class bodies are suffering because their bodies are not in fact 'theirs.'[8]

What this means is that our normal reading of 1 Corinthians 12:12–25 as a 'metaphor' is a mistake. It is not as if the church is, like the body, interconnected, needing all its parts even the inferior one. The church is the body from which we learn to understand our particular bodies. That is why Paul can argue that those who occupy positions of lower status are actually more essential and should be accorded more honor than those of higher status. As Martin observes, 'This is not a compensatory move on Paul's part, by means of which those of lower status are to be compensated for their low position by a benefaction of honor. Rather, his rhetoric pushes for an actual reversal of the normal, "this worldly" attribution of honor and status. The lower is made higher, and the higher lower' (96).

When we read Paul we best leave behind distinctions between the physiological and psychological that we have come to think of as obvious. Put colloquially, you have to get physical to read Paul. That is particularly true if we are to understand Paul's 'ethics' and why his ethics cannot be distinguished from his theology. Paul presumes the church is Christ's body so immorality is not like the body becoming ill or polluted, it is to make the body ill and polluted. So questions of a

---

[8] Martin provides an illuminating account of the relation between class and the aesthetics of the body in the ancient world. People in the lower classes were assumed to be ugly, which of course meant that people in the upper classes policed their lives through medical practices meant to insure that they be beautiful. Particularly important was how the infant body was treated, requiring quite detailed forms of swaddling (26–37). Against such a background one begins to appreciate how socially disruptive Paul's holding up the 'weakest' member must have been. For a suggestive account of how the rite of formation cannot help but create permeable boundaries, see L. Gregory Jones, *Embodying Forgiveness: A Theological Analysis* (Grand Rapids: Eerdmans, 1995), 182–97.

man having sexual relations with his stepmother (1 Cor. 5), for Christian men to use prostitutes (6:12–20), to eat meat sacrificed to idols (chapters 8–10), and the proper eating of the Lord's Supper (11:17–34) are all connected. For Paul all of these matters are a question of the purity of the body and avoidance of pollution. For a Christian man to visit a prostitute is equivalent to the body being invaded by a disease that threatens everyone since everyone is the body.

Crucial for Paul is maintaining the boundaries of the body. Martin observes that just as Christian healers cured diseases by casting out demons, so Paul demands the Corinthians cleanse the body by expelling those who pollute the church. Thus in 1 Corinthians 5:9–12 Paul tells the Corinthians they must not associate with the brother who is 'sexually immoral or greedy or an idolater or a slanderer or a drunkard or rapacious,' and in particular they are not to eat with such a man. Yet Paul says you may have to associate with such people who are not in the church since otherwise Christians 'would have to leave the cosmos entirely.' Paul does not fear the pollution of the church by contact between a Christian and non-Christian, but 'he does think that the disguised presence within the church of a representative from the outside, from the cosmos that *should* be "out there," threatens the whole body. The body of Christ is not polluted by mere contact with the cosmos or by the body's presence in the midst of the corrupt cosmos, but it may be polluted if its boundaries are permeated and an element of the cosmos gains entry into the body' (170).

The problem with modern readings of Paul, readings often meant to underwrite a concern with holiness, is they are far too spiritual. For example they assume that the problem with allowing someone who is sexually immoral to remain in the church is that they may tempt others to such immorality. Of course that may be true, but that is not how Paul thinks about these matters. He thinks it has to do with the very constitution of the body. It is not a question of whether sexual fidelity is or is not good for us. It is a question of the kind of body we are as the body of Christ. It is not a question whether we 'understand' why we should marry or not marry. It is a question of how our bodies are positioned for the upbuilding of the body of Christ.[9]

---

[9] Martin rightly criticizes modern Protestant attempts to make Paul an advocate of marriage, family, and heterosexual intercourse – e.g., why Paul really was not against marriage. According to Martin even more misleading are attempts to make Paul a supporter of a 'healthy view of human sexuality. As recent theorists of the history of sexuality have argued, the category itself – whether one is speaking of homosexuality, heterosexuality, or human sexuality in general – is a modern one, heavily indebted to psychology, psychotherapy, and the medicalization of the self so important to modern culture, especially since the nineteenth century. Paul does not speak of sexuality but of sexual actions and desires. And whenever the subject arises, Paul treats sex as potentially dangerous. If it cannot be completely avoided, it must be carefully controlled and regulated so as to avoid pollution and cosmic invasion' (211). Martin's account of desire should be required reading for all who would develop an 'ethics of sex' for

Holiness is not, for Paul, a matter of individual will. Holiness is the result of our being made part of a body that makes it impossible for us to be anything other than disciples. That is why the 'little things' matter. Whether one eats or does not eat meat sacrificed to idols matters because bodies do matter. How those 'little things' shape and are shaped by the body may well change. Indeed over-concentration on one 'little thing' may well be a way to overlook or ignore what is really destructive for the holiness of the body. Yet what Martin has helped us see is our bodies, what we do and do not do, our habits, as the subject of as well as that which makes possible sanctification.

The Wounded Body

The great difficulty with Martin's account of Paul's letter to Corinth is not whether he gets Paul right or wrong, but rather that we have no idea what to make of his account of the Pauline body. We can 'understand' what he is saying, but we cannot imagine it in relation to our own lives. Few of us experience our bodies as he suggests the Corinthians experienced theirs. Our churches certainly do not think sinners should be expelled because they threaten the integrity of the body. After all we join the church through voluntary commitment by which we mean we have made an intellectual choice to be a member of this church. The body just comes along as part of the package.

In truth we simply lack the resources, which is just another way to say examples, to imagine what Paul is talking about or how such a view of the body might fit over our own lives. Yet I think there is one place in our lives where Paul's understanding of the body is intensely exemplified – when we are sick. Sickness makes it impossible to avoid the reality of our bodies. When I am sick I am not a mind with a suffering body, but I am the suffering body. Illness may be the only time that we have the opportunity to discover that we are part of a story that we did not make up.

Arthur Frank observes that 'seriously ill people are wounded not just in body but in voice' (xii). The wound creates the need to tell stories because the diseased or injured body disrupts our old stories creating the need for new stories. Yet these stories are not something separate from our body but rather come out of our bodies. Just to the extent, however, stories give voice to our pain, make our body familiar, the body eludes language. Desperate to domesticate the alienation our hurt creates between our stories and our body, we are driven to reduce the body to a thing, the topic of the story, the not me (2–3). But in that reduction we lose our bodies as the source of who we are.

---

today. Particularly important is Martin's contention that Paul shows no concern for the 'propagation of the race' as the necessary presumption of Christian marriage (214).

Another name for this reduction, according to Frank, is called modern medicine. Such a medicine is so close to us, has taught us how to understand ourselves, we no longer sense its power over us. Frank calls our attention to the descriptive power of modern medicines by quoting a North African woman: 'In the old days folk didn't know what illness was. They went to bed and they died. It's only nowadays that we've learned words like liver, lung, stomach, and I don't know what!' (4–5).[10] What it means for this woman (and for us) to seek medical care is not only to agree to follow the regimens prescribed, but to tell her story in medical terms. To say how she feels, this North African woman is required to narrate her feelings in terms of a second-hand medical report. 'The physician becomes the spokesperson for the disease, and the ill person's stories come to depend heavily on repetition of what the physician has said' (6).

Such a medicine is the institutional form of the Cartesian soul/body dualism Martin was combating in his attempt to exemplify Paul's understanding of the body. Something like the Cartesian dualism is required if the authority by which physicians impose their specialized language on their patients is to be legitimated. Frank characterizes this modern, medicalized body as monadic since it refuses to offer its pain to others or to receive reassurance from others that they recognize our affliction. A monadic body is the body that modernist administrative systems desire since such bodies are all the more capable of being put through bureaucratic procedures. Moreover it is hard to see how modern medical practice, which has increasingly become bureaucratic, could admit any other understanding of the body since the disease model that grounds its practice presupposes just such an account (36).[11]

---

[10] Frank is quoting Pierre Bourdieu in his *Outline for a Theory of Practice*, 166.

[11] Frank rightly observes that postmodernity is contradictory since it is so often characterized by opposing tendencies happening simultaneously. For example 'one side of postmodernity is the hyper-rationalization that subsumes the individuality extolled by modernity. Modernist medicine's general unifying view was a beneficent rationalization carried out in the interest of a science that had cure as its objective. DRGs are a less-than-beneficent rationalization carried out in the interest of cost-containment and administrative control over medicine. DRGs represent the modernist project turning against itself. A different side of postmodernity is the presence of self-stories that provide models of reclaiming the self' (70–71).
Wendell Berry notes that the metaphor of the body as a machine is accurate in some respects but must be controlled by 'a sort of numinous intelligence.' But in most ways the body is not like a machine, 'the body is not formally self-sustained; its boundaries and outlines are not so exactly fixed. The body alone is not, properly speaking, a body. Divided from its sources of air, food, drink, clothing, shelter, and companionship, a body is, properly speaking, a cadaver; whereas a machine by itself, shut down or out of fuel, is still a machine. Merely as an organism the body lives and moves and has its being minute by minute, by an inter-involvement with other bodies and creatures, living and unliving, that is too complex to diagram or describe.' Wendell Berry, *Another Turn of the Crank* (San Francisco: Counterpoint), 94–95. Berry argues in this wonderful chapter called, 'Health is Membership' that he would like to purge his mind and language of terms like 'spiritual,' 'physical,' 'metaphysical,' and 'transcendental' – 'all of which

The monadic body, however, is capable of permutations that Frank displays through ideal types he thinks exemplify modernist options: the disciplined and the mirroring body. The disciplined body is characterized by self-control through which it seeks predictability by employing therapeutic regimens. Such regimens organize the body in the hopes that contingency can be avoided or at least compensated (41). The mirroring body is at once its own instrument and object of consumption, that is, the body consumes and consumption enhances the body. Medicine, for example, is consumed in the interest of cure. This body is called mirroring because it recreates itself in the images of others. Like the disciplined body the mirroring body fears contingency, not in the form of unpredictability, but in the form of disfigurement. Both bodies are monadic, acting alone in a world that judges them, 'but the judgements are made on different grounds: performance for the disciplined body and appearance for the mirroring body' (44).

Frank identifies another type, the dominating body, that is dyadic, not in a sense of being for others, but against others. For the characteristic feature of the dominating body is that it defines itself by force. When this body becomes ill, it gets mad, assuming the contingency of disease but never accepting it. The disciplined and mirroring bodies turn on themselves, but the dominating body turns on others (48–49).

These types constitute modernist stories in miniature that shape and continue to shape our bodies. Frank reminds us that these are types since few of us ever exemplify any of these types completely. Rather we embody them at different times in different circumstances, often several at the same time. Not to be forgotten, however, is that these are body types – that is, they remind us that just as there is no single thing called self, neither is there any single thing called body. Our bodies are under constant negotiation, shaped and reshaped by the stories in which we find ourselves.

---

imply that the creation is divided into "levels" that can be pulled apart and judged by human beings. I believe that the creation is one continuous fabric comprehending simultaneously what we mean by "spirit" and what we mean by "matter"' (90–91). Berry argues that the most important distinction is not between spirit and matter, but between the organic and the mechanical.

He confesses his views on these matters are shaped by his belief that it is straightforwardly true, as we are told in the Gospel of John, that God loves the world. 'I believe that the world was created and approved by love, that it subsists, coheres and endures by love, and that, insofar as it is redeemable, it can be redeemed only by love. I believe that divine love, incarnate and indwelling in the world, summons the world always toward wholeness, which is reconciliation and atonement with God. I believe that health is wholeness' (89).

For a much fuller account of these matters as well as how they impact on the development of medical ethics, see Joel James Shuman, 'Beyond Bioethics: Caring for Christ's Body' (PhD dissertation at Duke University, 1998). Shuman rightly argues that we must recover a Christian practice of medicine.

Note, however, how these types, these stories that reflect the monadic body, also shape how we as Christians now think of salvation and holiness. For illness think of sin which we try to overcome through performance, appearance, or more likely through dominion of others. Just as the monadic body in the name of independence becomes all the more subject to the power of medicine, so do we as Christians become what we fear just to the extent we assume salvation is about making us safe from being dependent.

Yet Frank contends these modernist stories that have legitimated and reinforced the power of medicine over our lives are now under challenge. He notes, 'The *postmodern* experience of illness begins when ill people recognize that more is involved in their experience than the medical story can tell' (6). Correlative to this attempt to reclaim our stories of our illness according to Frank is a different body – the communicative body. It is not just an ideal type, but an idealized type Frank commends exactly because it accepts its contingency as part of the fundamental contingency of life. If Frank is right about our discovery of such a body, it may moreover help Christians better understand what it means for our bodies to be made holy. One cannot help but hear theological resonance in Frank's account of the communicative body.

For example, he observes that the communicative body does not regard predictability as the rule but the exception. Accordingly there is no 'self' desperately seeking to control the body. While there may be aspects of the body that are not the self, where one ends and the other begins is not easily determined. For the communicative body, the 'body *communes* its story with others; the story invites others to recognize themselves in it. Thus the communicative body tells itself explicitly in stories. Reciprocally, stories are the medium of bodies seeking to approximate the communicative type' (50). For the communicative body illness is not something that must be overcome, nor simply chaos, but rather an occasion for the discovery that we are on a journey, a quest, through which we learn 'who I always have been' but did not know (129).[12]

The suggestion that the communicative body is not just an ideal but an idealized type is Frank's way of saying that this is the way we ought to be. Moreover he thinks this is the way we can be 'after modernity.' It requires that ill people, not caregivers, need to regard themselves as the heroes of their own stories. This requires that we understand that heroism is not to be identified with those that can 'do' something, but rather is to be found in those who persevere through suffering (134). What such a body offers is not victory, but testimony.

---

[12] I have had to telescope Frank's quite wonderful discussion of the restitution and chaos illness narratives. The plot of the former is 'I was healthy, I am sick, but tomorrow I will be healthy again.' The chaos story appears to have no plot, seeing illness as the disruption of all stories. These stories can and are told in quite different ways, but Frank is surely right to see them as basic plot lines that shape our bodies not only when we are ill but when we are well.

Our healing is not the overcoming of our illnesses, but rather our ability to share our going on with one another through the community stories create.

The imperative to receive testimony is, according to Frank, post-modern just to the extent that the witness must remain uncertain of what is received. Such uncertainty is required if we are not just to hear a story, but to be implicated in it. As Frank puts it, 'This reciprocity of witnessing requires not one communicative body but a *relationship of* communicative bodies. Ordinary speech, conditioned by thinking on the model of law courts, refers to "the witness" as if witnessing could be a solitary act. Witnessing always implies a relationship; I tell myself stories all the time, but I cannot testify to myself alone. Part of what turns stories into testimony is the call made upon another person to receive that testimony. Testimony calls on its witnesses to become what none of us are yet, communicative bodies' (143).

Frank's account of the 'wounded storyteller' is not located theo-logically or even in any specifiable tradition. In that way he remains ambiguously modern, that is, no longer confident of the modern self but yet has no alternative. He thinks we must reclaim from modern medicine the stories our bodies are trying to tell us, but the call for us to be the narrator of our own stories can be seen as but a new form of the modernist pretension that we can be our own creators. He quotes Paul Ricœur's suggestion that we must become 'the narrator of our own story without becoming the author of our life,' noting such a statement seems to require acceptance of divine authorship (176). Yet, at least in this book, he offers us no sign that he believes in such an authorship.

He rightly observes that the ethic of testimony requires the witness to speak 'outside the language of survival. Modernity disallows any language other than survival; the modernist hero cannot imagine any other way to be, which is why physicians are often genuinely baffled by criticism. People in postmodern times need different languages of meta-survival with various messages that death is all right. Clinical ethics needs these messages' (166). But 'various messages' can be but an appeal to modern presumptions to let pluralism reign – we get to choose the after life we like.

I confess I feel uneasy making these critical comments, given the testimony Frank has made through this book. I worry that my attempt to make Frank say where he stands is itself a modernist stance. Posing the question but reproduces the modernist assumption that what really matters is his 'consciousness.' What is important is that he is standing in stories that he cannot do without. For example consider his own reflections on Paul:

> The body's story requires a character, but who the character is is only created in the telling of the story. The character who is a communicative body must bear witness; witness requires voice as its medium, and voice

finds its responsibility in witnessing. What is witnessed is memory, specifically embodied memory, a memory of experience written into the tissues. St Paul, whose attitudes toward sexual embodiment are not popular, nevertheless expressed the embodiment of witness passionately. Paul knows he witnesses through his body: 'In stripes, in imprisonments, in tumults, in labors, in watchings, in fastings' (II Corinthians 6:5). Paul's ministry, to bring others into the body of Christ, is effected through rendering his own body available to suffering. This archetypal affinity of witness and bodily suffering cannot be evaded: Paul's unpopular message is that the responsibility of some is to find themselves called to the nexus of this affinity. (165–66)

So Paul's understanding of the body turns out to be the heart of Frank's perspective on illness. For Frank 'wounded storytellers' are moral witnesses, re-enchanting a disenchanted world. Through such stories we are reminded of our duties owed to the common sense world. The last line of Frank's book reads, 'illness stories provide glimpses of the perfection.' Yet is such perfection the perfection of Christ?

The Sanctified Body

I see no reason why we should try to give an answer in general to such a question. Rather we should be grateful that people like Frank have been forced to challenge modernist presumptions about the self, renewing their and our imaginations in the process.[13] I purposefully use the language of 'force' because I think that we do not develop new habits without being forced to do so. If we are to learn to think differently, we must have our bodies repositioned so that we have no other choice but to be what we were created to be.

Which is the reason I have chosen to focus on the body as the subject of sanctification. Not just the body, but the sick body. By suggesting that Frank's account might help us to imagine what it would mean for us to be in the Pauline sense the body of Christ, I am seeking to find the means to remind us that perfection is but another name for submission. The focus on illness is anything but accidental. For illness is the means by which we discover we are subject to the world of necessity, that we are fundamentally dependent beings, that we need stories that shape our dying. Perfection is the art of dying. To practice that art requires that we learn the art of living as embodied members of Christ's body.

The problem with the language and practice of holiness in modernity is that it has been far too spiritual. To become holy has been presented as something we could will, something we could become if we just tried hard enough. Using Frank's typology holiness has been shaped

---

[13] In an earlier book, *At The Will of the Body: Reflections on Illness* (Boston: Houghton Mifflin Co., 1991), Frank provides a wonderfully candid narrative of his own illnesses.

by disciplinary, mirroring, and dominating stories more than by the communicative story. As Christians we have assumed modernist paradigms to shape our accounts of holiness because they promised to put us in control of our existence and, in particular, of our bodies. As a result, our body's story, which is nothing less than the story of our desire for God, has been and is silenced.[14]

There are complex questions about the relation between the body and the body's stories that require further analysis.[15] I am sure the way to understand the way the body is storied is by looking more closely at how we are habituated. Indeed I suspect we are made perfect through our habits. So how we eat, with whom we eat, when we eat, what we eat are among the most important questions of 'ethics.' The monks have been right to think nothing is more important for the shaping of communities of holiness than how our days are structured. Nothing is more important for holiness than learning to speak and the use of that speech to speak the truth to one another in love.

If we are to be so habituated, we will be so only by God's grace which often is but another name for necessity. Illness is one of the last sources of grace just to the extent it forces us to need one another, to be communicative bodies, to be peasants. Perhaps that is why the most intense time in many Protestant worship services is when we share prayers for our own and the illnesses of others. Such times should not be depreciated, but they are not self-sustaining. For the body that we share with one another in prayer must become the body God shares with us in Eucharist. After all the Eucharist is the only true sanctified body.

I was a member of Broadway United Methodist Church when I lived in South Bend, Indiana. We were located in a poor section of town. As part of our struggle to move to every Sunday Eucharist, we had discovered we ought to provide a meal for the neighborhood after church. Most of the homeless who came to that meal did not come to church. One exception was an African-American lady. She was a classic bag lady.

[14] As part of his analysis of the various types Frank nicely shows what they imply about desire. For example he notes that the disciplined body lacks desire which but indicates its impossibility (41). The mirroring body produces desire, but what such a body wants is itself (44). The communicative body desires and so desiring must learn to live out of control (50).

[15] Some may be concerned that my account of the 'self' may be too physical risking some form of a reductionistic naturalism. These are complex question in philosophical psychology about which I cannot pretend competence. It is my own view, however, that modern theological accounts of the self have not been sufficiently naturalistic. Theologians until recently have always known that humans are also creatures which means we are animals. We should not be surprised, therefore, if neuroscience is capable of displaying our behavior in a predictive fashion. The mistake is to assume such a display being a sufficient reason to assume that all our behavior is 'determined,' whatever that would mean. For an account that nicely shows their complexity see Owen Flanagan, *Self-Expressions: Mind, Morals, and the Meaning of Life* (New York: Oxford University Press, 1996).

As a former EUB church we continued to have spontaneous prayer requests during the church's prayer. We would pray for the end of war, to end hunger, for better race relations, but few would ever expose our hurts or fears. We would ask for Aunt Rose's illness to be healed, but we would not say if we were ill. That was not the case with the bag lady. She would say, 'Lord, I am hurting, I have a cold, and I am frightened. Make these people help me.'

It did not take long for her to teach us we could so expose ourselves to one another. I believe that lady is a model for someone on the way to perfection. I believe that lady helped make us, Broadway United Methodist Church, Christ's body. That, I believe, is what the sanctified body looks like.

5

Going Forward by Looking Back: Agency Reconsidered

Why I Quit Worrying about Agency and Learned to Love Stories

To be asked to think again about agency feels like an exercise in nostalgia.* The work of rethinking settled thoughts is not irrelevant to questions of agency or at least to the account of agency I will provide in this essay. The focus on agency often involves an attempt to suggest an understanding of the self that secures our ability to act freely or responsibly given the decisions facing us. Such a view of agency is correlative of a view of the moral life that assumes such a life is constituted by prospective decisions. In other words, the crucial task of ethics is to provide an account of reason that helps the agent make the right decision in a manner that will not leave them determined by their past. In contrast, I will suggest that agency names those skills necessary to make our past our own, though it's often constituted by decisions we thought at the time were 'free' but which from our current perspective we can now see were made without our knowing what we were doing when we made them. In other words, I will argue that our moral lives are more properly constituted by retrospective rather than prospective judgements.

So in one sense nostalgia as a necessary component of memory may not be irrelevant for any consideration of agency. Indeed, I remember vividly my second year in divinity school, Gustafson's lecture on H. Richard Niebuhr's account of responsiveness in the introductory class in Christian ethics. He sympathetically criticized Niebuhr for failing to provide for our ability not only to respond but to act. I do not know whether that was the beginning of my concern to develop an account of agency, but I have no doubt that Gustafson's general perspective was crucial for my attempt to recover the importance of the virtues and character. In short, my own work has been made possible because of the gift, and gifts, of James Gustafson. Which is but a

* This essay was originally written to be included in a *Festschrift* honoring James Gustafson. We were assigned articles and mine was 'Agency.' See Lisa Cahill and James Childress (eds.), *Christian Ethics: Problems and Prospects* (Cleveland: Pilgrim Press, 1996).

93

reminder that any account of agency that excludes the givens of our life, which so often come in the form of gifts, is insufficient.

Of course, Gustafson would be the first to point out that his own work has been to some extent an attempt to develop the thought of H. Richard Niebuhr and, in particular, Niebuhr's account of the self. Many read and continue to read *The Responsible Self* as offering an alternative to other normative theories. Accordingly, they concentrate on the image of responsibility in the hope that such an image would produce a more adequate moral theory than deontological and teleological alternatives. Though obviously such readings of H. Richard Niebuhr are not incompatible with aspects of Niebuhr's work, Gustafson always rightly saw that in so far as Niebuhr's work can be said to have a center that center is the 'self.'[1]

In his excellent introduction to *The Responsible Self*, Gustafson observed that Niebuhr's 'ethics' had as one of its purposes to aid us in our 'struggle to achieve integrity. The personal situation of the moral man always involves an effort to come to wholeness and orderliness in life.'[2] Such an ethic also is an attempt to provide us with 'aid in accuracy in action' so that we might rightly describe that which we do and do not do. I too thought that that might be a promising way to develop Niebuhr's and Gustafson's focus on the self, and so I tried to develop their suggestions by employing the language of character, 'vision and virtue.'

That was how I was led to the language of agency. I thought such a language was required in order to provide an adequate account of character. Accordingly, I maintained, in *Character and the Christian Life*, that character is the qualification of our agency befitting our nature as creatures capable of self-determination. I was trying to have my cake and eat it too. That is, I was trying to find a way to sustain an account of moral continuity while not having our lives 'determined' by our character. After all, it seemed that character had to qualify something and I took that something to be our irreducible agency. I was trying to split the difference between Ryle's *Concept of the Mind* with its behaviorist implications and more Kantian accounts of the self that assumed that some aspect of the self must remain free from its own determination.

In order to try to sustain such an account of agency, I was drawn to philosophical work in action theory. If actions had an irreducible character, then some account of agency was implied that could avoid dualistic and behavioristic understandings of the self. I remember that

---

[1] This generalization is, of course, quite misleading. God, not the self, is the center not only of H. Richard Niebuhr's work, but also that of Gustafson. By calling attention to the 'self' I am but emphasizing what might be called the phenomenological center of Niebuhr's thought.

[2] James Gustafson, 'Introduction,' in H. Richard Niebuhr, *The Responsible Self: An Essay in Christian Moral Philosophy* (New York: Harper & Row, 1963), 16.

Gustafson was at the time quite skeptical about my attempt to develop a philosophical argument in support of agency that did not require an engagement with psychological and social factors. He was right to be skeptical, but my mistake was fundamentally philosophical.

I had mistakenly accepted the presumption of those who worked in action theory that a concept of agency could be derived from the notion of action *qua* action. Such analysis presupposes that 'action' or 'an action' is a coherent and conceptually primitive notion, but that was simply wrong. As I would later learn from MacIntyre:

> The concept of an intelligible action is a more fundamental concept than that of an action as such. Unintelligible actions are failed candidates for the status of intelligible actions; and to lump unintelligible actions and intelligible actions together in a single class of actions and then to characterize action in terms of what items of both sets have in common is to make the mistake of ignoring this. It is also to neglect the central importance of the concept of intelligibility.[3]

What MacIntyre helped me see is that you do not need an account of agency in itself to understand our ability to acquire character. Rather character is the source of our agency, that is, our ability to act with integrity. Interestingly enough, this puts me much closer to my other conversation partners in *Character and the Christian Life*, that is, Aristotle and Aquinas. We often forget that they had no account of agency or the 'self' as such. Rather they discussed the kind of issues we associate with the language of agency in terms of the voluntary and the involuntary. They needed no account of 'agency' or the 'self' to insure our ability to act in a manner that the virtues can be acquired. I began to understand that if the significance of habituation is appreciated then questions of agency become secondary.[4]

---

[3] Alasdair MacIntyre, *After Virtue* (Notre Dame: University of Notre Dame, 1984), 209. I discuss these mistakes more extensively in the 'Introduction' to the second edition of *Character and the Christian Life* (Notre Dame: University of Notre Dame, 1989), xiii–xxxiii.

[4] I am not suggesting that Aristotle and Aquinas have exactly the same views on these matters, but, when compared to more modern accounts of the self, their similarities are certainly more striking than their differences. Some might try to interpret Aquinas' account of the will as providing an analogue to our sense of agency, but I think such an interpretation mistaken. The will requires determination by reason to will properly just as reason requires movement of the will to do its work. Moreover, will and reason alike are impotent without habituation.

MacIntyre contrasts an Aristotelian and post-Kantian view by noting that the latter assumes we are entitled to hold people responsible for their actions if it is true that they could have done other than they in fact did and could have chosen other than they chose. Such a view is the ultimate oddity for an Aristotelian. For the Aristotelian the mark of the good person is that his or her character has been formed by training in the exercise of the virtues so that he or she often could not do or be other than virtuous in his or her choices and actions. 'We strive, if we aspire to be good, to be moved by the possession of good reasons to good actions. There is a causal chain stretching back from each good action far into our moral and psychological past. By contrast on the

Which also helps explain why I quit thinking about agency and began to think more about the narratives that constitute our lives. MacIntyre's account of intelligible action is a reminder that our ability to understand and identify what we or someone else is doing requires that we be able to place that episode in the context of a narrative. That such is the case is a reminder that human action evinces a historical character. 'It is because we all live out narratives in our lives and because we understand our own lives in terms of narratives that we live out that the form of narrative is appropriate for understanding the actions of others. Stories are lived before they are told – except in the case of fiction.'[5] I have tried to exhibit MacIntyre's point by telling the story of how I mistakenly thought I needed an account of agency to develop lessons I thought I had learned from Niebuhr and Gustafson. The telling of the story entailed no agency more determinative than the skills the story itself makes possible.

The 'Postmodern' Turn

The story I have just recounted occurred prior to what we now characterize as the 'postmodern' turn. Yet the development of post-modern accounts of the self helps me understand better why I had quit worrying about questions of agency, particularly from a theological point of view. For it is my own view that the doubts that postmodern thinkers have cast on questions of agency are a great theological resource for those of us committed to providing accounts of the Christian moral life in terms of the virtues and character. I am aware that such a suggestion will strike many as odd if not absurd given the anti-theological stance of many postmodern thinkers, but I hope to show that the postmodern turn was inevitable.

Put in quite general but, I believe, instructive terms, the anti-humanism associated with Nietzsche and Foucault is the only kind of atheism possible in modernity. Using MacIntyre's terms, the encyclo-pedists – that is, those committed to the Enlightenment project – could not help but produce the genealogist.[6] For if it was the project of the encyclopedist to put the human in the place of God, it was the task of the genealogist to be the thoroughgoing atheist desiring no god, including the human. If it is history all the way down, then it is equally

---

post-Kantian view there must be a decisive break in the chain of causes and reasons.' The Kantian requires that our capacity for moral agency be detached from all other capacities in the interest of freeing us from the limits of our past so that we might be equal. According to MacIntyre, this results in an attenuated, if not ghostly, account of moral agency. 'How Moral Agents Became Ghosts,' *Synthese* 53 (1982), 295–312.

[5] MacIntyre, *After Virtue*, 211–12.

[6] I am, of course, referring to MacIntyre's Gifford lectures, *Three Rival Versions of Moral Enquiry: Encyclopedia, Genealogy, and Tradition* (Notre Dame: University of Notre Dame, 1990).

the case, with respect to the 'self,' that it is 'masks' all the way down. God, 'the self,' and agency are each in their own way metaphysical fictions that we simply do not need.

In general, the theological response to this kind of atheism has been one of horror. It is one thing to deny God, but it is quite another to deny the self. If there is no 'substantive self' then there can be no universal moral principles. If there are no universal moral principles then everything is relative. So the loss of the 'self,' the loss of our agency, threatens the metaphysical presuppositions on which Christian ethics in modernity has been built. As one of my feminist students observed in a seminar in which we were reading Richard Rorty's, *Contingency, Irony, and Solidarity*, 'Just when women were claiming the power to be selves they now tell us such a thing does not exist. I suspect this is some kind of conspiracy to keep women in our place.'[7]

For theologians to come to the defense of modernist conceptions of the self in the interest of securing moral objectivity and moral agency strikes me as a deep irony.[8] As I suggested above, the creation of such a self was but part of the Enlightenment attempt to construe the world as intelligible without any need for the 'God hypothesis.' Ann Hartle makes this wonderfully clear through her analysis of Rousseau's *Confessions*. Rousseau's *Confessions* invite a comparison with Augustine and Plutarch. People, for Plutarch, are no more or less than who their cities tell them they are. If they are noble they are such because they are what others tell them they are.

In contrast, Rousseau saw clearly that Augustine presupposed that he is what he is for God. 'Only God can say what Augustine is. God sees in Augustine what even Augustine cannot see in himself. Augustine has his being from and through another: he is what God sees him to be.'[9] In opposition to Plutarch and Augustine, Hartle suggests that Rousseau's enterprise in his *Confessions* is to expose himself as he is to himself. In short, he claims to be able to see himself as he is by *feeling* his own existence. This feeling, moreover, is self-sufficient exactly

---

[7] Of course, such a response may not be fair to Rorty. His point is not that there is no self, but rather any self we may achieve is contingent. Thus 'to see one's life, or the life of one's community, as a dramatic narrative is to see it as a process of Nietzschean self-overcoming. The paradigm of such a narrative is the life of the genius who can say of the relevant portion of the past, 'Thus I willed it,' because she has found a way to describe the past which the past never knew, and thereby found a self to be which her precursors never knew was possible.' *Contingency, Irony, and Solidarity* (Cambridge: Cambridge University Press, 1989), 29. Such a view of overcoming is one that might be quite congenial with some aspects of feminist thought, but not others. It would certainly not sustain some of the essentialist claims about the nature of women's experience.

[8] I am aware, of course, that the 'self' and 'agency' are not equivalents, though they are often closely interrelated.

[9] Ann Hartle, *The Modern Self in Rousseau's Confessions: A Reply to St Augustine* (Notre Dame: University of Notre Dame Press, 1983), 4.

because it is private and unshareable.[10] Accordingly, Rousseau becomes one of the originators of the modern self, a self that migrates to become the noumenal self, a self that exists whether God exists or not.

The 'self' that theologians now rush to save is the 'sovereign self' that sought to be its own ground.[11] To be sure, Descartes, as is often pointed out, prepared the way for Rousseau. Descartes' 'ego' is irrefutably present to itself as pure extensionless consciousness requiring no acknowledgment or complicity with language or community. Another source of this distinctively modern view of the self, a source that in many ways is the opposite of the rationalist tradition, is Hobbes. In Hobbes the self is the center of assertion by which one defines oneself over against other such centers. Yet, as Joseph Dunne observes, Decartes' and Hobbes' pictures of the self proved capable of being combined through incorporation by each into an ideal of knowledge which was becoming available at the same moment of their emergence: 'Knowledge as explanatory and predictive with respect to its object and as residing in this newly masterful self as subject and knower – a subject, moreover, which could decisively extend its mastery by incorporating anything *in itself* which was not a pure faculty of knowing into the object-domain of knowledge.'[12]

Postmodernism names the vulnerabilities built into this view of the self and knowledge that were present from its inception. Descartes' account of the self's certitude could not help but create a corresponding unlimited doubt and in Hobbes the omnivorousness of our fellow-creatures means we must live in a world in which we cannot trust even ourselves. The masters of suspicion, Marx and Freud, each in their own way challenge the presumption of the self's transparency to itself, but do so within the humanism on which modernity is based. For again, as Dunne observes, neither Marx nor Freud is committed to the demise of the subject just to the extent that they each remain committed to the possibility of attaining truth about the human condition by disciplines that make possible an undeceived subjectivity.[13]

Postmodernism represents a more radical questioning than that propounded by either Marx or Freud just to the extent it denies subjectivity and correlative notions of agency altogether. Accordingly, the postmodern thinker does not try to reconcile what he or she may say about the self or agency with anything that is implicit in his or her

---

[10] I unfortunately cannot replicate the rich details Hartle uses to expose Rousseau's 'method' for discovering himself on his own terms. His attitude toward his death is particularly instructive as a forerunner of modernity's fear and fascination with death.

[11] I borrow the language of the 'sovereign self' from Joseph Dunne in his article, 'Beyond Sovereignty and Deconstruction: The Storied Self,' *Philosophy and Social Criticism* 21, 5/6 (1995), 137–57. As I hope will be clear, I am indebted to Dunne's analysis for much of what follows.

[12] Ibid. 138.

[13] Ibid. 140.

own act of propounding. The 'self,' like language itself, is but a sign that gets its meaning from other signs that get their meaning through their relationships of similarity and difference with other signs. The 'self' names our attempt at agency to name the play of the languages that speak through us.

As I noted at the beginning of this section, I regard these latter developments as theologically hopeful. The 'self' that postmodernists deny is the self created by the displacement of God.[14] In some ways such a self has surprising affinities with Christian accounts. As David Matzko has pointed out, who could be more 'decentered' than the Christian saints, since they cannot know who they are until God, through the church, tells them who they are?[15] That does not mean, however, that the 'decentered self' of the postmodernist is sufficient to sustain a practice as basic to the church as the naming of the saints. Indeed, I remain agnostic whether the genealogists can sustain their own project.[16] Yet there can be no question that the developments I

---

[14] I have obviously not done justice to the complexity of this story, particularly as told by Charles Taylor in his *Sources of the Self: The Making of Modern Identity* (Cambridge MA: Harvard University Press, 1989) Taylor is certainly right that in many ways the sources of the self we now call modern were present in some aspects of Christianity. I am not at all convinced, however, by his reading of Augustine as the source of 'inwardness' that finds expression in Descartes. To be sure, given modern developments it is easy so to read Augustine, but when Augustine looks 'internally' he finds God not self. I think such a reading is justified not only by *The Confessions*, but particularly in relation to Augustine's reflections on the Trinity. Aquinas in many ways remains the most able Augustinian in his insistence that only God is capable of moving the will non-violently.

[15] David Matzko, *Hazarding Theology: Theological Descriptions and Particular Lives* (PhD dissertation, Duke University, 1992). Matzko argues that sainthood is displayed in a narrative of the saint's life because those who tell the story of the saint are the primary agents in that narrative practice.

[16] See, for example, MacIntyre's suggestion that the genealogist's strategy of masking and unmasking may commit the genealogist to ascribing to the genealogical self a continuity of deliberate purpose and a 'commitment to that purpose which can only be ascribed to a self not to be dissolved into masks and moments.' *Three Rival Versions of Moral Inquiry*, 54. MacIntyre's argument is not an attempt to show that Nietzsche's or Foucault's positions are self-refuting but whether their own lives can be displayed fully in their own terms. The question must remain open whether their projects can be sustained, which is finally a question of whether they can be lived. For a compelling account of Nietzsche, see Alexander Nehemas, *Nietzsche: Life as Literature* (Cambridge MA: Harvard University Press, 1985). Equally interesting is James Miller's 'biography' of Foucault, *The Passion of Michael Foucault* (New York: Simon & Shuster, 1993). See in particular the discussion Miller's book occasioned in *Salmagandi* 27 (Winter 1993), 30–99. As usual, in his contribution to the symposium MacIntyre puts the issue well: 'We have good reason to be suspicious of any contemporary ethics of free choice, according to which each individual makes of her or his life a work of art. For something very like this aesthetization of the moral, which places the choices of each individual at the core of her or his moral life and represents these choices as an expression of that individual's creativity, is characteristic of advanced capitalist modernity. It provides a reinforcing counterpart to the bureaucratized careers of its elites, one which enables

have just sketched must be taken into account by those of us attempting to develop constructive accounts of Christian character.

Christian Character and Agency

Which brings me back to the story of how I learned to quit worrying about agency and love stories. For in some quite interesting ways the postmodernist challenges to substantive accounts of the self and correlative views of agency provide ways to help me spell out both what it means to say that character is our agency and why such a claim is crucial for helping us understand the kind of character we should hope is characteristic of Christians. To be a Christian is to be a member of a community with practices that are meant to make us faithful to our baptism. We therefore have a stake in accounts of the moral life by which we can be made accountable to engagements and promises we have made where we did not 'know' what we were doing.

For example, consider this passage from a letter from a friend (I have his permission to share it):

> Over the past week or so, I have been working on a rough autobiography in order to help my spiritual director determine how the hell I got the way I am. What has struck me in reading my draft is the inexplicable, unpredictable hurricane of grace. How did a Baptist kid born in southern Kentucky ever wind up being incorporated into the Mystical Body at the font of Our Lady Mediatrix of All Graces Church in the Bronx? My free will was certainly involved, but chiefly in consenting to follow the unprovoked leads opening in front of me. I'm not sure I had anything more to do with the fact that I am baptized than someone baptized when only a few days old. Sacramental theology tells us that it is Christ who baptizes; well, Christ tracked me down, pinned me in, and baptized me whether I wanted it or not.

Note that the problem is never one of explaining how, within patterns of stability, change is possible. On the contrary, the problem is explaining how, given the constant change that constitutes our lives, continuity is possible.[17] The answer, of course, is that not everything changes all the time, for if it did then we would have no way of knowing any change was happening. Yet that does not resolve the problem of the kind of continuity that should characterize our lives as Christians. What I believe is clear from the above is that such continuity is ill-

---

individuals to think of themselves as independent of their socially assigned roles, while they live out what is in fact one more such normalizing role. We therefore need to be told by those who endorse Foucault's standpoint just how Foucault's conception of ethics of care for the self and his implementation of that conception in his own life avoided this normalizing function' (60).

[17] For a fascinating set of reflections on change with which I am very sympathetic, see Stanley Fish, *Doing What Comes Naturally: Change, Rhetoric, and the Practice of Theory in Literary and Legal Studies* (Durham: Duke University Press, 1989), 141–60.

conceived as a 'core of selfhood, coated as it were with accumulated experiences but always capable of withdrawing itself from the latter into a transcendental point, an antecedent "I".'[18]

Put simply, story is a more determinative category than self. Indeed, our very notion of 'self' only makes sense as part of a more determinative narrative. We can only make sense of our lives, to the extent that we can make sense of our lives at all, by telling stories about our lives. To be able to 'make sense of our lives' is primarily an exercise, as I suggested above, of retrospective judgement. Such judgements are by necessity under constant negotiation just to the extent we must live prospectively, with a view to the future. We are able to go forward just to the extent we can look back.

The reason my life's story can never be 'set' is partly because I do not have a privileged perspective on my life.[19] Our lives as enacted narratives are too interconnected with other narratives for us to claim sole authorship. As MacIntyre has maintained, at most we are co-authors of our lives,[20] a point that helps us realize that the strong account of agency I originally thought necessary to sustain an account of character is equivalent to the fantasy that we can make our lives be

---

[18] Dunne, 'Beyond Sovereignty and Deconstruction', 143. This view of the self underwrites the presumption that any account of responsibility requires that we be able to 'step back' from ourselves and decide whether we are the selves we want to be. This view is well defended in William Schweiker's, *Responsibility and Christian Ethics* (Cambridge: Cambridge University Press, 1995), 163–67. Schweiker's position is complex. He argues that our capacity for self-designation necessary to be an agent requires the linguistic resources of some moral community in which others identify me as a responsible agent. The temporal character of the self is thereby duly acknowledged; yet Schweiker's ambition to develop a comprehensive account of responsibility means that our temporality is bounded by our ability to secure a standpoint outside our history. Thus he argues that, 'We are responsible for our actions and to others because in some basic sense we possess, or own, our actions and our lives. An agent is self-directed or autonomous if she or he exercises some measure of control over her or his life' 137. He thinks this to be equivalent to Aristotle's, Augustine's, and Aquinas' claim that the principle of voluntary action must be internal to the agent. That is the case only if you remember that for Aristotle and Aquinas our ability to act depends on our being habituated by the virtues. Of course, habits can also be bad, or in Aquinas' language, vices. A bad action is still an action and thus habitual for Aristotle. Yet such habits result in bad character. Thus Aristotle observes that one of the effects of being bad is that bad persons cannot even be constant in their badness. These are complex matters for Aristotle and Aquinas that I cannot pretend to have thought through. Aquinas does not develop Aristotle's account of moral weakness precisely because he has the Christian concept of sin – which he develops through an account of the vices understood as disordered habits. On reflection, it is clear that 'badness' and the moral psychology attending to its description, is even harder to characterize than 'goodness.' I think it is such exactly because, as Aquinas maintained, the vices are not connected in the manner of the virtues. I am indebted to Jim Childress for reminding me of these complex matters.

[19] In *Character and the Christian Life* I argued that the agent is privileged, but such a view I now think must be even more carefully qualified than the way I tried to put the matter there (see 104–106).

[20] Alasdair MacIntyre, *After Virtue*, 213.

anything that we want. This, of course, is a great terror – as nothing could be worse for us, at least as Christians, than to have such a fantasy fulfilled. At most, 'agency' names the skills correlative of a truthful narrative that enable us to make what happens to us our own, which includes 'decisions' we made when we thought we knew what we were doing but in retrospect seem more like something that happened to us.[21]

Examples are required if such abstract remarks are to be illuminated. Think, for example, of what it means for the church to witness the marriage of two people who make a promise to be faithful to one another for a lifetime. They allegedly 'know what they are doing' when they make such a promise. In other words, they are supposed to have been tested to indicate that they have the 'awareness' necessary for them to be held responsible for the 'decision' they are making at the time. But surely no one can know what it would mean to promise another person lifelong fidelity at any time in our lives, much less when we are young. I take it that is why the church insists that marriages must be witnessed, since by having the marriage witnessed we can hold the couple to a promise that they made when they could not have known fully what they were doing. By witnessing the marriage the church does not presume that the couple know what they are doing, though of course we try to help them understand what it means to make a promise when they cannot know what they are promising. Rather, the church trusts through the faithful lives they have exhibited among us to this point that the couple are the kind of people the church can trust to live into a promise they made when they did not exactly know what they were doing.

Marriage, of course, may be the most unhappy example of character given contemporary practice. But I take it that the 'breakdown' of marriage in our society is partly due precisely to an exaggerated sense of agency that underwrites the presumption that we should not be held responsible for decisions we made when we did not know what we were doing. The difficulty with such a view is that our lives are constituted by decisions we made when we did not know what we were doing. Such is the 'stuff' of character. Of course, lives with the appropriate regret and joy are possible only in communication which provides for forgiveness, penance, and reconciliation.

Sin and grace are among the skills the practice called Christian gives for making our lives our own. Retrospectively, we find our lives constituted by actions for which we can now only feel shame. For example, my early life was constituted by practices that allowed me to treat African-Americans in a manner that can only be called racist.

---

[21] I was struggling in my *The Peaceable Kingdom: A Primer in Christian Ethics* (Notre Dame: University of Notre Dame Press, 1983) to say something like this (see, in particular, 38ff).

The temptation is to relegate that part of my life to 'what I did before I knew better.' That was the 'determined' part of my life, the 'not me.' But if it was 'not me' then I cannot adequately account for the continuities of my life that presently constitute my character. 'Determinism' turns out to be a discourse necessary for people who no longer have the language of forgiveness of sin. My 'racism' was, and continues to be, 'me,' but to make it part of my life, part of my memory, in a way that constitutes my character I must accept forgiveness for it. So forgiveness of sin turns out to be an essential practice if I am to be capable of making my life my own.[22]

This is a reminder that Christians believe that our lives are constituted by gifts that we learn to make our own through the gift of God's very life in cross and resurrection instituted in baptism. Without participation in such a life the postmodernist may well be right that our lives are but the infinite play of signifiers signifying nothing. Yet Christians are a people who believe that the many narratives that constitute our lives finally have the *telos* of making us God's friends and, in the process, making us friends with one another and even friends with our own life. As John Macmurray observed, 'All meaningful knowledge is for the sake of action and all meaningful action is for the sake of friendship.'[23]

---

[22] For an account of forgiveness along these lines, see L. Gregory Jones, *Embodying Forgiveness: A Theological Analysis* (Grand Rapids: Eerdmans, 1995).

[23] John Macmurray, *The Self as Agent* (London: Faber & Faber, 1957), 15. Macmurray's work remains a gold mine of analysis and insight for anyone who would pretend to think seriously about the matters discussed in this essay.

6

Gay Friendship:
A Thought Experiment in
Catholic Moral Theology

Difficult Beginnings

'Do you believe in the virgin birth?' That was the question we were asked in Texas in order to test whether we were really 'Christian.' At least that was the way the challenge was issued during the time I was growing up in Texas. I confess I was never particularly concerned with how that question should be answered. I was not raised a fundamentalist, but I believed in the virgin birth. The problem for me was not believing in it but what difference it might make one way or the other whether I did or did not believe in it. My preoccupation was not with Mary's virginity, but with my virginity and how I could lose it. In the meantime, of course, we Texans had football to keep us from being too torn up by any anxieties that might come from questioning the virgin birth.

When I began my work as a Christian ethicist my attitude about the so-called 'homosexuality issue' was not unlike my earlier attitude about the virgin birth. I began my work in the midst of war – the Vietnam war – and in such a context sex did not seem to be *the* moral issue. Of course sex played a role in the student rebellion of the 1960s and questions about sex were at the center of debates about situation ethics. But given my concern to develop an ethics of virtue, I thought the concentration on sex, and in particular sexual acts, was a methodological mistake. Moreover the focus on sex as *the* question in ethics seemed to me an indication that any ethic so shaped was too determined by the concerns of the bourgeois. Therefore when homosexuality came along as *the* issue I resisted the presumption that this was a matter on which I had to have a 'position.'

Of course now no one, at least no one who teaches Christian ethics, is allowed to be indifferent about the status of homosexuality. It has become the equivalent to questions about the virgin birth in Texas in the 1950s. No matter where you are or with what subject you are engaged you can count on someone saying something like this: 'That is all well and good but what does what you have said have to do with homosexuality?'

The problem with such questions is not that they are unimportant, but when they are made 'the' question they have a distorting effect on the shape of Christian convictions. For example those who asked about the virgin birth were not concerned with the way questions of Mary's virginity are connected with Christological concerns, but rather were seeking to discover whether you believed the Bible is literally true. When the question of the virgin birth is raised in that context it cannot help but distort how Christian convictions should work, no matter what answer one gives to it. I have often felt the same kind of discomfort about the way the question of homosexuality is raised as 'the' moral problem today, precisely because the question seems wrongly posed.

Moreover, answers given to questions wrongly posed can have unexpected and unwelcome results. For example some of the arguments made on behalf of lessening the onus on homosexuality can also result in lessening the onus on lying and/or war. Moral descriptions are interrelated in manifold ways, not the least being whether our lives make sense. I suspect that part of the concern some have with the approval of homosexuality is how such approval may make practices such as lifelong fidelity in marriage as well as the narratives intrinsic to those practices unintelligible.

Of course many, particularly in liberal cultures, deny a connection between homosexuality and marriage. But that is not an option for Christians, since we must refuse to think of our lives as but the sum of individual decisions since that would result in alienating us from our own lives as well as isolating us from one another. We want our lives at least to make sense retrospectively, as well as to make possible a community called church that constitutes a common story.

Yet the great difficulty is even knowing how and where to begin to think about homosexuality. For example I served for a short time on the United Methodist Commission for the Study of Homosexuality. When we Methodists do not know how to think about an issue we appoint a committee to 'study' the matter, in hopes that some policy statement can be made for the whole church. The results are seldom encouraging since it does little good to pool ignorance in the hope that an outcome will be better than the process. Indeed it is usually the case that the result of a Methodist Commission turns out to be less than the sum of its parts.

I found that I had little to contribute to our deliberations since I did not think the moral status of homosexuality could be or should be determined by whether 'science' could establish the etiology of homo-sexuality. I had read enough Foucault to be extremely suspicious of that move. I was moreover increasingly suspicious of the very category 'homosexuality,' for the way that description was being used by both sides in the debate seemed to presume what we have come to call 'essentialism' – a position that I find philosophically problematic. I wondered even more what Christian practices would require the description 'homosexuality.'

I asked my colleagues on the commission why as Christians we needed to have a position on homosexuality. Did we not have everything we needed in descriptions like promiscuity and adultery? After all, the current ministry is not under any imminent threat from the ordination of gays, but rather is being undermined by adultery. So why do we not simply report back to the general church that we have in place all the moral language we need to deal with the problem of sexual morality? This recommendation was not only not acted on, it was not even taken seriously. It was assumed by both the anti- and pro-gay sides that the church had to have a position about homosexuality.

Of course we Methodists have to have a position about homosexuality because we do not have an adequate account of marriage. It seems we have to know how to think about homosexuality, else we might have to acknowledge we do not know how to think period. Whether you agree or disagree with Roman Catholics on this matter you at least have to acknowledge they have a consistent position. If every act of sexual intercourse is to be open to conception then it would seem the matter is fairly clear. Attempts to circumvent this 'conservative' position by describing 'sexual acts' as premoral seem to me to create as much trouble as the position they are trying to avoid.[1] Catholic conservatives and Catholic liberals seem equally to concentrate on 'acts' in the abstract.

I am going to try to provide an alternative way to think about these matters by suggesting the difference it might make if we approach the questions from the perspective of an ethic of virtue and in particular friendship. As my title suggests, I am aware that this way of beginning is 'experimental.' It is often alleged that those of us who work from the perspective of the virtues cannot deal with issues like homosexuality. I hope to show, however, that by beginning with what it means to be a virtuous friend we can better understand how Christians might think

---

[1] The argument works this way: homosexuality is a premoral or ontic evil, and all things being equal (or outside of any context) homosexuals should avoid evil actions by being celibate. However, if celibacy is not an option (because the person has a big sex drive), being in a committed relationship is better than being promiscuous. A committed relationship brings about the good of unitivity, so it is acceptable to do an evil thing (homosexual act) to bring about a greater good (unitivity). Therefore in such cases, although homosexuality is a premoral evil, in certain contexts it can be rendered moral. See, for example, Philip Keane's discussion of homosexuality in his *Sexual Morality: A Catholic Perspective* (New York: Paulist Press, 1977), 84–91. One cannot help but sympathize with Keane's attempt to create a space for gay people within Catholic moral theology. Yet the methodology used to create that space cannot help but create conceptual confusions – i.e., description of actions as premoral on the assumption that an action can be intelligible without an agent. I am indebted to Dr Kathy Rudy for helping me clarify this point.

about these matters in a way to avoid some of the unhappy alternatives so present today.

Yet my approach is 'experimental' in a manner that is quite unusual for me. Early in my time at Notre Dame I was confronted by a charismatic colleague who tried to convince me I needed to have a 'personal experience of Jesus.' I told her I was raised a Methodist, which meant that by the time I was twelve I had had enough experience to last me a lifetime. Actually my unease with appeals to experience as a warrant for theological language is because I remain an unreconstructed Barthian. I do not think Christian language gains its meaning because it describes 'experiences'. Yet I cannot deny that I begin with questions of friendship because that is the way that the question of homosexuality has come home for me.

For me friendship is not merely an 'experience.' Rather friendship is at the heart of my understanding of the moral life. Indeed, given my reservations about appeals to experience, I am sure I would have never been willing to engage with the issue of homosexuality if I had not discovered that I had friends who are gay. In some of these friendships at least, I did not know in the beginning or even through much of the development of the friendship that my friends were gay. Yet they are gay, and they are among the most faithful Christians I know. It has increasingly become the case, moreover, that I have developed friendship with gays, or better they have sought friendship with me, and that has become very important for my life.

One of the interesting things I have discovered is that my friends do not try to offer 'explanations' why they are gay. They are just gay. Just as the early church had to come to terms with the reality that gentiles, who probably should not have been followers of Jesus, were in the church, so we discover that gays are also in the church. Moreover they are there in a manner that would make us less if they were not there. I take that to be a stubborn theological reality that cries out for thought. I want to try to begin thinking through what such a 'fact' might morally entail by focusing on the moral significance of virtuous friendships.

Pretending to Be a Roman Catholic Moral Theologian

Before I explore the role of friendship for how we might think about homosexuality, I need to establish the context for my reflections. To do that I am going to pretend to be a Roman Catholic moral theologian. I am aware that few contexts would seem less happy for consideration of the issue of homosexuality as well as for the approach I am taking. Yet I believe that recent discussions by Roman Catholic moral theologians, in particular the promulgation of the encyclical, *Veritatis Splendor*, and the debate it has occasioned, provide one of the richest contexts for the kind of exploration I undertake.

I realize that such a claim will strike most people, and in particular Roman Catholics, as high folly, but at the very least Roman Catholic moral theology provides a context in which argument might count. By beginning with *Veritatis Splendor* I am at least able to begin with a tradition that knows there is more involved in thinking about sex than asking whether what we do with and to one another is an act of love. The problem with 'love,' of course, is that we have no idea how it is to be specified and as a result what might count as an exemplification of loving behavior. This becomes peculiarly problematic when we live in cultures in which some now think it reasonable to think thoughts such as: 'No one has the right to tell me what I can do or not do with my body.' For all of its problems, at least Roman Catholic moral reflection on these matters provides a context in which argument counts.

I need to warn you, however, that my credentials even to pretend to be a Roman Catholic moral theologian have been questioned by some. For example Richard McCormick, SJ criticizes a short essay I co-authored with David Burrell in which we praised the characterization in *Veritatis Splendor* of proponents of proportionalism as seeking an accommodation with the spirit of the age. McCormick says it is 'difficult to find language strong enough to condemn such motivational attribution. This is especially regrettable from authors who have played no significant role in these developments and manifest no realistic grasp of the problems, concepts, and language that surround them.'[2]

In a recent essay Joseph Selling echoes McCormick's complaint against amateurs who want to take sides in the current dispute between proportionalists and their 'conservative' opponents. Selling notes that proportionalists certainly never have doubted that there is such a thing as right and wrong, but rather are pastorally concerned to help individual persons come to terms with serious questions. He acknowledges that to the 'outside observer' such moral theology could appear as a capitulation to the 'individualistic, consumer, "anything goes" spirit of the times, but this would be a false impression.' He then clarifies what he means by 'outside observer' – they are 'anyone who did not follow the development of moral theology with a professional understanding. This would apply to theologians who were not specifically trained in that field or to non-theologians such as philosophers who knew a good deal about natural law theory or legal philosophy but relatively little about theological concepts such as grace (fundamental option), covenant (biblical theology, the meaning of sin as a theological concept) or pastoral care (diminished guilt, internal forum, material sin, or the lesser evil solution to moral dilemmas).'[3]

[2] Richard McCormick, SJ, 'Some Early Reactions to *Veritatis Splendor*,' *Theological Studies* 55, 3 (September 1994), 488.

[3] Joseph Selling, 'The Context and the Arguments of *Veritatis Splendor*,' in Joseph Selling and Jan Jans (eds.), *The Splendor of Accuracy: An Examination of the Assertions made by Veritatis Splendor* (Grand Rapids: Eerdmans, 1994), 21.

I know I am supposed to be intimidated by McCormick's and Selling's claims of insider expertise and knowledge, but I am going to 'damn the torpedoes' and try to provide an alternative to the debate as they understand it. I should say in some ways I am quite sympathetic to their claims of expertise. That is, I am sympathetic in the sense that I think part of their problem is they have been encouraged to think of themselves as 'experts.' At least one of the lessons we need to learn from recent debates in Catholic moral theology is that it is a dangerously over-determined tradition. For example, when you identify grace with a 'fundamental option,' and specify 'biblical theology' by a concept like 'covenant,' you have an indication that moral theology has become so specialized it is by no means clear what it means for it to be called theology.

Yet it is certainly true that I am an 'outsider' since I am a Protestant. I am also an outsider because I have not tried to participate in the proportionalist controversy, even though over the years I have tried to read the books and articles by proportionalists and their opponents. I have not taken sides mainly because I did not like the way the sides were constituted. I remember years ago that when I first read Louis Janssens, I was quite sympathetic with his concern to avoid a law-like account of morality, but quite unsympathetic with the way he was trying to provide an alternative. 'Fundamental option' seemed to be neither an option nor fundamental. In particular, I was suspicious of the lingering neo-Kantian presumptions about the self that were shaping the way Aquinas was being read. From my perspective, notions like 'fundamental option' could only seem attractive or necessary if one had forgotten how Aquinas understood the nature of practical reason, character, and the virtues.

In other words, what has bothered me about the proportionalists is not their attempt to provide an alternative to the 'old legalistic moral theology,' but that even in their attempt to provide an alternative to the legalist framework they continued to presuppose a law-like framework. Actions continued to be treated in abstraction from the virtues, but now in the name of pastoral sensitivities such actions are assumed to be infinitely re-describable. No doubt some of the ways the proportionalists put their case made them appear to be consequentialist, but that never seemed to me to be the crucial problem. Rather I have not been able to understand where they think descriptions come or what controls their use. Part of the difficulty, of course, is that those who have resorted to devices such as 'pre-moral' seem to have no sense that this is a problem.

The great achievement of *Veritatis Splendor* is to make the virtues central for the way the moral life is understood, as well as to suggest the interrelation between actions and virtues. This encyclical is often criticized for its failure explicitly to draw out the interconnections between Parts I and III and Part II. To be sure, one could have wished for a clearer display of the way the Christology in the first part should make a difference for the critique of the proportionalist in the second, but this encyclical is a remarkable achievement precisely in the manner in which it repositions the issues. Certainly the intent of the encyclical is conservative, but more important are the avenues it opens for fresh considerations of the Christian moral life including even matters such as homosexuality.

Martin Rhonheimer, in his article called '"Intrinsically Evil Acts" and the Moral Viewpoint: Clarifying a Central Teaching of *Veritatis Splendor*,' has come as close as anyone I know to getting the issue right.[4] He emphasizes the centrality in *Veritatis* of paragraph 78, where we get the characteristic Thomistic claim that the morality of an act depends on the 'object' which has been chosen by a deliberate will. This claim is elaborated in the following manner: 'In order to be able to grasp the object of an act which specifies that act morally, it is therefore necessary to place oneself *in the perspective of the acting person.*' The Encyclical goes on to argue that the object of a moral act cannot be a process or an event of the 'merely physical order' assessed by the power to bring about a state of affairs in the 'outside world,' but rather the 'object is the proximate end of a deliberate decision which determines the act of willing on the part of the acting person.' Thomas is then quoted to the effect that someone who robs to feed the poor has not acted uprightly since 'no evil done with a good intention can be excused.'

This argument immediately precedes the claim that there are 'intrinsically evil' actions, that is, actions that irrespective of the good intentions of the agent are incapable of being ordered to God. I confess I have always found the phrase 'intrinsically evil' mystifying. In a conversation with David Burrell some years ago I asked him if he thought a certain belief was 'absolutely true.' He challenged my use of the phrase 'absolutely true' by asking what 'absolutely' added if in fact the belief is true. In the same vein I continue to wonder what the qualifier 'intrinsic' adds to an action's being evil.

I realize this seems like a small matter, but I suspect the language of 'intrinsic evil' has led to some of the confusions concerning the character of practical reason – something that it is crucial to understand properly if we are to get these matters right. For 'intrinsic evil' makes it sound like certain actions are 'out there,' abstracted from agents, and they are to be evaluated either by their intrinsic nature or in terms of the consequences they produce. But that is exactly what Rhonheimer is suggesting cannot be done if we are to rightly understand *Veritatis*. That certain actions are evil makes sense only in a view of the moral life as a life shaped by the virtues in which human actions are understood from the perspective of the first person.

---

[4] *The Thomist* 58, 1 (1994), 1–39.

An ethic of the virtues requires an account of practical rationality and action in which an agent's 'action' is by its very nature intentional. If, as Aristotle maintains, we become just by acting justly, then the way we are so habituated requires that we must do that which we do in the way in which a virtuous person would do it. Rhonheimer observes that, from the viewpoint of the agent, actions are intentional not in the sense that I am aware of what I am doing, though I may be, but simply that I must be able to claim what I have done as mine. In contrast, from a third person perspective – that is, from the viewpoint of an observer – actions appear as events that are only contingently related to certain causes. Relying on this perspective, the proportionalists construe the moral life from the third person viewpoint and accordingly treat 'actions' as external bits of behavior to be judged good or bad, ironically, as if the agent did not exist.[5]

An ethics of the virtues must insist, therefore, that there are not two states of affairs when we act rationally: that is, an action-event and the resulting state of affairs, but rather that action and agency are inseparable. Accordingly the 'goods' intrinsic to our nature are not simply a set of givens nor are we the sum of our inclinations. Rather the goods sought by our desires 'constitute the proper practical self-experience of persons as a *certain kind* of being.'[6] The claim that certain actions

---

[5] Rhonheimer rightly argues that adherents of so-called 'teleological ethics' omit in principle an *intentional* description of particular types of actions which they later qualify on the basis of their decision-making procedures as 'right' or 'wrong.' By 'intentional descriptions' Rhonheimer is indicating the necessity of seeing the actions within a narrative required by the virtues. Because the proportionalists avoid this account of action they must describe actions as mere 'event.' They thus offer their theory as a solution to the problem of determining the right or wrong of such action, a solution, Rhonheimer nicely observes, that is required by their getting the problem wrong to begin with (35–36). Yet Rhonheimer rightly notes that the approach of the proportionalist 'is not different from traditional approaches that can be found in some classical manuals of moral theology. Some of them used to look at actions as physical processes or events, relating them afterwards to the "norm moralitatis," an extrinsic rule determining whether it is licit or illicit to perform such and such an "action." What most classical manuals failed to do was precisely to render intelligible what a human action is and that its moral identity is *included* in it because it is included in the *intentional* structure of an action' (38).

[6] Rhonheimer, 'Intrinsically Evil Acts,' 14. Rhonheimer provides a quite interesting account of the inclinations correlative of our nature as bodily beings for which I have deep sympathy. In doing so he is developing the contention in *Veritatis* that 'The person, by the light of reason and the support of virtue, discovers in the body the anticipatory signs, the expression and the promise of the gift of the self, in conformity with the wise plan of the Creator' (48). I think that Rhonheimer and the Encyclical are quite right to suspect an incipient gnosticism in the moral psychology of the proportionalist. I remain more agnostic than Rhonheimer, or the Encyclical, about the extent that the natural law can be known on the basis of the knowledge that comes through our body, but I have no reason in principle to deny such knowledge. For another treatment of *Veritatis* that rightly emphasizes the significance of the body for our knowledge of the goods see Alasdair MacIntyre, 'How Can We Learn What *Veritatis Splendor* Has To Teach,' *The Thomist*, 171–95. MacIntyre glosses the Encyclical this way: 'Moral direction is not

are always wrong is but a way of specifying that they can never be consistent with a good will, that is, with what a person of virtue would choose.[7] To be morally virtuous is not to will to do 'the right thing' time after time, but rather 'moral virtue is the habitual rightness of *appetite* (sensual affections, passions, and of the will, the rational appetite related to the various spheres of human praxis). An act which is *according* to virtue is an act which is suited to cause this habitual rightness of appetite which produces "the good person."'[8]

The virtue that is central to our ability to make our actions our own Aristotle calls *phronesis*, which Thomas develops as *prudentia*. Alasdair MacIntyre notes that the acquisition of this virtue requires the recognition of the rational authority of the precepts of the natural law and most especially the negative exceptionless precepts. We discover such precepts in the institutions and projects through which we seek variety of goods such as 'enduring relationships in the family and in friendship, goods of productive work, of artistic activity and scientific inquiry, goods of leisure, goods of communal politics and religion.'[9]

MacIntyre notes that an individual will have to learn how to discern and to order specific goods in each of these projects and activities in order to make the choices necessary for the goods to be achieved. Moreover, how those goods will be understood will differ from culture to culture. What according to MacIntyre will not vary is the kind of responsiveness by one human being to others which makes it possible for each to learn from the others' questioning. Such requirements are the preconditions for the kind of rational conversations we must have to discover the goods that come from our engagements with one another in which we need not fear being victimized.[10]

---

something to which the body is merely subjected as something alien and external. Physical activity is intelligibly structured towards the ends of the whole person, something that is rendered invisible by any reductive physicalism. It is the whole human person as a unity of body and soul which is ordered to its ends by natural law, when the human being is in good functioning order. The truth that is by being so ordered that the person is enabled and empowered – a bodily enabling and empowerment – is among those truths without a grasp of which an understanding of freedom cannot be achieved' (186). The crucial issue for me concerning Rhonheimer's and MacIntyre's accounts of natural law is, in the Encyclical's language, how 'the light of reason and support of virtue' is required for the so-called natural law.

[7] Ibid. 18–20.

[8] Ibid. 22.

[9] MacIntyre, 'How Can we Learn,' 183–84.

[10] Ibid. 184. MacIntyre's account of this process at once is historicist and non-relativistic. Thus he argues his account requires an understanding of truth that is more than warranted assertibility. 'In asserting that something is true we are not talking about warrant or justification, but claiming rather that this is in fact how things are, whatever our present or future standards of warrant or justification may lead us to state or imply, that this is in fact how things are, not from the point of view of this or that culture, but as such. Such assertions of course often turn out to be false, but once again what they turn out to be is not false-from-a-point-of-view, or false-by-this-or-

Rhonheimer, whose view of practical reason is quite similar to MacIntyre's, observes that our necessary commitments to promise-keeping and truthfulness require narrative display. For our refusal to break a promise leads us to discover new lines of action, alternatives, and hitherto unseen opportunities. 'To describe this we would need to tell a story. Virtuous actions are, in this sense, rendered intelligible only in a narrative context. But the right thing to do will always be the action which is consistent with the rightness of appetite, with the rightness of our will's relation to concrete persons with whom we live together in defined relationships.'[11]

In a follow-up article, 'Intentional Actions and the Meaning of Object: A Reply to Richard McCormick,' Rhonheimer further specifies the interrelation of the virtues, descriptions of actions, and the need for a narrative display.[12] He criticizes proportionalists for assuming that a basic action can be described and redescribed 'without looking at what the acting person chooses on the level of action (or "means"); rather, they concentrate on what he or she chooses in the order of consequences and on the corresponding commensurate reasons, all of which finally constitute the "expanded object".'[13] Rhonheimer observes, however, that such an expanded notion of object is not really a notion of 'object' at all, but rather its abolition. It is so because for Aquinas 'object' means the basic intentional content of a human act that is distinguishable from further intentions. In short, to speak of the 'object' of an act means that actions are not infinitely redescribable. At least they are not infinitely redescribable if a community is to be capable of sustaining virtuous lives.

Rhonheimer shows that the same behavioral pattern alone cannot decide everything. For example, he contrasts John, a college student who drinks whisky to induce temporary loss of consciousness in order to forget his girlfriend left him, with Fred, a soldier who drinks the same amount of whisky to avoid the pain of an emergency operation. Rhonheimer notes that while the behavioral pattern is identical, without indicating an intention, it is impossible to describe *what* John and Fred are doing, that is, what they are choosing.[14] Rhonheimer denies that this allows us simply to 'shift intention to and fro' since John cannot

---

that-set-of-standards, but simply false' (187). Yet truth is always a matter of being 'on the way' as the truth of the negative precepts of the natural law require construal through grace. Thus MacIntyre suggests, 'unless, unlike the rich young man, we respond to God's offer of grace by accepting it, we too shall be unable fully to understand and to obey the law in such a way as to achieve that ultimate good which gives to such understanding and obedience its point and purpose' (190).

[11] Rhonheimer, 'Intrinsically Evil Acts,' 26.

[12] Martin Rhonheimer, 'Intentional Actions and the Meaning of Object: A Reply to Richard McCormick,' *The Thomist* 59, 2 (1995), 279–311.

[13] Ibid. 294.

[14] Ibid. 297.

reasonably intend his act to be an act of anaesthesia. There are given contexts (shaped by circumstances and recognizable, as a morally significant contextual unity, only by practical reason) 'that *can* have if we choose a determined "kind of behavior," *independently* from *further* intentions.'[15]

When agents choose to act they necessarily do so under a description which is according to Rhonheimer 'precisely the description of an intent formed by reason.'[16] So the intention to have intercourse with someone who is not my spouse cannot be overridden by some further description that may involve doing so for obtaining some information necessary to save the lives of others. 'One can therefore describe concrete choices of kinds of behavior as wrong or evil independently from further intentions. Such descriptions, however, always *include* a basic intention, an intention that itself presupposes a given ethically relevant context without which no intention formed by reason, could come into being. This has nothing to do with the "expanded notion of object." But it includes a certain complexity that is due to the plurality and multiplicity of virtues that in turn reflect human life and its richness in relations between persons, including the differences of ethically relevant contexts.'[17]

Thus, against McCormick Rhonheimer maintains, for example, that it is possible without being a proportionalist to maintain there is a difference in the basic intentional content in the case of the following actions: simple killing for any end whatsoever, killing in self-defense, capital punishment, and killing in battle. These action descriptions differ not only because one might have different reasons for performing them, but because their intentional structure is different in each case. Their *structure* is different. Thus there is a difference between 'self-defense' and 'the choice to kill in order to save my life.' On some abstract level they may be identical, but from the acting person's perspective there is a different choice. 'In legitimate self-defense, what engenders my action is not a will or a choice for the aggressor's death. A sign of this is that I only use violence proportionate to stop his aggression. This may lead me to kill him, but the reason for my action is not wanting him to be

---

[15] Ibid. 299.
[16] Ibid. 283. The language of choice in Aquinas does not mean, as it does for us, decision. That is, choice is not a chronological state prior to action nor does choice describe a cognitive operation we associate with judging. For the end, for Aquinas, is the principle, not the conclusion, of practical wisdom. For Aquinas, acts shaped by virtuous habits involve judgement and choice but not as if one precedes the other. Aquinas' account of these matters in the *Summa*, I-II, Q.6–21, is descriptive and not prescriptive. Thus his circular account of the relation of 'will' and 'reason' is not vicious since neither 'will' nor 'reason' name separable faculties but rather are descriptions meant to illumine how we become virtuous through God's activity. I am indebted to Mr Michael Hanby for a seminal report on Aquinas' account of human action for the above account of choice.
[17] Ibid. 300.

dead (for the sake of saving my life); rather it is wanting to stop his aggression. Thus there is a difference of intention on the level of concrete chosen behavior, and that means, on the level of the object.'[18] Rhonheimer's (and MacIntyre's) account of *Veritatis Splendor* deftly opens the door for a fresh consideration of the way moral descriptions work. If, as Rhonheimer maintains, one has to analyze intentional contents as belonging to the structure of the virtues, then one has to consider why certain descriptions are privileged. Rhonheimer quotes the *Catechism's* teaching 'that there are certain specific kinds of behavior that are always wrong to choose, because choosing them involves a disorder of the will, that is, moral evil,' which I have no reason to dispute.[19] Yet the display of such acts requires a much thicker narrative than is usually supplied.

Which finally brings me back to friendship. An ethic of the virtues like that of *Veritatis Splendor* is unintelligible without friendship. That Aristotle devoted two books of the *Ethics* to friendship is hardly accidental. For Aristotle friendship is not just a necessity for living well, but necessary if we are to be people of practical wisdom. Through character-friendships we actually acquire the wisdom necessary, and in particular the self-knowledge, to be people of virtue. We literally cannot do good without our friends, not simply because we need friends to do good for but because the self-knowledge necessary to be good comes from seeing ourselves through our friendships.[20]

As Paul Wadell observes, friendship in Aristotle names the relationship by which we become good. The activity of friendship – and it is crucial that we understand it as an activity – is what trains us to be virtuous. 'By spending time together with people who are good, by sharing and delighting with them in our mutual love for the good we are more fully impressed with the good ourselves. Friendship is not just a relationship: it is a moral enterprise. People spend their lives together doing good because that is what they see their lives to be.'[21] In short friendship is an epistemological necessity, for moral goodness is

---

[18] Ibid. 302–303. One might think I would have a stake in challenging these distinctions since I am a pacifist. No doubt the practice of non-violence and the attending virtues might produce different kinds of descriptions, but the pacifist certainly has a stake in distinguishing different kinds of killing. For example, the pacifist certainly can (and should) maintain that self-defense is not the same as killing in war even if killing in self-defense is also not something the pacifist should do.

[19] Ibid. 307.

[20] For my more extended reflections on Aristotle's account of friendship see my 'Happiness, the life of Virtue and Friendship: Theological Reflections on Aristotelian Themes,' *Asbury Theological Journal* 45/1 (Spring 1990), 35–48. A revision of these essays with a much fuller account of the virtues has appeared in a book written with my friend, Professor Charles Pinches of the University of Scranton, called *Christians Among the Virtues: Theological Conversations with Ancient and Modern Ethics* (Notre Dame: University of Notre Dame Press, 1997), 3–54.

[21] Paul Wadell, CP, *Friendship and the Moral Life* (Notre Dame: University of Notre Dame Press, 1989), 62.

constituted through the ability of friends to name together those activities that constitute virtue as well as vice. Friendship names the practice necessary to sustain ongoing enquiry concerning the descriptions of the objects of our actions. For as MacIntyre suggests above, that which we learn to do and not do is discovered through such practices.

On Being Friends with Gay Christians

It is often said, 'Some of my best friends are gay, but that does not mean I approve of their being gay.' However, if Aristotle is right about the significance of friendship, then there surely must be something wrong with such a statement. If 'being gay' indicates a morally problematic mode of behavior then those who would be virtuous cannot afford to be friends with gay people. Of course it can be said that we all live morally ambiguous lives, so we should not expect too much of one another in such matters. But if 'being gay' names an immoral practice, then surely being a friend of gay people would not be a wise policy for those who would be moral.

Yet as I observed at the beginning, many of us find ourselves in Christian friendship with gay people. Consider an example, a fictionalized account of a real friendship. I have a friend who is a close friend of a lesbian couple who have lived faithful lives with one another for over twenty-five years. This couple have adopted and raised two children who are profoundly mentally handicapped. They are also committed Roman Catholics.[22] What should we call this relationship? Should my friend be their friend, and should I be his friend? Am I risking corruption through his friendship with gay Christians?

Of course the answer to such questions appears easy: 'It depends on the kind of people they are.' That is, it depends on the question of whether they are virtuous.[23] To be sure, that seems right, but I cannot act as if their being gay is irrelevant to their being virtuous. To distinguish between their being virtuous and being gay threatens to introduce a distinction between public and private which I take to be the destruction of any serious discussion of the virtuous life among Christians. Moreover such a distinction prevents the narrative from being truthfully told.

---

[22] I realize that this description could be contested since some might think that their claim to be Roman Catholic can only be a pose. If they were really Roman Catholic they would give up living together or at least refuse to sleep with one another. I cannot deny that their self-description as Roman Catholic must be complex, but I ask in the name of charity that their story be accepted in good faith.

[23] There is a crucial theoretical issue at stake here – that is the question of the unity of the virtues. Aquinas quotes Gregory to the effect 'that a virtue cannot be perfect as a virtue if isolated from the others: for there can be no true prudence without temperance, justice, and fortitude.' (ST, I-II, Q.65, 1). If these women are virtuous, even in Aquinas' sense as 'wayfarers,' then they cannot be said to be immoral in any simplistic sense.

Of course that does not mean that my gay friends think being gay should determine all they are or do. Indeed they tell me that one of the great problems with being gay in our current context is that such an identification becomes far too consuming. Sex, after all, just is not all that interesting, particularly as a defining characteristic that colors all of our activity. Gay people, like the rest of us, have more important things to do than to be gay.

Indeed that is one of the reasons I resist the very description 'homosexuality.' If there is something called 'homosexuality' then that must mean I have to be something called 'heterosexual.' I am not, of course, a heterosexual; I am a Texan – a philosophical joke meant to remind us that our identities are given through participation in practices that should serve the purposes of good communities. I remember when I first went to Notre Dame and was filling out the standard forms for employment, one of the forms asked me to indicate whether I was male, female, or religious. Now there is a mode of classification that could have produced a book from Foucault!

I, of course, understand that many will find this tack beside the point for consideration of the ethics of homosexuality. It is not about friendship, stupid – it is about sex and particular kinds of sex. Moreover, as I indicated at the beginning, if you believe that every sexual act must be open to conception then the game is up. I, of course, do not believe that, though I am unsympathetic with the 'spiritualization' of sex that I think informs many of the arguments made against the view that every sexual act must be open to conception. By 'spiritualization' I mean the peculiarly modern presumption that our sexual conduct has no purpose other than the meanings we give it and so are able to derive from it. Such a view seems to make us far too 'sexual.' A seminarian at Notre Dame once told me, 'We celibates can be happily sexually adjusted.' I told him I was married, had my share of sex, but I was sure I would never be happily sexually adjusted. What a terrible burden is put on sex: requiring it always to be fulfilling because it has no other purpose.[24]

---

[24] Wendell Berry observes the oddness in our time of associating 'sexual freedom' with the physical. 'In fact, our "sexual revolution" is mostly an industrial phenomenon, in which the body is used as an idea of pleasure or a pleasure machine with the aim of "freeing" natural pleasure from natural consequence. Like any other industrial enterprise, industrial sexuality seeks to conquer nature by exploiting it and ignoring the consequences, by denying any connection between nature and spirit or body and soul, and by evading social responsibility. The spiritual, physical, and economic costs of this "freedom" are immense, and characteristically belittled or ignored. Industrial sex, characteristically, establishes its freeness and goodness by an industrial accounting, dutifully toting up numbers of sexual partners, orgasms, and so on, with the inevitable industrial implication that the body is somehow a limit on the idea of sex, which will be a great deal more abundant as soon as it can be done by robots.' *What Are People For?* (New York: North Points Press, 1990), 191. This is perhaps a preamble to auto commercials where the car is suggested as something elegant to have an affair with.

Yet the purpose of sex cannot be known from sex. This, of course, locates my disagreement with the presumption that every act of sexual intercourse must be open to conception. Marriage as a practice of the church has as one of its purposes the readiness to receive children, but even that does not entail biological children. That marriage has such a purpose, moreover, I assume is part of the church's commitment to be hospitable to the stranger requiring all the baptized to consider ourselves parents whether we have biological children or not. I have always thought it quite appropriate that celibate priests be called 'Father.' It is a radical judgement on the presumption that biology constitutes fatherhood.

If every sexual act need not be open to conception, then it seems to me that *Veritatis Splendor* offers us a perspective from which to think about how we might narrate the relation between the two women I described. They are not promiscuous. The intimacy they share is oriented to upbuilding their lives for the good of their community. Just as we can discriminate between different kinds of killing through analogous comparisons, I do not see why we cannot see this kind of relationship analogous to what Christians mean by marriage.[25] The church after all does recognize the marriage of people who are beyond the age of childbearing. On what grounds are the women I described above excluded from such recognition?

The quick answer, of course, is that they are the same sex. They are homosexual. But here we see the wisdom of the Catholic tradition and why I spent so much time discussing *Veritatis Splendor*. Catholic moral theology has never thought that a *theory* about 'homosexuality' would determine these matters, but rather asked what kind of behavior is commensurate with being the virtuous person for the upbuilding of

---

[25] My friend Michael Quirk argues that the false assumption shared by proportionalists and their conservative critics is that, if description is a problem, it is a problem that a *theory* of moral description will solve. 'Proportionalism founders on its need for criteria to winnow out relevant from irrelevant descriptive considerations, and proper from improper weigh-ins; anti-proportionalism founders on its parallel need to come up with descriptions of moral species that are not relative to context or purposes at hand but are normative as such, and which are in some way self-applying to particular moral cases. Fortunately, there are practices of moral description that can provide a measure of stability for the act of moral description in the absence of readily available criteria: the ability to reveal the slave owner is at odds with his linguistic community's ascription of humanity to slaves, and hence at odds with himself, is a paradigm case of how practice can accomplish the winnowing-out of poor and false moral descriptions without reliance upon a prior set of theoretically-validated rules for doing so. There are only such rules as moral practice itself demands. And the lesson for theological ethics in all this is that the substitution of moral theory for an accounting of that which religious practice demands on its adherents – that is, for a "thick description" of the elements of the Christian life, the virtues they support, and the sorts of conduct that can be intelligibly narrated within the constraints of these virtues – will only serve the ignoble end of making disagreement and disunity more pronounced and intractable than it needs to be.' 'Why the Debate on Proportionalism Is Misconceived,' *Modern Theology* 13/4 (October 1997), 520. Quirk's point is obviously at the heart of the way I have tried to argue in this paper.

the church.[26] I am suggesting that it would at least be possible to understand the object of the relation between the women I described above as analogous to marriage. I would put the matter more strongly – if gay Christians are to have some alternative to the sexual wilderness that today grips all our lives, gay and non-gay alike, something like what I am suggesting must be found.[27]

Such a suggestion obviously involves a complex account of the interrelation of practices and their correlative virtues, the narratives that render such practices and virtues intelligible, and the institutions necessary to sustain such narratives. I cannot pretend to have done that work adequately in this paper. Rather I have tried to provide a beginning for such work – a beginning that surely begins by entering into enquiry with our gay friends in the hope that together we might discover how to live faithfully as God's people.

I need, however, to be candid. Just as marriage between those past child-bearing age may be an exception, so it may be that the recognition of faithful relations between gay people is an exception. But exceptions are not a problem for a community that is secure in its essential practices. The crucial question is how to live in a manner that the exception does not become the rule. Just as the married bear the burden of proof in the church, given the church's presumption that we do not have to be married to be Christians, so among the married those who cannot have biological children may well bear the burden of proof. Such a burden hopefully should be seen as a means for the upbuilding of the community of believers. By asking gays to help us understand how their lives contribute to our presumption as Christians that marriage is constituted by a promise of lifelong monogamous fidelity we might discover what a life-giving promise that is.

I am aware that gay Christians may think that they already have enough burdens. Why should they be asked to justify their lives in such

---

[26] I am, of course, aware that there are scriptural issues involved which I am ignoring. By doing so I do not mean to imply they are unimportant. Yet I do not think that the church's position on these matters can turn on any one text even one as important as Romans 1. The issue for me is not whether texts like Romans 1 'mean' what we mean by homosexuality, but rather how such texts are to be read in the light of the church's practices of singleness and marriage. Here I follow the rule that the more obscure texts should be interpreted in the light of the less obscure. The truth of the matter is the New Testament does not have that much to say about sexual conduct, which I suspect is an indication that Christian thinking about sex cannot be isolated from more determinative practices such as truth-telling, sharing goods, mutual correction that make the church the church.

[27] Of course, it can be said an alternative already exists – i.e., celibacy. I would not want to dismiss that alternative, for surely celibacy is a gift necessary for the church's practice. But as it is a gift, one cannot assume that everyone in the church has been given it. Simply because someone is gay does not mean they have the gift of celibacy. If they do, it is a great gift. Of course, all Christians, married and unmarried, are called to be chaste. Indeed I expect some of our current confusion about sex among Christians derives from our loss of any understanding of how chastity is intrinsic to marriage.

a manner? We certainly do not ask it of those who call themselves 'heterosexuals.' I can only say, 'This can only be asked of you because you are Christian and because we are friends.'

7

Characterizing Perfection: Second Thoughts on Character and Sanctification

What is Right and Wrong about Wesley

My attempt to use Wesley's account of sanctification to recover the importance of character for the moral life is but one aspect of my general admiration for Wesley's insistence on the empirical character of Christian convictions. Christianity, for Wesley, is about changed lives and any belief that does not serve that end held little interest for him. Moreover, this 'turn to the subject' was not an attempt on Wesley's part to avoid questions of the truth of Christian belief, but rather an attempt to locate the right context to ask the question of truth. For example, in 'A Plain Account of Genuine Christianity,' Wesley says, 'If, therefore, it were possible (which I conceive it is not) to shake the traditional evidence of Christianity, still he that has the internal evidence (and every true believer has the witness or evidence in himself) would stand firm and unshaken.' Still he could say to those who were striking at the external evidence, 'Beat on the "sack of Anaxagoras," but you can no more hurt my evidence of Christianity than the tyrant could hurt the spirit of that wise man. I have sometimes been almost inclined to believe that the wisdom of God has, in most later ages, permitted the external evidence of Christianity to be more or less clogged and encumbered for this very end, that men (of reflection especially) might not altogether rest there, but be constrained to look into themselves also and attend to the light shining in their hearts.'[1]

Wesley's attack on halfway Christians, on lukewarm belief, was not only an attempt to upgrade the morality of Christians but involved basic questions of the truth and falsity of Christian convictions. His insistence on integrity between what Christians believed and what they did was uncompromising because any temporizing on the part of Christians betrayed the character of their belief.[2] Christians, for Wesley,

---

[1] John Wesley, *A Plain Account of Genuine Christianity in John Wesley*, ed. Albert C. Outler (New York: Oxford University Press, 1964), 192. Hereafter cited as Outler.

[2] See, for example, Wesley's sermon, 'The Almost Christian,' in his *Forty-Four Sermons* (London: Epworth Press, 1964), 11–19. It is interesting that in this sermon Wesley says that sincerity is impossible for an 'almost Christian.' Indeed without a

are a pilgrim people undertaking an arduous but fulfilling journey. It is, therefore, unthinkable that those on that journey would not manifest some predictable and observable empirical change. Wesley's doctrine of perfection, for all of its difficulties, at least rightly denotes that there is an inherent contradiction to claim to be a Christian without that claim making a difference in our lives and how we live. The affirmation of such a change after all is not a statement about our ability but the sovereignty of God's grace over our sinfulness.

The difficulties with Wesley's doctrine of perfection are well known – how can sin remain in the 'perfect,' what would it mean for the perfect to sin in a manner that is not 'deliberate,'[3] and the inherent temptation to works righteousness always present in such a doctrine. Yet in spite of these difficulties I continue to think that Wesley was right to hold that the peculiar contribution of Methodists to the church universal lies in our struggle to recover the centrality of holiness as integral to the Christian life. I must admit, however, I often wish that Wesley might have hit upon a less troublesome notion than 'perfection' in order to express his convictions about the necessity of continued growth in the Christian life.[4] Perfection unfortunately conveys too much of a sense of accomplishment rather than the necessity of continued growth that was at the heart of Wesley's account of sanctification. Thus Wesley says, 'Yea, and when ye have attained a measure of perfect love, when God has circumcised your hearts, and enabled you to love him with all your heart and with all your soul, think not of resting there. That is impossible. You cannot stand still; you must either rise or fall; rise higher or fall lower. Therefore the voice of God to the children of Israel, to the children of God, is, "Go forward!" "Forgetting the things that are behind, and reaching forward unto those that are before, press on to the mark, for the prize of your high calling of God in Christ Jesus"!'[5]

Not only do I think Wesley was right to stress the centrality of such growth for any truthful account of Christian convictions, I think such an emphasis remains particularly significant for today. For we live in

---

'real, inward principle of religion, from which these outward actions flow,' it is not possible to be even an honest heathen (14). But sincerity is not sufficient to be a Christian since that requires love of God and neighbor. Thus Christian sincerity is formed by a different set of presuppositions than that of heathen honesty.

[3] Wesley, *A Plain Account of Christian Perfection*, in Outler, 286.

[4] William Cannon plainly states that 'Perfection is a weasel word in Christian theology,' since it at once sets a standard too high for attainment but yet maintains it is a possibility as a temporal goal. 'John Wesley's Doctrine of Sanctification and Perfection,' *Mennonite Quarterly Review* 35 (April 1961), 5–9. He is of course right as long as perfection is construed in the language of a 'goal.' The matter becomes quite different, however, once perfection is understood as a qualification of our character as I have tried to show in my *Character and the Christian Life: A Study in Theological Ethics* (San Antonio: Trinity University Press, 1975), 179–228.

[5] Wesley, 'Sermon on Faith,' quoted by Harold Lindstrom, *Wesley and Sanctification* (Nashville: Abingdon Press, 1946), 118–19.

the world that was just beginning to be born in Wesley's time – a world that no longer assumes that a religious, or in particular, a Christian, account of life is necessary for decent and upright living. What difference, if any, it makes to be a Christian becomes even more pressing in such a world. No account of the truth or falsity of Christian convictions can or should avoid that question, not because it is the question asked by the world, but because it is a question, as Wesley saw, that is at the heart of Christian faith.

Yet it does not seem possible for us to speak with the same confidence about perfection as Wesley. The fragmentation of our world, and the correlative fragmentation of our lives, makes us less sure than Wesley that we are in fact continually being sanctified. We are happier thinking of ourselves at best as troubled sinners and certainly not as righteous saints. Moreover, Wesley thought he could say in no uncertain terms in what the real change consisted. Thus those that walk after the spirit 'show forth in their lives, in the whole course of their words and actions the genuine fruits of the Spirit of God, namely, "love, joy, peace, long-suffering, gentleness, goodness, fidelity, meekness, temperance," and whatsoever is lovely and praiseworthy.'[6] Moreover, we are a bit embarrassed that Wesley thought the demands of 'perfect love' involved questions of what to wear, how to eat, how we are to entertain ourselves, and so on. Theologically it seems we are in a no-win situation. Like Wesley we feel the necessity to claim that being a Christian makes a difference, but we are less sure how to characterize perfection without resorting to vague generalities about 'being loving' or appearing overly moralistic by being too specific. For we have become acutely aware that 'the pious' too often lack the substance that makes their piety authentic.

In *Character and the Christian Life* I was intent to show that character might be a way of displaying perfection that might avoid these difficulties. For Wesley was not any less conscious than we of the hypocrisy of being a halfway Christian. If anything, he was even more concerned with the problem since he lived in an age when what it meant to be a 'better sort of person' was assumed equivalent to being a Christian. His doctrine of perfection was an attempt to challenge this assumption by insisting on the necessity of 'purity of intention' or 'a single eye' for the life of the Christian.[7] To be so determined meant that everything we are and do derives from a wholehearted devotion to God that precludes any ulterior motive – that is, what we do and do not do springs from our character as people devoted to God. By developing the notion of character I tried to suggest a means

---

[6] John Wesley, 'The First-Fruits of the Spirit,' in *Forty-Four Sermons*, 87.

[7] See, for example, my *Character and the Christian Life*, 198–99. Though Wesley often used the language of 'internal' to talk about the subject of perfection, in fact the 'intention' that is purified is everything we are and do. Thus contrary to our assumption, Wesley's sense of 'internal' was quite public.

of characterizing concretely the subject and form of such whole-heartedness.

Yet I have never felt completely happy with that attempt, as character remains far too abstract a notion. I think part of my difficulty has to do with Wesley's way of characterizing perfection. For even though Wesley's account of sanctification is inherently teleological,[8] he was unable to find the appropriate means to suggest how our being on a journey also requires results in the particular kind of singleness characteristic of Christians.

In this respect I think his problem was similar to the difficulty which Alasdair MacIntyre has called to our attention in respect to the virtue of constancy. According to MacIntyre constancy is a relatively recently identified virtue displayed in its most compelling form in the novels of Jane Austen. Constancy is that quality that allows us to reaffirm the unity of the self across and through our many different loyalties and actions.[9] It is akin to the Christian virtue of patience and the Aristotelian virtue of courage, but it is not the same as either. For constancy results from the recognition of the particular kind of threat to integrity presented by the modern world, a recognition patience does not require. Moreover, constancy requires a sense of self-knowledge based on a recognition of the necessity of repentance since the constant person is acutely aware that the generally agreed upon manner of behavior, which is quite right in itself, can also be a snare that only gives the illusion of constancy.

It would be fascinating in itself to explore in what ways Wesley's sense of perfection is like and unlike MacIntyre's (and Austen's) sense of constancy. Certainly I think it is no accident that novelists and theologians at that time seemed equally concerned to explore the difference between those who are genuinely moral and those who have but the appearance of morality.[10] Yet equally interesting for our purposes is MacIntyre's observation that constancy is quite different from other virtues such as justice, patience, courage, and so on. Such virtues can be spelled out in reference to concrete practices, but

[8] For example, Lindstrom suggests 'In regarding love to God in this aspect of man's reunion with Him, Wesley has logically to make Him ultimately the sole object of human love. All else becomes a means to this end. Further, as love is considered a gradual growth, it follows that love to God as well as already involving fellowship with Him must also be seen as a progress towards an ever more perfect fellowship with Him' (189). Or again, 'The Christian, as in William Law and the mystics, is above all (for Wesley) a pilgrim, his life on earth a journey, the destination Heaven. And the path he must travel to reach his goal is the path of sanctification, of real empirical change in man' (218).

[9] Alasdair MacIntyre, *After Virtue* (Notre Dame: University of Notre Dame Press, 1981), 225.

[10] It would be particularly interesting to pursue this theme by comparing and contrasting Wesley's concern for perfection and the concerns of the 'realistic' novelists of the nineteenth century. For the latter were acutely concerned with the problem of integrity or constancy as the hallmark of the moral person.

constancy cannot be specified 'at all except with reference to the wholeness of human life.'[11] So unless there is a '*telos*' which transcends limited goods or practices by constituting the good of a whole human life, the good of a human life conceived as a unity, it will both be the case that a certain subversive arbitrariness will invade the moral life and that we shall be unable to specify the context of certain virtues adequately.'[12]

I think that MacIntyre's point about the difficulty of characterizing constancy is almost exactly parallel to Wesley's stress on perfection. To characterize perfection adequately requires a 'reference to the wholeness of a human life,' but that is obviously no easy matter. It is, moreover, made even more difficult when you are attempting, as Wesley was, to remain faithful to Reformation insights concerning justification and yet maintain the priority of a teleological understanding of Christian existence. For example, Gilbert Meilaender has noted that there are in Christian tradition two pictures of the Christian life which are not necessarily irreconcilable, but are certainly not easily harmonized – namely, that of life as a journey and as a dialogue.[13]

When the Christian life is pictured as a dialogue, ethics becomes but an attempt to explicate the divine verdict on human life by exposing our status as sinners. In these terms it is very difficult, Meilaender observes, to make sense of notions of progress in righteousness. In contrast, when the Christian life is pictured as a journey, 'as the process by which God graciously transforms a sinner into a saint, as a pilgrimage (always empowered by grace) toward fellowship with God,'[14] progress is an essential element of the Christian life. Righteousness is not just a right relation with God, but becoming the sort of person God wills us to be. Meilaender suggests that the tension between these two pictures of Christian existence cannot be overcome, nor should we try to overcome it.[15] Yet Wesley did try to overcome it by clearly making his

---

[11] MacIntyre, *After Virtue*, 189.

[12] Ibid.

[13] Gilbert Meilaender, 'The Place of Ethics in the Theological Task,' *Currents in Theology and Mission* 6 (August 1979), 199.

[14] Ibid. 200. Meilaender's account of dialogue is too Lutheran for me. After all, a dialogue can be an ongoing conversation in which one can certainly make progress.

[15] Ibid. 210. Meilaender in good Lutheran fashion wants to maintain that these two emphases should always be kept in dialectical tension, though he hints that, at least for dogmatic theology, the journey metaphor is primary. I think he is right about that, but I would go even further and suggest that the metaphor of dialogue only makes sense as a necessary and continuing part of the journey. In that sense I think Wesley and the whole sanctificationist tradition are more nearly right. The problem, however, is that when either justification or sanctification becomes an independent theological notion something has gone wrong. Thus 'perfection' displays justification and sanctification not vice versa. For a more extended argument defending the secondary nature of justification and sanctification see my *The Peaceable Kingdom: A Primer in Christian Ethics* (Notre Dame: University of Notre Dame Press, 1983). I think part of the difficulty with the last chapter of *Character and the Christian Life* was my concentration on

teleological framework primary and then making justification but one step along the road.

As a result he fell into the unfortunate language of 'stages' in an attempt to characterize perfection. Thus in his sermon, 'The Scripture Way of Salvation,' he enumerates the stages of justification and sanctification as: (1) the operation of prevenient grace; (2) repentance previous to justification; (3) justification or forgiveness; (4) the new birth; (5) repentance after justification and the gradually proceeding work of sanctification; and (6) entire sanctification.[16] The problem with his scheme, of course, is that it is too neat, for Wesley was acutely aware that our lives can hardly be laid out with such exactness. Stages overlap and we regress.

But even more troubling, the language of stages is simply insufficient to characterize the kind of *telos* that Wesley was attempting to reclaim through his insistence on perfection.[17] For if perfection can be characterized only by 'reference to the wholeness of a human life' then the language of stages is far too abstract. Rather, what is required is the actual depiction of lives through which we can be imaginatively drawn into the journey by being given the means to understand and test our failures and successes. That such is the case, moreover, reflects the kind of journey that Christians are asked to undertake. For the *telos* of the Christian life is not a goal that is clearly known prior to the undertaking of the journey, but rather we learn better the nature of the end by being slowly transformed by the means necessary to pursue it. Thus, the only means to perceive rightly the end is by attending to the lives of those who have been and are on the way.

In order to develop this point I want to call our attention to a work well known to Wesley, namely Williams Law's, *A Serious Call to a Devout and Holy Life*. It is generally acknowledged that in spite of his differences with Law's account of the atonement as well as Law's alleged mysticism, Wesley was deeply influenced by Law's view of Christian perfection.[18] I certainly have no reason to challenge that assumption as I think my analysis of Law can only substantiate Law and Wesley's common vision. Yet I want also to suggest that Wesley missed what was perhaps the most important aspect of *A Serious Call to a Devout and Holy Life* by his failure to learn from Law's character studies what

---

justification and sanctification as abstracted from any account of what kind of journey Christians are asked to undertake.

[16] Lindstrom, *Wesley and Sanctification*, 113.

[17] In an interesting way the same difficulty of 'stage' language is reappearing in much of the literature influenced by Kohlberg.

[18] For what remains one of the best treatments of Law's influence on Wesley, and in particular their differences concerning the atonement, see Lindstrom, *Wesley and Sanctification*, 55–60. Also see Lindstrom's discussion of how closely Wesley followed Law's account of perfect love, 161–83.

was crucial to his account of perfection. For as I shall try to show, those character studies are not simply 'examples' that can be left aside or ignored, but are essential to the substance of Law's account of Christian perfection.

By pursuing this line of inquiry, moreover, I hope to indicate perhaps some of the kind of work we need to do if we are to be worthy heirs of Wesley's heritage. My calling attention to Law is not meant as a fundamental criticism of Wesley, but rather to suggest the means to work out Wesley's own best insights in a different, but I think compatible, direction. In the process I hope to show that Wesley and Law's account of the Christian life is particularly significant today if we are to meet the challenge of saying what difference being a Christian might make – and thus why it is we believe our faith to be true.

What Is Right about Law's, *A Serious Call to a Devout and Holy Life*

In order to understand the place of characterization in *A Serious Call* it is necessary to have a sense of the structure of the entire book. Law obviously thought a great deal about how the book should be shaped, as he was intent on the book's becoming an exercise that might put one on the path to holiness. The book begins, therefore, with a general claim that devotion signifies a life given or devoted to God, not just in performance of certain religious duties, but in all the ordinary actions of our life. Indeed the problem is that so many Christians are 'strict as to some times and places of devotion, but when the service of the church is over, they are but like those who seldom or never come there. In their way of life, their manner of spending their time and money, in their cares and fears, in their pleasure and indulgences, in their labor and diversions, they are like the rest of the world. This makes the loose part of the world generally make a jest of those who are devout, because they see their devotion goes no further than their prayers, and that when they are over, they live no more unto God, till the time of prayer returns again; but live by the same humour and fancy, and in as full an enjoyment of all the follies of life as other people.'[19]

---

[19] William Law, *A Serious Call to a Devout and Holy Life*, with an introduction by Geoffrey Bromiley (Grand Rapids: Eerdmans, 1966). All page references to this work will appear in the text in parentheses. There are several editions of *A Serious Call*, the most recent being in the *Classics of Western Spirituality*, ed. Paul Stanwood (New York: Paulist Press, 1978). I have used Bromiley's edition because I find his notes most helpful. In the last chapter of *A Serious Call* Law returns to his theme claiming 'because in this polite age of ours we have so lived away the spirit of devotion, that many seem afraid even to be suspected of it, imagining great devotion to be great bigotry; that it is founded in ignorance and poorness of spirit, and that little, weak, and dejected minds are generally the greatest proficients in it: It shall here be full shown that great devotion is the noblest temper of the greatest and noblest souls, and they who think it receives any advantage from ignorance and poorness of spirit are themselves not a little, but

According to Law, however, it is as absurd to suppose holy prayers without a holiness of life as to suppose a holy life without prayers. Either 'reason and religion prescribe rules and ends to all the ordinary actions of our life, or they do not: If they do, then it is as necessary to govern all our actions by those actions, by those rules, as it necessary to worship God' (5).[20] Thus if self-denial or humility are essential to our salvation then they must be made part of every aspect of our lives.

For Law the problem is how to explain how it has come to pass 'that the lives even of the better sort of people are thus strangely contrary to the principles of Christianity' (11). His answer is quite simple. It is not that they want to live a life of devotion, but due to the frailty of the flesh, fail to do so. Rather it is that they plainly lack the intention or desire to live a holy life. Thus some will say 'that all people fall short of the perfection of the Gospel, and therefore you are content with your failings. But this is saying nothing to purpose. For the question is not whether Gospel perfection can be attained, but whether you come as near it as sincere intention and careful diligence can carry you' (19). Not to pursue perfection is not only irreligious but irrational life, as the Scripture makes clear, 'our salvation depends upon the sincerity and perfection of our endeavors to obtain it' (20).[21]

Moreover it is not possible to distinguish between states of life, excusing some from holiness because they are involved in worldly pursuits. Holiness is required by all, clergy, businessmen and women alike. Indeed most of the employments of life are by their nature lawful

---

entirely ignorant of the nature of devotion, the nature of God, and the nature of themselves' (299).

[20] Though Law and Wesley were often identified as religious enthusiasts who had no use for reason, both maintained that everything they advocated was based on rational grounds. Thus Law says, 'If we had a religion that consisted in absurd superstitions, that had no regard to the perfection of our nature, people might well be glad to have some part of their life excused from it. But as the religion of the Gospel is only the refinement and exaltation of our best faculties, as it only requires a life of the highest reason, as it only requires us to use this world as according to reason it ought to be used, to live in such tempers as are the glory of intelligent beings, to walk in such wisdom as exalts our nature, and to practice such poetry as will raise us to God; who can think it grievous to live always in the spirit of such a religion, to have every part of his life full of it, but he that would think it much more grievous to be as the angels of God in heaven?' (47–48).

[21] Of course, it was this kind of language that made Wesley shudder as it had an unmistakable Pelagian ring. Yet Wesley was not far from a similar view, even though he explicitly rejected Law's view that Christ's atonement was a representational act in the name of mankind that still requires our own mortification. Once a theological view of salvation is accepted, I think it is very hard to avoid something very much like Law's account of the matter. To do so in no way undermines the priority of God's grace, but rather it is a reminder that God's grace is a form of forgiveness that graciously gives us a way to go on – that is, grace is just the invitation and opportunity to take part in the journey of God's people.

so long as we engage in them only so far, and for such ends, as are suitable to beings that are to live above this world. 'This is the only measure of our application to any world business; let it be what it will, when it will, it must have no more of our hands, our hearts, or our time, than is consistent with an hearty, daily, careful preparation of ourselves for another life' (32).

The man of the world is no less required to be truthful and honest in all his dealings than those concerned more directly with 'spiritual' matters. The same is equally true of humility as it must become a 'general ruling habit' extended to all our actions and designs. For Law observes that we:

> . . . sometimes talk, as if a man might be humble in some things, and proud in others; humble in his dress, but proud of his learning; humble in his person, but proud in his views and designs. But though this may pass in common discourse, where few things are said according to strict truth, it cannot be allowed when we examine into the nature of our actions. It is very possible for a man that lives by cheating to be very punctual in paying for what he buys; but then everyone is assured that he does not do so out of any principle of true honesty. In like manner, it is very possible for a man that is proud of his estate, ambitious in his views, or vain of his learning, to disregard his dress, and person, in such a manner as a truly humble man would do. (38–39).

Christian perfection, therefore, is the attempt to extend a 'regular and uniform piety' (40) to all the actions of our common life. What is crucial, therefore, for Law and Wesley is the singleness of intention, the constancy of character, that makes our behavior consistent with a life devoted to God.

Law next turns to those who are free from the necessity of daily toil by the owning of estates and fortunes, suggesting they must consider themselves devoted to God in even a higher degree. It is not enough that they do occasional acts of humility, devotion, or justice, but rather they must live by habitual exercise of charity to the utmost of their power (55). Those with such advantages, however, are particularly tempted to have their soul destroyed by the misuse of innocent and lawful things.

> What is more innocent than rest and retirement? And yet what more dangerous than sloth and idleness? How lawful and praiseworthy is the care of a family! And yet how certainly are many people rendered incapable of all virtue by a worldly and solicitous temper? Now it is for want of religious exactness in the use of these innocent and lawful things that religion cannot get possession of our hearts. And it is the right and prudent management of ourselves as to these things that all the arts of holy living chiefly consist. Gross sins are plainly seen, and easily avoided by persons that profess religion. But the indiscreet and dangerous use of innocent and lawful things, as it does not shock and offend our consciences so it is difficult to make people at all sensible of the danger of it. (60–61).

More people are kept from a 'true sense and state of religion by a regular kind of sensuality and indulgence than by gross drunkenness' (65).[22]

In the context of discussing the special responsibilities of those with a secured living Law treats especially the role of women. But in doing so he continues his theme of the need to bring every rule and action under the intention to live completely devoted to God. Thus, it is not enough to be but a little vain for to be vain in one thing means we are vain in all things (76). Like the good high church Puritan he was, Law does not refrain from treating the place and use of clothes.[23] To be sure, as he admits, such matter can be trivial, but it is nonetheless as impossible 'for a mind that is in a true state of religion to be vain in the use of clothes as to be vain in the use of alms or devotions' (77). To be plainly and soberly dressed is but to manifest the plainness and simplicity of the Gospel. That Law would take the time to deal with such matters denotes the thoroughness of his concern to bring all our behavior under the single rule of the Gospel.

Having argued for the necessity of forming all our behavior in accordance to our devotion to God no matter what our state of life, Law addresses the objection that such a life cannot help but be dull and lifeless. On the contrary, such a life is the only true and interesting one, for true piety rightly directs our passions to their true good. When that is missing we are beset by trouble and uneasiness that is founded on our mistaken want of something or the other (103).

> The man of pride has a thousand wants, which only his own pride has created; and these render him as full of trouble as if God had created him with a thousand appetites without creating anything that was proper to satisfy them. Envy and ambition have also their endless wants, which disquiet the soul of men, and by their contradictory motions render them as foolishly miserable as those that want to fly and creep at the same time. (104)[24]

[22] Though we tend at best to regard Law's and Wesley's concern with dress, how we eat, and our modes of entertainment with embarrassed bemusement, I think we do so by sacrificing a certain kind of seriousness. Law is perfectly right that it is the small habits that finally corrupt, not our large sins. Moreover, he was by no means narrowly moralistic about such matters, thinking they could be clearly determined by a general rule or practice. His concern was not that all Christians dress alike, indeed he explicitly criticized such an assumption, but that our dress denote a simplicity that marks the simplicity of our character.

[23] As a non-juror and with his high view of the sacraments, Law obviously appeared as the very opposite of the Puritans, but one cannot help being impressed by how much his understanding of the Christian life parallels classical Puritan presentations such as Bunyan's.

[24] Samuel Johnson, who acknowledged Law's influence, interestingly gives as one of his examples of the lengths men will go to avoid boredom as the attempt to fly. See his *History of Rasselas, Prince of Abyssinia* in *The Selected Writings of Samuel Johnson*, ed. Katharine Rogers (New York: A Signet Classic, 1982), 170–73. Indeed, I suspect Law's influence on Johnson was not only profound in terms of Johnson's own views of

The Shaping of Holiness by Prayer

The challenge that Christian holiness is life-denying cannot be countered just by showing the misery brought on by worldly desires. Rather what is required is a depiction of the life of holiness that is compelling and attractive. And it is to that task that Law turns in the second half of his book. His discussion is shaped around the times of our daily prayers with a corresponding virtue associated with each time. The result is a comprehensive account of the Christian life seldom equalled.

He begins by countering all objections that it is not possible to take the time for such a regular devotion by suggesting it is impossible not to take the time if we truly believe we have a destiny beyond this world. For devotion is 'nothing else but right apprehensions and right affections toward God,' and, as such, we void life of interest and adventure if we fail to develop such affections through devotion (162).[25] Not only would we engage in daily devotions, but we should have some fixed subject which is our chief matter of prayer at that particular time of day. Thus 'as the morning is to you the beginning of a new life, as God has then given you a new enjoyment of yourself and a fresh entrance into the world, it is highly proper that your first devotions should be a praise and thanksgiving to God as for new creation; and that you should offer and devote body and soul, all that you are, and all that you have, to His service and glory' (155).

Indeed Law insists that we ought to chant our prayers for singing unites the soul and body in a manner nothing else can do. For the 'soul has no thought or passion but the body is concerned in it; the body has no action or motion but what in some degree affects the soul' (169). Since we are neither all soul nor body, and seeing that we have no habits that are not actions both of our souls and bodies, 'It is certain that if we would arrive at habits of devotion or delight in God, we must not only meditate and exercise our souls, but we must practice and exercise our bodies to all such outward actions as are conformable to these inward tempers' (171).

---

religious life, but also in the style in which he wrote. Anyone familiar with Johnson's *Rambler* and *Idler* cannot help but be struck by Johnson's use of character studies that imitate closely Law's method in *A Serious Call*. Moreover, it is my suspicion the moralist tradition, represented by Taylor, Law, and Johnson, found its ultimate home in the eighteenth- and nineteenth-century novelist. For their development of character, realistic though it is, is never without moral purpose. Indeed, Trollope could not resist, which he might well have done, calling his minor characters by stereotypical names – e.g., Lawyer Too Good in *The Last Chronicle of Barset*. Moreover, central to Austen, Eliot, and Trollope was the problem of how true vision requires repentance and forgiveness – themes at the heart of Law's and Wesley's concern with perfection.

[25] The significance of this should not be overlooked, for Law never understood holiness as consisting of the denial of the passions, but rather as the passions finding their true end.

At nine o'clock Law suggests the subject of our prayers ought to be humility. He devotes more space to his discussion of humility than to any of the virtues he treats in the last part of the book. He does so because 'a humble state of soul is the very state of religion,' but it is essential we rightly understand the nature of humility. For humility does not consist in having a worse opinion of ourselves than we deserve, 'but as all virtue is founded in truth, so humility is founded in a true and just sense of our weakness, misery, and sin. He that rightly feels and lives in this sense of his condition lives in humility' (183).

Humility, for Law, comprises nothing less than the Christian taking a stance against the spirit and temper of the world. For the world is built on false assumptions that fuel envy, pride, and power which the Christian cannot help but reject.[26] It is no accident that it is in this context that Law makes appeal to the life of Christ, and in particular his cross. For it 'was the spirit of the world that nailed our blessed Lord to the cross, so every man that has the spirit of Christ, that opposes the world as He did, will certainly be crucified by the world some way or the other. For Christianity still lives in the same world that Christ did: and these two will be utter enemies till the kingdom of darkness is entirely at an end' (199). That many assume that the world has become Christian, according to Law, only makes the world a more dangerous enemy by having lost its appearance of enmity. 'Its outward profession of Christianity makes it no longer considered as an enemy, and, therefore, the generality of people are easily persuaded to resign themselves up to be governed and directed by it. There is nothing, therefore, that a good Christian ought to be more suspicious of, or more constantly guard against, than the authority of the Christian world' (201).

The subject of our prayer at noon is universal love. But before treating that subject directly Law returns to his contention that all people, those in business, those of 'figure' or dignity, must engage in the practice of daily prayer.

> For it is the very end of Christianity to redeem all orders of men into one holy society, that rich and poor, high and low, masters and servants, may in one and the same spirit of piety become a 'chosen generation, a royal

---

[26] For example, Law argues that envy is built into our educational system so that it unavoidably becomes our way of life, even though 'envy is acknowledged by all people to be the most ungenerous, base, and wicked passion that can enter into the heart of man. And is this a temper to be instilled, nourished, and established in the minds of young people? I know it is said that it is not envy but emulation that is intended to be awakened in the minds of young men. But this is vainly said. For when children are taught to bear no rival and to scorn to be out-done by any of their age, they are plainly and directly taught to be envious. For it is impossible for any one to have this scorn of being out-done, and this contention with rivals, without burning with envy against all those that seem to excel him or get any distinction from him. So that what children are taught is rank envy, and only covered with a name of a less odious sound' (207–208). Part of Law's great power was his ability to locate and reveal our vices that we have learned to call by less odious names.

priesthood, a holy nation, a peculiar people,' that are to show forth the praises of Him Who hath called them out of darkness into His marvelous light (1 Pet. 2:9). (242)[27]

It is natural that he should return to this theme in the context of stressing the significance of universal love, for his account of such love is uncompromising. The 'greatest idea that we can frame of God is when we conceive Him to be a being of infinite love and goodness, using an infinite wisdom and power for the common good and happiness of all His creatures' (243). And since we are to live in the image of such a God, it is our duty and privilege to look upon all people in the same manner. There are other loves that may be tender and affectionate, but unless they derive their source from this kind of love they lack piety – they are loves of 'humor, and temper, or interest, or such a love as publicans and heathens practice' (244).

Law readily admits that our power of doing external acts of love and goodness is restrained, but we must do what we can to heal the sick, relieve the poor, and be a father to the fatherless. For the love required by God is not any natural tenderness, which is more or less in people according to their constitutions, but that larger principle of the soul, founded in reason and piety, 'which makes us tender, kind, and benevolent to all our fellow-creatures, as creatures of God, for His sake. It is this love of all things in God, as His creatures, as the images of His power, as the creatures of His goodness, as parts of His family, as members of His society, that becomes a holy principle of all great and good actions' (247–48).

Only on the basis of such a love can we rightly learn to love ourselves. For while we must detest and abhor many of our past actions and honestly admit our folly, we must nonetheless not 'lose any of those tender sentiments toward ourselves' as we are required to love ourselves as God has loved us. For even though we cannot do all we need to do as lovers of ourselves and others, we can still pray for others thus

---

[27] While I could not take the time to do it in this paper, it would be fascinating to study Law's and Wesley's understanding of church and society. For each, almost in spite of himself, shares more with certain forms of the disestablished church than the church to which they were both so loyal. The relationship between Wesley and the Anabaptists has often been suggested, but never subjected to rigorous analysis. There is certainly no doubt, however, that Wesley's (and Law's) understanding of regeneration was very similar to that of Menno Simons and many others of the early Anabaptists. See, for example, Harold Bender's and Franklin Littell's articles in the special edition of the *Mennonite Quarterly Review* 35 (April 1961) that was specifically directed to explore the relation between these two traditions. I suspect the most determinative difference is that the Anabaptists never lost sight of the fact that, scripturally, the kind of perfection required was non-violence and forgiveness. Yet Law and Wesley were uncompromising in their insistence that perfect love particularly required love of the enemy, though they did not draw the same implications about violence as the Anabaptists. See, for example, Wesley's sermon 'The Marks of the New Birth,' in *Forty-Four Sermons*, 170. I am indebted to the Michael Cartwright for suggesting some of the similarities between Wesley and the Anabaptists.

forming a universal friendship with ourselves and others in God's life. It is because we can so pray that Christians have been raised to a state of mutual love that 'far exceeds all that had been praised and admired in human friendship' (256).[28]

At three o'clock our prayers should be concerned with resignation to God's will. For the 'whole nature of virtue consists in conforming to, and the whole nature of vice in declining from, the will of God' (272). Resignation is the great enemy of all our fears and envies for it requires us to learn to see that nothing that has happened in our lives is without value.[29] There can be no room, therefore, for envy since we know that we have lacked nothing that is necessary for our salvation.

Finally at evening prayer we are to confess all our sins for it is necessary to repent of our sins as otherwise the guilt of unrepentant sins will continue with us. Such confession requires the most stringent self-knowledge. Thus, as every man has something particular to his nature, some stronger inclinations to some vices than others, it is necessary that these particularities should never escape a severe trial at evening repentance (89).

Through his discussion of daily prayer Law has attempted to provide an account of the virtues necessary for Christian living.[30] The 'single-ness,' the 'purity,' the constancy that is the soul of Christian living is formed by humility, love, resignation, and repentance. The interrelation and interdependence of these virtues are what is necessary for Christian

---

[28] Though he does not develop a conceptually explicit argument, it seems clear Law believes that only on the basis of such a love is it possible for our lives to have the kind of singleness required for living as a Christian. Yet while perfection requires perfect love, it is not identical with perfect love since it also requires humility, resignation, and repentance. Nor is perfection simply the combination of these virtues, though we cannot be perfect without them. Law does not attempt to account for the interrelation of these virtues in a conceptually satisfying manner. Yet, as I hope to show, that is not a major difficulty as instead he attempts to display characters who exhibit perfection by their formation by these virtues.

Law does not deal with the tension between universal love and our more particular loves and duties. He is simply not alive to that alleged tension because he understands 'universal love' as loving as God loves. Thus any tension between our concrete loves and our love for all people is resolved for him by intercessory prayer.

[29] Law's relatively brief treatment of resignation should not be taken as a sign of its lack of significance or his lack of insight about it. Indeed, I think it is one of the best parts of his book. For example, I think he is right to employ the notion of resignation rather than the usual, 'conforming our life to God's ill.' For he sees that our lives are not so much lived prospectively by our conforming to a prior command of God. Rather, resignation is the virtue by which we learn to look back upon our lives and affirm in all that we have done and that has happened to us that God is present. By that means we can learn to praise God as much in our suffering as in our success and thus to be able to make sense of – that is to narrate – our lives.

[30] By treating the matter in this way I do not mean to suggest that Law's insistence on the actual practice of prayer is secondary to the development of these virtues. Certainly, because of my own lack of such practice, I am tempted to interpret Law in that manner, but that would not only be unfair to Law, but I suspect would undervalue the practice of prayer for living the moral life of the Christian.

perfection. They give the means and skills for constant examination that provides the means for us to be less subject to the sins of pride, envy, and disregard of others.

For Law as for Wesley love is the crucial and central virtue – love that loves all as God loves. Yet love of itself is not sufficient to bring all our behavior under a single principle unless it has the humility that derives from our recognition and repentance of our own sinfulness. But humility is not sufficient unless it results in a recognition that God has given us everything we need to make our lives our own to be content with our calling in life. For it is just such contentment, such resignation, that is the necessary condition for our being at home with who we are, our character, that makes possible the singleness of life called perfection.

The analysis I have provided of Law's *A Serious Call to a Devout and Holy Life* may seem to add relatively little to Wesley's account of perfection. Certainly Law's account is more systematic than Wesley's occasional sermons, but almost everything Law has said can be dug out of Wesley in one place or another. Yet there is an added dimension to Law's account that I have as yet to expose – namely, his constant use of character studies to enliven his account of the Christian life. For it is insufficient only to assert the interrelation of humility, love, resignation, and repentance: the way they interrelate to form holy lives must finally be depicted.

Law's Characters

Most of *A Serious Call to a Devout and Holy Life* is dedicated to the portrayal of a large cast of characters meant to illumine negatively and positively the nature of the Christian life. Thus we soon learn to know Penitens, Calidus, Serena, the two unforgettable sisters Flavia and Miranda, Fulvius, Coelia, Flatus, Succus, Octavius, Cognitus, Negotius, Classicus, Comecus, Paternus, Matilda, Eusebia, Claudius, and Ouranius. Their names alone are enough to indicate that Law wants to do no more than draw certain stereotypes that are easily recognized, but yet these 'stereotypes' often take on unexpected life due to Law's acute insight into character.[31] Moreover, the liveliness of these characters is crucial to the depiction of perfection that Law is trying to elicit in his readers.

The basis for such a claim finally rests on the total effect of Law's book and a discussion of each character. I cannot attempt to show

---

[31] Certainly Law's characterizations never came close to those of the great novelists of the eighteenth and nineteenth centuries. His studies are like the first introduction of a character in a novel without the subsequent story required for the development of character – developments that often require us to reassess our first impressions. Of course, it was just such reassessments which Jane Austen was so concerned with in her novels, since she also was fascinated by the moral problem of distinguishing true virtue from the appearance of virtue in a society where everyone was taught the outward skills of a gentleman or lady.

how Law's depiction of each character fits into the total purpose of his book, but I want to take at least a few examples to illumine how he works. Many of Law's characters are negatively drawn. For he tells us:

> Examples of great piety are not now common in the world; it may not be your happiness to live within sight of any, or to have your virtue inflamed by their light and favour. But the misery and folly of worldly men is what meets your eyes in every place, and you need not look far to see how poorly, how vainly men dream away their lives for want of religious wisdom. This is the reason that I have laid before you so many characters of the vanity of a worldly life, to teach you to make a benefit of the corruption of the age, and that you may be more wise, though not by one sight of what piety is, yet by seeing what misery and folly reigns, where piety is not. (128)

Law introduces Flavia so that we can see the problems of those who have the benefit of an estate. Flavia is the wonder of all her friends because she manages a moderate fortune so well. She is more genteel than ladies with twice her fortune. She is always in fashion and never misses an arrangement that can be a diversion. She is very orthodox, often attending church and receiving the sacrament. She once thought highly of a sermon against pride and vanity as she was sure it was directed at Lucina, who she thinks tries to be finer than she is. She is charitable if she likes the person making the request, but when she gives her half-crown she tells him that if he knew the milliner's bill she just received he would know what a great deal it is to her. When she hears a sermon on the necessity of charity she is sure the man preaches well since she applies nothing to herself remembering her half-crown. As for the poor themselves, she will accept no complaints from them, thinking them all cheats and liars. She buys all the books of wit and humor, but will read a book of piety only if it is short and written well and she can borrow it. Law suggests that Flavia would be a miracle of piety if she were half as careful for her soul as her body. The rising of a pimple in her face, the sting of a gnat, can make her keep to her room for two or three days. She is so over-careful of her health she has the misery of never being able to think of herself as really well. As a result she must spend a great deal on sleeping-draughts, drops for the nerves, and so on. And yet Flavia is considered by herself and all as a paradigm of a Christian, being especially careful to allow no work on Sunday. She even turned out a poor old widow from her home for mending her clothes on Sunday night (61–63).

Flavia is obviously presented in an unsympathetic light, but she is no less real for that. We have met Flavias, and we know the Flavia that is in each of us. And as a result we are stung by Law's judgement that Flavia's whole life is in opposition to the tempers and practices necessary for our salvation. For Flavia, according to Law, is suffering from her good fortune as it has filled her whole life with indiscretion, and 'kept her from thinking what is right, and wise, and pious in everything else'

(64). She is the paradigmatic example of that 'regular kind of sensuality' that ultimately corrupts our lives by leaving us with the illusion that we are living rightly.

Then there is Flatus, whom Law treats as a counter to the claim that a life of holiness is a life devoid of interest and desire. Flatus is rich yet always uneasy, always searching for an illusive happiness. Each time you meet him he has some new project in his head, and it, at that time, is that for which he has always looked. At first his great interest was in fine clothes, and he spent hours seeking out the best tailors, but this ultimately did not answer his expectations and he turned to gaming. This satisfied him for a while, but by the fate of play, he was drawn into a duel where he narrowly escaped death, and thus he no longer sought happiness amongst gamesters. Next he gave himself over to the diversions of the town, and you heard him talk of nothing but ladies, drawing rooms, and balls. But he unluckily fell into a fever, grew angry at strong liquor, and abandoned the happiness of being drunk. Next he tried hunting, building new kennels, new stables, but soon learned to hate the senseless noise and hurry of hunting. Anyway, his attention was drawn away to rebuilding his estate, and he spent much time with architects endlessly discussing details, but the next year he left his house unfinished, complaining of masons and carpenters. Flatus even became interested in scholarly pursuits, but soon abandoned them to live on herbs, and so on (118–19).

Law has told us that a life not directed by holiness is hollow, but we cannot see that hollowness nearly so well without the life of Flatus. For we need his depiction to be able to see that pattern of his life that may be more or less reflected in our own lives. Though Flatus is certainly overdrawn, Law suggests his mode of life is 'one of the most general characters in life; and that few people can read it without seeing something in it that belongs to themselves. For where shall we find that wise and happy man who has not been eagerly pursuing different appearances of happiness, sometimes thinking it was here and sometimes there?' (122)[32] The major difference between most of us and Flatus is that, whereas Flatus is continually changing, most of us become satisfied with one form of false happiness, such as heaping of riches or seeking of status. But in fact we are no better and just as silly as Flatus.

Law not only portrayed negative characters, but he also tried to depict those we can and should admire. That he did so is not accidental, for he must show that the life of piety is more attractive and interesting than its opposite. That is no easy matter since generally sin makes a better story than virtue, but Law was surprisingly successful in portraying the virtuous. That he saw he must do so results, at least partly, from his

---

[32] Johnson's *Rasselas* is but an extended commentary on this point. Thus the book concludes, after a fervid search for the choice of life that can bring happiness, with Rasselas's sister concluding, 'To me the choice of life is become less important: I hope hereafter to think only on the choice of eternity' (256).

understanding of the close interrelation of soul and body. For he knows that our souls must be reached through the body as our imaginations must be stirred if we are to live rightly. Thus, he recommends in light of the fact that our imaginations have great power over our hearts and can affect us greatly with their representations, that 'at the beginning of your devotions, you were to imagine to yourself some such representations as might heat and warm your heart into a temper suitable to those prayers that you are then about to offer unto God' (177).[33]

Law's depictions of virtuous characters are meant to serve just that purpose. They are to stir our imaginations so we might envision the possibility of a life of perfection. Thus, in contrast to Flavia he depicts Miranda, the sister of Flavia, who seeks to live as a sober and reasonable Christian. Though her mother forced her to be genteel, to live in ceremony, to be in fashion, to be in every polite conversation, to hear the profaneness of the playhouse, she now remembers that life only as a way to atone for by contrary behavior. She does not divide her duty between God and neighbor, but considers all due to God. She divides her fortune accordingly between herself and several poor people. But she does not give foolishly, as she will not give a poor man money to go to see a puppet show since she will not allow herself to spend money in the same manner. She thinks it foolish for a poor man to waste what is given to him on trifles when he wants food and clothes. So she holds herself to the same disciplines as if she were equally poor.

Law commends Miranda's life to us, not because of its good effects, but because of its constancy. For 'there is nothing that is whimsical, trifling, or unreasonable in her character, but everything there described is a right and proper instance of a solid and real piety. It is as easy to show that it is whimsical to go to Church, or to say one's prayers, as that it is whimsical to observe any of these rules of life. For all Miranda's rules of living unto God, of spending her time and fortune, of eating, working, dressing, and conversing, are as substantial parts of a reasonable and holy life as devotion and prayer' (76).

Miranda may seem too good to be true, but Law does depict his characters' struggles with envy and pride. Thus in discussing the demands of universal love he portrays Ouranius, a priest, who labors in a small country village.[34] Every soul under his care is dear to him as he prays for them as well as himself. He never thinks he can love or do enough for his flock, and he visits everyone in his parish with the same piety with which he preaches to them.

---

[33] In the light of his understanding of the moral significance of the imagination, it is a bit of a puzzle why Law (as well as Wesley) had such a negative attitude toward art and, in particular, the novel. I suspect it has much to do with the fact that they were acquainted with the worst examples – thus Law's antipathy to opera because it portrayed non-serious love.

[34] Bromiley suggests that Law probably drew more heavily on autobiographical insights for the presentation of Ouranius than any other of his portrayals (226).

Yet when Ouranius first became a priest it was not so. For he had a haughtiness in his temper that bred a contempt for all foolish and unreasonable people. But slowly and surely he has 'prayed away this spirit.' Now rude, ill-natured, or perverse behavior on the part of any of his flock, rather than betraying him to impatience, only brings in him a desire to pray to God for help. It would strangely delight us to see, Law alleges, 'with what spirit he converses, with what tenderness he reproves, with what affection he exhorts, and with what vigour he preaches; and it is all owing to this, because he reproves, exhorts, and preaches to those for whom he first prays to God' (259).

Such a spirit has invaded his whole life, for when he first came to his little village every day was disagreeable to him since such a parish did not seem worthy of his talents. The parish was full of mean people who were unfit for the conversation of a gentleman. He stayed at home and wrote notes on Homer and Plautus, but devotion had got the government of his heart. Now rather than his days being tedious, he wants more time to do the variety of good for which his soul thirsts. He has come to love the solitude of the parish because he hopes that God has placed him and his flock there to make their way to heaven. He not only converses with poor people, but attends and waits on the poorest kind of people. For it now means more to him to be considered a servant to all than a gentleman.

Enough has perhaps been said to suggest the importance of such characters for Law's overall project. They are not just 'examples' of what can be said more abstractly about perfection. They are necessary exhibits of perfection exactly because becoming perfect is such a nuanced affair in which we are constantly tempted to self-deception. We cannot simply decide to love universally and will ourselves free of envy. We must be drawn from our envy by the skills we can learn from others. For perfection requires the 'wholeness of a human life' for us to properly have sense of it. Law tried to supply that 'wholeness' through his characterizations.

To be perfect requires knowledge, but it is not knowledge like that embodied in a rule or principle. Rather, it is the kind of knowledge we know as judgement – that is, a sensitivity to particulars and their implications that cannot be taught by a general theory. Knowledge of what is valuable and worthy involves such judgements (303). But we can acquire that knowledge only by attending to those who have paid the price for it. Thus Law provides us with characters to inspire our imagination, that we might learn the skills to have selves capable of being perfected.

Characterizing Perfection

Where has all this got us? I have tried to suggest that Law's use of characterization of perfection is more appropriate than Wesley's use of the language of stages. It is so because the journey of the self denoted by perfection requires display by concrete lives that adequately reflect the ambiguity as well as accomplishment of those seeking well-lived lives. The 'singleness' that perfection demands is no easy matter, as the closer we come to embodying it, the more we are beset by temptations that deny its character. By attending to good lives we develop those skills necessary for ridding our lives of envy and pride and rendering them more accessible to love, making possible the repentance necessary to being perfect. Yet what are we to make of such depictions for us? At the very least such portrayals are a reminder that Christianity only makes sense as a way to teach us to live and die.

Put differently, perfection names the *telos* any adequate account of the Christian life requires. Moreover, it places that emphasis rightly – for the teleology is not one of moral decisions or justifications, but of the self. It may be the language of perfection is archaic, but I think little will be gained by trying to replace it by more contemporary terms such as 'maturing' or 'wholeness.' What is required is not the 'updating' of the language, but rather the imaginative endeavor to learn how to characterize perfection in a manner similar to Law's.

Such characterization can be accomplished, however, if we are able to identify those who are in fact living the life of perfection. And in that sense our task is quite different from that of Law or Wesley. For their problem was how to distinguish authentic holiness from counterfeit in a polite age where everyone could at least claim to be if not look like a Christian. Our task is to locate within the anarchy of endless 'lifestyles' that kind of life characteristic of Christians. Even though Christians will differ from one another in what they do, they are nonetheless a people on the same journey, one that requires the same virtues and character of all. We know in fact that many are on that journey. What we lack is the courage and ability to depict their lives for our and the world's benefit.

Little has been said to this point about the communal context of a life of perfection, but the demand to locate and characterize lives of perfection is fundamentally a communal task. For the journey that Christians undertake is the journey of a people. The growth of their individual lives, which certainly is also a journey, is intelligible only within the movement we call the church. It is perhaps one of the church's most important tasks to identify those people who in a compelling manner embody in their lives that larger journey. I suspect that this is constantly done in churches in an informal manner. I am simply suggesting that at least part of the humble service of theology might be to learn to do this in a manner that we might have the benefit that comes from learning to characterize perfection.

8

Timeful Friends:
Living with the Handicapped

L'Arche is special, in the sense that we are trying to live in community with people who are mentally handicapped. Certainly we want to help them grow and reach the greatest independence possible. But before 'doing for them,' we want to 'be with them.' The particular suffering of the person who is mentally handicapped, as of all marginal people, is a feeling of being excluded, worthless and unloved. It is through everyday life in community and the love that must be incarnate in this, that handicapped people can begin to discover that they have a value, that they are loved and so lovable.[1]

Individual growth towards love and wisdom is slow. A community's growth is even slower. Members of a community have to be friends of time. They have to learn that many things will resolve themselves if they are given enough time. It can be a great mistake to want, in the name of clarity and truth, to push things too quickly to a resolution. Some people enjoy confrontation and highlighting divisions. This is not always healthy. It is better to be a friend of time. But clearly too, people should not pretend that problems don't exist by refusing to listen to the rumblings of discontent; they must be aware of the tensions.[2]

Our focal point of fidelity at l'Arche is to live with handicapped people in the spirit of the Gospel and the Beatitudes. 'To live with' is different from 'to do for.' It doesn't simply mean eating at the same table and sleeping under the same roof. It means that we create relationships of gratuity, truth and interdependence, that we listen to the handicapped people, that we recognize and marvel at their gifts. The day we become no more than professional workers and educational therapists is the day we stop being l'Arche – although of course 'living with' does not exclude this professional aspect.[3]

---

[1] Jean Vanier, *Community and Growth* (London: Darton, Longman & Todd, 1979), 3.
[2] Ibid. 80.
[3] Ibid. 106.

On the Ethics of Writing about the Ethics of the Care of the Mentally Handicapped

Every time I write about the mentally handicapped I make a promise to myself that it will be the last time I write about this subject. Yet here I am breaking my promise once again. I published my first essay on the mentally handicapped over twenty years ago. I have continued to speak and write about the mentally handicapped ever since. Surely, one would think, by now I have said all I have to say. Of course, such an attitude, that is, that I have said what I have to say, is that of an intellectual. People who really care about the mentally handicapped never run out of things to say, since they do not write 'about' the mentally handicapped precisely because they do not view the mentally handicapped as just another 'subject.' They write for and in some sense with the mentally handicapped.

To be able to write for and with the mentally handicapped requires that you know people who are mentally handicapped. By 'know' I mean you must be *with* the handicapped in a way they may be able to claim you as a friend. I was once so claimed, but over the last few years I have not enjoyed such a friendship. So when I now write about the ethics of caring for the mentally handicapped, I fear I am not talking about actual people but more of my memories of the mentally handicapped. When they become an abstraction, moreover, we can begin to think we must provide 'reasons' for their existence or, worse, discover meaning in why we care for them. Jean Vanier, as the passages above make clear, feels no need to find meaning in why l'Arche homes exist.

I call attention to the tension I feel in yet once again writing about the mentally handicapped, because my difficulty illustrates the challenge facing all who care for them. How do we care for the mentally handicapped without allowing the reasons we are tempted to give for such care to distort what should be our relation to those for whom we care? To make the question even more difficult – 'How do we care for the mentally handicapped in such a manner which would forestall our felt need to provide reasons why we should care for the mentally handicapped, thereby rendering their lives unintelligible?' After all, both the existence and care of those of us who are considered 'normal' is not thought to require justification. Why is the existence and/or care of the 'mentally handicapped' singled out as presenting a special problem?

In truth my difficulty about writing about the mentally handicapped did not begin with my isolation from the handicapped. From the beginning I have always felt a bit duplicitous when I addressed the subject of the mentally handicapped and their care. In fact, I have not ever really written about the mentally handicapped. No matter how much I care for the mentally handicapped, I have been haunted by the presumption that my 'interest' in them and my writing about them has been part of an intellectual agenda that makes them useful to me. Once I had been drawn into the world of the mentally handicapped, however, it did not take me long to realize they were the crack I desperately needed to give concreteness to my critique of modernity. No group exposes the pretensions of the humanism that shapes the practices of modernity more thoroughly than the mentally handicapped.

Our humanism entails we care for them once they are among us, once we are stuck with them; but the same humanism cannot help but think that, all things considered, it would be better if they did not exist. As modern people we think we are meant to be autonomous beings. In view of such an overpowering presumption, how do we make sense of those among us whose very existence can be nothing but dependence? We live in cultures for which rationality and consciousness are taken to be the very essence of what makes us human. What are we to make of those who will never, even with the best efforts, be able to read or write? Should they be considered human?

Examples of how the mentally handicapped render problematic some of the most cherished conceits of modernity are legion. For example, in his *Life As We Know It: A Father, a Family, and an Exceptional Child*, Michael Berube tells of the birth and care he and his wife have given to their Down's syndrome son, Jamie. His is a wonderful story of how two college professors found their lives reshaped by their son's disability. I have nothing but admiration for the way they have accepted and cared for their son. The story Berube tells of their struggle to keep Jamie alive and to secure appropriate medical care is at once as inspiring as it is humane.

Moreover, Professor Berube has read his Foucault. He knows that some of the most humane forms of 'treatment' may be but forms of control. He even knows that the most humane accounts of justice in modernity, such as those of Rawls and Habermas, cannot help his son. That such accounts of justice require that we shed our individual idiosyncrasies make the existence of his son irresolvably problematic. As Berube puts it,

> There isn't a chance in the world that James Lyon Berube could come to the table independently of 'interests,' independent of cognitive and social idiosyncrasies legible to all, independent of either a genetic makeup or a social apparatus that constructs him as 'abnormal.' The society that fosters Jamie's independence *must* start from an understanding of his dependencies, and any viable conception of justice has to take the concrete bodies and 'private,' idiosyncratic interest of individuals like Jamie into account, or it will be of no account at all.[4]

[4] Michael Berube, *Life As We Know It: A Father, a Family, and an Exceptional Child* (New York: Pantheon Books, 1996), 248. Berube may not appreciate the considerable differences between the accounts of justice by Rawls and Habermas but I think he rightly intuits that such differences in the face of the mentally handicapped do not amount to much.

Berube criticizes Rawls and Habermas for succumbing to 'a curious Enlightenment fantasy, the idea that once we boil away all the idiosyncrasies and impurities of the irrational human race, we can come up with some perfectly neutral, rational, disinterested character who can play the language-game of justice as if it were a contest in which he or she had no stake.'[5] Yet Berube's criticism of Rawls and Habermas rings hollow in the light of his own narrative. He either cannot or does not choose to make intelligible his admirable commitment to Jamie.

For example, with great candor Berube tells us that he and his wife are as pro-choice after the birth of Jamie as they were prior to his birth. Indeed, he notes that they intentionally did not use amniocentesis, assuming they would 'just love the baby all the more' if the baby was born with Down's syndrome. He confesses such a stance was 'blithe and uninformed' and that if they had known that their child's life 'would be suffering and misery for all concerned' they might have chosen to have an abortion.[6] Berube notes, however, that it is extremely difficult to discuss Jamie in this way. Just as it was hard to talk about him as a medicalized being when he was in the ICU, it is still harder 'to talk about him in terms of our philosophical beliefs about abortion and prenatal testing. That's partly because these issues are so famously divisive and emotionally charged, but it's also because we can no longer frame any such questions about our child now that he's here.'[7]

'Now that he is here' is the nub of the matter. Berube does not pretend to be able to do more than represent Jamie 'now that he is here.' Indeed, he takes that as his ethical and aesthetic task – to help us imagine Jamie and to imagine what he might think of our ability to imagine him. Just as the Berubes look forward to the day that Jamie might be able to eat at the 'big' table, to feed himself tacos, burgers, and pizza, to set the table even if such a setting is somewhat 'random,' so Berube's job 'is to represent my son, to set his place at our collective table. But I know I am merely trying my best to prepare for the day he sets his own place. For I have no sweeter dream than to imagine – aesthetically and ethically and parentally – that Jamie will someday be his own advocate, his own author, his own best representative.'[8]

How sad. All Berube can imagine for Jamie is that he be 'his own author.' That Berube can imagine no other future is not his fault. His imagination but reflects the same limits that formed the conceptions of justice he found so unsatisfactory. What other possibility could there be in a world in which God does not exist? What other politics is available for those like the Berubes when the church has been reduced to reinforcing the sentimentalities of contemporary humanism? Berube

5 Ibid. 247.
6 Ibid. 47.
7 Ibid. 48.
8 Ibid. 264.

has been gifted with Jamie, but he lacks the practices of a community that would provide the resources for narrating his own and Jamie's life.

That is the 'crack' I have exploited in the interest of a theological agenda. In short, I have used the 'now that he is here' as a resource to illumine Christian speech. As Christians we know we have not been created to be 'our own authors,' to be autonomous. We are creatures. Dependency, not autonomy, is one of the ontological characteristics of our lives. That we are creatures, moreover, is but a reminder that we are created for and with one another. We are not just accidentally communal, but we are such by necessity. We were not created to be alone. We cannot help but desire and delight in the reality of the other, even the other born with a difference we call mentally handicapped.

Our dependency, our need for one another, means that we will suffer as well as know joy. Our incompleteness at once makes possible the gifts that make life possible as well as the unavoidability of suffering. Such suffering, moreover, may seem pointless. Yet, at least for Christians, such suffering should not tempt us to think our task is to eliminate those whose suffering seems pointless.[9] Christians are, or at least should be, imbedded in a narrative that makes possible a sharing of our lives with one another, that enables us to go on in the face of the inexplicable.

For Christians the mentally handicapped do not present a peculiar challenge. That the mentally handicapped are constituted by narratives they have not chosen, reveals the character of our lives. That some people are born with a condition that we have come to label as being mentally handicapped does not indicate a fundamental difference between them and the fact that we must all be born. The question is not whether we can justify the mentally handicapped, but whether we live any longer in a world that can make sense of having children. At the very least, Christians believe that our lives are constituted by the hope we have learned through Christ's cross and resurrection that makes morally intelligible bringing children into a world as dark as our own.

I have not made these arguments to try to convince people constituted by the narratives of modernity that they should believe in God. Such an argument could not help but make God a *deus ex machina* which not only demeans God, but God's creation as well. Rather, my concern is to help Christians locate those practices that help us understand better why our willingness to welcome the mentally handicapped should not be surprising given the Triune nature of the God we worship. In other words, I have used the mentally handicapped as material markers necessary to show that Christian speech can and in fact does make

---

[9] For my reflections on these matters see my *Naming the Silences: God, Medicine, and the Problem of Suffering* (Grand Rapids: Eerdmans, 1990). The second edition of the book was retitled *God, Medicine, and Suffering*.

claims about the way things are. Theologically thinking about the mentally handicapped helps us see, moreover, that claims about the way things are cannot be separated from the way we should live.

By subjecting the mentally handicapped to this agenda, one might object, am I not also exemplifying the desperate attempt I have criticized in others to find some 'meaning' in the existence and care of the handicapped? I would obviously like to answer with a quick denial, but as I indicated above, the question continues to haunt me. That it does so, I think, is partly because I am not sure how one rightly responds to such a challenge. What sense are we to make of the care given to the mentally handicapped in a world of limited resources? I think the answer requires the reshaping of the question – a reshaping, I believe, gestured at in the work of people like Jean Vanier. For we will only know why we do what we do by the exemplary lives of those like Vanier who teach us how to live with those we call the mentally handicapped. So I can do no better than to turn our attention to his work.

On 'Using' the Mentally Handicapped

Before I turn to Vanier, however, I want to expose a narrative that I suspect may inform and shape questions about the 'use' of the mentally handicapped – that is, the kind of problematic that has shaped what I have just said about my own dis-ease with my use of the mentally handicapped. It is, moreover, a narrative that I think is particularly pernicious, not only for the care of the mentally handicapped, but for any human relations, including our relations to animals and nature. This narrative received its most eloquent expression as well as its most adequate defense in the second formulation of Kant's Categorical Imperative – 'Act so that you treat humanity, whether in your own person or in that of another, always as an end and never as a means only.'[10]

For many, such an imperative seems to embody our highest ideal. Kant certainly did not think of it as an ideal, but rather thought such an imperative constitutive of any moral act that deserves the description, 'moral.' Unfortunately this results in the creation of the realm of 'morality' that moderns assume can be distinguished from economics, politics, or, more importantly, manners. Once such a realm exists, some people then think they have to think about the 'ethics' of the care of the retarded.

The power of this narrative, that is, that we should treat one another as ends and not means, is revealed for modern people by the very fact we cannot imagine anyone seriously challenging it as a statement of what we should at least always try to do. One may doubt the existence of God, but it seems everyone agrees that we ought never to treat one another simply as a means. The way we often put the matter is that

[10] Immanuel Kant, *Foundations of the Metaphysics of Morals*, trans. Lewis White Beck (New York: Liberal Arts Press, 1959), 47.

every human being should be treated with dignity. Of course, like most abstractions, it is very hard to know what it means to treat others as ends. That most human relations require we treat one another as means does not seem to call into question the assumption that we ought not so to do. Whatever the difficulty may be in concrete specification of treating another as an end, we continue to think we all would prefer to be treated as an end not a means.

This seems particularly to be the case when it comes to the mentally handicapped. We presume that the improvement in the care of the mentally handicapped over this century derives from our commitment to treat them as persons deserving respect – that is, as ends in themselves. There is, of course, the troubling problem of whether the mentally handicapped possess the characteristics necessary to be counted as persons. If they do not, for example, possess minimal forms of rationality, can they be considered persons deserving respect? Is the care of such beings then to be considered supererogatory? Such questions may be considered too theoretical to be of interest, but if resources become scarce, questions about the care of the mentally handicapped can begin to have frightening implications.

The language of means and ends often has peculiar power in the treatment the mentally handicapped actually receive. The ethic that often shapes critiques of institutionalization of the handicapped, that creates the demand for their normalization, that requires they receive appropriate medical treatment, is one that assumes they too should be treated as ends not as 'means only.'[11] That any restrictions on the mentally handicapped should be the 'least restrictive' seems to require that the mentally handicapped are to be treated as far as possible like anyone else.

Yet what 'as far as possible' means is not easily determined. For example, Michael Berube observes how the Foucauldian question haunts the humanities:

> Is it wrong to *speak for* others, to assume that one can represent the interests of another in a faithful and transparent way? How can one be an advocate for the mentally retarded while believing that institutions never die and that every act of representation is also an act of usurpation? Is there no way to have faith in Camelot, in Special Olympics, in Advocacy?[12]

Berube answers that whatever he may believe about the history of madness, sexuality, incarceration, it is impossible to act as a Foucauldian when it comes to Jamie.

---

[11] It is important to note that Kant quite sensibly assumed that it is sometimes permissible to treat people as means. What the Imperative excludes is that treatment as a means occludes their status as ends. Of course this but creates the problem of how we are to know when someone has ever been treated as a 'means only.'

[12] Berube, *Life As We Know It*, 112.

We *have* to act, for both theoretical and practical reasons, in the belief that these agencies can benefit our child, even as the sorry history of institutionalization weighs on our brains like a nightmare. To act in any other way, to indict all such institutions across the board, would be to consign Jamie to the kind of self-fulfilling prophecy that follows from unearned cynicism: *We know they can't help, so why bother?* It would be hard to imagine a more irresponsible attitude toward his life's prospects.[13]

Yet Berube knows, as every parent of the mentally handicapped knows, that they are caught in what seems an irresolvable conundrum. In order for your child to receive appropriate care they must be labeled – retarded, handicapped, Down's syndrome – but the labels can become self-fulfilling prophecies; or worse, the labels can legitimate the intervention of others into their children's lives that often only benefits the agents of intervention. This becomes particularly troubling when the agent of intervention is an institution called the state. Parents want their child treated as an end, with respect, but in a social ethos dominated by an ethic of respect their children can only be treated as a means.

Which I think brings us back to Kant and why the second formulation of the Categorical Imperative is not only inadequate to help us understand the place of the mentally handicapped but for any account of morality. For what is often forgotten is that Kant's formulation of the Categorical Imperative presupposes an account of existence that is without ultimate *telos*. What purpose there is results from human freedom now understood as an end in itself. Humanity is forced to impose meaning on a mechanistic world whose only meaning is to be found in our existence as humans. Human behavior is subject to mechanistic explanation as any part of nature. We remain ends only to the extent we can will ourselves to be such.

What such a view of the world cannot do is to allow us to ask, 'What are people for?'[14] Such a question presupposes that creation, all that is,

---

[13] Ibid. 113. Berube observes that what saves the unavoidability of Jamie being a subject is that they as parents have the benefit of seeing Jamie's agents face to face. 'They *are* agents: they are defined by their agency (in both senses), and Jamie is their agentless object, the name repeated a thousand times in the eight-inch stack of medical prognoses, cognitive evaluations, and assorted therapy reports that constitute the subject known as Jamie Lyon Berube. But they also happen to be our neighbors and friends. Rita Huddle, Jamie's first speech therapist at DSC, is also the mother of two of Nick's friends in tae-kwon-do class, where we run into her regularly; Nancy Yeagle, his first occupational therapist, is also the mother of one of his playmates at day care as well as the spouse of the chef at a local Italian restaurant Jamie's quite fond of. And Sara Jane Annin, his case worker, is not only a friend and confidante, but the mother of *two* children with Down's syndrome' (113–14).

[14] This question is the title of Wendell Berry's wonderful book, *What Are People For?* (San Francisco: North Point Press, 1990). The essay in the book that bears this title concerns the view by the 'governing agricultural doctrine' of the government, universities, and corporations that there are too many people on the farm. Berry argues that this doctrine continues to be held even though the migration of people from the

has a purpose that is not a function of our self-generating will. On such a view human beings have a *telos* that allows a distinction to be drawn between 'man-as-he-happens-to-be and man-as-he-could-be-if-he-realized-his-essential-nature. Ethics is the science which is to enable men to understand how they make the transition from the former state to the latter.'[15] Such a transition, moreover, requires a community, and the purpose of the community for which we are created is nothing less than friendship with one another.

From such a perspective we can begin to appreciate how few resources the means/ends manner of thinking provides for helping us understand the care of the mentally handicapped. Of course, we 'use' the mentally handicapped, but we are here to be of use to one another. The notion that any use we make of one another can only be justified if it is done voluntarily can now be seen as one of the peculiar sentimentalities of modernity that results in self-supervision that is all the more tyrannical since what we do is allegedly what we want to do. That the mentally handicapped are subject to care for their own good – a good they may not have chosen – is not an indication that such care is misguided, but rather requires that the goods that such care is serving be properly named. After all, they (like us who are not retarded) exist to serve and to be served for our mutual upbuilding.

As Christians we should not feel embarrassed to discover that the mentally handicapped among us help us better understand the narrative that constitutes the very purpose of our existence. That such is the case does not 'justify' their existence, but then their existence no more than our existence from a Christian perspective requires justification. We are free to help them just to the extent we no longer feel the necessity to justify their existence. The form such 'help' takes can only be discovered relative to the tasks of the community necessary to sustain the practices for the discovery and care of the goods held in common. Put in terms I used above, Christians do not use the mentally handicapped as an affront to a world without purpose, but we should not be

---

farms hurts the land and the cities. Yet 'the great question that hovers over this issue, one that we have dealt with mainly by indifference, is the question of what people are *for*. Is their greatest dignity in unemployment? Is the obsolescence of human beings now our social goal? One would conclude so from our attitude toward work, especially the manual work necessary to the long-term preservation of the land, and from our rush toward mechanization, automation, and computerization. In a country that puts an absolute premium on labor-saving measures, short workdays, and retirement, why should there be any surprise at permanence of unemployment and welfare dependency? Those are only different names for our national ambitions' (12).

[15] Alasdair MacIntyre, *After Virtue*, 2nd edn. (Notre Dame: University of Notre Dame Press, 1984), 52. MacIntyre observes that Kant in the second book of the second *Critique* does acknowledge that a teleological framework is necessary for his ethics to be intelligible (56). The teleology Kant presumed was, of course, anthropocentric not theocentric.

surprised that the Christian refusal to abandon the mentally handicapped to such a world will be seen as an affront.

We must confess as Christians, however, that our care of the mentally
handicapped has been shaped more by the means/end narrative than
by that of Christ. As a result, in the name of care we too often subject
the handicapped to therapies based on mechanistic presumptions that
promise 'results' rather than community. That is why the alternative
Vanier represents is so important. For l'Arche offers an imaginative
portrayal of what a purposive community might look like in which the
mentally handicapped serve and are served.[16]

Vanier's Wisdom

I am aware, of course, that I will be accused of romanticizing Vanier
and the l'Arche movement. Yet as Vanier reminds us,

> Too many communities are founded on dreams and fine words; there is
> much talk about love, truth, and peace. Marginal people are demanding.
> Their cries are cries of truth because they sense the emptiness of many of
> our words; they can see the gap between what we say and what we live.[17]

No community can be self-correcting in principle. Criticism is possible
only when there are those present who constitute a critical edge. Vanier,
whose own presence for l'Arche creates a problem just to the extent
some may think l'Arche depends on him, is surely right to suggest that
communities like l'Arche at least have some purchase of being truthful
to the extent they understand that truth often is spoken by those who
cannot speak.[18]

Such communities are by necessity constituted by the practice of
hospitality. This is not always easy, given Vanier's understanding of

---

[16] Put metaphysically, the practices that constitute l'Arche rightly assume that being
is prior to knowing. Questions about what 'meaning' the mentally handicapped may or
may not have are questions shaped by habits that assume the priority of epistemological
questions. Berube's 'now that he is here' reveals that the priorities of being cannot be
repressed. I am indebted to Dr Brett Webb-Mitchell for calling my attention to this
connection.

[17] Vanier, *Community and Growth*, 200.

[18] One cannot help but think Vanier is thinking about his own role in l'Arche when
he observes, 'I am sometimes a bit worried by communities which are carried by a
single strong shepherd or a solidly united team of shepherds. As these communities
have no traditions, no history and no constitutional control by a recognized legal
authority, there is hardly any check on their activities. The leaders may develop a taste
for their role, seeing themselves as indispensable, and so unconsciously dominating
others. There is also the risk of mixing community and spiritual power. It is good and
useful if these spiritual shepherds quickly hand over direction of the community to
someone else, so that they can be freer to exercise their gift of priest and shepherd,'
Ibid. 176. He observes he is concerned about communities without any traditions who
refuse to accept external authority. They will not outlive their founder for long and, if
there is no external control, the founder will be in danger of making some serious
mistakes (86).

community as a grouping of people 'who have left their own milieu to live with others under the same roof, and work from a new vision of human beings and their relationships with each other and with God.'[19] Such communities can easily become ingrown and protective, but for a community that has learned to live with the handicapped such protectiveness can only be destructive. The crucial question is not whether people are to be welcomed, but who is to make the decision who is to be welcomed and how. According to Vanier, in l'Arche communities those best able to discern who should be welcomed are the handicapped. 'They have been in the community for a long time, often for longer than the assistants, and sometimes longer than the person in charge. It is important to consult these handicapped people before we welcome someone in distress.'[20]

I am never sure how to characterize Vanier's observations about l'Arche. It seems right, however, that most of what he has to tell us takes the form of aphorisms – that is, short bursts of hard won wisdom not easily systemized or brought to a point. Wisdom is constituted by judgements about matters that matter. Yet to be wise requires that we be part of traditions that form people like Vanier, who can say what we all might see or experience, but lack the ability to say what we see. In short, if Vanier had not spent years living with the mentally handicapped he would not have acquired the skills now to speak with and for the handicapped.

The wisdom that he shares with us, gentle though it is, cannot help but disrupt our lives. We read Vanier because we want to know how to do, if not be, good; but in knowing how to do good, we also discover that the subject is not the mentally handicapped but us. For the great shock for many of us who want to be of help to the handicapped, because we think they are weak, is to discover our own weakness. As Vanier observes,

> It is always easier to accept the weakness of handicapped people – we are there precisely because we expect it – than our own weakness that often takes us by surprise! We want to see only good qualities in ourselves and other assistants. Growth begins when we start to accept our own weakness.[21]

What, moreover, could be more threatening for the handicapped than for them to expose our own sense of helplessness and loneliness?

To be able to be with the mentally handicapped without being 'helpful' is what l'Arche is about. It is slow work. Indeed, to be capable of such work means, as Vanier puts it, we have 'to be great friends of

---

[19] Ibid. 2.
[20] Ibid. 197. Vanier observes that to welcome is not primarily to open the doors of our house, but to open our hearts by becoming vulnerable.
[21] Ibid. 88.

time.'²² We have to become not only friends of time, but friends of those who make such time possible. And to make such time possible is to call upon one who, though outside of time, has entered into our time to be with us and to befriend us. We have to learn how to receive the friendship the mentally handicapped offer to us.

> When friendship encourages fidelity, it is the most beautiful thing of all. Aristotle calls it the flower of virtue; it has the gratuity of the flower. On the dark days, we need the refuge of friendship. When we feel flat or fed up, a letter from a friend can bring back peace and confidence. The Holy Spirit uses small things to comfort and strengthen us.²³

Our care of the mentally handicapped and their care of us is one of the small things we do for one another. 'Community is made of the gentle concern that people show each other every day. It is made of small gestures, of services and sacrifices which say "I love you" and "I'm happy to be with you".'²⁴ Vanier confesses that when he feels tired he goes to La Forestière. La Forestière is a house in his community where none of the nine or so people who live there can talk and most cannot walk. They must express their hearts and emotions through their bodies. The assistants at La Forestière cannot work at their own rhythm, but at that of the handicapped.

> Things have to go at a pace which can welcome their least expression; because they have no verbal skills, they have no way of enforcing their views by raising their voice. So the assistants have to be the more attentive to the many non-verbal communications, and this adds greatly to their ability to welcome the whole person. They become increasingly people of welcome and compassion. The slower rhythm and even the presence of the handicapped people makes me slow down, switch off my efficiency motor, rest and recognize the presence of God. The poorest people have an extraordinary power to heal the wounds in our hearts. If we welcome them, they nourish us.²⁵

²² Ibid. 80.
²³ Ibid. 135. Vanier's remarks on friendship are particularly interesting given his philosophical training. He wrote his dissertation at the Institut Catholique in Paris on Aristotle's ethics. He knows well that for Aristotle character friendship would be impossible between those thought to be 'normal' and the 'handicapped.' One cannot help but think that Vanier's life exemplifies how Aquinas' contention that the goal of life is to be befriended by God explodes Aristotle's understanding of friendship. I am indebted to Brett Webb-Mitchell's account of Vanier as well as his study of l'Arche in his *L'Arche: An Ethnographic Study of Persons with Disabilities Living in a Community with Non-Disabled People* (PhD dissertation: University of North Carolina, 1988). Since writing his dissertation, Webb-Mitchell has published a series of books that explore the theological significance of the mentally handicapped and, in particular, how friendship with the handicapped is possible. See his *God Plays Piano, Too* (New York: Crossroad, 1993), *Unexpected Guests at God's Banquet* (New York: Crossroad, 1994), and *Dancing with Disabilities* (Cleveland: United Church Press, 1996).
²⁴ Vanier, *Community and Growth*, 26.
²⁵ Ibid. 139–40.

We, that is those of us external to the world of l'Arche communities, are tempted to characterize their work in heroic terms. But that is not how they understand what they do. As Vanier observes, love does not mean doing extraordinary things, but rather knowing how to do ordinary things with tenderness. He calls our attention to the significance of Jesus' 'hidden life' – the thirty years he spent in Nazareth when no one knew he was the son of God. He lived family and community life in humility working with wood and having his life constituted by the small happenings of such a village. Jesus' hidden life is the model for all community life.[26] In his life we are given the time to be friends of the timeful friends we call the mentally handicapped.

Doing Things with Vanier

To call attention to Vanier's witness is dangerous just to the extent it is so powerful. He and his friends' presence is too strong for most of us. We cannot imagine reproducing his work in our lives. It requires too much time, it requires too much 'labor intensive involvement,' it requires people willing to have their lives turned inside out, it assumes that what Christians believe about the world is true and can be lived. For many such requirements and assumptions seem utopian.

Yet they cannot be utopian because l'Arche communities exist. No doubt those in l'Arche often are less than they would wish, but that such a wish forms their desires indicates that they do not think they are pursuing some unrealizable ideal. Moreover, their witness remains crucial for the rest of us who are not part of their community; for without such examples our imaginations lack the resources to know that what we have become used to doing is not done by necessity. Without l'Arche anything I or any other theologian might have to say could not help but be empty. L'Arche literally gives weight, gives body, to the story of the world we Christians know as Gospel.

Because Vanier and his friends are so embodied by and in the story of Christ, they feel no need to give meaning to the lives of the mentally handicapped. They feel no need to justify the care they give to the mentally handicapped. They do not think they need to justify their 'use' of the mentally handicapped. Such questions and problems do not arise because you do not need to ask such questions about your friends. Friends need no justification. Friendship is a gift and, like most significant gifts, it is surrounded by mystery. We finally cannot explain friendship anymore than we can explain our existence. We can only delight in our friends.

Without such delight our care of the mentally handicapped cannot help but seem pointless. Without delight the professional skills we gain to try to help the mentally handicapped can too quickly become part

[26] Ibid. 220.

of a mechanistic world of control. Vanier and his friends are certainly not disdainful of the wonderful technologies that have been developed to help the handicapped.[27] Rather they see that such technologies can too easily become ends in themselves, no longer serving friendship.

Yet is all this finally just 'too Christian'? Vanier, after all, is obviously a person shaped by Catholic practice and thought.[28] How can what is learned in l'Arche be possible in a secular and pluralist world? I do not know for sure how Vanier would answer, but I suspect his answer might be something like this. What is possible in l'Arche is possible anywhere we find people willing to learn to live with the mentally handicapped. After all, the God that is celebrated in l'Arche is God. Such a God knows no boundaries. If such a God can make the mentally handicapped claim some of us as friends, surely such a God will be found among those who know not God. That such is the case after all is why what Christians believe about the world is called 'good news.' For is it not wonderful to discover in a world as terrible as this that God has created the time, given us friends of time in time, so that we might learn to be friends with one another and, yes, even God.

---

[27] Ibid. 106.

[28] Vanier observes, 'As I think of all the communities throughout the world, struggling for growth, yearning to answer the call of Jesus and of the poor, I realize the need for a universal shepherd, a shepherd who yearns for unity, who has clarity of vision, who calls forth communities and who holds all people.

'I was deeply touched by the election of John-Paul I and even more touched by the election of John-Paul II. How long will it take before people realize this deep need? How long will it take for Catholics to understand the depths of their gifts and to be confounded in humility? How long will it take Catholics to recognize the beauty and gift in the Protestant churches, especially their love of Scripture and of announcing the Word? And one day will Protestant churches discover the immensity of riches hidden in the Eucharist?

'Yes, I yearn for this day.' (104)

9

In Defense of Cultural Christianity: Reflections on Going to Church

Culture, Theology, and the Church

One of the most important questions you can ask theologians is where they go to church.[1] For if theologians do not go to church, they may begin to think their theology is more important than the church. Theology can too easily begin to appear as 'ideas,' rather than the kind of discourse that must, it if is to be truthful, be embedded in the practices of actual lived communities. That is one of the reasons I do not do 'systematic theology.' Systems can be quite beautiful but also easily subject to ideological perversions.

In liberal cultures it is almost impossible to resist the temptation to think of Christianity as a system of beliefs. For example, the distinction between the private and the public leads Christians, both liberal and conservative, as well as non-Christians, to think of 'religious' beliefs as having purchase primarily on our subjectivities. That is why Billy Graham is concerned with our souls and not our money.[2] Christians assume that if we get our 'beliefs' right, we will then know how to act right, to know what we ought to do with our money, our possessions.[3]

---

[1] I make this claim in *In Good Company. The Church as Polis* (Notre Dame: University of Notre Dame Press, 1995), 223.

[2] The Revd Chris Ayers, 'When is the last time you wanted to kill your preacher,' *Charlotte Observer* (forthcoming). Chris Ayers, a Southern Baptist preacher in Charlotte, North Carolina, asks in his editorial why Billy Graham is so popular when Jeremiah, Jesus, and Peter were not. He ends his courageous editorial – 'Billy Graham is Charlotte' – by asking, 'Have we organized our churches so that prophetic preaching is highly unlikely?'

[3] The assumption that my money is 'mine' is, of course, a reflection of capitalist practice. Capitalism names those material practices that make Christianity appear first as belief and only secondarily as embodied. What I am attempting in this paper is similar to Robert Inchausti's project exemplified in his *The Ignorant Perfection of Ordinary People* (Albany: State University Press of New York, 1991). Inchausti narrates the lives of Gandhi, Solzhenitsyn, Wiesel, Mother Teresa, King, and Walesa in an effort to describe a form of resistance he calls 'plebeian postmodernism.' One who represents such a view 'honors the concrete deed before the abstract stance and the claims of the family before the fictions of the state. [Such a view] judges the quality of one's practice by the good it concretely accomplishes rather than by the party it serves, the money it makes, or the coherence of the theory upon which it is based' (13).

I have been trying to think and write about Christianity in a manner that does not reproduce Christianity as a set of beliefs that one may or may not have. This does not mean, for example, that questions about God's Trinitarian nature are unimportant. Yet something has gone wrong when questions about Trinity have no purchase on how we make as well as what we do with our money. I am less interested in what people, including myself, 'think.' I am much more interested in what is shaping our desires or, if you prefer, our bodies.

Accordingly, I find myself increasingly attracted to what might be called cultural Christianity. We were taught in the liberal seminaries of mainline Protestantism in America to be critical of Christians who were Christians because they were Irish or Italian.[4] No book better exemplified this general attitude and stance than H. Richard Niebuhr's *Christ and Culture*.[5] Niebuhr's famous types made invisible the culture

---

[4] Such views were not explicitly anti-Catholic, though such sentiments were often close to the surface. Less obvious was the class bias against 'cultural Christianity.' I will have more to say about these matters in the next section.

[5] H. Richard Niebuhr, *Christ and Culture* (New York: Harper Torchbooks, 1951). I realize this way of understanding Niebuhr's work is contentious, but Niebuhr's understanding of 'Christ' reflects the displacement of Christian practice capable of cultural embodiment. Niebuhr exemplifies the attempt of Protestant liberalism to save some 'meaning' for Christianity in the aftermath of the loss of the church's social power. With his usual insight and candor, John Dewey observed that the greatest change in Christianity has not been due to the challenge of science, though that has been the focus of attention, but rather: 'the change in the social center of religion has gone on so steadily and is now so generally accomplished that it has faded from the thought of most persons, save the historians, and even they are especially aware of it only in its political aspect. . . . There are even now persons who are born into a particular church, that of their parents, and who take membership in it almost as a matter of course; indeed, the fact of such membership may be an important, even a determining factor in an individual's whole career. But the thing new in history, the thing once unheard of, is that the organization in question is a *special* institution, within a secular community. Even where there are established churches, these are constituted by the state and may be unmade by the state. Not only the national state but other forms of organizations among groups have grown in power and influence at the expense of organizations built upon and about a religion. The correlative of this fact is that membership in associations of the latter type is more and more a matter of the voluntary choice of individuals who may tend to accept responsibilities imposed by the church but who accept them of their own volition,' *A Common Faith* (New Haven: Yale University Press, 1960), 61. Niebuhr's *Christ and Culture* simply accepts this displacement as a *fait accompli*. I do not think it possible or desirable to return to a Christendom model of the church. What may be possible, and it is the strategy behind this paper, is now to use some of the leftovers of Christendom as resources for a church capable of saving us from 'our own volition.' That is, we may discover that we have been more shaped by what we 'choose' than what was present in the initial choice. So 'cultural Christianity,' which once named the way Christians made a home for themselves, now becomes a way for Christians to know how to survive without a home. For the most compelling critique of Niebuhr's *Christ and Culture* see John Howard Yoder's 'How H. Richard Niebuhr Reasoned: A Critique of *Christ and Culture*' in Glen Stassen, D. M. Yeager, and John Howard Yoder, *Authentic Transformation: A New Vision of Christ and Culture* (Nashville: Abingdon, 1996), 31–89.

that produced the assumption that Christ, or at least 'radical monotheism,' was itself not a culture. I have a new rule of thumb: anytime the phrase 'X and/or Y and culture' occurs (as in 'Christ and culture'), you know a mistake has been made. Such a phrase cannot help but reproduce the presumption of liberal cultures that there is a place to stand free of culture.

Niebuhr's account of 'radical monotheism' was an attempt to save theology from sociological reductionism. Given the events of his time, he was also trying to insure American Christians would not make the mistake of German Christians. But the very means he used to secure 'transcendence' ironically provided the theological justification for the spiritualization of Christianity.[6] By 'spiritualization,' I mean simply the attempt to make Christianity intelligible without that set of cultural habits called church.[7] As a result Niebuhr, like many Protestant liberals,

---

I wrote this chapter prior to the publication of Kathryn Tanner's *Theories of Culture: A New Agenda for Theology* (Minneapolis: Fortress Press, 1997). We are in Tanner's debt for her accounts of the development of the notion of culture and in particular her critique of modernist accounts of culture as self-contained units. While I am quite sympathetic to her alternative account of culture, I find her suggestions for the church to be a voluntary society naive. She will no doubt think I do so because I must look from her perspective like a post-liberal who draws a far too impermeable boundary between the church and the world. Yet I think she is able to 'take the high ground' against those she characterizes as post-liberals because her discourse remains at such an abstract and formal level – a strategy quite common to modernists but odd for one claiming as she does to have left modernism behind. Tanner, like James Gustafson, is concerned with Christian self-righteousness or, put differently, with the exaggerated claims made on behalf of the Christian difference. They ask where the evidence is, the empirical confirmation of such a difference. I believe such a question is easily answered once we have eyes to see. The church exists, lives are transformed, God is present among us. That God is so present can never be an occasion for boasting, but rather for Christians to celebrate the goodness of our Lord. But such goodness is known by the existence of people whose lives only make sense in the light of what God has done in Christ and the church. For Gustafson's query – 'What is the evidence?' – see his 'Don't Exaggerate,' *Christian Century* 114/30 (29 October 1997), 964–65. I suspect standing behind the concerns of Tanner and Gustafson is H. Richard Niebuhr's account of radical monotheism – a god that turns out to be so sovereign that he cannot be incarnated.

[6] 'Ironically' because Niebuhr, unlike his brother Reinhold, had a quite impressive sense of the importance of the materiality of the church at least in his early work. This is particularly apparent in his 'Toward the Independence of the Church' in *The Church Against the World* (Chicago: Willett, Clark, & Co., 1935), 123–56. In that essay he continued to challenge the capitalist betrayal of the church he had begun in *The Social Sources of Denominationalism* (New York: Meridian, 1972) which was first published in 1929. From my perspective, *The Kingdom of God in America* (New York: Harper, 1959) represents a reactionary development just to the extent Niebuhr's increasing 'idealism' (that is, the stress on transcendence) makes the church less necessary to his theology.

[7] I am indebted to Raymond Williams' analyses of culture in his *Key Words: A Vocabulary of Culture and Society* (New York: Oxford University Press, 1976), 76–82. Williams developed, through his wide-ranging work, an account of the materiality of culture that avoids the unsatisfactory base/superstructure distinction of Marxism.

betrays a cultural Christianity in service to a social order that needs 'religion' to be 'spiritual' and transcendent in order that it may not become a challenge to the material practices necessary to the sustaining of a capitalist social order.

Which is but a reminder that it is not a question of whether or not Christianity is culturally embodied but rather what kind of culture Christian practices produce. I am convinced, moreover, that the only way to discover such practices is to try to describe what goes on in actual churches.[8] Put quite simply, I want to ask if congregations can sustain a culture able to provide some resistance to the world that threatens to reduce Christianity to mere 'belief.' As a way to explore this question, or better, questions, I am going to describe where I go to church.

Going to Church

I go to church at Aldersgate United Methodist Church in Chapel Hill, North Carolina. I have been a member of Aldersgate for seven years.[9] When I first moved to Durham to teach in the Divinity School at Duke, I attended a number of Methodist churches. Most Sundays I left the services angry, not only because the liturgy was so thin but because of the stupidity displayed in the sermon. I am a layman who happens to be a theologian – a dangerous combination. A theologian is tempted to believe that his or her task is to 'make Christianity up.' I need to be reminded that God thinks me up.

For two years I belonged to a new church begun in Durham as part of the attempt to stem the tide of lost membership. I mistakenly assumed that such a new church offered the opportunity to 'get things right.'

Williams helps us see that all forms of signification must be analyzed within the actual means and conditions of their production and reproduction. For a discussion of Williams on this point, see John Eldridge and Lizzie Eldridge, *Raymond Williams: Making Connections* (New York: Routledge, 1994), 45–75.

For one of the most discerning discussions of these matters in a Christian perspective, see Nicholas Lash, *A Matter of Hope: A Theologian's Reflections on the Thought of Karl Marx* (Notre Dame: University of Notre Dame Press, 1982). Lash argues that Christian materialism is required because our relation to God is mediated. Such mediation frees history from necessity based on cause and effect. So the Christian stance toward the future cannot be 'to wait and see what happens' (137). Christian hope names the conviction that in Christ we find our lives narratable, that is to say, hopeful.

[8] 'Description' is, of course, anything but innocent. The methodological assumptions that often shape the 'sociology' governing such descriptions reproduce the kind of 'spiritualization' of the church for which I am trying to provide an alternative. The following description will seem quite naive, as that is exactly what I want it to be.

[9] It is interesting how language functions in this context. I claim to be a member of Aldersgate. One can also say that we belong to such and such church. I prefer 'member' because such language is more physical, as in 'bodily member.' There is nothing wrong with the language of belonging, but one can belong to many organizations without being a member.

Yet the church quickly reproduced the habits of mainstream Methodism – it was going to be a place where people found 'meaning' for their lives and the men played softball. The church was obviously going to be quite successful attracting upwardly mobile young couples. Realizing there was nothing I could do to stop this church from being successful, I began to look again.

My wife, who is also a Methodist minister, besides her work at Duke as Director of Continuing Education and Summer Programs, knew of a church in Chapel Hill that was ministered by a friend she had known in seminary. The church is quite modest but I was struck by the seriousness and integrity of everything the minister, the Revd Susan Allred, did. Moreover, the congregation, usually about a hundred members on a 'good Sunday,' seemed genuinely to care about worship. By that I mean they believe it important to be reminded of the name of the God we worship, confess sin, have three readings of Scripture and a Psalm, a sermon that attends to the Scripture for the day, prayer and thanksgiving in response to the Word.

Though we live at some distance from the church, we 'liked the church' and sought membership. We were, quite frankly, looking for a church that would not demand much energy or time. We are, after all, busy professionals. But we have found ourselves pulled into the church more than we anticipated, not only because we admire our minister but over the years we have come to know and be known by the people in the church. So, for example, Paula, my wife, simply cannot say 'no' when asked to lead worship as part of the church's nursing home ministry.

It is important to note that the church is in Chapel Hill. Chapel Hill is a university community, which means that the educational level of the church is a bit higher than many Methodist churches. It is also a transient community, so our size not only depends on whether the University of North Carolina is in session, but we also constantly lose members who have come to the area universities to study.[10] We have, for example, lost members who failed to receive tenure. Such times never fail to occasion mourning in the congregation.

The church is thirty years old and was once thought to be potentially one of the strong new churches in the district. However, after a promising start, that has proved not to be the case; at least that does not seem to be the case if you measure success with numbers and money as the Methodist church tends to do. We are a land-locked church and we lack financial resources to do anything about it. Yet our membership spans generations, with many of the original members still in the church. Over the past ten years, the church has attracted younger members so the church is now filled with children. Our 'educational space' would be considered inadequate, but somehow we continue to 'make do.'

---

[10] The church consists of people loyal to the University of North Carolina. Since Paula and I are 'Duke people,' we have to endure a good deal of friendly abuse.

Our worship area is the normal regimented pews with the choir stalls at the front. It is not an attractive sanctuary but at least its simplicity insures there is no ugliness – for example, the American flag is nowhere to be seen. Given the simplicity of our space it makes all the difference who is and is not present on any Sunday morning. We need everyone we can get. A missing body is not overlooked, particularly if it is the member who is 96 years old. The congregation is largely white, middle-class, but we differ widely in age. Though we appear homogeneous, there is a great tolerance, or better, enjoyment of our differences. For example, it is a small but, I think, telling matter that some of us do not 'dress up' to come to church because we do not dress up to go anywhere.

The congregation probably tends to be on the liberal side. Many of the members are involved in serving meals at the Community Shelter, AIDS ministries, and we support the North Carolina Council of Churches. The latter is quite significant, since the Methodist Conference of North Carolina withdrew support from the Council when the Council accepted two churches whose membership is largely gay. Though little is made of it, Aldersgate has quite prominent gay members who are valued by almost everyone in the congregation. They are valued because they are 'just like us,' that is, they work with the kids, sing in the choir, play softball (our team has both men and women), and lead worship.

As I indicated, we have been increasingly drawn into the congregational life, but in truth we were first attracted to the church by Susan Allred. She never does anything where God does not matter and it is the God whom we worship as Christians. She would not describe herself as theologically sophisticated, but she has something much more important than theological sophistication – that is, she has a wonderful appreciation for the seriousness of theological speech and, in particular, the importance of how that speech is shaped by worship. She never fails to remind us where we are in the Christian year, calling attention to the difference church time does and should have for our lives. Her preaching is always scriptural and she has a wonderful way of narrating our lives together as Christians by and through the scriptural texts.

Like most Methodist churches we celebrate the Eucharist once a month. Susan Allred usually celebrates the Eucharist at the beginning of Advent or Lent, but these are not sufficient to make us think something is odd when we do not celebrate. I use every opportunity to urge the church to move to more frequent Eucharist practice and I am not without hope that some day I will prevail. I am also trying to convince the church that putting up Stations of the Cross could not hurt our sanctuary.[11]

---

[11] My graduate assistant, Kelly Johnson (in critiquing a first draft of this paper) asked, if we had such Stations: 'Would you use them?' – a good question that could only come from a Roman Catholic. I can only respond that if they were there, if we only looked at them, that would at least be a start to challenge the rationalism of Protestant worship.

I assume Aldersgate is a very typical example of a mainline Christian church. It is a 'Sunday church,' as most of us seldom see one another through the week. We do business at various committee meetings and find other times to get together. But Sunday morning remains the central event for us as a people. We cannot claim to know one another well, though there are some very close friendships within the church. It has certainly been the case that Paula and I have come to know many of the members in a manner that we feel claimed by them, as I hope they feel how important they have become for us.

In fact, one of the high points of our liturgy is always the prayers of the people. There we learn of one another's lives as through our prayers we reveal our sufferings and our joys. This person is having an operation, or their mother has just died, another has separated from their spouse, and so on. Through the prayers we learn to have our lives lifted up to God and, thus, to one another. That is how slowly we learn of and from one another's stories.

Aldersgate is not a distinctive church. We are not the kind of church where one would expect to find 'resident aliens.' Most of us are there because in some way or another what we do on Sunday morning 'pleases us.' In other words, we are there because we have selected Aldersgate as a good 'church,' a 'church with a warm heart' as our motto reads – a motto, I might add, I particularly dislike.

So I go to church at Aldersgate because I like the church which, of course, bothers me. No matter what its peculiar attractions may be, it is finally part of a capitalist economy that means my involvement at Aldersgate is but another consumer choice. Therefore, in my own ecclesial life I reproduce the kind of church shopping I otherwise wish to defeat. The practices that sustain our worship of God at Aldersgate are, as a result, too easily undermined by the alleged voluntary culture that forms our lives separate from worship. I will argue, however, that this description of my membership at Aldersgate does not do justice to the complexity of my – and I believe most of the congregation's – involvement with the church. We voluntarily join the church, but such a 'joining' is finally inadequately understood as a

---

The materiality of medieval Catholicism could lead to abuse but it also served to remind Christians that Christianity is about the formation of the body. As Miri Rubin observes in her wonderful *Corpus Christi: The Eucharist in Late Medieval Culture* (Cambridge: Cambridge University Press, 1991), 'the whole structure of the church, the approval of secular authorities, the very naturalness of being the only place of worship and of a comprehensive world view preached and taught frequently, was empowered in the claim of sacramentality and in the practice of an exclusive right of mediation. A Christian narrative of sacramentality was the dominant tale which embraced man, the supernatural, order and hierarchy, sin and forgiveness; it punctuated life, marriage, birth and death' (8–9). Stations of the Cross might at least remind Protestants that Jesus' death was not the result of 'a difference of opinion' or an example of a 'failure to communicate.'

'choice.' The difficulty of how to understand how that happens – that is, how our 'choice' becomes something that happens to us – is what I want to try to describe.

The Church as a Non-Voluntary Community

In order to try to name the complexity, the cultural shaping potential of a church like Aldersgate, I suggest we think of such a church as non-voluntary. By 'non-voluntary' I am attempting to name a set of practices that offers an alternative to the assumption that our membership in the church must be either voluntary or determined. Because we have assumed these descriptions are the only ones available, Protestants in particular have put far too great a weight on our 'true' participation in the church. As a result, we lose the resources to name the disciplines necessary to resist the church's becoming a 'life option,' another consumer preference, because we fail to note how we became Christians in spite of ourselves. That is, we lack the means to learn we were chosen before we chose.

By employing the notion of 'non-voluntary' I hope to name how we might think of an alternative to the unhappy choice between voluntary or coerced behavior.[12] Elsewhere I argue that Christianity is extended training meant to help us discover and name those practices and narratives that hold us captive, but that we fail to see how they do so exactly because we think we have chosen them.[13] In other words, the great task before Christians today is to unmask the invisibility of those stories that constitute our lives which we assume, wrongly, are commensurate with our being Christian. How, for example, can churches maintain disciplined forms of examination of people who wish us to witness their marriages when the same people can easily be married at a church that does not require they be so examined.[14] Even more pressing, how can we witness marriages when we assume that divorce is for many of them inevitable?

[12] The notion of 'non-voluntary' action raises fascinating issues in philosophy of action and moral psychology. Such issues go back to Aristotle's account of 'choice' in his *Nicomachean Ethics* that is still unsurpassed. The analysis I provide in Chapter 9 is my continuing attempt to think about these matters.

[13] In particular, see my *Dispatches from the Front: Theological Engagements with the Secular* (Durham: Duke University Press, 1994), 164–76; and *Where Resident Aliens Live; Exercises for Christians* (Nashville: Abingdon Press, 1996).

[14] That such a discipline is required is due to the presumption that Christian marriage is a commitment to lifelong monogamous fidelity. How would anyone ever know what they were doing when they made such a promise? That is why the church insists we must know, we must examine, who the couple are before we are willing to witness their making such a promise. For it will be the church's duty to hold the couple to a promise they could have not known what they were doing when they made it. We must have some sense that the habits of their baptism have shaped the couple's life so that they will find the church's mutual support for the keeping of such promises a joy.

I confess one of the reasons I probably over-romanticize Catholicism as an option to mainstream Protestantism is that Catholicism still maintains at least some habits I assume are characteristic of cultural Christianity.[15] In many of its settings Catholicism is not 'a church' but a culture which formed and forms bodies to inhabit the world in a distinctive fashion.[16] Such formation was materialist to the core, since it was never a matter of whether one had all the beliefs right but rather whether one prayed, obeyed, paid, and died rightly.[17] Salvation was not some set of ideas but being part of a people constituted by material practices that shaped one's life in a manner that made one part of God's great communion.

Of course, Protestants learned to critique Catholic cultural formation primarily for its alleged perversions. Such a church was and is called authoritarian and alleged to underwrite the worst forms of oppression. Catholic Christianity allegedly failed to challenge the status quo and

[15] See, for example, my *In Good Company: The Church as Polis* (Notre Dame: University of Notre Dame Press, 1995), 19–31.

[16] I do not mean to suggest that mainstream Protestantism does not reflect a culture, but that is just the problem – Protestantism more reflects a culture than creates a culture. In this respect it is interesting to compare Catholic and Protestant *kitsch*. Catholic catalogues sell, for example, 'egg rosaries, moulded 1 1/4" diameter egg (plastic) contains a delightful moulded cord rosary. Comes in an assortment of pink and blue rosaries, sold 36 eggs per box, 39 cents' (*Autom*, March 1996, 33). How wonderfully material. As my colleague Professor Brett Webb-Mitchell points out, Catholics in New York during the Pope's visit were selling 'Pope on a rope' shower soaps. Protestants just do not have that kind of possibility. For example, people at the Methodist General Conference would be surprised if Cokesbury was selling 'General Conference on a rope' or even 'Bishop on a rope.' I am indebted to Dr Mary Collins for calling my attention to the wonders of the *Autom* catalogue. (I confess I ordered a wonderful chasuble from the catalogue for my wife because she often presides at Eucharist.)
I suspect that Catholic *kitsch* continues to draw on the habits of the body correlative to the Christian understanding of the resurrection of the body. For example, Caroline Walker Bynum argues in her *The Resurrection of the Body in Western Christianity, 200–1336* (New York: Columbia University Press, 1995), 'for most of Western history body was understood primarily as the locus of biological process. Christians clung to a very literal notion of resurrection despite repeated attempts by theologians and philosophers to spiritualize the idea. So important indeed was literal, material body that by the fourteenth century not only were spiritualized interpretations firmly rejected; soul itself was depicted as embodied. Body was emphasized in all its particularity and physicality both because of the enormous importance attached to proper burial and because of the need to preserve difference (including gender, social status, and personal experience) for all eternity. But the "other" encountered in body by preachers and theologians, storytellers, philosophers and artists, was not the "other" of sex or gender, social position or ethnic group, belief or culture; it was death' (xviii). Bynum's book is a wonderful account of the interaction of piety and theology and, in particular, how the piety of the 'simple' was often more profound than the theology of the day. I am sure little hangs on rosaries in plastic eggs, but that Catholic hospitals continue to bury fetuses of early miscarriages is a practice that I suspect, if lost, would change the character of Catholic theology.

[17] What could be more important than 'dying rightly'? That Christian bodies are no longer shaped by baptism results in the medicalization of our deaths. No longer able to make our deaths our own, 'assisted suicide' begins to sound like good news.

accepted far too readily the structures of power written into a feudal social order. When the church enjoyed such cultural power, when people had no choice not to be Christian, the church far too easily became an end in itself, confusing what was good for the church with what is good for God's kingdom.

I have no stake in denying that such perversions may well have taken place and in practice continue to take place. But I think such a critique provides a far too comforting narrative for those of us who assume that Protestantism constitutes a strong alternative. The so-called voluntary church nicely underwrites patterns of domination characteristic of capitalist social orders with much less basis for critique than was provided by the Catholic church. At least that church had an account of the just wage and usury that could challenge corrupt economic practices. Given the voluntarism of mainstream Protestantism, we have no such resources other than vague calls for something called social justice. Accordingly, the Gospel in mainstream Protestantism becomes an 'ideal' which lacks any material specification.

I am of course aware that Catholicism, particularly in America, has increasingly come to look like mainstream Protestantism. The Catholics now think they too ought to 'choose' to be Catholic. So they tend to view their Catholicism as simply that form of religious life they prefer perhaps because of their upbringing. Yet there remains in Catholicism a sense that Christianity is finally not something that I get to make up my mind about but rather a set of practices to which I must submit my life. To be sure, this can lead to quite unhappy results, but it also remains a resource for the constitution of disciplined communities that have power of resistance against that order of necessity called freedom.

The problem in the mainline Protestant churches is that we no longer can imagine what it would mean to obey. Laity and ministry alike think they can be Christians without training. They think it is their duty to think for themselves, even (perhaps especially!) in matters religious. Such a view underwrites the presumption that 'religious' names their personal relationship with God. Accordingly, the mainstream churches are not able to maintain any account of authority that would sustain the formation of those who have come to the church as a self-selection process but who must, if we are to live faithful to the Gospel, discover disciplines necessary for the transformation of our lives.

I am aware that the 'voluntary character' of being a member of the church seems intrinsic to the very character of Christianity. The church is God's promise to the Jews sent to the Gentiles. Intrinsic to the character of the church therefore is witness and conversion. We have learned to describe conversion as the making of a voluntary commitment, but such a description fails to do justice to the complex character of Christian conversion. Christians discover that what they thought they had done voluntarily has in fact been done to them, since they could not have known what they were doing by being baptized when they were baptized. That is why Christianity is an extended set of skills learned through imitating others, an imitation that is meant to help us make our baptisms our own over a lifetime. Such skills can become virtues sufficient to help us resist the powers that would otherwise determine our lives. The challenge is how to maintain that process, a process for becoming holy, without the process being perverted by the presumption that I am doing what I have chosen to do.

I do not pretend to have an adequate response to the challenge. Will Willimon and I call for Christians to rediscover their alien status,[18] which of course invites the question, 'Where is this church that you and Will Willimon talk about?' 'Where did it ever exist in Christian history?' 'Where does it exist today?' 'How can it exist today?' Given my own theological commitments, I cannot respond to such questions by underwriting the distinction between visible and invisible churches. That is exactly the kind of spiritualization I am trying to avoid.[19] Nor can I put off the question by suggesting that because I am a theologian I can talk about what the church ought to be, not what it is. The 'is' has to exist for me. It must exist at Aldersgate United Methodist Church, even though those of us who attend there believe we are there because we have chosen to be there and yet by being there we are made more than our choice.

Returning to Aldersgate: A Sermon with Commentary

I believe that God's church does exist at Aldersgate United Methodist Church in Chapel Hill, North Carolina. I believe, moreover, that Aldersgate United Methodist Church embodies material practices that hopefully can force me to live faithfully, to ways of life I have not chosen. Moreover, I believe that Aldersgate makes me at least something of a Christian by teaching me how to speak Christian speech by listening to other Christians speak.[20] After all, few activities are more physical than speech.

---

[18] Stanley Hauerwas and William Willimon, *Resident Aliens: Life in the Christian Colony* (Nashville: Abingdon, 1989). I am indebted to Will Willimon for helping me learn how to write for Christians. That theologians now write primarily for other theologians in the universities is an indication of the material malformation of Christian practices. I am not in the least critical of those who try to write for a 'popular audience.' I simply wish I were better able so to write.

[19] David Yeago attributes the 'spiritualization' of Christian practice to a misreading of Luther's understanding of justification, the law/Gospel distinction, and the articulation of the so-called 'Protestant Principle.' See his 'Gnosticism, Antinomianism, and Reformation Theology: Reflections on the Costs of a Construal,' *Pro Ecclesia* 2, 1 (Winter 1993), 37–49.

[20] I am often struck by the prayers of my fellow lay members. Recently at a Staff-Parish meeting, in which we were trying to discern with our minister whether she should seek reappointment to Aldersgate for another year, I was stunned when the chair of the meeting simply announced that this was something we ought to pray about. The chair is a woman in her late fifties who works for H & R Block. She began to pray and the

In order to exemplify such speech, I offer a sermon preached by Susan Allred at Aldersgate on 17 March 1996.[21] There was nothing 'special' about this particular Sunday or the sermon other than that it was preached while I was trying to think through this paper. When I heard it all I could think was, 'Well, that says it all.' I will, therefore, interrupt her sermon with short commentaries on why I find her sermon so hopeful. That such a sermon was preached suggests, I think, much about the body of people who must exist to make such a sermon possible.

A Sermon preached by the Revd Susan L. Allred, at Aldersgate United Methodist Church, Chapel Hill, on 17 March 1996

My dear friends in Christ, have you ever seen such a full plate of Scripture readings in your entire life – a banquet of the rich food that seems to last forever. There were thirteen verses from 1 Samuel (on the anointing of King David by Samuel), the reading of one of our favorite Psalms, the twenty-third, a great passage about light from Ephesians, and then fifty-one verses from John's Gospel, the entire ninth chapter. What has happened to our minister! These are the readings for the fourth Sunday in Lent (Year A).

What's going on! It's Lent – it's mid-Lent; the church's pilgrimage to Jerusalem to experience again Christ's death and resurrection continues and intensifies! Three weeks from today is Easter! As Christians we are baptized into Christ's death and resurrection and Easter means baptismal renewal. It is a time to celebrate anew that through baptism we have been anointed (just like biblical kings) to be part of a Royal Priesthood, a sign of our being chosen by God. We have been chosen and adopted as God's own people so that we may proclaim God's mighty acts. We believe that at the early church's first baptisms a song was sung whose words are recorded for us in 1 Peter 2:9–10: 'But you are a chosen race, a royal priesthood, a holy nation, God's own people, in order that you may proclaim the mighty acts of him who called you out of darkness into his marvelous light. Once you were not a people, but now you are God's people; once you had not received mercy, but now you have received mercy.' Do we know how to proclaim God's mighty acts today?

Since we worshiped together a week ago, a member of our congregation has died. Those of you who could rearrange your work schedules and other commitments gathered in this worship space on Friday for a Service of Death and Resurrection for Roy Smith. Roy's body was cremated and we brought his ashes into the sanctuary in a box and we placed them on a

---

prayer was eloquent and direct. I was literally in tears, moved by her unapologetic presumption that God could be asked to help us. What a wonderful gift for a theologian to learn that such speech is possible and perhaps begin to learn to imitate it.

[21] Susan Allred graciously gave me permission to use her sermon. In the first draft of this paper I reproduced the sermon without commentary. I am indebted to Tex Sample for suggesting why it is important to indicate how I heard the sermon.

table in this central aisle and covered them with a beautiful white satin cloth with an embroidered gold cross, the colors of Easter, and we said these words in the service: 'As in baptism Roy put on Christ so in Christ may Roy be clothed in glory.'

Susan Allred begins noting the lengthy passages of scripture we have taken the time to read. This obviously means the service is going to 'run over,' be longer than an hour. Yet she does not apologize; rather, she reminds us that this is what you would expect a royal people to do. We have all the time in the world because we are a people who have been baptized into Christ's death and resurrection. We are no longer a people lost in time but rather a people who can take time in a lost world to enjoy what God has done for us.

Taking time shapes our bodies. We can be at rest. It is, therefore, particularly appropriate that Susan Allred reminds us that one of our members died during the week. Notice we did not have a funeral, but a 'Service of Death and Resurrection.' This is the church's language that narrates our lives, names who we are as the baptized, reminds us whose time we are in. We can take the time to hear the Scripture, worship God, care for one another because our death, our body, has been shaped by our baptism.

When the blind man in the Gospel lesson was anointed he received sight. A study of baptismal practices in the church's early history reminds us that anointing was a familiar practice. We also know that baptism was often referred to as illumination. At an early date in the church, we know that the newly baptized one was given a lighted candle and these words were spoken: 'You are the light of the world. Let your light shine.' At your baptism you were anointed and set apart so that you may declare the wonderful deeds of him who called you out of darkness into his marvelous light.

When God called us Gentiles to be grafted into God's family he made of us a royal nation – 'Once we were no people, but now we are God's people.' Once we had not received mercy but now we have received mercy. We have been called out of darkness into God's marvelous light! It is appropriate for us as Christians because of our baptisms to consider ourselves as royalty, but do we often think of ourselves in that way? One writer expresses our claim to royalty with these words: 'The Queen of England, at her coronation, was dressed in priestly garments and anointed with oil. We are not less royalty and priests because of our baptism, our coronation as Christians.'[22] But there are also 'risks of baptism.' There are 'consequences of commitment.'

The healing of the blind man in John's Gospel is about learning to see what God is doing in the world. The fact that the story *begins* with Jesus taking clay from the earth and placing it on the eyes of the blind man

---

[22] Soards, Dozeman, McCabe, *Preaching the Revised Common Lectionary* (Nashville: Abingdon Press, 1992), 71.

reminds us from the beginning that this is a story about God's creative work in the world – just as God formed clay to create humanity so Jesus makes mud. From the dust of the earth we were formed and God continues to be a creative God in our lives. Through Jesus God helps us to see what life is intended to be. Jesus came to make God known in the world.

The blindness in Chapter 9 of John's Gospel is about people who can technically see but can only see what is literally and simply before them. The story is about sight and non-sight, especially those who are blind to God's work in Jesus. To make them see who Jesus was truly constituted a *miracle*, a divine healing! One commentary on the text rightly recalls Paul's experience on the Damascus Road when he was suddenly blinded. 'When the scales drop from his eyes, he who thought he saw everything now saw for the very first time. We speak of this as a conversion experience, a turning around, not so much a second chance but rather as the first time to get it right.'[23]

How fortunate we are that God has called us to live in community. We do not have to travel the road of discipleship alone! God calls us to live in community with one another and to show each other the light. We are called to be priests to one another and to the world, walking together in the light.

Clay that sees – that is what we are reminded we are: clay that sees! We can now see and in our seeing we become God's light for the world. Heady claims to be made about this modest group of people at Aldersgate United Methodist Church in Chapel Hill, North Carolina. But Susan Allred reminds us that God – miracle of miracles! – God has made us royalty in a town that does not believe anyone does or should rule. To see God's rule requires nothing less than miracle, which turns out to be us.

Which turns out to mean we are certainly going to need one another. To be God's light means darkness is revealed as darkness which has no use for the light. If we are going to survive we will need one another. As bodies, as clay that sees, we are not called to be heroines or heroes, but to 'live in community.' As we learn to minister to one another, to be bodily present to one another, we become God's witness to the world of the salvation wrought in Christ. How good it is to need one another.

Having said all these things which we believe about our priesthood as baptized Christians, I remind you again of the consequences of our commitment.

This congregation is filled with many faithful disciples of Jesus Christ, but it still isn't easy living together. At a recent meeting of the Administrative Board we focused on the ways we as a congregation can do a better job with financial stewardship. We are all baptized Christians – named and anointed – but aware that planning for a faithful ministry

[23] Peter J. Gomes, *Proclamation 6*, Series A, Lent (Fortress Press, 1995), 50.

brings up differences of opinions. We do not all think alike. We have different personality styles and we have to learn to *talk* to one another.

We all know the membership vows by heart. I will be loyal to the United Methodist Church and uphold it by my: *Prayers, Presence, Gifts,* and *Service.* (We have those four words memorized.) We promised to support the church in those ways. We want to support our missionary family in Liberia, to support our ministries at the Shelter for the Homeless, Willow Springs Nursing Home, activities of our United Methodist Women, The Reconciling Church Movement, and today 13 members of our congregation, having finished an intensive training program, will receive the name of an AIDS patient who will become our 'Care Partner.'

It is never easy to talk about money in the church. As a community our vision of what God is calling us to do in outreach ministries beyond ourselves and increasing our own programs has outgrown our pocketbooks. God has given us a vision but our pledges continue to stay the same. We must increase our pledges in order to support this vision that God has given us. These are hard discussions but we must work through them as a congregation! These are difficult discussions but they are necessary. Can those who are pledging pledge more? Will persons who have not pledged find a way to make a pledge to the 1996 budget? Will those who thought a gift from a graduate student was so small it would not make a difference now be able to see that *all* sizes of gifts are needed for the ministry of Christ's church?

Money! I thought the sermon was about important theological issues – baptism, death, light – but it turns out it is about money. But what could be more appropriate than to be reminded that God wants our money? – that our money is not 'ours,' but rather but a mode of our service for one another and for the world? Money, particularly in a capitalist economy, becomes one of our most determinative spiritual realities. The task is to demythologize money's mythic power by making it a mode of service. The simple reminder that we are behind in our budget at least puts us on that road.

Moreover, note Susan Allred's realism. She knows we do not agree, that we have to learn to talk to one another. Yet she makes us more than we are individually by reminding us that all the ministries of the church make up the one body of Christ. We do not get to withhold our money in support of those ministries with which we do not agree. This is no democratic institution. It is a community of Christ's body through which we are made subservient to one another. We are not called on to be agreeable but to expose our differences, believing as we do that we are constituted by a unity made possible by God.

Back to 'Christ's Body the Church' at Aldersgate. What does it mean to be faithful disciples? I like the increasing feeling we have that it's OK to ask for the church to pray for us when we experience times of discernment. We are learning to listen to God's wisdom and the wisdom of the church on our decisions. In addition to the supportive community we experience through worship, confession, praying for one another and listening together to God's word, we have in the United Methodist Church a special process called 'candidacy' for persons who believe that God is calling them into the ordained ministry of the church. All of us are ordained by our baptisms to be in the ministry of Jesus Christ but there is a process for persons to seek discernment as to whether they are being set aside by God for an ordination of Word, Sacrament and Order.

In recent months, a member of our own church, Joy McVane, has invited us into a period of discernment in her life concerning God's call to ordained ministry. We have entered into some early stages of this process with Joy. She has met with the Staff-Parish Committee and the Charge Conference and was unanimously approved. Recently she was approved before the District Committee on Ordained Ministry and was certified as a candidate for ministry in our denomination. In the fall she plans to enter Duke Divinity School for a minimum of three years of study. It is our privilege and honor to continue to be companions and Christian friends for Joy as she continues this journey. We will pray for her family and for our life together with them here at Aldersgate.

By holding up Joy McVane, Susan Allred moves us from money to ministry. In some churches that may seem to be a stretch, but not at Aldersgate. Because Sunday after Sunday we are reminded what it means to be God's people, we know that money and ministry cannot be separated. Accordingly, Joy McVane placed herself under our care and was appropriately examined by the Staff-Parish Committee. As a member of that committee I can testify that she was seriously examined not just for her own self-understanding but more important, for how her sense of ministry was confirmed by how her life contributed to the upbuilding of the church at Aldersgate. Note that we were reminded that our examination of Joy was but part of the process of our learning to share our lives with one another through prayer.

Our joy concerning Joy, however, was tempered by Susan Allred's next reading us a letter from a former member of the church. He had also decided to enter the ministry as a so-called 'late vocation.' He discerned that serving put too great a strain on him and his family. The letter was addressed to his current congregation but was also meant to be read to us announcing his decision to discontinue the process. That he thought it right to share his decision with us was a wonderful testimony that he felt he could trust us. Just as we had supported his decision to enter the ministry, so he knew we would support his decision to leave the ministry. He knows, moreover, that he would be welcome to return to us. That was made unmistakable by the last two paragraphs of the sermon:

In view of Joy's newly announced candidacy and Billy's announced changes, let us continue to open ourselves to God's love and grace through Jesus Christ so that we may have eyes to see how God is working in our community. God will show us how we are to support and love one another. God will continue to shape us by the story of his great love for us through Jesus.

God is continuing to work in our midst! We know this to be true *because* this is God's church! It was not our idea that all of us would end up here at Aldersgate Church to share our lives so deeply with one another. The promise is clear: God through Christ will lead us to Easter to renew our baptisms and will help us to see more clearly what God has yet to teach us about God's story. Long before we went in search of God, God came in search of us. While we were yet sinners Christ died for us. On that day of crucifixion we became God's royal people through Christ!

One Sermon Does Not Make a Culture, but It Is Not a Bad Place to Start

I am aware that this sermon is insufficient evidence that Aldersgate United Methodist Church is a culture capable of resisting the culture of choice. But neither is the sermon the product of the Revd Susan Allred's peculiar genius. If Roy Smith, Joy McVane, and Billy did not exist, this sermon could not be preached. Yet in the preaching, their lives, all our lives, receive specification as part of the church's life and, thus, part of Christ's life. The sermon may sound like 'ideas,' but from beginning to end the sermon is unapologetically material and bodily as Roy's cremated body is placed on a table in the central aisle.

Of course, most of us at Aldersgate continue to think 'our bodies are our own.' Most of us at best remain about half-Christian, possessed as we are by practices that give us the illusion we are in control of our lives.[24] But Aldersgate remains for me a sign of hope, a small island of cultural Christianity, where we get hints of what it means to be part of God's salvation, God's church. For as the Revd Susan Allred often reminds us, the church is not some idea she has had, it is God's church.[25]

---

[24] Since Susan Allred is now more the author of this paper than I am, I told her the only thing I could do is give the stipend I received for writing the paper to the church and that is what I did. We, after all, need the money and I need examples if the argument of the paper is to make sense of a material practice. It is a frightening thing to realize that working on an essay requires me to live differently. I am not sure I like that.

[25] I am indebted to Ms Kelly Johnson and Mr David Cloutier, and especially to Tex Sample, for reading and critiquing earlier drafts of this paper. Ms Sarah Freedman, surely one of the most theologically sophisticated secretaries in the world, patiently put the paper in readable shape.

Part III

SPEAKING TRUTHFULLY IN, FOR, AND AGAINST THE WORLD

10

The Non-Violent Terrorist:
In Defense of Christian Fanaticism

On Being a Fanatic

We live in a time in which extremity has become the norm. Whatever else the description 'postmodern' does, it gestures for many the un-avoidability, if not the legitimacy of the exaggerated. In such a context many quite understandably seek moderation. Extremity may for a time be exhilarating, but it is hard to live on a daily basis. I suspect among the reasons some find the way I do theology so distasteful is when all is said and done, it is just too extreme.

For example, I was asked to speak at a conference entitled 'Christian Ethics Between Radicalism and Fanaticism.' In the letter inviting me to address the conference the purpose of the colloquium was said to be an attempt 'to analyze the necessity and the dangers of the radicalism of (Christian) ethics.' I assumed, as a self-identified fanatic, I was to represent 'the necessity' of Christian radicalism.[1] Yet I was asked in particular 'to deal as an ethicist with the question of the tension between the radicality of the gospel in sociopolitical, peace and ecological matters and the risk of becoming a fanatic. How can you live out the radicality of the Christian message without becoming intolerant?' This, of course, put me in something of a bind because I believe Christians in our time cannot avoid being identified as fanatics. Moreover, I believe there is nothing wrong with intolerance if you are the kind of Christian radical I believe we are called to be.

Yet such a position cannot help but appear as extreme for those worried about Christians acting responsibly in the world as we know it. Fanatics and radicals are seldom thought to be responsible. In other words I realize I bear the burden of proof. I am, therefore, going to try to make an unapologetic case for Christian radicalism by providing a defense of what to many is the clearest case of fanaticism – terrorism. I

---

[1] The conference was sponsored by the Catholic University of Louvain. I am extremely grateful to the organizers of the conference, particularly Dider Pollefeyt, for their wonderful hospitality and their intellectual seriousness. For the avowal of my 'fanaticism' see my *Dispatches from the Front: Theological Engagements with the Secular* (Durham: Duke University Press, 1994), 5.

realize this will seem a bizarre strategy for a pacifist, but I hope to show why non-violence cannot help but appear as a terrorist tactic by those who want to make the world safe for war.

In the light of what many take to be the moral anarchy of our culture, it is comforting to think that there is a strong moral consensus about some things – e.g., child pornography and terrorism. Therefore my attempt to provide a justification of terrorism, at least a kind of theological terrorism, cannot help but seem unsettling. Yet I want to try to show that insofar as most continue to believe that war is a necessary instrument for the maintenance of goods of the human community, then terrorism cannot be automatically subject to moral condemnation.

I want to be candid, however, about where my argument is meant to lead. I want you to be, like me, a pacifist. As a pacifist I obviously think that war and terrorism are not compatible with Christian discipleship.[2] Yet many Christians think that, though war is terrible, under certain conditions it may not only be justified but a duty. Those that would so justify war for Christians usually assume that terrorism is beyond justification. I will try to show that the attempt to save war as a moral project by distinguishing war from terrorism will not work. In short, if you think terrorism is prohibited, then so is war. Christian non-violence, therefore, cannot help but appear as fanatical just to the extent it challenges the assumed 'normality' of war and violence.

The discussion of the ethics of terrorism, however, is meant to provide a context for what I take to be the worry of many when confronted with the position I seem to represent – namely, how can the radical character of the Gospel be reclaimed without making Christians irrelevant or, worse, intolerant. The kind of radical Christocentric ethics I am trying to develop, at least to some, seems to threaten the ability of Christians to act constructively in a world already far too divided. In such a divided world what is needed, it is argued, is a universal ethic capable of resolving conflict. In contrast, I will try to show that if Christians are to help such a world live more peacefully, we can only be what we are – those who worship Jesus Christ, the Son of God. For that is the basis of our 'radicalism' as Christians – i.e., we are not radicals because we assume a radical stance on this or that issue that the world understands as radical, but because any stance we assume must be witness to the God of Jesus Christ.

---

[2] Violence and non-violence are descriptions of behavior that requires analogical display. In other words we do not just 'know' violence or non-violence when 'we see it.' Peace too often is just another name for the absence of overt hostilities. For an exchange about the 'meaning' of non-violence see Paul Ramsey, *Speak Up For Just War or Pacifism* (University Park: Pennsylvania State University Press, 1988) and my response in the 'Epilogue.' In *Dispatches From the Front* I argue that we cannot know what violence (and war) is absent the practice of non-violence. This may appear a 'small point,' but I think its significance is often overlooked. From a Christian perspective non-violence is not an exception to war, but rather war and violence are conceptually and in practice parasitical on non-violence.

The 'Ethics' of Terrorism

'One community's terrorist is another community's martyr' is the kind of generalization that is as true as it is false. Yet it is not a bad place to begin thinking about terrorism just to the extent such a statement reminds us that any description of terrorism implicates a set of moral practices and presumptions. James Burtchaell rightly argues that it is:

> misleading to address the ethics of terrorism and response to terrorism by accepting without question the fashionable presumption that terrorism is a development so discontinuous with the traditions of warfare that it deserves unconventional moral scrutiny. On the contrary, terrorism, like the many enlargements of violence before it, is a lineal descendent of traditional warfare. It can best be understood and evaluated by analogy with conventional conflict. And I am increasingly of the opinion that it raises not old questions about new kinds of combat but new questions about old forms of war. It is warfare's newest and most sobering progeny.[3]

It is interesting to reflect on the Israeli/PLO conflict in the light of Burtchaell's claim that it is by no means easy to distinguish war from terrorism. The government of Israel found it useful to call the PLO a 'terrorist organization' because they sometimes killed schoolchildren on buses. Yet the state of Israel was brought into power by an extended and very well organized terrorist campaign. It is easy to forget that those who later became politicians in Israel at one time in their lives blew up the Prince David Hotel. To this day Israel assumes it has the right to bomb Palestinian refugee camps in retaliation for 'terrorist attacks,' but such bombing is not considered terrorism even though the camps house women and children. Is the bombing perpetrated by an established government by definition not terror?[4] Now that the PLO is a government with land does that mean former acts of 'terrorism' are now war?

It has been assumed that a strong distinction can be made between terrorism and war to the extent the former fails to observe the civilized

---

[3] James Tunstead Burtchaell, *The Giving and Taking of Life: Essays Ethical* (Notre Dame: University of Notre Dame, 1989), 211–12.

[4] For example, the definition of terrorism by the United States Department of Defense assumes that terrorism is defined as use of violence by those outside a duly constituted government. Thus 'terrorism is the unlawful use or threatened use of force or violence by a revolutionary organization against individuals or property, with the intention of coercing or intimidating governments or societies, often for political or ideological purposes.' Yet as Burtchaell points out, such definition leaves no room for state terrorism directed to its own population or to another state (Ibid. 213). In 1954 the US Government engineered the overthrow of the duly elected government in Guatemala, for instance, and has since made every effort to have an obviously terrorist control 'duly constituted,' while having to overlook its massacres of 100,000 Guatemalans, the 'disappearing' of countless others. (It's interesting that in US news reports those Guatemalans who protest or defend themselves are routinely labeled 'rebels.') Burtchaell provides other definitions from the FBI, International Law Association, and others which only help one see that no 'definition' of terrorism can be made to do the work of analysis.

rules of war, and in particular, engages in attacks on civilians. Yet from the 'terrorist' point of view distinctions between combatants and non-combatants are not easily maintained. For example, some years ago there was general outrage against those who raided a white man's Rhodesian farm and slaughtered his wife and children. Yet from the perspective of those who had conducted the raid, those killed – women and children alike – had been 'washed, dressed, schooled, and conveyed abroad and entertained and cultivated by dint of the occupation of *their* land and low-paid labor of *their* backs and the deprivation and humiliation of *their* children. It had been the white children's father's rifle that violated them and their homeland, but it was his family that lived good-naturedly on his violence. How could he be guilty and they be innocent?'[5]

Such examples are but reminders that often those who are called terrorist use violence because they have been denied any other alternative by the 'recognized government.' Of course this goes to the heart of the attempt to distinguish between terrorism and war, since any such distinction gains its moral warrant from the assumption based in just war theory that there is a continuity between the police function of the state and its war-making potential. The justification of war is but an extension of the right of the state to punish. The latter is possible because it is the disciplined use of violence for the good in common including the good of the one punished. Which is but a reminder, as Paul Ramsey emphasized, that just war is not so much a casuistry to determine if a war meets prior determined criteria, but rather is an account of state action required for the protection of the innocent.[6] So war is but a continuation of the justice internal to the state transposed to relations between states.

There are, however, some strong reasons to doubt that war is but a continuation of the police function of the state. The latter includes not only a prior agreement on what a crime may be, but also requires the criminal be caught, a decision be made of degree of guilt, the appropriate punishment, as well as the carrying out of the punishment. It is instructive to note that the police do not carry out any of the last

[5] Ibid. 221. My use of this example is not meant to suggest it is impossible to distinguish between combatants and non-combatants. Just war thinkers have rightly emphasized the importance of that distinction. Yet that distinction in itself is not sufficient to distinguish war from terrorism.

[6] In *Christian Ethics and the Sit-In* (New York: Association Press, 1961), Ramsey says, 'democracy means justifiable and limited resistance (and thus it refines and establishes procedures for making a justifiable revolution, which is in principle to apply to domestic politics the same line of reasoning that drove Christians in the early centuries of this era to justify and limit warfare for the resistance and correction of evil' (93). Later in the same book he observes that democracy is nothing more than *justum bellum*, 'both in its origin in Western history and in the principles of Christian ethics requiring participation in it as a form of regularized struggle between man and man in the midst of which alone we have in this fallen world any life with man preserved unto a higher and more open fellowship' (104).

functions, whereas in war all the functions are carried out by the same agent. In short, war lacks exactly the prior institutions and practices that limit the violence intrinsic to the police function of the state and, at least to some extent, make such violence less arbitrary. Yet as we noted above, it is just the assumption of such continuity that has underwritten the distinction between war and terrorism.

Of course it may be objected that this way of thinking about terrorism leaves out the most important aspect of just war reflection – i.e., the principle of non-combatant immunity. Those called terrorist, however, do not necessarily attack non-combatants, but if they do they are not without some moral response. Such an attack may be an attempt to make clear the kind of war they understand they are forced to wage – namely a war of the desperate that must use selective targeting in non-selective ways.

In this respect it is particularly important to remember that even attacks on civilians by alleged terrorists are not indiscriminate. Who gets blown up by a bomb on a bus may be indiscriminate, but that the bomb was planted on a bus is not indiscriminate. Rather, such bombing may be tied to policy objectives that may even make such a bombing analogous to the defense of civilian deaths on just war grounds of indirect effect; for alleged terrorist strategies are meant – like war itself – to make people prefer peace, or at least order, rather than continue the conflict. Therefore the 'random violence' of the terrorist is anything other than random just to the extent it is used in the interest of making the adversary sue for peace. Indeed, the terror of terrorism is often designed to brutalize those who must fight the terrorist so that the very means to fight the terrorist becomes self-defeating.

Accordingly, James Burtchaell argues that terrorism will increasingly be seen not as an anomaly but as one of the degenerate progeny of conventional war. He calls attention to three distinct reactions to weapons development, such as the machine gun, elicited in this century. Some thought such weapons so horrendous they were inherently immoral. Others thought them so terrible they would make war less likely. Still others thought such weapons only made clear how horrible war has always been. Burtchaell concludes that terrorism justifies all three conclusions as it is indeed savage and inhumane. Yet so is war. So 'inquiry into the nature and ethical imperatives of terrorism is sound only if we do not imagine that it is inhumane by contrast with war, which is humane. Conventional warfare is conventionally inhumane.'[7]

Yet this is a conclusion from which most of us would recoil. But if the above discussion of terrorism has taught us anything we must ask who is the 'us' doing the recoiling. Max Stackhouse represents what I take to be the most persuasive answer to that question – the 'us' must be the universal voice of humanity. Stackhouse argues that we are at a

---

[7] Burtchaell, *The Giving and Taking of Life*, 231.

loss to respond to terrorism because some no longer believe in a universal ethic. According to Stackhouse,

> Ethically, we are in an age in which there is grave doubt among theologians, philosophers, jurists, and social scientists as to whether any universal principles exist which can be reliably known and used by the international community to define torture or terrorism as wrong. To be sure, many say that terrorism and torture are terrible. But when the question is posed as to whether there are any universal absolutes, or whether there are intrinsically evil acts, or whether there are cross-cultural values which could be the basis for declaring such practices to be inherently wrong we find only doubt and skepticism.[8]

According to Stackhouse without such a universal ethic we have no means to challenge the assumed right of nation-states to make decisions on the basis of self-interest.

Stackhouse's concern to counter the 'relativism' he thinks to be the cause of our inability to condemn terrorism could be meant as a critique of me.[9] Since I am alleged to hold the view that no universal ethic exists, I represent a form of confessional theology that has no basis for saying why terrorism is wrong.[10] As Stackhouse puts the issue:

> If we believe terrorism and torture are in fact fundamentally contrary to the truth and justice of God and ought to be stopped everywhere, we must recognize that the theological foundations on which many contemporary contextualist and confessionalist theologies rest are inadequate to this task, whatever their contributions to other areas. Sadly, they do not have the cross-cultural, intellectual or moral amplitude to address these issues.[11]

---

[8] Max Stackhouse, 'Torture, Terrorism and Theology: The Need for a Universal Ethic,' *Christian Century* 103, 29 (8 October 1986), 861.

[9] Stackhouse's most sustained criticism of my position can be found in his 'Liberalism Dispatched vs. Liberalism Engaged,' *Christian Century* 112, 29 (18 October 1995), 962–67. Though this article takes the form of a review of my book, *Dispatches from the Front*, it is a wholesale attack on what he takes to be my position. What Stackhouse thinks I must think is only what someone like Stackhouse can think I think because of the way he thinks. For example, in his review he suggests that I think religious claims are immune to rational criticism. I certainly do not think that to be the case, though I should like to know more what he thinks rational criticism to be. I mention this point since it relates to the general argument of this essay. I certainly have a stake in rational criticism though I am quite suspicious of appeals to rational criticism in the abstract.

[10] For a response to the charge I am a 'confessionalist' see my 'Failure of Communication or A Case of Uncomprehending Feminism,' *Scottish Journal of Theology* 50, 1 (March 1997). This article is a response to Gloria Albrecht's review of my book, *In Good Company*. I find it interesting that Stackhouse and Albrecht share the view I must be a 'confessionalist' since they are, politically, at other ends of the spectrum. I think, however, this is but an indication of how deeply each of them is embedded not only in political liberalism but more importantly in theological liberalism.

[11] Stackhouse, 'Torture, Terrorism and Theology', 862. Stackhouse's assumption that we must have a reason for knowing why terrorism is wrong is, of course, part of the problem. Such a view fails to see that the question is not justification but description.

Without such a cross-cultural vision, Stackhouse argues we will be plunged into a Hobbesian world where all contend against all, a world in which only might makes right. Stackhouse thinks, however, we do not live in a world devoid of universal principles. Such principles are those found in democratically authorized constitutions, which Stackhouse believes to be the harbingers of the 'enormous transformation' the world is currently undergoing toward the creation of a 'universal civilization.'[12] Stackhouse argues that those who do not recognize the universality of such democratically authorized constitutions should be regarded as not yet fully rational or, worse, morally perverse. A surprisingly intolerant conclusion for someone so committed to tolerance.[13] Yet it is a conclusion that helps make intelligible my willingness to describe myself as a terrorist – from a perspective such as that of Stackhouse, people like me threaten the project to free the world of war because of our unwillingness to assume a universal stance.

Epistemological Crises and War

So how are we to go on? If we are to be 'responsible' must we be able to provide, as Stackhouse argues, an ethic of universal principles so that we can distinguish between war and terrorism? Or are we condemned, as I am alleged to be, to represent a 'local' or 'restricted' morality, even one called Christian, which cannot provide a basis for rational agreements so we might avoid war? I certainly do not think such an alternative to be our only choice, but to show why I will need to explore Alasdair MacIntyre's account of what he calls epistemological crises. In doing so I shall have to ask your patience as it may not be immediately clear how issues of war and terrorism (much less why I characterize my own position as one of Christian fanaticism) are clarified by what at first appears to be a way of understanding scientific disputes.

Terrorism is one of those descriptions that works within the practices of a community that make the question, 'What is wrong with terrorism?' distinctly odd. Torture works much the same way as do words like murder and, perhaps, abortion. That such words exist can give the impression that a universal ethic of principles exists to justify their use. But such descriptions as descriptions need no justification.

[12] Ibid. 863. Stackhouse develops this position in his, *Creeds, Society, and Human Rights: A Study in Three Cultures* (Grand Rapids: Eerdmans, 1984).

[13] The very day I was writing this paragraph I received my copy of *The New York Review of Books* XLIV, 1 (9 January 1997) which carried a review by William McNeill of Samuel Huntington's, *The Clash of Civilizations and the Remaking of World Order*. McNeill quotes Huntington to the effect that 'Western belief in the universality of Western culture suffers from three problems: it is false; it is immoral; and it is dangerous.' According to McNeill Huntington thinks it false because other civilizations have other ideals and norms; it is immoral because imperialism is the logical consequence of universalism; it is dangerous because such universalistic assumptions make war more likely. 'Decline of the West?', 18. Though I have other things to say, certainly Huntington has said some of what needs to be said in response to Stackhouse.

Yet by the time I am finished I hope to have shown you why MacIntyre's account is crucial for helping us recognize that nothing could be more rational than the peace it is our privilege and obligation to witness as Christians and why such a peace, from the world's perspective, may be thought to be a form of terrorism.

MacIntyre's account of epistemological crises is a correlative of his traditioned account of rationality. According to MacIntyre, it was the central aspiration of the Enlightenment to provide standards and rational justification that any rational person, that is a person independent of all social and cultural particularities, would or should accept without recourse to appeals to authority.[14] This ideal has been impossible to maintain because it has proved impossible to secure agreement on precisely those principles which were to be undeniable by all rational persons. Yet what is particularly troubling is that any attempt to provide an alternative account of rationality to that of the Enlightenment continues to be judged deficient by the failed standards of that same Enlightenment standard.

Yet MacIntyre argues that an alternative account of rational inquiry is possible as that 'embodied in a tradition, a conception according to which the standards of rational justification themselves emerge from and are part of a history in which they are vindicated by the way in which they transcend the limitations of and provide remedies for the defects of their predecessors within the history of that same tradition.'[15] Such a view of rationality is historical, since any attempt to justify it is to narrate how the argument has gone so far; accordingly, any subject needing justification is itself a concept with a history; which means that there can be no denial of the diversity of traditions of enquiry.

For those schooled on Enlightenment presuppositions this last point is particularly troubling. From such a perspective it is assumed that MacIntyre cannot avoid relativism and, in spite of his denials, may even advocate relativism.[16] Moreover this view it is alleged has disastrous political results because if there is no alternative to relativism then we are condemned to live in a world of war. Absent any way of securing agreements between people who otherwise share nothing in

[14] Alasdair MacIntyre, *Whose Justice? Which Rationality?* (Notre Dame: University of Notre Dame, 1988), 6.

[15] Ibid. 7. Not enough attention has been paid to the form MacIntyre's argument takes in this book. He cannot provide any argument to end all arguments with those who want to assume Enlightenment views since his own account of rationality can only be displayed. The narrative detail concerning the Scottish Enlightenment in the book is not MacIntyre simply showing he understands Stair, Hutchenson, and Hume, but rather is necessary for his defense of how rationality requires narrative.

[16] This charge simply will not go away no matter how many times the point is made that the very 'problem of relativism' has been created by the epistemological theories that claim to be our only hope against relativism. MacIntyre's account of relativism as an option that depends on the development of cosmopolitan cultures seems exactly right. Ibid. 389–403.

common other than their rationality, then it seems the only recourse for resolving disputes is war.

Yet MacIntyre argues that traditions may be able to resolve conflicts not only within the tradition itself but between traditions. In this respect, it is important to attend to the anti-Cartesian and anti-Hegelian aspects of MacIntyre's account of traditions. For MacIntyre, unlike Cartesians, assumes that traditions begin not from unassailable self-evident truths, but rather are contingent. Moreover, in contrast to Hegelian presumptions that each tradition must share with all other traditions some final rational state, for MacIntyre 'traditions are always and ineradically to some degree local, informed by particularities of language and social and natural environment, inhabited by Greeks or by citizens of Roman Africa or medieval Persia or by eighteenth-century Scots, who stubbornly refuse to be or become vehicles of the self-realization of *Geist*. Those educated or indoctrinated into accepting Cartesian or Hegelian standards will take the positivity of tradition to be a sign of arbitrariness. For each tradition will, so it may seem, pursue its own specific historical path, and all that we shall be confronted with in the end is a set of independent rival histories.'[17]

Yet this suggestion is belied by 'one particular kind of occurrence in the history of traditions' which MacIntyre calls 'epistemological crises.'[18] Such crises can occur in the history of particular persons, groups, and for a whole tradition. Indeed, such a crisis in a tradition may well find itself manifest in our inability to tell the stories of our lives with narrative coherence. To share a culture means we share schemata which are at once constitutive of and normative for intelligible actions – i.e., it means we can 'get' a joke. Yet it may happen that an individual may come to recognize the possibility of different possibilities of interpretation which present an alternative rival schemata of what is going on around him or her. MacIntyre suggests that Shakespeare's *Hamlet* exemplifies in the person of Hamlet as well as the question of how to interpret the play, *Hamlet*, the problem of having too many schemata for interpretation.[19] That such a crisis may occur does not mean it can always

---

[17] Ibid. 361. That a tradition is contingent, however, does not mean MacIntyre believes it impossible to arrive at first principles. Indeed, he believes Aquinas exemplifies how the articulation of such principles is possible. See MacIntyre's, *First Principles, Final Ends and Contemporary Philosophical Issues* (Milwaukee: Marquette University Press, 1990).

[18] MacIntyre first developed his account of epistemological crises in his 'Epistemological Crises, Dramatic Narrative and the Philosophy of Science,' *The Monist* 69, 4 (October 1977), 453–72. This essay has been reprinted in Stanley Hauerwas and L. Gregory Jones (eds.), *Why Narrative?: Readings in Narrative Theology* (Grand Rapids: Eerdmans, 1989), 138–57. References to this article will be to *Why Narrative?*.

[19] Ibid. 138–41. It is important to note that MacIntyre's account of epistemological crisis is not an invitation to resume the Enlightenment presumption that before we can know anything we must first have an account of how we know. As Nicholas Lash nicely puts the matter – epistemology is what we do when things go wrong: *The*

be resolved since it may, as it was in the case of Hamlet, make it impossible for him and/or us to understand what is going on around us. Such a lack of understanding may make it impossible for us to make our own lives intelligible and may even lead, as it did for Hamlet, to madness (or to the necessity to feign madness). Yet even that description may be too comforting since it assumes in such a situation we are able to distinguish normality from madness.

A new narrative is required for the resolution of an epistemological crisis. Such a narrative must enable the agent to understand both how they could have intelligibly held their former beliefs and how they may have been misled by them. When historically founded certitudes are rendered problematic, new concepts are required to enrich our schemes to furnish solutions to problems that seem intractable; an explanation must be given why the tradition had, before these new resources were available, seemed sterile or incoherent; and these tasks must be carried on in a fashion in which the new conceptual resources are seen in continuity with the tradition as articulated to that point.[20] MacIntyre suggests the way the Catholic doctrine of the Trinity was resolved in the fourth century is a good illustration for the resolution of an epistemological crisis. Aquinas providing the means in which Aristotle could be received into an Augustinian framework is, of course, MacIntyre's crucial exemplification of a successful resolution of an epistemological crisis.[21]

Relativism now appears as the doctrine that denies the possibility of epistemological crises occurring, but by the very fact that such crises occur we can now see that relativism as a position is a mistake. MacIntyre, however, is willing to concede to the relativist that over long periods of time rival traditions, both internally and in relation to one another, may develop without encountering more than minor epistemological crises. Yet when this happens such traditions will be unable to encounter their rivals in a way to defeat them.[22] Moreover,

---

Beginning and End of 'Religion' (Cambridge: Cambridge University Press, 1996), 112–16. It is not quite right to think an epistemological crisis always indicates something has gone wrong, but at the very least a crisis indicates some sense that we have a problem.

[20] MacIntyre, *Whose Justice? Which Rationality?*, 362.

[21] See in particular MacIntyre's account in his *Three Rival Versions of Moral Enquiry: Encyclopaedia, Genealogy, and Tradition* (Notre Dame: University of Notre Dame Press, 1990), 105–26. By focusing on these examples I do not mean to distract attention from the compelling examples that MacIntyre uses that come from the history of science. Yet one suspects that MacIntyre's account of epistemological crisis was first illumined for him from theology and, in particular, Newman. I mention this to suggest that inherent in MacIntyre's account of these matters is, I suspect, a very promising way to appreciate at once the difference and the similarity between the kind of knowledge gained through theology and that gained through science. Not the least result could be that the current prejudice against the former in favor of the latter might be challenged without recourse to Kuhn.

[22] MacIntyre, *Whose Justice? Which Rationality?*, 366.

there is nothing to prevent a tradition from degenerating into a self-contained enclave to avoid recognizing it is being put into question by rival traditions. 'This is,' MacIntyre observes, 'part of the degeneracy of modern astrology, of some types of psychiatric thought, and of liberal Protestantism.'[23]

MacIntyre's concession that for long periods of time traditions of very different kinds can co-exist without bringing their conflicts and disagreements to rational resolution makes clear that an epistemological crisis, while possibly quite painful, is even more importantly a great achievement. Our problem is not that Christians come into conflict with the world in which we live, but that we do not. Indeed, from this perspective war can now be seen as a failure to sustain the kind of conflict MacIntyre describes as an epistemological crisis – war is necessary when traditions are unable to recognize the crises they create for one another. This is not to deny that a war might be the form an epistemological crisis might take or that terrorism could be construed as a desperate way to force a conflict that is otherwise denied. Yet war and terrorism usually are not well known for providing 'conceptual schemes' which allow continuity with the past to be named.

Witness as Theological Terrorism

MacIntyre's account of epistemological crises is crucial if we are to avoid the unhappy choice between Stackhouse's appeal to universal principles and war. Moreover, if MacIntyre is right, then we can better appreciate why Christian non-violence cannot help but be seen from advocates of both those alternatives as a form of terrorism. For Christians have been sent out into a world of war to challenge the necessity of war armed only with the weapons of love. Put differently, that Christians are first and foremost called to be witnesses by necessity creates epistemological crises for those who do not worship the God of Jesus Christ. (Of course, I also want to create such a crisis for those who do worship Christ but think they can still participate in war.) Such crises may for long periods be irresolvable and the tension created tempt all involved to violence. That Christians must resist such temptations is not because such violence may not, at least for a while, seem to provide 'peace,' but because the peace provided is not the peace of Christ.

Christian witness so understood is particularly threatening to those that assume, like Stackhouse, that our only alternative to war and

---

[23] MacIntyre, in *Why Narrative?*, 147. MacIntyre no doubt takes great pleasure in providing these three candidates as examples of degenerate traditions. I only wish the list might be taken as a wonderful joke. However, I fear it is unfortunately all too true.

terrorism is to represent a universal alternative.[24] That narrative, in spite of its great desire for peace, cannot help but attempt to silence those who represent 'particularistic' traditions. 'Particularists,' particularly those who refuse to accept the marginalization offered by such universalists, cannot help but appear as fanatics and/or terrorists who threaten what appears to be our only hope for peace. From the perspective of liberal Christianity, Christians who insist on the 'politics of Jesus'[25] cannot but appear like Islamic fundamentalists – not a bad place to be from my perspective.

Witness can be understood as a universal imperative, but it is such as an expression of hope rather than an assured result. As Emmanuel Katongole observes, 'witness involves the affirmation of the hermeneutical significance of the presence of others. Because human beings are not accidentally culturally mediated, but necessarily so, truth does not come as a correspondence to an independently existing reality. Rather, truth is an interpretative performance realized through and within the cultural linguistic practice. This historical nature of truth mitigates against any epistemological singularity or self-sufficiency. Witness, as the form of contact between historically constituted traditions, affirms the realization that no one tradition is in possession of *the* truth. If that were the case, contact with other traditions would take the often preferred form of enforcement and imposition.'[26]

[24] It is my view that the significance of MacIntyre's argument in his *Three Rival Versions of Moral Enquiry* has yet to be appreciated. For what MacIntyre attempts in that book is to create an epistemological crisis for the encyclopedist and genealogist. The form MacIntyre's argument takes is as important as its content. Put simply, MacIntyre fights fair just to the extent his argument takes the form of a narrative that invites further response. MacIntyre's work, therefore, must have the same essential incompleteness he so insightfully suggests in *Three Rival Versions* (124) is the heart and soul of Aquinas' *Summa*.

[25] I am, of course, referring to the title of John Howard Yoder's *The Politics of Jesus* (Grand Rapids: Eerdmans, 1994). This is the second edition of the book that contains Yoder's update from the 1972 edition. For a wonderful attempt to work out the politics of a perspective like Yoder's within current discussions in political theory, see Thomas Heilke, 'On Being Ethical Without Moral Sadism: Two Readings of Augustine and the Beginnings of the Anabaptist Revolution,' *Political Theory* 24, 3 (August 1996), 493–517. Heilke develops the anabaptist practice of the ban as an alternative to the politics of violence. He notes such a 'politics' may not seem such to those who assume that the 'effort to sustain a hegemonic, territorial, sovereign entity, embodied in a physical collective of human beings and articulated to action for its own self-preservation' constitutes the only entity that deserves the name 'political' (513). Such a view of politics helps make clear why the church cannot help but appear as a threat to such 'politics' – the church is a polity that represents no such collective but is at once at home and not at home in all such politics. The church, like many terrorist organizations, can be understood as an international conspiracy against all politics based on 'self-preservation.'

[26] Emmanuel Katongole, *Particularity and Moral Rationality: Questioning the Relation between Religion and Ethics with Reference to the Work of Stanley Hauerwas* (PhD dissertation: Katholieke Universiteit, Leuven, 1996), 208–209. Katongole's claim

It is important to observe that witness in no way is meant to avoid the importance of argument. Yet to have an argument requires that Christians first listen to what the other has to say. Such listening, moreover, may well cause us to learn better what we have to say. Such listening may even create epistemological crises within Christian self-understanding. Yet that is the risk we must take, since our tradition is unintelligible if we fail to be witnesses for the peace that God has secured for the world in Jesus Christ. In that name and that name alone is at once the legitimation as well as the necessity of our witness.

Which finally must bring us back to questions of war and terrorism. Does the position I have tried to sketch in this paper mean Christians must finally accept the inevitability of war and, perhaps even, our inability to distinguish war from terrorism? I certainly see no reason why such a conclusion must follow from what I have said. Christian witness is an alternative to war just to the extent Christian witness establishes connections between those who have no reason to be connected. Such connections in themselves cannot insure peace because, contrary to liberal sentimentality that assumes if people only come to know one another better violence is less likely, the exact opposite may be the case. Rather, what is crucial are the narrative connections Christian witness makes possible, believing – as we do – that the story of Christ is the end of all stories.

Such connections, which I believe are but another word for church (for we must not forget the Christian word for universal is 'catholic'), give Christians the resources for distinguishing war from terrorism. For as the analysis above suggests, to be able to distinguish war from terrorism does not finally rest on conceptual distinctions, important as they are; but rather, through the sharing of stories we are enabled to

---

that truth does not come as a correspondence to an independent reality I take to be a rejection of crude correspondence theories of truth, that is, theories that MacIntyre characterizes as conceiving a realm of facts independent of judgement or of any other form of linguistic expression. MacIntyre rightly suggests that there is much to be said for correspondence theories and one understands that the relation between mind and its objects is given expression in judgements. See his *Which Justice? Which Rationality?* (Notre Dame: University of Notre Dame Press, 1988), 354–60. For a particularly strong defense of realism from an anti-foundational perspective, see Frederick Will, *Pragmatism and Realism* (Lanham MD: Rowman and Littlefield Publishers, 1997). Will says (36–37), 'Concepts and speech do not need extreme measures to introduce them to the world, they have the world as their home. We do not begin with language or thought apart from things or objects and then face the problem of how we manage to speak or think of these; they were there, engaged in and literally constitutive of practices from the start. Without them the practices would not exist.' Will later observes that because knowledge of objects is gained through practices, some philosophers conclude the artifacts are dependent on the practices themselves. Will pronounces, rightly, that such a conclusion is 'perverse' because 'cognitive practices are designed to discover and disclose objects, not to produce them' (104).

see that the children of my enemies are not my enemies. Such a 'seeing' is an achievement that requires the slow work of those who must learn to wait in a world of war, knowing as they do that God would not have God's kingdom accomplished through violence. Without such a fanatical people we literally would be without hope.

II

No Enemy, No Christianity: Preaching between 'Worlds'

I am just postmodern enough not to trust postmodern as a description of our times. The very description 'postmodern' cannot help but privilege the practices and intellectual formations of modernity. For example, calling this a postmodern age reproduces the modernist assumption that history must be policed by periods. Modernity creates something called the 'Middle Ages' which we all know can be safely left behind. The very description 'postmodern' is far too comforting, since it gives the illusion that we know where we are in contradiction to the postmodernist's epistemological doubt that such knowledge is unavailable.

Modernity was created by a deliberate rejection of the past, but ironically modernity is now our past. Accordingly, 'Postmodernity is still in the line of modernity, as rebellion against rebellion is still rebellion, as an attack on the constraints of grammar must still be written in grammatical sentences, as a skeptical argument against the structures of rationality must still be put rationally.'[1] As Reinhard Hütter observes, 'it belongs to the ironies of modernity that exactly those who are most modern increasingly claim postmodernity as modernity's most recent advance.'[2]

I confess that, as a theologian, I take perverse delight in the controversies surrounding postmodernism. Modernity, or at least the intellectual formations of modernity, sought to secure knowledge in the very structure of human rationality. Accordingly, God was relegated to the 'gaps' or denied altogether. Postmodernists are, thus, the atheists that only modernity could produce. Modernity said that God is a projection of the ideals and wants of what it means to be human so let us serve and worship the only God that matters – that is, the human. Postmodernists, in the quest to be thorough in their atheism, now deny that the human exists.[3]

[1] J. Bottum, 'Christians and Postmoderns,' *First Things* 40 (February 1994), 29.

[2] Reinhard Hütter, 'The Church as Public: Dogma, Practice, and Holy Spirit,' *Pro Ecclesia* 3, 3 (Summer 1994), 334.

[3] Bottum puts the matter well: 'The premoderns said that without God there would be no knowledge, and the postmoderns say we have no God and have no knowledge. The premoderns said that with the purposefulness of final causation, all things would

I do find it puzzling, however, to watch theologians, both conservative and liberal, come to the defense of the human, the rational, objectivity, the 'text,' 'moral values,' science, and all the other cherished conceits of the modern university in the name of 'humanism.' It is as if Christians have forgotten that we also have a stake in atheism. Christians do not believe in the 'human,' we believe in God – a God we believe, moreover, who intends to kill us all in the end. So we Christians do not oppose nuclear weapons because they threaten to destroy 'mother earth,' but because the God we serve would not have one life unjustly killed even if such a killing would insure the survival of the human species. Indeed, it is not clear that we Christians even know what the human species is or what status it may have since we have surer knowledge that we are creatures than that we are human.

Christians, therefore, have little stake in the question of whether we live in a postmodern time. For us, any divide in history, the way we tell the story of how we have come to the place where we are, requires a reading of God's providential care of God's creation through the people of Israel and the church. Israel and the church are not characters in a larger story called 'world,' but rather 'world' is a character in God's story as known through the story that is the church. Without the church there is no world to have a story. From my perspective, postmodernism but names an interesting set of developments in social orders that are based on the presumption that God does not matter.[4]

The imperialistic character of these claims for the significance of the church does not mean that it is unimportant for Christians to under-stand that peculiar development called modernity. Rather, as I just suggested, we must narrate the modern/postmodern divide on our terms. That, I fear, is what we have not done well in modernity. Christians' attitudes toward modernity have primarily been char-acterized by a sense of inferiority. As John Milbank observes, 'The

---

be equally valueless, and the postmoderns say there is no purpose and no value. The premoderns said that without an identity of reality and the Good, there would be no right and wrong, and the postmoderns say there is neither right nor wrong. Though they disagree on whether God exists, premoderns and postmoderns share the major premise that knowing requires His existence,' 'Christians and Postmoderns,' 29. Of course, in fact, as I am sure Bottum would acknowledge, one of the interesting aspects of many 'postmodern' intellectuals is their moral passion.

[4] For a similar account see Robert Jenson, 'How the World Lost Its Story,' *First Things* 36 (October 1993), 19–24. Jenson suggests, 'There is little mystery about where the West got its faith in a narratable world, neither is there much mystery about how the West has lost this faith. The entire project of the Enlightenment was to maintain realist faith while declaring disallegiance from the God who was that faith's object. Modernity was defined by the attempt to live in a universal story without a universal storyteller. The experiment has failed. It is, after the fact, obvious it had to: if there is no universal storyteller, then the universe can have no story line. If there is no God, or indeed if there is some other God than the God of the Bible, there is no narratable world' 21. My only difficulty with Jenson's account is that I doubt 'the West' has always been 'there.'

pathos of modern theology is its false humility.'[5] Our preaching and theology has been one ceaseless effort to conform to the canons of intelligibility produced by the economic and intellectual formations characteristic of modern and, in particular, liberal societies.

Christians in modernity thought their task was to make the Gospel intelligible to the world rather than to help the world understand why it could not be intelligible without the Gospel. Desiring to become part of the modernist project, preachers and theologians accepted the presumption that Christianity is a set of beliefs, a worldview, designed to give meaning to our lives. As a result, the politics of Christian discourse was relegated to the private in the name of being politically responsible in, to, and for liberal social orders.[6] We accepted the politics of translation believing that neither we nor our non-Christian or half-Christian neighbors could be expected to submit to the discipline of Christian speech.[7]

Ironically, the attempt to make Christianity intelligible often sought support from those philosophical and literary theories that attempted to protect discourse from translation – the most prominent example being new criticism. Under the influence of new criticism, some thought that Christianity could be conceived as a beautiful poem that is its own justification. Such a poem, of course, could and should illumine the human condition, but just to the extent that the poem provided such illumination, all attempts to make the poem 'do something' must

---

[5] John Milbank, *Theology and Social Theory: Beyond Secular Reason* (Oxford: Basil Blackwell, 1990), 1.

[6] Postmodern people are not necessarily post-liberal. Indeed, the great problem is that, given the lack of a definitive alternative to liberalism, too often postmodernism becomes but another form of liberalism. One of the wonderful things about the work of Stanley Fish is his unrelenting attack on liberalism. In particular, see 'Liberalism Doesn't Exist,' in his *There's No Such thing as Free Speech and It's a Good Thing Too* (Oxford: Oxford University Press, 1994), 134–38. As Fish puts the matter, 'A liberalism that did not "insist on reason as the only legitimate path of knowledge about the world" would not be liberalism; the principle of a rationality that is above the partisan fray (and therefore can assure its "fairness") is not incidental to liberal thought; it *is* liberal thought, and if it is "softened" by denying reason its priority and rendering it just one among many legitimate paths, liberalism would have no content. Of course it is my contention that liberalism doesn't have the content it believes it has. Rather it is a very particular moral agenda (privileging the individual over the community, the cognitive over the affective, the abstract over the particular) that has managed, by the very partisan means it claims to transcend, to grab the moral high ground, and to grab it from a discourse – the discourse of religion – that had held it for centuries' (137–38). The internal quote is by Stephen Carter, who is also the subject of Fish's critique.

[7] By the politics of speech, I mean something as simple as the description of my position as 'provocative.' 'Provocative' is one of the favorite words of liberals enshrining the politics of being willing to consider all views but to adhere to none. Provocative is the speech act of liberals that insures their ability to 'step back' from any engagement that might suggest they have a conviction that might make them intolerant. For an argument as to why a 'language in use' cannot be translated, see Alasdair MacIntyre, *Whose Justice? Which Rationality?*, 370–88.

be condemned as crass. Paul Tillich and Reinhold Niebuhr, in quite different ways, gave theological warrant to the high humanism intrinsic to the powerful set of suggestions associated with such formalist theories. What could be more comforting to the modern consciousness than to discover that 'ultimate concern' or 'sin' are essential and unavoidable characteristics of the human condition? You do not even need to go to church to learn that. Reading Shakespeare will do just as well, if not better.

The humanistic presumptions of new criticism nicely fit the aestheticism of the middle class that dominates Christianity in America – at least the Christianity that produces intellectuals like us. That is why I take it that contemporary preaching is still dominated by formalist presumptions, even if the preachers (or the teachers of homiletical theory) think they have theoretically left such theories behind. New critical habits are hard habits to break because they fit so well the class interests that dominate the seminary cultures in which most of us are located.

In particular, new critical assumptions hide from us how our theological presumptions are shaped by class interests. Frank Lentricchia, in his *Modernist Quartet*, makes the fascinating suggestion that the modernist writer defined himself against the standards of the mass market by becoming the champion of radical originality and the maker of a 'one-of-a-kind-text.' He observes, however, that 'the modernist desire in Frost and Eliot – to preserve an independent selfhood against the coercions of the market, a self made secure by the creation of a unique style – is subverted by the market, not because they wrote according to popular formulas, but because they give us their poems as delicious experiences of voyeurism, illusions of direct access to the life and thought of the famous writer, with the poet inside the poem like a rare animal in a zoo. This was the only commodity Frost and Eliot were capable of producing: the modernist phenomenon as product, mass-culture's ultimate revenge on those who would scorn it.'[8]

In like manner, the preaching and theology shaped by new critical presumptions to illumine the human condition hid from us that the human condition we were illuminating was that of the bourgeois. That is why the sermon meant to illumine our condition, which is often eloquent and profound, is also so forgettable and even boring. Insights about the human condition are a dime a dozen. Most days most of us would rightly trade any insight for a good meal.

The high humanism of contemporary theology and preaching not only hid the class interest intrinsic to such preaching, but also reinforced the presumption that Christians could be Christians without enemies. Christianity, as the illumination of the human condition, is not a

---

[8] Frank Lentricchia, *Modernist Quartet* (Cambridge: Cambridge University Press, 1994), 112–13.

Christianity at war with the world. Liberal Christianity, of course, has enemies, but they are everyone's enemies – sexism, racism, homophobia.[9] Yet liberal versions of Christianity, which can be both theologically and politically conservative, assume that what it means to be Christian *qua* Christian is to have no enemies peculiar to being Christian. Psalms that ask God to destroy our enemies and their children, such as Psalm 109, can appear only as embarrassing holdovers of 'primitive' religious people. Equally problematic are apocalyptic texts that suggest Christians have been made part of a cosmic struggle.

'Cosmic struggle' sounds like a video game the children of the middle class play. Most of us do not go to church because we are seeking a safe haven from our enemies; rather, we go to church to be assured we have no enemies. Accordingly, we expect our ministers to exemplify the same kind of bureaucratic mentality so characteristic of modern organizational behavior and politics. I sometimes think that there is a conspiracy afoot to make MacIntyre's account of the manager in *After Virtue* empirically verifiable.[10]

That the manager has become characteristic of liberal politics should not be surprising, but I confess I continue to be taken aback by the preponderance of such character types in the ministry. Of course, I should not be surprised that a soulless church produces a soulless ministry devoid of passion. The ministry seems captured in our time by people who are desperately afraid they might actually be caught, at one point or another in their ministry, with a conviction that might curtail future ambition. They therefore see their task as to 'manage' their congregations by specializing in the politics of agreement by always being agreeable. The preaching such a ministry produces is designed to reinforce our presumed agreements since a 'good church' is one without conflict. You cannot preach about abortion, suicide, or war because those are such controversial subjects – better to concentrate on 'insights,' since they do so little work for the actual shaping of our lives and occasion no conflict.

I confess that one of the things I like about the Southern Baptists (and many things about the Southern Baptists I worry about) is that they have managed to have a fight in public. At least fundamentalists believe they are supposed to have strong views, and they even believe they are supposed to act on their convictions. The problem with most of the mainstream churches is that we do not even know how to join an argument – better to create a committee to 'study the issue.'

If postmodernism means anything, it means that the comforting illusion of modernity that conflict is, can be, and should be avoided

---

[9] These are, of course, the enemies produced by the egalitarian presumptions of liberalism. They may be Christian enemies, but if they are, the narrative and practices that produce them are quite different and change how they are to be described.

[10] Alasdair MacIntyre, *After Virtue* (Notre Dame: University of Notre Dame Press, 1984), 73–76.

is over. No unbiased viewpoint exists that can in principle insure agreements. Our difficulty is not that we have conflicts, but that modern people have not had the courage to force the conflicts we ought to have had. Instead, we have comforted ourselves with the ideology of pluralism, forgetting that pluralism is but the peace treaty left over from past wars that now benefits the victors of those wars.

Hopefully God is using this time to remind the church that Christianity is unintelligible without enemies. Indeed, the whole point of Christianity is to produce the right kind of enemies. We have been beguiled by our established status to forget that to be a Christian is to be made part of an army against armies. It has been suggested that satisfaction theories of the atonement and the correlative understanding of the Christian life as a life of interiority became the rule during the long process we call the Constantinian settlement.[11] When Caesar becomes a member of the church the enemy becomes internalized. The problem is no longer that the church is seen as a threat to the political order, but that now my desires are disordered. The name for such an internalization in modernity is pietism and the theological expression of that practice is called Protestant liberalism.

In contrast, I am suggesting that our preaching should presume that we are preaching to a church in the midst of a war – a position you may find odd to be advocated by a pacifist. I hope the oddness, however, might encourage you to re-examine your understanding of Christian non-violence – which, if you were like me, was probably shaped by Reinhold Niebuhr. Who more than the Christian pacifist knows Christians are in a war against war? Moreover, as a pacifist, I do not need something called the human condition illumined when I am preparing to face the enemy. Rather, I need to have a sense of where the battle is, what the stakes are, and what the long-term strategy may be. Yet that is exactly what most preaching does not do. It does not help us locate our enemy, because it does not believe that Christians should have enemies. In the name of love and peace, Christian preaching has but reinforced the 'normal nihilism' that grips our lives. We have a difficult time recognizing the wars which are already occurring or the wars that should be occurring because we think it so irrational that some should kill others in the name of 'values.'

James Edwards has argued in his *The Plain Sense of Things: The Fate of Religion in An Age of Normal Nihilism* that nothing charac-terizes the nihilism that grips our lives better than the language of 'values.' Nihilism is not a philosophical conspiracy designed by Nietzsche and some French intellectuals to undermine the good sense of liberal Americans – indeed, Nietzsche was the great enemy of nihilism. Rather, nihilism is now become the normal condition of our lives to the extent

---

[11] Denny Weaver, 'Atonement for the Nonconstantinian Church,' *Modern Theology*, 6 (July 1990), 307–23.

that we all believe that our lives are constituted by what Edwards calls 'self-devaluating values.' All our values are self-devaluating because we recognize their contingency exactly to the extent that they are values. As Edwards puts it, 'normal nihilism is just the Western intellectual's recognition and tolerance of her own historical and conceptual contingency. To be a normal nihilist is just to acknowledge that, however fervent and essential one's commitment to a particular set of values, that's all one has: a commitment to a particular set of values.'[12]

Normal nihilism is not, however, a condition that grips only intellectuals, but rather forms everyone in liberal social orders. Edwards, for example, suggests that one could not want a better exemplification of normal nihilism than the regional shopping mall. In the mall, one not only sees alternative values tenuously jostling one another, but our very participation as consumers means we also indirectly act as the creator of those values. 'In air conditioned comfort one can stroll from life to life, from world to world, complete with appropriate sound effects (beeping computers; roaring lions). Laid out before one are whole lives that one can, if one has the necessary credit line, freely choose to inhabit: devout Christian; high-tech yuppie; Down East guide; great white hunter. This striking transformation of life into lifestyle, the way in which the tools, garments, and attitudes specific to particular times and places become commodities to be marketed to anonymous and rootless consumers: they are the natural (if also banal) expressions of our normal nihilism.'[13] Nihilism is the result of having so many compact discs from which to choose that, no matter which ones we choose, we are dissatisfied because we cannot be sure we have chosen what we really wanted.

The moral challenge is not consumerism or materialism. Such characterizations of the enemy we face as Christians are far too superficial and moralistic. The problem is not just that we have become consumers of our own lives, but that we can conceive of no alternative narrative. We lack the practices, and hence the imagination, that could make such a narrative intelligible. Put differently, the project of modernity was to produce people who believe they should have no

---

[12] James Edwards, *The Plain Sense of Things: The Fate of Religion in an Age of Normal Nihilism* (University Park PA: Pennsylvania State University Press, 1997), 47.

[13] Ibid. 50. The shopping mall is almost a perfect image to suggest Fred Jameson's analysis of postmodernism in his *Postmodernism: or, The Cultural Logic of Late Capitalism* (Durham: Duke University Press, 1991). As Jameson suggests, our postmodern condition is the phenomenon of late capitalism so 'if the ideas of a ruling class were once the dominant (or hegemonic) ideology of bourgeois society, the advanced capitalist countries today are now a field of stylistic and discursive heterogeneity without a norm. Faceless masters continue to inflect the economic strategies which constrain our existences, but they no longer need to impose their speech (or are henceforth unable to); and the postliteracy of the late capitalist world reflects not only the absence of any great collective project but also the unavailability of the older national language itself' (17).

story except the story they choose when they had no story. Such a story is called the story of freedom and is assumed to be irreversibly institutionalized economically as market capitalism and politically as democracy.[14] That story, and the institutions that embody it, is the enemy we must attack through Christian preaching.

I am aware that such a suggestion cannot help but be met with disbelief. You may well think I cannot be serious. Normal nihilism is so wonderfully tolerant. Surely you are not against tolerance? How can anyone be against freedom? Let me assure you that I am serious; I am against tolerance; I do not believe the story of freedom is a true or good story. I do not believe it is a good story, because it is so clearly a lie. The lie is exposed by simply asking, 'Who told you the story that you should have no story except the story you choose when you had no story?' Why should that story be determinative for your life? Simply put, the story of freedom has now become our fate.

For example, consider the hallmark sentence of the *Casey* decision on abortion – 'At the heart of liberty is the right to define one's own concept of existence, of meaning, of the universe, and of the mystery of human life.' Remember that was written by political conservatives. Moreover, it is exactly that view of freedom that John Paul II so eloquently condemns in the encyclical, *Veritatis Splendor*. A view of freedom, like that embodied in Casey, according to John Paul II, assumes we must be able to 'create values' since freedom enjoys 'a primacy over truth, to the point that truth itself would be considered a creation of freedom.'[15]

In contrast, John Paul II, who is not afraid to have enemies, reminds us that the good news of the Gospel, known through proclamation, is that we are not fated to be determined by such false stories of freedom. For the truth is that we are not free to choose our own stories inasmuch as we are God's good creation. Freedom lies not in creating our lives, but learning to recognize our lives as gift. We do not receive our lives as if they were a gift, but rather our lives are gift. We do not exist and then God gives us a gift, but our existence is gift. The great magic of the Gospel is providing us with the skills to acknowledge our life as

[14] For a more developed account, see my *Dispatches from the Front: Theological Engagements with the Secular* (Durham: Duke University Press, 1994). Edwards notes, 'The only stories available to us to explain the values we hold (or better, that hold us) are causal stories: stories told by intellectual historians or by psychoanalysts, not by theologians or philosophers. Under the compulsion of our carefully nurtured will to truth – our commitment to what Nietzsche calls "intellectual cleanliness" – we have lost our confidence in those metanarratives that promise us escape from contingency. And with that we also lost any sense of a genuine autonomy or self-possession' (47). This explains the peculiar combination in modernity of assertion in the autonomy of the individual with an equally strong sense that when all is said and done our lives are determined by forces we have not chosen. For my attempt to challenge the presuppositions that result in such an unhappy account, see my *Wilderness Wanderings: Probing 20th-Century Theology and Philosophy* (Boulder: Westview Press, 1997).

[15] This quote comes from paragraph 35 of the encyclical.

gift, as created, without resentment and regret. Such skills must be embodied in a community of people across time, constituted by practices such as baptism, preaching, and Eucharist, which become the means for us to discover God's story for our lives.

The very activity of preaching, that is, the proclamation of a story that cannot be known apart from such proclamation, is an affront to the ethos of freedom. As a church, we stand under the word because we know we are told what we otherwise could not know. We stand under the word because we know we need to be told what to do. We stand under the word because we do not believe we have minds worth making up on our own. Such guidance is particularly necessary for people like us who have been corrupted by our tolerance.

The liberal nihilists are, of course, right that our lives are contingent, but their account of contingency is unintelligible. Contingent to what? If everything is contingent, then to say we are contingent is simply not interesting. In contrast, Christians know their contingency is a correlative to our status as creatures. To be contingent is to recognize that our lives are intelligible only to the extent that we discover we are characters in a narrative we did not create. The recognition of our created status produces not tolerance, but humility. Humility derives not from the presumption that no one knows the truth, but rather is a virtue dependent on our confidence that God's word is truthful and good.

Ironically, if you preach with such humility in the world we currently inhabit you will more than likely be accused of being arrogant and authoritarian. To be so accused is a sign that the enemy has been engaged. After all, the enemy, who is often enough ourselves, does not like to be reminded that the narratives that constitute our lives are false. Moreover, you had better be ready for a fierce counter-offensive as well as be prepared to take some casualties. God has not promised us safety, but rather participation in an adventure called Kingdom. That seems to me to be great good news in a world that is literally dying of boredom.

God has entrusted us, God's church, with the best story in the world. With great ingenuity we have managed to make that story, with the aid of much theory, boring as hell. Theories about meaning are what you get when you forget that the church and Christians are embattled, in particular embattled by subtle enemies who win easily by denying any war exists. God knows what God is doing in this strange time between 'worlds,' but hopefully God is inviting us again to engage the enemy through the godly weapons of preaching and sacrament. I pray that we will have the courage and humility to fight the enemy, in Walter Rauschenbusch's wonderful words, with 'no sword but the truth.' According to Rauschenbusch, such truth:

> . . . reveals lies and their true nature, as when Satan was touched by the spear of Ithuriel. It makes injustice quail on its throne, chafe, sneer, abuse, hurl its spear, tender its goal, and finally offer to serve as truth's vassal.

But the truth that can do such things is not an old woman wrapped in the spangled robes of earthly authority, bedizened with golden ornaments, the marks of honor given by injustice in turn for services rendered, and muttering dead formulas of the past. The truth that can serve God as the mightiest of his archangels is robed only in love, her weighty limbs unfettered by needless weight, calm-browed, her eyes terrible with beholding God.[16]

May our eyes and our preaching be just as terrible. Indeed, may we preach so truthfully that people will call us terrorists. If you so preach you will never again have to worry about whether a sermon is 'meaningful.'

---

[16] Walter Rauschenbusch, *The Righteousness of the Kingdom,* ed. Max L. Stackhouse (Nashville: Abingdon Press, 1968), 92.

12

Christians in the Hands of Flaccid Secularists: Theology and 'Moral Inquiry' in the Modern University

On Being a Theologian and Ethicist with Two Stories

I am a Christian theologian who teaches ethics. I could alternatively say that I am a Christian ethicist, with the hope that most people would concentrate on the noun and not the qualifier but that probably wouldn't help matters much. In fact, many people have become and still do become Christian ethicists because they do not like theology. They think justice is something worth thinking about or even advocating or doing, but they do not like or they see little point in thinking about matters as obscure and seemingly as irrelevant as the Trinity. Such a deliberately non-confessional view of ethics, moreover, appears more acceptable in the modern university where it is generally thought to be a 'good thing' to study ethics, but it is not a good thing to be a theologian or to do theology. These days, theology just doesn't sound like a discipline appropriate to the university.

Yet I prefer to be a theologian. Or better, I simply cannot think of myself as anything but a theologian despite the fact that a theologian is not a good thing to be if you also want to be a respected academic. Yet being a theologian has become a habit for me that I cannot nor do I wish to break. I am also an ethicist, but I do not make much of that claim. (After all, 'ethicist' is such an ugly word.) Of course, there are also intellectual reasons why I do not desire to claim the title 'ethicist.' Quite simply, ethics too often names what many take to be the useful remains of past Christian practices and beliefs. Such a view of ethics serves liberal social orders well, but it distorts the character of Christian convictions. Accordingly, I have tried – through my teaching and my writing – to show that 'ethics' cannot and should not be abstracted from 'theology.'

Yet even given such an understanding of theology and ethics, it would be reasonable to assume that I might have some useful insights to offer about theology's contributions to the recent call for a renewal of moral inquiry in the contemporary university. After all, moral inquiry surely must be at the heart of what anyone does who teaches Christian ethics. That, however, is not the case. Why that is not the case involves a complex history of an equally complex interrelation of theology and the modern university, something I cannot fully develop here, but I can offer one or two cursory remarks.

At least part of that history is suggested by the phrase 'moral inquiry.' Of course, one should not read too much into a phrase; but then again grammar is not innocent. The use of the phrase 'moral inquiry' without any further qualification can misleadingly suggest that moral inquiry exists in and of itself and that it is, moreover, a 'good thing.' I do not believe, however, that moral inquiry *qua* moral inquiry or its close kin, critical intelligence, exist or even if they do exist – which they do not – that they are good things. Yet it is just such grandiose abstractions that are produced and reproduced by the knowledges that constitute the legitimating discourses of the modern university. Moreover, the presumption that the goal of the university is to sponsor such an unqualified account of moral inquiry is at least part of the reason why theology is no longer considered a legitimate university discipline.

First, two stories to set the stage for the other stories I have to tell. One day, out of the blue, I received a call for which academics live. It was from a senior editor of one of America's most prominent middle-brow magazines. He had just read my recent book, *After Christendom? How the Church Is to Behave If Freedom, Justice, and a Christian Nation Are Bad Ideas* and he said he liked it.[1] Not only did he like it, he thought it was time I wrote for his magazine. I could not believe it. No American theologian since Reinhold Niebuhr had written for such magazines. I thought I was about to become famous.

I recovered from my excitement just enough to ask how he had ever heard of me. It seems that he had gone to one of the very good small schools in the east. In an introductory course in modern theology he had read one of my books, was intrigued, and, even though he was not religious, he had made it a point to read my books ever since. Of course I was flattered and gratified. I had finally been discovered – and by the secular world no less. Indeed, he was interested in me because I was so unapologetically Christian.

How could I resist the invitation to write for his magazine under those conditions? I told him, however, I did not want to write an article that made me appear as a good Christian for the secularist – namely, the kind that criticizes Christianity in a way which only reinforces secular prejudices. Some Catholics have made careers for themselves by doing precisely that. Because they cannot say enough bad about the church, they are considered 'good Catholics' by *The New York Times*.

[1] Stanley Hauerwas, *After Christendom? How the Church Is to Blame If Freedom, Justice, and a Christian Nation Are Bad Ideas* (Nashville: Abingdon Press, 1991).

While I have plenty of criticisms of my own regarding the church, particularly liberal Protestantism, I was not about to write an article that was just another bashing of Christianity, even liberal Christianity. So I asked the editor to give me some time to think through the kind of article I might write and he readily agreed.

A few weeks later I called him to try out my initial idea. I said, 'I think I have a terrific title – "Christians in the Hands of Flaccid Secularists."' There was a long silence on the other end of the phone. I waited. Finally, 'That's interesting.' I said, 'You do not get it, do you?' 'Get what?' 'That the title is a play on Jonathan Edwards' famous sermon, "Sinners in the Hands of an Angry God."' 'I'm afraid I didn't read much nineteenth-century stuff.' At that point, I knew that this was not going to work. I told the editor, 'I do not know how to write even half-serious theology for people who no longer have sufficient knowledge to tell which God it is that they no longer believe in.'

That is the problem with modern atheism; it is just so uninteresting. Of course, we can hardly blame atheists for that, since Christians have for some time been offering atheists less and less to disbelieve. Believers and atheists too often come across as equally flaccid. The problem is how do you teach theology in universities to students who have been taught to think, like this bright young editor, that, in the name of being educated, all positions are 'interesting.' Theology for such people cannot help but be more 'information.'

Second story. In response to appointments in the English and Literature Departments at Duke, some of the Duke Faculty founded a chapter of the National Association of Scholars. They were concerned with what they understood to be the lack of scholarly objectivity among their ranks, not to mention the moral nihilism they alleged was intrinsic to this new breed of scholar. Matters got rather heated, with the usual mix of personality conflict becoming confused with intellectual issues. The Provost of the University thought it wise for some of us involved in the dispute to spend a day in a retreat getting to know one another. I should say that I was identified as one of the supporters, if not a representative, of the nihilistic barbarians the NAS meant to challenge.[2]

The day started by the Provost suggesting that we go around the table introducing ourselves and saying a bit about our field and our peculiar interests. As is usually the case, this proved to be extremely interesting, as you cannot help but be fascinated with the work of highly intelligent people – e.g., the botanist who spends her life trying to understand why markings on butterfly wings differ. She may be a member of the NAS, but what finally matters is her work. It happened that I was one of the very last of the group of about fifteen to speak. I

---

[2] For my critique of the NAS statement of purpose, see my *After Christendom*, 133–52.

thought to myself, 'How can I explain to someone who studies butterfly wings that I spend most of my time thinking about God?' Butterfly wings not only seem more interesting, but you also seem to know what you are doing when you are studying butterfly wings. I suspect, however, that this sense of 'knowing what you are doing' is found more among those who are external to such kinds of study than those who are actually engaged in the activity.

I thought all I could do was be honest. So I began by remarking that it was not clear that I should be among this group of academics, because I am not an intellectual. I am a theologian. Theology names an office of a community called the church and is in service to that community. So as one who occupies that office I am not free to think about anything I want to think about. Rather I am charged, for example, with the task of thinking about the Trinity and why Christians think their lives make no sense if God is not Triune. I observed it is, therefore, clear who I serve, but I would like to know who each of my colleagues around the table serve.

That question, I believe, is the hardest question facing those of us who find ourselves in the university. Moreover, our inability to answer that question is the reason we are equally uncomfortable with the question of the moral significance of what we do. We know that what we do is shot through with moral presuppositions that cannot help but shape ourselves and those we teach, but to acknowledge that invites conflicts between competing moralities, conflicts we fear not subject to resolution. The recent modern university managed to avoid such conflicts by maintaining, in one form or another, the ideology of 'knowledge for knowledge's sake.' But intellectual developments and changing demographics have shown us that this ideology is no longer a workable 'solution.' Yet we continue to take shelter in modernist notions of 'objectivity' in order to avoid questions of who we serve or what the university is meant to do.[3]

---

[3] John Patrick Diggins' account of Henry Adams wonderfully suggests the dilemma before the university. Diggins observes that 'although Adams found teaching a challenging vocation, he also felt that the purpose of education was not only to impart the facts of history but to interpret their meanings as well. Like the philosopher Charles S. Peirce, Adams sensed the dilemma of trying to teach when there are no truths to be taught. Thus Adams pondered the responsibilities of being in a position of intellectual authority and having nothing authoritative to say,' *The Promise of Pragmatism: Modernism and the Crisis of Knowledge and Authority* (Chicago: University of Chicago Press, 1994), 68. In the 'Conclusion' of *The Promise of Pragmatism*, Diggins praises Veblen, who long before Pierre Bourdieu and other French postmodernists 'exposed higher education as a system of status rivalry and class pretension, "a study of total depravity." But in the end Veblen failed and judged himself a failure. The indulgent America he found developing in the 1890s continued its "invidious distinction" between wealth and work in the 1990s, and higher education has become a cushy residence of bureaucratic administrations and sinecured professors – the leisure of the theory class' (469).

That is why the one question you cannot ask around the modern university is 'whom do we serve?' or 'what is the university for?' The easy answer, of course, is that the university has many purposes and serves many constituencies. So the university is simply one further example of American pluralist politics which is assumed to need no justification. You can probably get away with that answer as long as you have enough resources to spread the wealth. But as resources become scarce we begin to see that 'pluralism' hides the fact that some are more equal than others. Pluralist ideology tries to hide their inequalities because they lack moral and intellectual justification given the presumptions of liberalism.

I should like to think that theologians are particularly well positioned to join our colleagues in the university to think through these matters. I do not assume, of course, that even if we were able to 'think them through,' we would have resolved the fundamental challenge facing the university in this culture. For the decisive problem is the gulf between what we do in the modern university and why people support us in those activities.[4] To set aside some people who do nothing with their lives but think about the Trinity requires, first, that you have a people who live lives that would be unintelligible if God is not the Father, Son, and Holy Spirit. Such a people must think their lives *hinge* on Trinity. A tension always exists between such a people and those they set aside to be theologians.[5] But our current problem is not that kind of tension. Rather, our problem is we no longer have the practices that would make such a tension intelligible. The reasons why that is the case are complex but I at least now want to try to suggest how theology lost its servant status and accordingly became unintelligible.

---

[4] The growth and significance of medicine in the modern university, not to mention the allied sciences that allegedly support medicine, is a fascinating example of one place where there seems to be a close correlation between people's desires and the university. This contrasts sharply with the blatant lack of correlation between the practice of theology and the university. No one much cares whether a theologian may or may not be heretical, but people do care whether a physician is qualified. I tell my students that if you want to have some sense of what the politics of medieval Catholicism was like you need only hang around the major medical centers associated with universities. People no longer believe that their salvation depends on priests, but they sure as hell believe that they do not want to die and they think, usually quite unrealistically, that medicine can significantly prolong their life, which accounts for the enormous prestige and power of medicine and medical knowledge in the university. However, this prestige and power is just as likely to corrupt a flourishing intellectual life, which was the case in the past for theology, as it is to engender it.

[5] The problem for many of us today who would be or want to be theologians is that most Christians, particularly in the mainline Protestant denominations, couldn't care less that we think about the Trinity. In 'Christians in the Hands of Flaccid Secularists' I had planned to argue that one of the problems with these who trumpet Christianity as an alternative to secular presuppositions is that the Christianity they trumpet too often has little relation to Christian orthodoxy.

How Theology Managed to Become a 'Curiosity' in the University

In his article, 'On the Intellectual Marginality of American Theology,' Van Harvey observes that many American intellectuals regard theology as something 'akin to astrology.'[6] Even worse, Harvey observes that theology is thought to be not only obscurantist but divisive because it constitutes a threat to the common discourse on which our democracy rests. Yet he notes that even secularists might think theology something worth having around, if only to remind us of the contribution that Christian theology has had in the past, not to mention giving us a more sophisticated presentation of those who persist in being Christian. Without theology, Christians will only say what they believe crudely and dogmatically and thus be even less likely to make any significant contributions to the public discussion.[7]

The burden of Harvey's argument, then, is that the marginality of theology in the modern university is largely the fault of theologians. By their willingness to underwrite every new theological movement, Protestant theologians virtually destroyed theology as an intellectually respectable discipline. As a result, theology has no recognizable center that would enable one to discern the good from the bad. Theologians, like most Christians in a democratic culture, have an inordinate fear of being distinctive because people may otherwise think that we really do

---

[6] Van A. Harvey, 'On the Intellectual Marginality of American Theology,' in Michael Lacey (ed.), *Religion and Twentieth Century Intellectual Life* (Cambridge: Woodrow Wilson International Center for Scholars and Cambridge University Press, 1989), 172. Hereafter page references to Harvey's article will appear in the text.

[7] Brian Gerrish observes that 'the place of theology in the modern university can be defended only where its abdication as queen of the sciences is presupposed. Granted that Christian theology can no longer provide, as it did in the Middle Ages, the unifying principles of the entire system of human knowledge, can it nonetheless claim a legitimate, if humbler, place in the university? It may be that theology has its own small niche, along with other arts and sciences, in an academy that has become in principle more egalitarian. But it may also be that the ancient crown of theology has been quietly encased in the museum of history.' 'Ubi Theologia, Ubi Ecclesia?: Schleiermacher, Troeltsch, and the Prospect for an Academic Theology,' in Joseph Mitsuo Kitagawa (ed.), *Religious Studies, Theological Studies, and the University Divinity School* (Atlanta, Georgia: Scholars Press, 1992), 71. As will be clear, I take a more aggressive stance than either Harvey or Gerrish on behalf of theology and its role in the modern university. I do so not because I think theology should again try to be 'the unifying principle of the entire system of human knowledge.' I do not have any idea, given our current state of knowledge, what such an aspiration would mean. Yet I see no reason why theology should be 'humbled' in the university in principle since I refuse to accept the presumption that the material convictions that characterize the work of theology are epistemologically at a disadvantage in principle *vis-à-vis* other disciplines in the university. Gerrish observes that 'it is easy to see why the citizens of a secular and pluralistic university could still be anxious about the possibility of a divided loyalty. History has taught them that the church, when weary of argument, will reach for a stick' (73). To which I have two responses: (1) today the 'sticks' are certainly in quite different hands; and (2) since I believe that Christians must be non-violent, I am committed to waging the war peacefully but no less conflictually.

believe something is at stake in our being Christian. So theologians, in a vain attempt for acceptance, try as much as possible to make theology look like history, or sociology, or psychology, or some other acceptable university discipline. This seldom works since theology often imitates those disciplines in their weakest forms.

Harvey, I think, rightly suggests that the shovels theologians used to dig their own graves can be located in the 'professionalization' of divinity schools and the changing definition of the theologian's role. Drawing on Stephen Toulmin's account of a discipline as the intellectual side of a profession, as well as Burton Bledstein's *The Culture of Professionalism* – a book that maps the growth of, as well as the professionalization of, the university in the late nineteenth century – Harvey observes, 'Given this picture of the professionalization of the university in America and the scientific ethos that came to dominate it, a hypothesis regarding the causes of the marginality of theology immediately suggests itself: because the university became the institutional matrix for intellectual life in America, and because the ethos of the university was scientific and hostile to everything that did not lend itself to rational adjudication, theology was necessarily pushed to the margins of intellectual life. Because the universities provided the basis of cognitive authority and served the function of containing divisiveness, theology, resting as it does on religious faith and giving rise to controversy, was simply excluded from the university' (181).[8]

The only problem with this hypothesis, according to Harvey, is that it fails to account for the fact that since the early nineteenth century most of the theologians in this country have been located in divinity

---

[8] For a more complex account of the relation between Protestant Christianity and the university, see George Marsden, *The Soul of the American University: From Protestant Establishment to Established Nonbelief* (New York: Oxford University Press, 1994). Marsden's book is an interesting case study of the problem facing theology. He notes that the stance of 'methodological atheism' assumed by many Christians when engaged in their disciplines contributed to the loss of any sense that theological conviction might matter. Yet his book assumes just that stand; see, for example, my review of Marsden, 'Missing from the Curriculum: Review of George Marsden's *The Soul of the American University,' Commonweal* CXXI, 16 (23 September 1994), 19–20. Douglas Sloan has documented the inability of the Protestant mainstream to provide a compelling account of Christian convictions as a knowledge capable of attention in the university. Indeed, the very theologians who seemed to revitalize Protestant theology in the second half of this century – Paul Tillich, Reinhold Niebuhr, and H. Richard Niebuhr – in different ways underwrote what Sloan rightly characterizes as a two-realm theory of truth. That theory Sloan argues, could only end in the further marginalizing of theology from the university. According to Sloan, the two-realm theory juxtaposed the truth or science, that is, objective results obtained by discourses and empirical reason to truths of faith, religious experience, morality, meaning, and value. The latter are assumed to be grounded in feeling, ethical action, convention and 'common human experience.' Yet, as Sloan suggests, the latter knowledges are on the defensive in the modern university – and I might add, rightly so. Sloan's book is *Faith and Knowledge: Mainline Protestantism and Higher Education* (Louisville: Westminster/John Knox Press, 1994).

schools.[9] As a result, the above description of how theology became marginal fails to account for the way in which developments in theological disciplines themselves played an important role in theology's loss of credibility. In particular, the sickness of theology can be attributed to theology becoming almost totally oriented to the training of people for the ministry and the specializations that were assumed to be appropriate to that task. Such specialization resulted in theology losing its claim to be a knowledge that should matter outside seminary cultures.

In the late nineteenth century, seminaries, under the influence of Schleiermacher, divided their curriculum into four main parts: biblical studies, church history, dogmatics or Christian doctrine, and practical theology (183).[10] Such divisions only reinforced the assumption that theology was a subject-matter, like law and medicine, for professional training. Theology was no longer considered a subject having to do with the clarification of the faith of the ordinary believer and, as a result, could no longer be considered essential for, in the sense of being integral to, our culture or our politics.

Yet the 'retreat' to the seminary by no means meant that theology was made safe but irrelevant. Rather, theology passed through a great intellectual crisis precipitated, according to Harvey, by two autonomous but closely interrelated movements: 'the rise of biblical criticism, especially of the New Testament, and the criticism of speculative metaphysics and theology proposed by Kant' (186). In the immortal words of Ernst Troeltsch, 'give the historical method an inch and it

---

[9] Bruce Kuklick observes, 'when theology withdrew from the center of the college to a professional school, at the margin of the academic community, the tiny but growing American university weakened its continuity with the past and the tradition of classical learning. In the ancient universities, theology had been responsible for animating schools of higher learning with a sense of their comprehensive calling. The professionalization of theology in the United States was thus an early and potent symbol of the fragmentation of knowledge and culture.' *Churchmen and Philosophers: From Jonathan Edwards to John Dewey* (New Haven: Yale University Press, 1985), 87.

[10] Harvey is summarizing Edward Farley's analysis of this development in his *Theologia: The Fragmentation and Unity of Theological Education in America* (Philadelphia: Fortress Press, 1983). Schleiermacher basically followed Kant by arguing that the faculties of medicine, law, and theology were justified within the universities not because they were sciences but because they were of service to the state. Thus the study of theology was justified because it served the needs of the public who were understood to have religious needs. Harvey notes that there was a fatal flaw in this argument when brought to the United States, as the same argument that was used to justify theology in Germany could be used to exclude theology from the university in America. Alasdair MacIntyre's account of the exclusion of theology from English universities in the name of creating 'unconstrained agreements' is another fascinating aspect of this story. See his *Three Rival Versions of Moral Enquiry: Encyclopedia, Genealogy, and Tradition* (Notre Dame: University of Notre Dame Press, 1990), 216–36.

will take a mile. From a strictly orthodox standpoint, therefore, it seems to bear a certain similarity to the devil.'[11]

That was not, however, the way the matter was first seen. Rather, many thought history was the way theology was to regain intellectual and moral force, not only in the university but in America as a whole. No one better exemplified this attitude than Walter Rauschenbusch, the great representative of the Protestant social gospel, in an essay called, 'The Influence of Historical Studies on Theology.'[12] Rauschenbusch begins his article by observing that the dominance of historical studies in the theological curriculum is only very recent. In the Middle Ages systematic theology dominated, but, since the Reformation, theology became the study of the Bible.[13] History entered with exegesis, yet, according to Rauschenbusch, it would be a mistake to limit the significance of history to the study of the Bible. For history has an essential place in all theological sciences, since it 'irrigates and fertilizes all other departments.' Rauschenbusch observes that just as a biblical book gets its significance 'only in connection with its historical environment, so any interpretation will be more penetrating and fruitful the more the interpreter knows of contemporary history.'

Of course, Rauschenbusch's use of the phrase 'contemporary history' is ambiguous. It can mean either the history that we are currently experiencing or the way we now do history. Rauschenbusch probably conflated both meanings since he believed that the development of 'scientific history' was an advance peculiar to our living in a 'modern time.' He asserts that 'human life is continuous, and a subsequent period of history is always the most valuable interpreter of an earlier period.' That is why history is a moral science for Rauschenbusch, since it allows us to recover the 'real' intent of the prophets and Jesus without the qualifications of later developments. Lyrically he exclaims, 'When we have been in contact with the ethical legalism and the sacramental superstitions of the Fathers, we feel the glorious freedom and the pure spirituality of Paul like a mighty rushing wind in a forest of pines. When we have walked among the dogmatic abstractions of the Nicene age, the Synoptic Gospels welcome us back to Galilee with a new charm,

---

[11] Ernst Troeltsch, 'Historical and Dogmatic Method in Theology,' in James Luther Adams and Walter Bense (trans. and eds.), *Religion in History* (Minneapolis: Fortress Press, 1991), 16. For a helpful account of Troeltsch's attempt to amend Schleiermacher's understanding of the role of theology in the university, see Gerrish, 'Ubi Theologia, Ubi Ecclesia?', 75–83.

[12] Walter Rauschenbusch, 'The Influence of Historical Studies on Theology,' *The American Journal of Theology*, 2 (January 1907), 111–27.

[13] Rauschenbusch's suggestion that systematic theology dominated the Middle Ages is an extraordinary misreading. No medieval theologian would have had the slightest idea what systematic theology might be. Aquinas thought his theological work was primarily to be found in his commentaries on Scripture. Systematic theology, in other words, was primarily the creature of Protestant scholasticism combined with the presuppositions of German idealistic philosophy.

and we feel that their daylight simplicity is far more majestic and divine than the calcium light of the creeds.'[14]

According to Rauschenbusch, the sense of continuity and development characteristic of historical studies is essential for all theological sciences. Indeed, 'it is interesting to imagine how the course of Christian history would have been changed if the leaders of the early church had only had a modern training in history.'[15] In effect, that was the great insight of the Reformers as they appealed to original historical sources against the falsifications and legends produced by the church. The scientific study of history is the necessary means for training the scientific temper and critical faculty of theologians. Ancient and medieval civilizations had no 'real' natural science or training in historical criticism and consequently theology was dogmatic and credulous. Fortunately, we are obviously not so limited, benefiting as we do from the development of modern history over the last century. For, as Rauschenbusch reminds us, 'modern history is only about a hundred years old; its mission is only begun.'[16]

I have taken the time to summarize Rauschenbusch's article because it remains so relevant. Most people in theology or the academic study of religion would find Rauschenbusch's progressivist assumptions embarrassing, but they continue to assume accounts of the importance of history not unlike his. These are habits that constitute the working assumptions of theologians not easily left behind. Just to the extent that theology can become history, it has a chance of being a respectable discipline within the university. To question the importance of history for theology would be equivalent to questioning Rauschenbusch's presumption that Protestantism is superior to Catholicism. Of course, most religious thinkers or academics who think about religion no longer have any good reason to believe in the superiority of Protestantism, so history is simply privileged as a challenge to what they take to be a Catholic understanding of truth. History was – and for many still is – the way Protestants displaced Catholicism while no longer believing what the Reformers believed.

Yet Troeltsch was right that history could not be put to such service without changing the very subject-matter of theology. According to Troeltsch, history requires three essential aspects: 'the habituation on principle to historical criticism; the importance of analogy; and the mutual interrelation of all historical developments.'[17] The first of these requires that all judgements in the realm of history are at best judgements of probability. 'It is obvious that the application of historical

---

[14] Ibid. 115. As I hope is obvious, Rauschenbusch used history as a critique of Catholicism with its 'magical' assumptions about sacraments and its hierarchical church government.

[15] Ibid. 117.

[16] Ibid. 126.

[17] Troeltsch, 'Historical and Dogmatic Method in Theology', 13.

criticism to religious tradition must result in a profound change in one's inward attitude to it and in one's understanding of it.'[18] Analogous occurrences are the key to historical criticism, since analogical comparisons require the presumption that history is generally both consistent and repeatable. Troeltsch rightly saw no reason to exclude Jesus or Jesus' resurrection from this principle.

Accordingly, all you have left is to try to make Christianity intelligible within the confines of the historical developments we now call Western civilization. No longer can or does the theologian try to make a case for God, since the metaphysics necessary for such a venture is allegedly defunct and any claims about revelation cannot be considered given the epistemological constraints that form the modern university. So all that is left for theology is to become 'a phenomenology of the collective consciousness of a determinative religious community.'[19] Theologians, particularly as New Testament scholars and church historians, can no longer study the Resurrection as if Jesus might have actually been raised, but now they study the beliefs and behaviors of people who believed in the Resurrection.[20]

It is my hope that this analysis of the marginalization of theology in the modern university illumines why theologians are hesitant about drawing any moral implications from their work. This is particularly true of those who find themselves in university departments of religious studies. Such departments are often comprised of people who are willing to study a religion on the condition either that it is dead or that they can teach it in such way as to kill it.[21] The last thing they would want

---

[18] Ibid. 13.

[19] Harvey, 'On the Intellectual Marginality of American Philosophy', 189.

[20] There are actually some good reasons why this way of working is not necessarily antithetical to a Christian understanding of truth, given that our faith depends on the testimony of reliable witnesses. Of course, that does not mean that Christians believe any less in the miracles that those witnesses report. For a wonderful account of the philosophical status of testimony, see Alasdair MacIntyre, 'Hume, Testimony to Miracles, the Order of Nature, and Jansenism' in J. J. MacIntosh and H. Meynell (eds.), *Faith, Skepticism and Personal Identity* (Calgary: University of Calgary Press, 1994), 83–99.

Moreover, if as John Milbank maintains, there can only be a science of the particular, then history, 'written history, which produces exceptions to the supposed universal rule; lived history, which permits us always to enact the different,' is theology's ally! See his *Theology and Social Theory* (Oxford: Basil Blackwell, 1990), 260.

[21] For a more extended set of similar *ad hominem* comments on the contemporary study of religion, see my 'A Non-Violent Proposal for Christian Participation in the Culture Wars,' *Soundings* LXXV, 4 (Winter 1992), 477–92. For a very helpful account of the current similarities and differences between the free-standing seminary, university diversity, schools and departments of religious studies in colleges and universities, see Joseph Kitagawa's, 'Introduction' to Joseph Mitow Kitagawa (ed.), *Religious Studies, Theological Studies and the University – Divinity School* (Atlanta, Georgia: Scholars Press, 1992), 1–36. Kitagawa observes that the lack of a clear self-understanding of the objective, scope, perspective, and methodology of religious studies leads some to conclude that almost any approach to religion – psychological, sociological, ethical, philosophical,

to acknowledge is that they might actually practice what they teach, because such an acknowledgment might suggest that they are less than 'objective.' Of course, that is why theology is not seen as an appropriate discipline in most departments of religion. To be sure, such departments may think it important to study the practice and faith of such figures as Thomas Aquinas, Maimonides, al-Farabi, or Karl Barth, but they would not think it appropriate to hire such people to teach in a department of religious studies.[22]

Yet ironically many of these departments continue to think it important to teach 'ethics.' That they do so is partly the result of a tradition begun by Walter Rauschenbusch and carried on by Reinhold and H. Richard Niebuhr, Paul Ramsey, James Gustafson and a host of others. Rauschenbusch, of course, wrote unembarrassedly of Christianizing the social order,[23] but such a sentiment would be thought outrageous by most currently working in the 'field' of Christian ethics. Under the influence of Reinhold Niebuhr, Christian ethicists began to talk more of love and justice as the building of social ethics. Matters more strictly theological could be left in the background.

James Gustafson has observed that many people who are now writing in the area generally known as 'applied ethics,' e.g., medical ethics, business ethics, environmental ethics, are often people with theological

---

and even 'semi-theological' – is 'tolerated in religious studies, as long as it avoids such non-academic religious features as faith, piety, and truth-claims' (7). Yet Kitagawa documents that there are 'fuzzy edges' between the sites for the study of religion and theology. In particular, scholars at free-standing, church-oriented divinity schools often pursue the same intellectual agendas determined by departments of religious studies with the result that those they train for the ministry are not prepared well for that task. Of course, it is a mistake to assume that theology gains its purpose from training people for the ministry. All the essays in this volume are important for helping us to understand better the role of theology in the current university. Joseph Hough, Jr's essay, 'The Marginalization of Theology in the University,' is particularly important. Hough suggests that at least one of the justifications for theology in the university is the contribution that theology can make to the 'common discourse' of the university. I would be sympathetic to that justification if I thought that the university had a 'common discourse.' The association of theology with the task of training people for the ministry is largely an accident of history, not something intrinsic to the service that theology is to render to the church.

[22] It would take me too far afield to look at the development of religious studies as an alternative to theology. Suffice it to say that religious studies departments as they developed after 1950 usually assumed the fourfold structure of the Protestant seminary. This was usually found to be unsatisfactory since not appropriate space was given to Judaism, Islam, and the so-called Eastern Religions. So departments felt the need to become more 'pluralistic,' but too often such pluralism lacked any intellectual rationale. Some tried to make something of 'religion,' but no definition or phenomenology of religion has been found to pass muster. Nor has there been any agreement about what kind of methodology is most appropriate to the subject-matter of most departments though as I suggested above the primary methodology tends to be historical.

[23] Walter Rauschenbusch, *Christianizing the Social Order* (New York: The Macmillan Company, 1921).

training.[24] Yet he notes that whether theology has anything to contribute to these areas is less than clear. For a few, such as Paul Ramsey, the theological authorization for the ethical principles theologians use is explicit, but 'for others, writing as "ethicists," the relation of their moral discourse to any specific theological principles, or even to a definable religious outlook is opaque. Indeed, in response to a query from a friend (who is a distinguished philosopher) about how the term "ethicist" has come about, I responded in a pejorative way, "An ethicist is a former theologian who does not have the professional credentials of a moral philosopher."'[25]

In fact, many who were once Christian ethicists now describe themselves as 'religious ethicists' though it is by no means clear to what the adjective 'religious' refers. My own view is that the term 'religious' works primarily as a distinguishing disciplinary marker for those who work within the university, i.e., those who do 'religious ethics' may be able to get a job in a religious studies department, but they certainly will not find a place within a philosophy department.[26] 'Religious' also is necessary as a generic term, since many of the issues addressed in these areas involve the development of policy that makes any particularistic identifications a matter of embarrassment. If Christian ethicists are to be players within the constraints of a liberal social order for the formulation of public policy, then the 'Christian' qualifier must be suppressed.

Christian ethics, a discipline one would assume to be committed to moral inquiry, turns out to be quite deceptive. Just to the extent that most people in the field are willing to make normative recommendations, they do so not as Christian theologians, but as 'ethicists.' As a result, courses in Christian ethics, if they are taught at all, increasingly appear like philosophy courses helping students to distinguish between meta-ethics and normative ethics for the purpose of helping the student

---

[24] James Gustafson, 'Theology Confronts Technology and the Life Sciences,' *Commonweal* 105, 12 (16 June 1978), 386. For a wonderful critique of the very idea of 'applied ethics,' see Alasdair MacIntyre, 'Does Applied Ethics Rest on a Mistake,' *The Monist* 67 (1984), 498–513.

[25] Gustafson no doubt feels some ambiguity in making this criticism, since, in doing so, he is criticizing many of his own students. That a good number of Gustafson's students are ambivalent about theology's relation to ethics should not be surprising, given the fact that Gustafson has authored a volume entitled, *Can Ethics Be Christian?*, a title that certainly gives something less than a resounding affirmative answer to the nature of that relation. I should also say that Gustafson is my teacher as well, one to whom I owe everything, including our considerable theological differences.

[26] For a devastating critique of the notion of religion see Talal Asad, *Genealogies of Religion: Discipline and Reasons of Power in Christianity and Islam* (Baltimore: Johns Hopkins University Press, 1993). Asad observes, 'the suggestion that religion has a universal function in belief is one indication of how marginal religion has become in modern industrial society as the site for producing disciplined knowledge and personal discipline' (46).

whether they should be primarily utilitarians or deontologists. So ethics becomes a further clarification of the students' 'values' under the assumption that the clearer they are about their values the better chance they have to be morally good – an assumption, of course, that cannot stand much philosophical interrogation. Of course, if all other justification for teaching ethics fails, the 'ethicist' can always claim to teach the history of Christian ethics. In doing so, they can introduce students to important subjects such as just-war theory or past understandings of the Christian's relation to the state. The clever students, if they are so inclined, might use such courses as aids in forming their own moral judgements, but that is the student's own business and should not be the object of the course. So ends the story of how teaching theology in the modern university has come to an end.

The Difference God Makes

Given the character of the modern university, the subsequent nature and 'place' of theology and/or religious studies, the kind of students that come to the university, and the practices that produce those students, I think there is nothing we can do that is more morally important than to be what we were trained to be – theologians. Our task is very simple: to show the difference that God makes about matters that matter. Fortunately, this is not a self-generative project, for as a Christian theologian I am not required to be creative. Theologians are to be faithful, believing as we do that our faith has been handed on to us by our mothers and fathers through the ages. So my first task as a theologian is to direct my students to those witnesses whose lives shine more brightly than mine ever could.

I am aware that such an understanding of 'moral inquiry' will seem quite offensive to many who want to recommend a return to 'moral inquiry' in the university. When I taught at the University of Notre Dame, one of my best friends was a biologist who was Jewish. His family was Reform and fairly observant. Walking across campus one day, I observed that it must be about time for his oldest son's bar mitzvah. He said he was not going to have a bar mitzvah, preferring to let his son 'make up his own mind' when he was older. I exploded, asking how could he want to let his son make up his own mind in the face of the thousands of Jewish martyrs who died at the hands of Christians' persecution. I said at least raise your son as an atheist, as that would suggest you have some convictions. He had his son's bar mitzvah.

In like manner, I cannot conceive of what it would mean to teach theology as if God did not matter. Of course, there are pedagogical issues that should not be avoided. I teach primarily in a divinity school that is part of a university. Undergraduates take my divinity school courses, but I do not change my courses to accommodate their presence.

I assume that most of them are Christians, though one Jewish student, as a result of one of my courses, decided to become a rabbi. If I were to teach an undergraduate course, I would not be less 'theological,' but I would not teach the course the same way I teach a course for those preparing for the ministry. Indeed, part of the course would involve them in trying to understand why teaching a course in Christian theology is a problematic undertaking in the contemporary university.

Yet pedagogy should not determine what is taught. You cannot teach about God as if God does not matter, anymore than you can raise a child as a Jew as if going through bar mitzvah does not matter. What is crucial is that the course be taught with the intellectual seriousness commensurate with its subject. Challenges, such as Troeltsch's understanding of history, must be met. The displacement of religious practice into the realm of the private by the political arrangements of liberalism must be located and critiqued. The liberal production of 'ethics' as an autonomous subject must be questioned and conceptual alternatives suggested.

Providing such alternatives has been the focus of much of my own work. To expose the moral practices intrinsic to theological convictions requires the display of conceptual resources that, at least until very recently, were largely ignored in ethical theory. Much of my work has involved the attempt to recover the importance of the virtues and correlative account of practical rationality, the role of narratives and practices for the display of morally worthy lives, and what kinds of communities are necessary to sustain such lives. Much of this work, I would hope, can be and even should be of interest to many who do not share my theological convictions. Yet for me such work is finally to be judged by whether it serves to help me better understand the God Christians worship and the difference that that worship should have for our lives.

All of this requires hard intellectual work that I confess, given my own abilities, dwarfs me. Yet I think that not to try, even in the rather foreign territory theologians today must work, would be cowardly. Moreover, it is just so much fun to be a theologian for the simple reason that nothing could be more interesting than God. One of the great advantages for those of us who would teach theology in the current university is that we are finally free. When universities were explicitly if vaguely Christian, theology taught in the candid manner I am advocating could not be free, since theology was to be done in a manner that underwrites the presumption that the way things are is the way things are supposed to be. But Christians are no longer in power, at least they are not in power as Christians, so we can now take the risk of teaching theology, if we are able, as edification. The problem, given recent intellectual developments, is not that theology is a problematic subject for the university, but that those of us who teach theology do so in such unimaginative ways.[27]

I am not suggesting that the classroom is the place to make Christians. The classroom is a far too coercive context for that. My reservations in this respect do not arise because I believe in academic freedom or even in the right of the student to 'make up their own minds.' My concerns are theological, since I believe that non-violence is intrinsic to Christian convictions about Jesus' cross and resurrection. The presentation of those convictions in a violent manner would therefore belie the character of God and thus be a theological mistake.

Christian theology, after all, is finally reflection on the stories of God found in the Christian Scriptures and developed through the traditions of the church. Christians do not have a 'morality' per se, but rather our morality is embedded in the stories that require constant retellings. Telling a story, particularly stories like those Christians tell of God's dealings with them, is a frightening business since in the tellings one frequently has the story retold in a manner that is surprising and challenging to the teller. That is one reason violence is antithetical to the telling since the very character of the story requires the Christian to be open to such retellings.

Therefore, when Christian theology is taught in the university, that teaching must include a presentation of the extraordinary diversity of the 'tellings' that have been part of Christian history. Such a presentation is not simply 'historical,' but rather the moral enterprise intrinsic to the story itself. For the story requires that the diversity of gifts that have been present throughout Christian history in order to appreciate that the nature of the God Christians worship is known only through those diverse witnesses. So, for example, as a Christian committed to non-violence, I must also tell of those Christian lives who thought that they were obligated to kill, that injustice not be allowed to flourish.

So to teach Christian theology requires that the student be initiated into an ongoing conversation across the centuries to better know how to worship the God of Jesus Christ. Indeed, as Robert Orsi reminds me, ethics is a performance, a conversation, whose form cannot be separated from the material convictions that conversation embodies. The story theology seeks to tell requires an enactment commensurate with its content. So if the student is to be initiated into the practice of non-violence, how that is done makes all the difference.[28]

---

[27] I suspect that the best theology being done in universities today is done in subjects that are not seen as theology. That is perhaps the way it should be.

[28] I am indebted to Dr Robert Orsi of Indiana University for a wonderful commentary on this paper at the colloquium sponsored by the Wilson Center on the Revival of Moral Inquiry in the University for which this paper was prepared. Orsi pointed out to me that the two stories at the beginning of my paper, as well as the story involving my Jewish colleague at Notre Dame, were conversation stoppers. I certainly did not mean for my questions at the meeting I described with my colleagues at Duke to be a

But why would any university, particularly secular universities, want the discipline of theology represented in the curriculum? There can, in principle, be no answer to that question, since the question will be a different question given the differences between universities. Indeed, I take it to be one of the illusions of the current academy that some universal called 'the university' exists 'out there' and that it is the aim of each university to try, to a greater or lesser extent, to embody it. What I believe can be said, however, is that any university devoid of serious theological discourse will lack a resource that may make some contribution to lessening the moral impoverishment of all of our lives but, in particular, the lives of our students.[29]

conversation stopper but rather one that advanced the conversation. However, I certainly can see how my reaction to the young editor, as well as my response to my Jewish colleague could be seen as attempts to stop the conversation. Indeed, I think, on reflection, I did not respond as well as I should to the young editor. What is important to see, however, is that Orsi's reactions help me understand the power of such narratives and how important it is to tell them well. I am in his debt.

[29] I am indebted to Professor Owen Flanagan, Dr Jim Fodor, and Dr Scott Saye for their criticism and help with this essay.

13

Christian Schooling
or
Making Students Dysfunctional

An Address for the Opening of the School Year
at King College (Bristol, Tennessee)

We assume, that is, those of us privileged to make up the modern university, that truthful knowing requires freedom. Accordingly academic freedom is assumed to be the hallmark of the contemporary university. Yet I do not believe that freedom – particularly the kind of freedom celebrated in liberal cultures like our own – is the necessary condition for truthful inquiry. Nor do I think academic freedom to be the defining mark for the university – particularly universities that would be Christian. Christian inquiry aimed at knowing more truthfully the world presumes that such truth results not from unconstrained freedom but from our being made part of a people who possess the skill to name lies as lies.

Christian thinking about the relation of truth and freedom should begin with texts like Colossians 2:8–15 – a good text, I think, for the beginning of a school year.

> See to it that no one takes you captive through philosophy and empty deceit, according to human tradition, according to the elemental spirits of the universe, and not according to Christ. For in him the whole fullness of deity dwells bodily, and you have come to fullness in him, who is the head of every ruler and authority. In him also you were circumcised with a spiritual circumcision, by putting off the body of the flesh by the circumcision of Christ; when you were buried with him in baptism, you were also raised with him through faith and power of God, who raised him from the dead. And when you were dead in trespasses and the uncircumcision of your flesh, God made you alive together with him, when He forgave us all our trespasses, erasing the record that stood against us with its legal demands. He set this aside, nailing it to the cross. He disarmed the rulers and authorities and made a public example of them, triumphing over them in it.

As modern people we have to confess that we are not quite sure what to do with language about 'the powers' and/or 'elemental spirits of the universe.' If any language in the New Testament needs demythologizing we think it must be language like that. 'Elemental spirits' sounds like figures from 'Dungeons and Dragons' or some fantasy game. The idea that 'elemental spirits' might still be lurking around we find hard to believe, particularly if we are in the process of being educated. After all, is not education the means we use to free ourselves from false notions?

Yet it is just a presumption that makes the language of the powers so crucial for helping us understand why the kind of schooling we receive as Christians is quite different than secular schooling. What it means to be free as a Christian is to be free from being determined by the modern notion that education can free us from the powers and elemental spirits of the universe. Put simply, the kind of education as professors we represent and as students you receive is exactly what Paul would identify as an 'elemental spirit,' a 'power!'

To be sure, those powers, though fallen, are and remain God's good creation. But exactly because they are part of God's good creation their perversion is all the more dangerous. For example, the most determinative evil that we do to one another is usually done in the name of a good. 'We had to drop the atomic bomb to save lives' is one of the best examples I know of what it feels like to be in the grip of such powers. For Christians to be free means that through Christ we have been given the means to resist such necessities.

For us, that is, for those of us who no longer believe in the powers, except as metaphors, nothing makes us more captive to just those same powers than the language of freedom. We think our task is to be free to be what we want even if we think what we want is to be Christian. As a result, we fail to see that nothing is more destructive, nothing makes us less free, than to have to do what we want to do. Indeed, I can think of no better description of hell than the condition of always having to do what I want to do.

As a way to challenge such a view of freedom, I start my classes by telling my students that I do not teach in a manner that is meant to help them make up their own minds. Instead, I tell them that I do not believe they have minds worth making up until they have been trained by me. I realize such a statement is deeply offensive to students since it exhibits a complete lack of pedagogical sensitivities. Yet I cannot imagine any teacher who is serious who would allow students to make up their own minds.

For example, think about the completely different set of presumptions for courses in the sciences. Would you trust a physics instructor who thought she or he could teach physics in a manner that students could make up their own minds about whether atoms do or do not exist? Do you think you could study molecular biology and doubt the existence of cells? Can you study geology and wonder whether a strong distinction can be made between different kinds of rocks? Why is it students are ready to submit to authority in the sciences but yet think they ought to be able to make up their minds when they take courses in the humanities and, in particular, theology? Are sciences 'objective' in a way that the humanities are not? I certainly do not think that is the case.

Part of our problem is that the idea of objectivity, which is mistakenly assumed to be exemplified in the sciences and an elusive goal for the humanities, is a deeply flawed notion. In the name of objectivity the assumption has been underwritten that knowledge is only good insofar as that which is known is freed from any tradition of inquiry. Yet the sciences work well exactly because they exemplify a traditioned mode of inquiry which, moreover, requires the student to be capable of participating in such a tradition. If students are to become good scientists they must be willing to have their lives transformed through that activity; they must be transformed, moreover, not simply because of the current social power of science but because of its beauty. The activity of science, as distinguished from the results of science, is sustained because of the elegance and beauty of what is discovered. The discovery of such beauty requires our lives be adequate for its recognition.

When I tell students that they do not have minds worth making up I intend not only to challenge the liberal presumption that the more choices we have the greater our freedom, but also to remind them that the mind is not something that exists in the head. Rationality is not an innate capacity with which we are born. Rather 'mind' names a skill, or better, sets of skills that have been acquired across generations and to which, if we are lucky, we are made party. To receive an education, and note that you must receive it, means that you must submit your life to a lifelong process of training. Inquiry is never over but rather exists within an ongoing tradition through which you discover why certain arguments are good arguments and others are not. That is why there can be no rationality that is free from a tradition. To master a subject, therefore, requires that one learns the history of the subject in which the telling is under constant re-negotiation. Indeed, one of the greatest weaknesses of the teaching of sciences is that too often a science is taught abstracted from the history which has constituted that science to this point.

You may well ask what all this has to do with the powers, those elemental spirits of the universe. I think this. Ironically no institution is more supportive of the powers today than universities, including those sponsored by the churches, and the knowledge the universities legitimate and in turn by which they are legitimated. Unfortunately, so much of what you will learn in the university will be designed to teach you that the way things are is the way things were meant to be or have to be. Education names the process through which the inevitabilities, the necessities, of our life are named. One of the ironies is that we have learned to give the name 'freedom' to the process in which we learn to name the necessities.

This is particularly the case in universities determined by capitalism. For example, we do not have students at the university anymore. We have consumers. Accordingly, university curriculums are under the constant demand that they be relevant. There is nothing in itself wrong with relevancy, but if that means that students at Christian universities think learning marketing is more important than learning about debates at the Council of Nicaea concerning the Trinity, then relevancy is clearly a problem. We Christians believe that nothing is more important than worshipping Trinity if we are to be free of the powers that determine the necessity we call consumer choice. Only by being initiated into the Christian tradition concerning the economy called 'trinity' does one have a chance of being freed from the necessities called 'economics.' For Christians know that the love displayed in God's life is not a zero-sum game but one of overflowing plenitude.

I know you will find such a claim outrageous. You will charitably think I am exaggerating to make a point. But I tell you I am completely serious. No necessities grip our lives more completely than those now enshrined in that discipline called 'economics.' We must remember that once there was no economics distinguishable as a separate practice from other aspects of our lives, and accordingly economics could not be distinguishable from politics. Now, of course, we cannot think what it would mean to view our world without assuming our lives are consti-tuted by something called 'the economic realm.' That presumption is, moreover, instantiated and legitimated by the discipline of economics in the modern university. Yet the very assumption that we can distin-guish between economics and politics is already one that from a Christian perspective is deeply problematic.

For example, I was once giving a talk in the business school at a university in Texas. This university was sponsored by a conservative denomination and they wanted their business school to be 'ethical.' Accordingly, they endowed a lectureship in business ethics and I was asked to give the yearly lecture on ethics. My lecture was entitled 'Why Business Ethics Is A Bad Idea.' In it I argued business ethics is but a form of quandary ethics popular in universities but having little to do with any serious moral engagement. Such courses in ethics assume that decisions are more important than character for determining the nature of the moral life. As a result we get the dreaded courses in 'applied ethics,' which usually turn out to deal with issues we never will nor should confront.

Prior to the lecture there was the obligatory dinner. During that dinner the associate dean of the business school told me she was a member of a church that grew by 100 to 200 members each Sunday. After the lecture she observed that she found my lecture very pessimistic. Surely there was something they could do to make the teaching of business more ethical. I said I thought there was but one had to start a good deal earlier than the university and the business school. For example, I suggested that before they let anyone join her church they ought to have them turn to the congregation and say what they made in public. 'I make $75,000 a year and I would like to be a member of Second Baptist Church.' 'I make $35,000 a year and I would like to be a member of Second Baptist Church.' She observed that they could not do that because that would be invading people's privacy.

I thought, 'Where are the fundamentalists when you need them?' After all, Ananias and Sapphira were smitten because they had lied about the proceeds they had received from the selling of their property. Obviously, the early church knew nothing of a distinction between politics and economics, between the public and the private. Yet our colleges now have departments of politics and departments of economics which assume that they are separate knowledges in which questions of the goods of a particular community can be divorced from questions of the distribution of those goods.

Of course we, that is, we Americans, need departments of economics to exist because if they exist then we assume that we know something like an economic realm must exist that is subject to its own 'laws.' Moreover, in order for economics to be a predictive science, we increasingly live as well as think about our lives as if we are utilitarian calculators. To live in any other way threatens to make rational choice methodologies, so important to the explanatory power of contemporary economics, not work. We become interest-seeking units of desire in order to sustain the predictive power of economics. Not so to think of ourselves would render our trust in those experts we call economists unintelligible.

The power of this way of thinking about the world can be illustrated by modern Christian concerns about justice. Christians today want to be good capitalists and yet also to be concerned about the poor. So we think the way to do both is to learn more and more about economics in order to make our economic systems more just. As a result, Christian calls for justice accept economics as an unavoidable sphere of our lives and thus assume that the market as we know it is a necessity.

With the best will in the world we try to increase the distributive shares of the economy in the hope that the poor will receive more than their allotted share. So justice turns out to be a way we comfort ourselves with the illusion that we can help the poor by subjecting them to the same economic modes of thought and practices that dominate our own lives. We simply cannot envision the possibility that capitalism, and the economic sciences that are meant to make capitalism inevitable, might be the kind of powers, the 'elemental spirits,' that Paul knew threatened the lives of the Colossians.

If you do not believe that your life is determined by such a power, note what you fear. We are people whose lives are determined by the fear of 'not having enough.' That is not accidental but rather the result of the institution of the capitalist market-place. Finally everything, including our bodies and in particular our blood, becomes property that is subject to exchange value. The Trinitarian conviction that God's creatures cannot be 'used up,' since gift only produces greater gifts, is subverted by the 'market.' After all, without the presumption of scarcity, we fear the economy will not be forced constantly to grow and expand.

Alasdair McIntyre suggests in the 'Introduction' to the second edition of his *Marxism and Christianity* (London: Duckworth, 1995) that the injustice of capitalism is quite a separate matter from capitalism's power to generate material prosperity for more people than any economic system in human history.[1] McIntyre acknowledges that capitalism has produced great wealth, but capitalism's ability to do so is irrelevant as rebuttal to the essential injustice of capitalism. Of course, he points out it is not only that individuals and groups should not receive what they deserve from capitalism but rather 'they are educated or rather miseducated to believe that they should aim and hope for not what they deserve but whatever they may happen to want. They are in the vast majority of cases to regard themselves primarily as consumers whose practical and productive activities are no more than a means to consumption. What constitutes success in life becomes a matter of acqui-sition of the consumer goods, and thereby that acquisitiveness which is so often a character trait necessary for success in capital accumulation is further sanctioned. Unsurprisingly, *pleonexia*, the drive to have more and more, becomes treated as a central virtue. The Christian theologians in the Middle Ages had learned from Aristotle that *pleonexia* is the vice that is counterpart to the virtue of justice. And they had understood, as later theologians failed to do, the close connection between the developing of capitalism and the sin of usury. So it's not after all just general human sinfulness that generates particular individual acts of injustice over and above the institutional injustice of capitalism itself. Capitalism also provides systematic incentives to develop a type of character that has propensity to injustice'.[2] MacIntyre further observed that even those who succeed by capitalist standards, that is, the rich, are from a Christian point of view placed in an almost impossible position for entering into the Kingdom of Heaven.

From such a perspective we can begin to appreciate how the university helps us believe that the way things are is the way things have to be. We simply cannot imagine any economic order that does not reproduce capitalist presuppositions that scarcity is the necessary condition to sustain an economy. We cannot conceive of any alternative for how we exchange goods or for how we care for one another that does not reproduce that necessity. Of course those are exactly the results that

---

[1] Alasdair MacIntyre, *Marxism and Christianity* (second edition) (London: Duckworth, 1995), V–XXXI.
[2] MacIntyre, pp. 13–14.

are intended. It is not a question, of course, of trying to go back to some simpler age, since on reflection we discover that no past age really was all that simple.

Of course, part of the difficulty of trying to unthink necessities that we find in modern economic thought is the very notion of unthinking them is insufficient – they are, after all, powers. Certainly, it is important that our imaginations are transformed in order that we might be able to envision at least some alternatives. Hopefully that might happen at the university and looking at past behavior might be the helpful stimulant for the imagination. For example, MacIntyre points out that what we mean by the market is quite different from past understandings of markets. For in pre-modern societies markets were auxiliary to production in a manner that production was not primarily for the market but for local needs. That is, markets provided a useful means of exchange for what was surplus to the local need. So one was not forced to participate in the market. In contrast, modern market relationships are imposed both on labor and small producers.

So it's not simply a question of transforming knowledge but rather whether a Christian university is supported by a community with practices that force us to reshape our imagination and our knowledges. For example, think how the knowledges taught in the modern university reinforce the inevitability of violence. In the name of 'realism' we try to help students see the inevitability of war as a characteristic of an international system or lack thereof. Of course, we do that partly because it becomes our task to show that the wars America fought in the past were necessary because we do not want to demean the sacrifices that were made through those wars.

Indeed, the very fact that we teach American history as if one of the main players in modernity is a character called 'America' rather than God already embodies the atheism necessary to legitimating such violence. In such respects the issues raised by multi-culturalism are but a side issue for Christians. Of course, African-Americans, native Americans, Chinese, Mexican-Americans, women, should have a voice that is not just a question of voice but what story they tell as Christians. For example, it would be interesting to think how Augustine would write the city of God when the city of the world is not named Rome but America. That strikes me as the kind of intellectual accomplishment that is demanded of us as Christians in the modern university, both as teachers and as students.

I am aware that many of you will find all this just too, well, 'radical.' You may well think I must be kidding, as surely it is part of the modern university's function to give students power in the world in which we find ourselves. Yet I am suggesting that if we are not to be taken captive through philosophies and empty deceits of which Colossians speaks, then the Christian university will be one that takes the risk of making the students who come to us profoundly dysfunctional when it comes to living in the world as we know it. But if you are profoundly dysfunctional, then you might also be free of the necessities that dominate your lives and all our lives today. To be free of those necessities means you have been subjected to a truthful training that hopefully will help you be a faithful citizen in that commonwealth called church.

14

For Dappled Things

Being the smart people I know you to be I assume most of you have just discovered one of the most important survival skills an academic needs – that is, how to get through commencement exercises without dying of boredom. It has been some years since you went through a commencement. You had forgotten how long they can be. You forgot to bring anything to read. Desperate, you turned to the Commencement program and to your delight discovered the listing of the dissertation titles. Even better, you discovered your dissertation title. Then you thought, 'I can get through the rest of this event by reading the other dissertation titles.'

Of course that is when the trouble begins. You are on the brink of having your PhD conferred – which surely puts you among the brightest of the bright in this society – but you discover not only do you not have a clue what most of the other dissertations are about, but you cannot even read their titles with understanding. After discounting the hypothesis that this might have to do with your limitations, you then begin to wonder about the institution from which you are graduating. For you could understand just enough about some of the titles to make you wonder what kind of university would allow someone to graduate with a PhD working on this kind of stuff. Just remember the person sitting next to you is probably thinking the same thing about your dissertation.

All of which is to say, 'Congratulations on the completion of your work and welcome to the rest of your life!' I realize that some of you will not stay in the university, but from this moment on, for better or worse you are citizens of the university. You owe us. I realize this is not a time to tell you, 'You owe us,' but if we are to continue to be a place that can graduate people who cannot understand the person next to them at graduation, we are going to need your help. We need you to help us tell those who are not part of the university why they should want to support communities and institutions who produce people like you and me.

The humbling experience of not being able to communicate with the person next to you is not something that is peculiar to this occasion. It is in the character of the modern university. I served on a committee in the university for some years that required me to be confronted by people from other disciplines. When I first heard about random walks, I thought this must be someone's project from the School of the Environment to lay trails in Duke Forest. Imagine my surprise to discover 'random walks' is a subject in the Department of Mathematics. Then there was tribology. I thought surely this was an area in the Program in Literature dealing with the Star Trek episode about 'Tribbles.' That is, I thought it possible this was another profound probing by cultural studies to illumine the production and reproduction of the capitalist subtext. It turns out the subject does have to do with capital, since it involves oil. For tribology is the study of friction and oil can reduce friction. There is, moreover, a *Journal of Tribology*, so we know it must count as an academic discipline!

Some within the university, and many external to the university, think the fact that we cannot understand one another's dissertation titles is surely an indication that something has gone wrong with the contemporary university. They assume what is wrong with the university is nicely exemplified by occasions like this. What could I possibly say that would be of interest to such a diverse group? Yet this occasion but reproduces the everyday politics of most universities, whether they be large or small, research universities or liberal arts colleges. When faculties come together to discuss matters of common concern, we discover the only matters about which we have a common concern are which parking lot we got assigned, the conditions of Card Gym, or perhaps, health insurance. The issue is no longer the two cultures made famous by C. P. Snow, but the many cultures both between departments and within departments. Departments often are names for diverse methodologies which share nothing in common other than perhaps proximity of offices and labs.

Yet I am not convinced that such a view of the university, and/or of your work in it, is justified. This is an odd position for me to take since I am a theologian. Theology may once have aspired to be the queen of the sciences, but such an ambition today by any discipline would only be laughable. Moreover, theology – like philosophy and, I think, many of the humanities – is a discipline where there is nothing new to learn. For us all the 'data' is in. So we cannot pretend to produce the kind of knowledges that seem to legitimate the current proliferation of disciplines. The problem for theology is how to understand what we know by attending to those in our past who struggled to say what defies saying. That, of course, requires being initiated into a discipline, which means theologians also write dissertations with titles that are not immediately understood.

Our inability to read and understand one another's dissertation titles is not in itself a sign that something has gone wrong, but rather a testimony to the discipline, the sheer hard work, necessary to understand a few things well. That you are all receiving a common degree at this time indicates you share more in common than your dissertation titles suggest. You have each submitted yourselves to the discipline of the past and current masters of your craft in order that you exemplify in your own life the passion of your subject.

I realize, of course, that the language of passion may seem far too dramatic to characterize the years you have spent in your doctorate work. Drudgery may seem closer to the mark. Yet surely passion must infuse the drudgery; for otherwise how are we to explain the exactness of your dissertation titles? Such exactness is required by the details – details, moreover, that can be appreciated only by those who have submitted themselves to the discipline necessary to see why such details matter. That you have now made those details matter surely suggests that at one time and at one place you fell in love. Or put differently, at one time and at one place you were possessed with the desire to want to know, for example, why butterfly wings differ, how songbirds sing, or why Trollope is the greatest English novelist. The reason you cannot easily communicate what you have learned is that the truth is in the details of such study, details that can only be appreciated by undergoing the discipline you have undergone.

But why would anyone want to undergo such discipline? Stanley Fish explains it this way:

> Literary interpretation, like virtue, is its own reward. I do it because I like the way I feel when I'm doing it. I like being brought up short by an effect I have experienced but do not understand analytically. I like trying to describe in flatly prosaic words the achievement of words that are anything but flat and prosaic. I like savoring the physical 'taste' of language at the same time that I work to lay bare its physics. I like uncovering the incredibly dense pyrotechnics of a master artificer, not least because in praising the artifice I can claim a share in it. And when those pleasures have been (temporarily) exhausted, I like linking one moment in a poem to others and then to moments in other works, works by the same author or by his predecessors or contemporaries or successors. It doesn't finally matter which, so long as I can *keep going*, reaping the cognitive and tactile harvest of an activity as self-reflexive as I become when I engage in it.[1]

But remember Stanley also reminds his students when they express admiration for Milton's poetry that Milton does not want their admiration: he wants their souls.

[1] *Professional Correctness: Literary Studies and Political Change* (Oxford: Clarendon Press; New York: Oxford University Press, 1995), 1b.

Fish's account may be peculiar to literary criticism and, no doubt, other literary critics would be quite critical of his understanding of why he does what he does. Yet I think he rightly indicates why many of us are attracted to the details of our disciplines. I have noticed, for example, that the highest accolade one mathematician can give another is to describe her work as 'deep.' A physicist's work must be 'elegant.' Yet just to the extent our work attains such beauty, it becomes hard for us to understand one another, though we may and should come to appreciate what each other does. Yet such appreciation is hard won and even harder for those who are not part of the world we call the university. Which means they (that is, those not part of our world) can rightly ask why they should pay for Stanley Fish to get such pleasure from the study of poetry?

There is no easy answer to this question, though I think there are answers. We can begin by observing that there exists no intrinsic tension between a Fish-like understanding of our work and our work being useful. I was once giving a lecture at Iowa State University (long before the wonderful novel *Moo* had been written). Since I am a compulsive jogger, I was running around the campus in the dark of the early morning. I passed a huge building that was fronted by enormous Greek columns, but because of the dark I could not read the inscription above the columns. I came around later after the sun had come up and discovered that chiseled in marble above those columns was the word, 'MILK.' I thought, what a wonderful way to organize knowledge! Indeed I hope that chairs of the Departments of Physics and/or English at Iowa State University report to the Dean of the School of Milk.

Yet as useful as the study of milk is, such usefulness often cannot provide adequate justification for the practices actually required for such study. For milk, no more than poetry or virtue, is not an end in itself but rather gains its significance as part of a network of needs and goods that represent a community's traditions. The university represents those set aside to serve and remember those goods through the patient love of details. Why we should be paid, or better – privileged, to do such work is because we believe the world in which we live would be the poorer if people like us and our passions did not exist. As those who have been privileged to have been given the time for the work represented by this ceremony, you now have the duty to help those not so privileged understand our passions as a contribution to our common goods.

That we cannot read one another's dissertation titles, therefore, may not be a sign of failure, but rather an indication we are rightly reflecting the truthful differences that make our world so beautiful. Such beauty makes it difficult for us to understand one another and in the process we are humbled not only by having to acknowledge all that we do not know, but even more by that which we have tried to know. And humility is that virtue most required if we are truthfully to tell one another what we know but do not understand. Moreover, I believe God enjoys the details, and we would not truthfully reflect God's creation if we hid the differences required by the details. Accordingly, I can do no better than to close with the words of Gerard Manley Hopkins:

> Glory be to God for dappled things –
>> For skies of couple-colour as a brinded cow;
>> For rose-moles all in stipple upon trout that swim;
> Fresh-firecoal chestnut-falls; finches' wings;
>> Landscapes plotted and pieced – fold, fallow, and plow;
>> And all trades, their gear and tackle and trim.
> All things counter, original, spare, strange;
>> Whatever is fickle, freckled (who knows how?)
>> With swift, slow; sweet, sour; adazzle, dim;
> He fathers-forth whose beauty is past change:
>> Praise Him.[2]

And so, I pray, may your life and work be dappled, as you go forth from this place.

---

[2] 'Pied Beauty,' *Modern American and Modern British Poetry*, edited by Louis Untermeyer (New York: Harcourt Brace, 1955), p. 425.

PART IV

SERMONIC ILLUSTRATIONS

15

Practice Preaching

Can (or Should) We Practice Preaching?

'Practice Preaching?' What could that mean? To practice preaching seems as odd as the suggestion that someone might 'practice homosexuality.' How in the world would you practice being a homosexual? I understand how you might practice baseball, but how can you practice homosexuality?[1] Is preaching closer to baseball than being a homosexual? I think preaching is closer to baseball than homosexuality, but why will take some explaining.

Ken Woodward, in a recent article in *Commonweal* called 'Ushering in the Age of the Laity: Some Cranky Reservations,' observed, 'When journalistic colleagues discover that I am a Roman Catholic they always ask, "Are you practicing?" to which I invariably reply: "I stopped practicing a long time ago," which is to say, I just go out and do it.'[2] Surely preaching is like being a Roman Catholic. That is, you just go out and

---

[1] Actually, 'practicing homosexuality' is not as odd as it may sound. I suspect homosexual relations are no less complex than any human relation. To be sustained they require a great deal of practice. Marriage names that institution for Christians through which we are given the time to develop practices we name as love. That same-sex relations are denied that institution make such relations all the harder.

[2] In Woodward, 'Ushering in the Age of the Laity: Some Cranky Reservations,' *Commonweal* CXXI, 15 (9 September 1994), 9. Woodward goes on to observe, 'What is it about Roman Catholicism, I've often wondered, that takes so much practice? I mean, it's not like learning to play the piano. Why is it you never hear of a practicing Presbyterian? Or a practicing Pentecostal? "Observant" won't do either, as in the sentence, "He's an Observant Jew." I know lots of practicing Catholics who are not terribly observant. "Born again" simply doesn't fit Catholics, implying as it does that one has been "saved" through accepting Jesus as his "personal Lord and Savior." Now I think we all need to be converted – over and over again, but having a personal savior has always struck me as, well, elitist, like having a personal tailor. I'm satisfied to have the same Lord and Savior as everyone else. Besides, Catholics can never be certain they are saved, even if they went to Notre Dame, which is one of the reasons Catholicism is so interesting.' For my reflections on why Catholics might be asked whether they are 'practicing' see my 'A Homage to Mary and to the University Called Notre Dame,' *In Good Company: The Church as Polis* (Notre Dame: University of Notre Dame Press, 1995), 81–90.

do it. So to suggest that one should practice preaching does not seem quite right.

I have argued, however, that being a Christian is very much like learning how to be a practitioner of a craft. For example, in *After Christendom*, I suggested that we ought to think of making disciples the way a bricklayer is trained.[3] I did so to emphasize that Christianity is not so much a set of beliefs that are meant to give our lives meaning, but rather, to be a Christian is to be initiated into a community with skills, not unlike learning to lay bricks, that are meant to transform our lives. To be initiated into a craft requires, of course, apprenticeship to a master through which we learn the basic habits of the craft sufficient for us to practice the craft as well as to discover the innovations necessary for the craft to have a future.

The notion of craft and the skills essential to the craft are natural to me, of course, as someone who has emphasized the importance of the virtues as the way to display the nature of the Christian moral life. The virtues, as Alasdair MacIntyre reminds us, are correlative to the notion of practice. By practice, MacIntyre means 'any coherent and complex form of socially established, cooperative human activity through which goods internal to that form of activity are realized in the course of trying to achieve those standards of excellence which are appropriate to, and partially definitive of, that form of activity, with the result that human powers to achieve excellence, and human conceptions of the ends and goods involved, are systematically extended.'[4] Preaching, I believe, is such a practice since it is essential to the church's very being. The church preaches because by its very nature the church cannot do otherwise. Preaching is not an activity done for some other purpose, some other reason, that is not already intrinsic to preaching itself. Accordingly, preaching requires and develops virtue in a community sufficient to sustaining preaching as essential for what that community is about. Which is but a reminder that preaching is fundamentally a political activity insofar as the church, through its preaching ministry, discovers the good we have in common.

It may still be objected that the idea that we ought to try to practice preaching does not seem like a good idea. Most congregations would not want to be subject to someone 'practicing preaching.' Most crafts require that beginners learn to practice, but few of us desire to be the guinea pigs on whom such beginners practice. Surgeons must be initiated into the craft of surgery by operating on someone for the first time, but few of us wish to be that patient.

---

[3] Stanley Hauerwas, *After Christendom* (Nashville: Abingdon Press, 1991), 93–112. I develop the ecclesial significance of this point in my *In Good Company: The Church as Polis*.

[4] Alasdair McIntyre, *After Virtue*, second edition (Notre Dame: University of Notre Dame Press, 1984), 187.

Yet, the analogy of surgery is wrong for preaching. For as I suggested above, using MacIntyre's account of practice, we must remember that preaching is not what a preacher does, but rather it is the activity of the whole community. Preaching as practice is the activity of the church that requires the church to be as able listeners, as well-schooled and well-crafted hearers, as the preacher is the proclaimer. Indeed, I suspect one of the great difficulties of preaching in the church today is the preacher's presumption that those to whom they preach do not have ears well-trained to hear. As a result, preaching is not the practice of the community but rather, as it so often is, an exercise in sentimentality.

The Authority of the Practice

Preaching as the practice of the whole church is an authoritative practice. Through the proclamation of the Gospel, the church stands joyfully under the authority of the Word. Preaching as a practice of the whole community, therefore, can never be understood as that time when the preacher gives his or her opinions about this or that or shares with a congregation unique or peculiar insights they have learned. You know, or the one to whom you are listening knows, that you have abandoned preaching authoritatively if the sermon involves telling the church some bit of the wisdom discovered through our children. That is the surest sign the sermon is not the practice of the church and has become instead an exercise meant to reinforce middle-class religiosity.

For preaching to be a practice intrinsic to the worship of God requires that the preacher, as well as the congregation, stand under the authority of the Word. That is why preaching should rightly follow a lectionary. To preach from the lectionary makes clear that preaching is the work of the church and not some arbitrary decision by the minister to find a text to fit a peculiar theme that currently fits the preacher's subjectivity. Rather, the exercise of the ministry of proclamation requires the minister to make clear that the Word preached is as painful to him/her as it is to the congregation. Such an acknowledgment makes clear that preaching is not just another speech but rather the way this people here, including the preacher, is formed into the Word of God.

The practice of preaching as the practice of authority, particularly in our culture, cannot help but be prophetic. It is a mistake to think that prophetic preaching occurs when the preacher holds up a specific moral challenge to the congregation. On the contrary, preaching as a practice is prophetic when it is done with authority. Where else in our culture do you find a people gathered in obedience to a Word they know they will not easily hear?

Such an exercise of authority is anomalous in liberal cultures which assume that all forms of authority cannot help but be authoritarian. As I have put the matter elsewhere, the story of modernity is that we should have no story except the story we chose when we had no story.[5] People schooled on that story cannot help but think no one has the right to stand in authority over them. So the very idea that they should be trained to be faithful hearers of the Word proclaimed seems anomalous.

It is important to note that this is not simply another attack on American individualism. To be sure, we live in a destructively individualistic culture and society. But I have put the issue in the language of story exactly because I think it illumines our difficulties better than the notion of individualism. The difficulty is not that we are just individualistic but that we believe that there is actually a place from which we can choose our story. That, of course, is a story that we did not choose and which determines us to be people who are interminably self-deceived.

In contrast, preaching as the practice of the church is a constant reminder that the church is constituted by people who have learned that they have not chosen God. Rather, we are a people who have been chosen by God which, at the very least, means we discover that we are a people constituted by a story that we have not chosen. This is a story we could not have 'made up.' Accordingly, to be a good hearer, to practice preaching, requires that we be schooled to be creatures. To be a creature means we must learn that our lives are gifts of a gracious God. I do not say that we receive our lives as a gift because that would mean we already existed prior to the reception of our lives as a gift. The fact is that our very lives are gift. That we are so constituted requires the constant practice that comes through receiving the Word of God through preaching.

So preaching as one of the essential practices of Christian worship is a prophetic reminder to a culture bent on denying our status as creature. In preaching, the church has been given the gift of prophecy, through which we are made more than we could be. As in the account of practice suggested above by MacIntyre, we know we are made more than we could ever imagine through preaching. That is why, I suspect, those who are set aside for the preaching ministry of the church often discover they acquire a power they did not know they had by being forced to proclaim the Word of God. To acknowledge that power can be frightening as we fear what it may mean for our lives. The joy, however, is to know what it will mean for the up-building of the whole church as God makes us more than we could ever be through the proclamation of God's Word.

The Story that Requires that Preaching Be Practiced

It should be obvious that preaching as a practice required by and for the church is not separable from what preaching is about. Preaching is

---

[5] Stanley Hauerwas, *Dispatches from the Front: Theological Engagements with the Secular* (Durham: Duke University Press, 1994), 164–76

the proclamation of the Word of God as found in the people of Israel and the life, death, and resurrection of Jesus of Nazareth. Preaching, therefore, is the practice that is meant to help us locate our lives in God's story. To do that, preaching must be about God's story through the explication of the scripture. Scripture is, of course, comprised of many stories – all of which, the church has taught us, help illumine the Gospel.[6]

In the 'introduction' to William Willimon's and my book *Preaching to Strangers*, I suggested that most preaching today fits what George Lindbeck has characterized as an experiential-expressivist view of religion.[7] The fundamental assumption of the experiential-expressivist view is that different religions are diverse expressions of a common experience. Such a view, of course, has been the very center of Protestant liberal theology as exemplified by such theologians as Paul Tillich and Reinhold Niebuhr. From this perspective, the Gospel is seen as a provocative account of the human condition. Such theology, and the preaching that it produces can be extraordinarily powerful as well as popular in a culture formed by the story that one should have no story except the story one chooses when one has no story.

Moreover, preaching in the experiential-expressivist mode can be quite artful. Literary examples are a natural resource as the preacher oftentimes finds Kahlil Gibran more insightful than the Gospel of Mark. Moreover, such a view of preaching seems better able to show the relevance of preaching to the 'real-life situations' of people as well as to contemporary social problems.

But for all its aesthetic and artful qualities, such preaching is not the practice of preaching required by the church. That practice is proclamation since it requires that the preacher and hearers be confronted by a Word that does not illumine what they already know but rather tells us what we do not know – and indeed, could not know on our own. That is why it must be done over and over again. Repetition is the key to helping us understand the material content of what it is we practice when we preach. It is the practice of the story of God that is not about the illumination of the human condition but rather about the proclamation of God found in the people of Israel and the life of Jesus of Nazareth. These are not general truths but rather a story that can be known only through hearing it proclaimed amidst that body of

[6] As Robert Jenson puts it – 'The story of the sermon and the hymns and of the processions and of the sacramental acts and of the readings is to be God's story, the story of the Bible. Preachers are the greatest sinners here: the text already is and belongs to the one true story, it does not need to be helped out in this respect. What is said and enacted in the church must be with the greatest exactitude and faithfulness and exclusivity the story of creation and redemption by the God of Israel and Father of the Risen Christ.' 'How the World Lost Its Story,' *First Things* 36 (October 1993), 22.

[7] William Willimon and Stanley Hauerwas, *Preaching to Strangers* (Louisville: Westminster/John Knox Press, 1992), 1–13.

people gathered in the hopes that we will be faithful hearers of God's story.

Preaching is that practice meant to help us locate our lives, our stories, in God's story. But preaching is not meant to stand alone; rather, it is surrounded by and sustained within the whole liturgy of the church. Preaching is that part of the church's liturgy through which we are reminded of the story that shapes all that we do from gathering to sending forth. That is why preaching finally requires it be sealed by that other practice essential to worship, that is, the Eucharist. Word and table are forever bound together as those practices necessary for us to understand we are the baptized people of God. Through baptism we have been made the people of God capable of that strange but wonderful practice called preaching. What a wonderful gift.

16

Reformation Is Sin

Sermon for Fig Tree Assembly, NY,
Sunday, 29 October 1995

A Sermon for Reformation Sunday
in Honor of Robert Wilken

Joel 2:23–32 ✤ 2 Timothy 4:6–8, 16–18 ✤ Luke 18:9–14

I must begin by telling you that I do not like to preach on Reformation
Sunday. Actually I have to put it more strongly than that. I do not like
Reformation Sunday, period. I do not understand why it is part of the
church year. Reformation Sunday does not name a happy event for the
Church Catholic; on the contrary, it names failure. Of course, the church
rightly names failure, or at least horror, as part of our church year. We
do, after all, go through crucifixion as part of Holy Week. Certainly if
the Reformation is to be narrated rightly, it is to be narrated as part of
those dark days.

Reformation names the disunity in which we currently stand. We
who remain in the Protestant tradition want to say that Reformation
was a success. But when we make Reformation a success, it only ends
up killing us. After all, the very name 'Protestantism' is meant to denote
a reform movement of protest within the Church Catholic. When
Protestantism becomes an end in itself, which it certainly has through
the mainstream denominations in America, it becomes anathema. If
we no longer have broken hearts at the church's division, then we cannot
help but unfaithfully celebrate Reformation Sunday.

For example, note what the Reformation has done for our reading
texts like that which we hear from Luke this morning. We Protestants
automatically assume that the Pharisees are the Catholics. They are
the self-righteous people who have made Christianity a form of legalistic
religion, thereby destroying the free grace of the Gospel. We Protestants
are the tax collectors, knowing that we are sinners and that our lives
depend upon God's free grace. And therefore we are better than the

Catholics because we know they are sinners. What an odd irony that the Reformation made such readings possible. As Protestants we now take pride in the acknowledgement of our sinfulness in order to distinguish ourselves from Catholics who allegedly believe in works-righteousness.

Unfortunately, the Catholics are right. Christian salvation consists in works. To be saved *is* to be made holy. To be saved requires our being made part of a people separated from the world so that we can be united in spite of – or perhaps better, because of – the world's fragmentations and divisions. Unity, after all, is what God has given us through Christ's death and resurrection. For in that death and resurrection we have been made part of God's salvation for the world so that the world may know it has been freed from the powers that would compel us to kill one another in the name of false loyalties. All that is about the works necessary to save us.

For example, I often point out that at least Catholics have the magisterial office of the Bishop of Rome to remind them that disunity is a sin. You should not overlook the significance that in several important documents of late, John Paul II has confessed the Catholic sin for the Reformation. Where are the Protestants capable of doing likewise? We Protestants feel no sin for the disunity of the Reformation. We would not know how to confess our sin for the continuing disunity of the Reformation. We would not know how to do that because we have no experience of unity.

The magisterial office – we Protestants often forget – is not a matter of constraining or limiting diversity in the name of unity. The office of the Bishop of Rome is to ensure that when Christians move from Durham, North Carolina, to Syracuse, New York, they have some confidence when they go to church that they will be worshipping the same God. Because Catholics have an office of unity, they do not need to restrain the gifts of the Spirit. As I oftentimes point out, it is extraordinary that Catholicism is able to keep the Irish and the Italians in the same church. What an achievement! Perhaps equally amazing is their ability to keep within the same church Jesuits, Dominicans, and Franciscans.

I think Catholics are able to do that because they know that their unity does not depend upon everyone agreeing. Indeed, they can celebrate their disagreements because they understand that our unity is founded upon the cross and resurrection of Jesus of Nazareth that makes the Eucharist possible. They do not presume, therefore, that unity requires that we all read Scripture the same way.

This creates a quite different attitude among Catholics about their relation to Christian tradition and the wider world. Protestants look over Christian tradition and say, 'How much of this do we have to believe in order to remain identifiably Christian?' That's the reason why Protestants are always tempted to rationalism: we think that

Christianity is to be identified with sets of beliefs more than with the unity of the Spirit occasioned through sacrament.

Moreover, once Christianity becomes reduced to a matter of belief, as it clearly has for Protestants, we cannot resist questions of whether those beliefs are as true or useful as other beliefs we also entertain. Once such questions are raised, it does not matter what the answer turns out in a given case. As James Edwards observes, 'Once religious beliefs start to compete with other beliefs, then religious believers are – and will know themselves to be – mongerers of values. They too are denizens of the mall, selling and shopping and buying along with the rest of us.'

In contrast, Catholics do not begin with the question of 'How much do we need to believe?' but with the attitude 'Look at all the wonderful stuff we get to believe!' Isn't it wonderful to know that Mary was immaculately conceived in order to be the faithful servant of God's new creation in Jesus Christ! She therefore becomes the firstborn of God's new creation, our mother, the first member of God's new community we call church. Isn't it wonderful that God continued to act in the world through the appearances of Mary at Guadalupe! Mary must know something because she seems always to appear to peasants and, in particular, to peasant women who have the ability to see her. Most of us would not have the ability to see Mary because we'd be far too embarrassed by our vision.

Therefore Catholics understand the church's unity as grounded in a reality more determinative than our good feelings for one another. The office of Rome matters. For at least that office is a judgement on the church for our disunity. Surely it is the clear indication of the sin of the Reformation that we Protestants have not been able to resist nationalistic identifications. So we become German Lutherans, American Lutherans, Norwegian Lutherans. You are Dutch Calvinist, American Presbyterians, Church of Scotland. I am an American Methodist, which has precious little to do with my sisters and brothers in English Methodism. And so we Protestant Christians go to war killing one another in the name of being American, German, Japanese, and so on.

At least it becomes the sin of Rome when Italian Catholics think they can kill Irish Catholics in the name of being Italian. Such divisions distort the unity of the Gospel found in the Eucharist and, thus, become judgements against the church of Rome. Of course, the Papacy has often been unfaithful and corrupt, but at least Catholics preserved an office God can use to remind us that we have been and may yet prove unfaithful. In contrast, Protestants don't even know we're being judged for our disunity.

I realize that this perspective on Reformation Sunday is not the usual perspective. The usual perspective is to tell us what a wonderful thing happened at the Reformation. The Reformation struck a blow for freedom. No longer would we be held in medieval captivity to law and

arbitrary authority. The Reformation was the beginning of enlightenment, of progressive civilizations, of democracy, that have come to
fruition in this wonderful country called America. What a destructive
story.

You can tell the destructive character of that narrative by what it
has done to the Jews. The way we Protestants read history, and in
particular our Bible, has been nothing but disastrous for the Jews. For
we turned the Jews into Catholics by suggesting that the Jews had sunk
into legalistic and sacramental religion after the prophets and had
therefore become moribund and dead. In order to make Jesus explicable
(in order to make Jesus look like Luther – at least the Luther of our
democratic projections), we had to make Judaism look like our characterization of Catholicism. Yet Jesus did not free us from Israel; rather,
he engrafted us into the promise of Israel so that we might be a people
called to the same holiness of the law.

I realize that the suggestion that salvation is to be part of a holy
people constituted by the law seems to deny the Reformation principle
of justification by faith through grace. I do not believe that to be the
case, particularly as Calvin understood that Reformation theme. After
all, Calvin (and Luther) assumed that justification by faith through
grace is a claim about God's presence in Jesus of Nazareth. So
justification by faith through grace is not some general truth about our
need for acceptance; but rather justification by faith through grace is a
claim about the salvation wrought by God through Jesus to make us a
holy people capable of remembering that God's salvation comes through
the Jews. When the church loses that memory, we lose the source of
our unity. For unity is finally a matter of memory, of how we tell the
story of the Reformation. How can we tell this story of the church
truthfully as Protestants and Catholics so that we might look forward
to being in union with one another and thus share a common story of
our mutual failure?

We know, after all, that the prophecy of Joel has been fulfilled. The
portents of heaven, the blood and fire, the darkness of the sun, the
bloody moon have come to pass in the cross of our Savior Jesus Christ.
Now all who call on that name will be saved. We believe that we who
stand in the Reformation churches are survivors. But to survive we
need to recover the unity that God has given us as survivors. So on this
Reformation Sunday long for, pray for, our ability to remember the
Reformation – not as a celebratory moment, not as a blow for freedom,
but as the sin of the church. Pray for God to heal our disunity, not the
disunity simply between Protestant and Catholic, but the disunity in
our midst between classes, between races, between nations. Pray that
on Reformation Sunday we may as tax collectors confess our sin and
ask God to make us a new people joined together in one mighty prayer
that the world may be saved from its divisions.

17

The Cruelty of Peace

SERMON FOR ADVENT SERVICE, 8 DECEMBER 1995,
AT DUKE CHAPEL

Isaiah 11:1–10 ✢ Romans 15:4–13 ✢ Matthew 3:1–12

Advent is something Christians are not very good at. We do not have the knack for it. Advent, after all, is about waiting and waiting is hard for us.

Indeed, Advent cannot help but appear like a game to us, an awkward prelude to Christmas. At Advent we Christians return to our childhood – particularly as childhood is shaped by Christmas. Like children, we love the build-up necessary to create the excitement of opening presents around the tree. This Christmas we know we want a bicycle. We let our parents know we want a bicycle. We are pretty sure we are going to get our bicycle, but we tell ourselves we will not get it because such pretense will only increase our excitement. So we enter into a period of waiting in which we pretend we will not get what we want so that when we get our bicycle we will really be surprised. It is as if we become characters in a play we have written for ourselves, all the while denying our authorship precisely because such a denial is crucial to our getting what we want. Of course, nothing can finally be more dissatisfying than to get what we want. But we don't often think about that.

That Christians play the game of waiting called Advent seems structured into our very faith. After all, we believe the Messiah has come. Thus in Romans, Paul quotes Isaiah who declares that 'The root of Jesse shall come, the one who rises to rule the Gentiles; in him the Gentiles shall have hope.' Are we not, after all, the people who believe the promise to Israel has been fulfilled? Are we not, after all, the people who believe that Jesus is the new David who has finally brought us peace? So we Christians rightly play the game of Advent, play the game of waiting, knowing that it has to be only a game because our Savior has come. Peace is possible. We have gotten what we want.

I have even written a book called *The Peaceable Kingdom* whose center is this text from Isaiah 11. Surely I believe that such a peace has come to pass through the birth of Jesus of Nazareth. Surely I believe it right for us as Christians to have our imaginations charged with the images of Isaiah 11. We would live at a time when the wolf shall live with the lamb, the leopard will lie with the kid, the calf with the lion, and a little child shall lead them.

I confess I love the paintings of Edward Hicks that portray such a kingdom, where Quaker and Indian are reconciled, where children play amidst the leopards, and where the tigers and wolves and sheep lie together. I'm particularly fond of Hicks' painting of Noah's ark where we catch sight of the wolves, the lambs, the lions, the cattle, proceeding into the ark that will be their salvation from the flood. But what will they eat? They will eat, of course, hay – as Hicks assumes that the results of the Fall had not yet gone so far that the animals had ceased being vegetarian. Hicks rightly saw that the ark is the great prototype of God's new salvation given to us through Jesus of Nazareth. How wonderful is God's peace.

Of course, part of the difficulty is that these images of the peaceable kingdom are too strong. If lambs actually lie down with wolves, they are foolish indeed. In effect, calves and lions do not respond to a child's leadership. Nor, for that matter, do we live at peace with one another. That we do not is particularly embarrassing for Christians. Thus in the early centuries Jews took pleasure in reminding us that not all are convinced that this Jesus is the root of Jesse. For if this Jesus is the root of Jesse then why is it that this peace of Isaiah does not exist?

As Christians we confess that this challenge makes us very nervous. Could it be that our faith is, in fact, false? Could it be that this Jesus is not, after all, the Messiah? So we Christians deliberately act to make this peace a reality. We are determined not to have a tree under which there is not present a new bicycle. Of course, peace is an ideal, but it's an ideal for which we must work. So Jesus becomes the great idealistic leader beckoning us toward a peace that does not exist but will exist if only we work hard enough at it. Our faith may be based on the existence of an idealistic dreamer. But by God, we will make it true!

Such a peace, of course, cannot help but be cruel. It is cruel because it makes us a people willing to do almost anything to achieve what we take to be this ideal of peace. War becomes a means to achieve peace. And when our idealism is thwarted, when war does not bring peace but just another war, we become cynical. Our cynicism roots profounder violence than would ever have been present if we had never hoped in the ideal of peace.

Nowhere is such cruelty more manifest than in Christian relations with the Jews. The Jews are such an embarrassment. We, after all, worship their Messiah whom they refuse to acknowledge as their Messiah. They do not, it turns out, believe in the ideal of peace. So there's only one thing for us to do as Christians – that is, replace them. In this century that displacement has turned out to be just another word for murder. As a result, many of us recoil at the words from John the Baptist, 'Even now the ax is lying at the root of the trees . . . the chaff he will burn with unquenchable fire.' Those words, after Holocaust, rightly terrify us.

So we cannot deny that our inability to wait as Christians has had deadly cruel results. Which should remind us that something desperate has gone wrong in how we Christians understand Advent. Something desperate has gone wrong in how we Christians have read texts like this from Romans. For note, Paul does not assume that Jesus came a servant to the circumcised, that Jesus confirmed the promises given to the patriarchs, in order that the Jews might be left behind. Rather, Paul presumes that Jesus is the root of Jesse making us Gentiles part of the promise to Israel. Paul assumes that through Jesus we Christians have been made Jews – Jews who have learned to wait because they know they are not the author of the play. They are not called upon to make God's promise true. They are called to faithful waiting.

Which reminds us as Christians: God's peace is not some ideal for which we must strive. God's peace is not the cruelty that comes from not getting our bicycles. Rather, peace is the name given by God to God's creation of God's Kingdom, that makes it possible for some of us in a world of war, in a world in which God's very creation is at odds with itself, to be able to live at peace with one another. So Paul tells us that what was written in former days was written for our instruction so that by steadfastness and encouragement of the Scriptures we might have hope. Such hope, Paul says, enables us to live in harmony with one another in accordance with the peace of Christ Jesus as found in cross and resurrection. This peace is no distant ideal but a reality that we are asked to live out here and now through eucharistic presence.

At Advent we are not asked as Christians to play at waiting. At Advent we are not asked as Christians to try to imagine what it must feel like to be Jews. No, at Advent we discover again that God has, through Jesus, grafted us into the waiting tree of Israel. At Advent we discover as Christians that we are God's patience, which is but another name for God's peace. As Gerard Manley Hopkins reminds us in his wonderful poem, 'Peace':

> When will you ever, Peace, wild wood dove, shy wings shut,
> You round me roaming end, and under be my boughs?
> When, when, Peace, will you, Peace? – I'll not play hypocrite
>
> To own my heart: I yield you do come sometimes; but
> That piecemeal peace is poor peace. What pure peace allows
> Alarms of war, the daunting wars, the death of it?
>
> O surely, reaving Peace, my Lord should leave in lieu
> Some good! And so he does leave patience exquisite,

> That plumes to Peace thereafter. And when Peace here does house
> He comes with work to do, he does not come to coo,
>   He comes to brood and sit.[1]

At Advent we discover that God would not have God's peace accomplished by our effort to make the kingdom true. At Advent we discover God's kingdom is truth through God's making us a people capable of waiting peaceably in a world at war. At Advent we discover that Christians are called to appear in the world as John the Baptizer who came out of the wilderness to proclaim, 'Repent, for the Kingdom of Heaven has come near.' At Advent Christians discover that God has given us everything we need to be a people capable of waiting peaceably, through this meal of reconciliation, through which we become for the world God's very body, so that the world may know God's peace is not some unrealistic set of expectations but God's peace is us. Hurry then to this table of waiting, this table of peace, where God turns our stony lives to bread.

---

[1] 'Peace,' *The Poems of Gerard Manley Hopkins* (Fourth Edition), edited by W. H. Gardner and N. H. MacKenzie (Oxford: Oxford University Press, 1970), p. 85.

18

Living on Dishonest Wealth

For Fred Herzog

Jeremiah 8:18–9:1 ✢ Psalm 79:1–9 ✢ 1 Timothy 2:1–7
Luke 16:1–13

The distinction between public and private so necessary to sustain our liberal political and economic practices is unknown in the New Testament. For example, in the Book of Acts Ananias and Sapphira were struck dead because they refused to reveal honestly to the church what they had made on the selling of property. The early church seems to have known nothing of the distinction between the public and the private, particularly when it came to money matters. The truth of the matter is that as Christians today we would sooner tell one another, if it were absolutely necessary, what we do in our bedrooms before we have to tell one another what we make. Which is but an indication of what we really care about.

But the text for this Sunday simply will not let us avoid that which we really care about – that is, our money and our property. Of course, it is such an odd text that clever people like us find ways to make this parable die the death of a thousand qualifications. After all, the parable just seems out of character for those of us who would be Christian. Is Jesus really commending the dishonest steward? It certainly seems that he is, insofar as we are told, 'Make friends for yourself by means of dishonest wealth so that when it is gone, they may welcome you into an eternal home.' What in the world are we to make of that? So we become fascinated by questions about how to interpret this parable in such a way that it might be seen as commending dishonesty and we forget that Jesus is making a claim about our money.

Moreover, the bit of wisdom that follows the parable gives us something to think about – namely, only those faithful in a little can be trusted to be faithful in much. And, conversely, those who are dishonest in a little can also certainly be expected to be dishonest in much. So Jesus tells us that if we have not been faithful with our

249

dishonest wealth, how can he trust us with the Gospel? The Gospel, it seems, is what this is really about. Money is just an example in service to this larger issue.

Or, often interpretations of this parable concentrate on the final verse where we are told that no slave can serve two masters. We are told, it seems, that we must choose between God and wealth, which usually turns out to mean we should not try to find our security in our money. In other words, the advice about two masters is usually interpreted as an attitude problem. We should not trust in our money but rather we ought to trust in God. So it really does not matter whether we have a lot of money because the issue involves the attitude we take toward the money we have and not the money as such. But if it's just an attitude problem, I would much rather have an attitude problem about a Porsche than my '83 Toyota Corolla with the dent in the fender.

I think such readings, however, have no basis in this text. Jesus does not suggest that the problem is the attitude we take toward God and/ or wealth. Rather he tells us quite frankly that if we have money we are in trouble when it comes to getting into the Kingdom of Heaven. It is just hard to be saved when you have a lot of money. We do not particularly like to hear that because we know, that is, we white Americans, that we have a lot of money. Of course, we do not have the money of the really rich in this society but if you are white and an American, you are rich. Indeed, I think we put up with the really rich in an effort to convince ourselves that compared to them we are not 'really' rich. Therefore, we tell ourselves, we do not have a problem about being rich for the simple reason that we are not 'really' rich.

Yet I do not think the realism of Jesus in this parable will let us off the hook. As people who have money, we simply have to acknowledge that it is also dishonest money. We tell ourselves that we have worked hard, and we no doubt have, and we deserve what we have got. But the very fact that we have been able to work hard, and thus assume that we deserve what we have gotten, is because we are white Americans. We have had the good luck to be born into good homes that had the habits that would make us a success in the kind of economic world in which we find ourselves. But the luck of our birth is based on the fact that our wealth is the result of dishonest appropriation.

I am, of course, enough of a Marxist to believe that all capital is unjust to the extent capital is appropriation from those who have had the misfortune of being born without property. Most capitalists are not themselves unjust; they simply inherit the practices of injustice. The truth of the matter is that all wealth is the result of murder. Consider, for example, the presumption that the land we currently stand on is ours. What made it ours? What made it ours is of course the killing of native Americans so that we could appropriate the land for our purposes. In Hegel's words, 'history is a slaughter-bench.'

Which brings us back to the stark realism of this parable. Jesus does not presume that we live in a world where we get to choose between honesty or dishonesty. Rather, we live in a world in which we cannot help but be possessed by dishonest habits and unjust systems. Jesus tells us 'No slave can serve two masters,' which seems to presume that we have a choice between being a slave and not being a slave. The truth of the matter is that Jesus presumes that we are in fact enslaved. Moreover, we are never more enslaved than when we think we are masters of our destiny, when we think that we can choose between being honest or dishonest in how we handle our wealth.

I imagine that by this point you're beginning to have a good deal of sympathy with those who insist we must maintain a distinction between the private and the public. This all just sounds too pessimistic. Surely there is some salvation in this. After all, aren't sermons supposed to be 'good news?' Has God really abandoned us to a world of such dishonesty and injustice? Is all we have left a Jeremiah-like response of mourning? 'The harvest is past, the summer is ended, and we are not saved.' And if we are not saved, what in the world are we doing here this Sunday?

I wish I had a good answer to that question. I have no doubt that in the cross and resurrection of Jesus of Nazareth we are a people who have been constituted for God's salvation of God's creation. I believe that such a people is rightly called church. I believe, moreover, that such a people have been given the means to discover, even in our enslavement to the powers that rule this world, ways of being of service to one another as God's good people. I believe one of the ways we are of service to one another is by telling one another the truth. The truth that we are enjoying the results of injustice cannot be avoided. Moreover, I cannot even pretend that the knowledge of the truth that we are enjoying the fruits of injustice will save us. It's more likely to make us even less able to acknowledge who we are because we do not know what to do with that knowledge, the knowledge that we are a people who flourish because others do not.

Being generous with our wealth is a good. But our generosity will not save us. Rather what we must face is the only thing that can save us is that our God is a generous God who offers us forgiveness of our sins – sins that are all the more powerful because we cannot will our way out of them. We are caught, but God has freed us from our 'caughtness' through Jesus Christ and this church. God has made us part of God's very life through Word and Sacrament. Through Word and Sacrament let us be consumed as a people who are seldom captured by God's generosity. To be so consumed, after all, means that we have no reason to tell one another lies about our righteousness.

So our salvation begins with the confession of the sin of our dishonesty and in that confession we no longer need to pass on histories of righteousness that deny that we come from injustice. Let us therefore seek to be reconciled with ourselves and with our brothers and sisters, asking one another to help us understand what we are to do with the fact that we are wealthy, and yet still God's people. Our salvation is that God has given us one another and in that giving we discover that we are no longer slaves, but friends of one another and of God and perhaps even friends with those who suffer because we are wealthy. That does, indeed, seem to be 'good news.' Amen.

19

God's Grandeur

Genesis 28:10–19a ✤ Romans 8:12–25
Matthew 13:24–30, 36–43

Creation groans; creation is in travail, even bondage – these are strong images. Such images capture our imaginations even though we have no idea what they mean. Our temptation, that is, those of us shaped by the attempt to domesticate nature, is to think Paul must be referring to what we call 'the environmental crisis.' Nature, it turns out, is just so hard to control. The good we try to do here has terrible results there. It seemed like a good idea to build levees to protect the towns along the Mississippi. No one meant to flood the corn fields of Iowa, but then we had no idea it would rain that much. And then, of course, there is all that we still have not understood well enough to control – hurricanes, tornadoes – but we are working at being better predictors. So groaning, travailing, bondage must mean, 'nature's out of whack.' If nothing else, groaning refers to those scenes we sometimes see on television when nothing else is on – of a snake swallowing a rabbit.

This way of reading these images is as understandable as it is wrong. But why it is wrong also indicates the distance between the world we inhabit, the lives most of us live on a day-to-day basis, and how Paul understands our situation as Christians. Such a distance is suggested by our assumption that these images of creation in agony are about nature. We assume this even though the text says nothing about nature. Rather Paul speaks of creation, a creation that 'waits in eager longing for the revealing of the children of God.' I realize that many of you may well think I am making too much of what is just a semantic distinction. Is not nature but another way to talk about creation?

The answer is no, nature is not just another way to say creation; for while creation encompasses nature, when you say nature you have not said creation. That is particularly the case today among enlightened folk like you and me. For notice that the very terms I used above to describe 'the environmental crisis' presuppose that 'nature' is a problem for 'us.' Who is that 'us' who somehow presume to stand apart from nature? Does not that 'us' name those who assume they have become, or must become, their own creators?

Notice that in the passage we read from Romans, creation does not name a reality from which 'we' can distinguish ourselves. Rather Paul tells us that we too groan inwardly, waiting as we do for adoption, for the redemption of our bodies. From Paul's perspective everything, dust, trees, hurricanes, cats, cows, lions, bugs, and even 'us' are creation. There is no creation over which we are to exert control. Rather we are but part of God's creation, distinctive only to the extent God invites us to share God's enjoyment of creation.

Which is but a reminder how far we are from being able to acknowledge our existence as creatures. I know we think of ourselves as Christians, particularly in this place on Sunday morning, but we live our lives at best as deists. Deism was that peculiar philosophical development of recent centuries that only a fading Christianity could have produced. The founders of this country were more deist than Christian, believing as they did that God names that 'something' that must have started it all but left the hard work to us. For the deist God was and is that great watch-maker in the sky, or at least somewhere 'up there,' that put the watch in existence, wound it up, and expected us to do the rest. This view nicely comports with capitalist economies which thrive on the view that most human behavior can be predictive if everyone just thinks of themselves as arbitrary units of desire.

In such a deist world nature names all that which is dumb. 'Dumb' is another way of saying we need to find a way to subject nature to human interest. We even begin to think of our bodies as nature. We have thus come to view ourselves as minds that inhabit a rather complicated machine called body. Such mechanistic views of nature and our bodies not unexpectedly have produced romantic reactions. Accordingly, we hear a great deal about our need to respect 'mother earth' or the importance of 'getting in touch with our bodies.' Such romantic expressions can sound like a rediscovery of the importance of creation but I fear they are at best a pale reflection of the Christian doctrine of creation. A beautiful sunset, particularly in Texas, is wonderful. But such sunsets, even in Texas, are not in themselves a testimony to creation. Moreover, snakes do eat rabbits and, even more disturbing, the bodies with which we are supposed to get in touch are subject to sickness, wear out, and die.

Creation does not mean that in spite of everything nature is wonderful; rather, 'creation' means that all that is is because God would have it so. In the words of Gerard Manley Hopkins:

The world is charged with the grandeur of God.
   It will flame out, like shining from shook foil;
   It gathers to a greatness, like the ooze of oil
Crushed. Why do men then now not reck his rod?
Generations have trod, have trod, have trod;
   And all is seared with trade; bleared, smeared with toil;
   And wears man's smudge and shares man's smell: the soil
Is bare now, nor can foot feel, being shod.

And for all this, nature is never spent;
   There lives the dearest freshness deep down things;
And though the last lights off the black West went
   Oh, morning, at the brown brink eastward, springs
Because the Holy Ghost over the bent
   World broods with warm breast and with ah! bright wings.[1]

Being the clever people you are, you will have noticed that Hopkins speaks of nature, but here it is not dumb but rather 'never spent.' For that 'dearest freshness deep down things' is all creation's longing for its maker. Rocks, toads, cats, clouds, dirt, wolves, and yes, even you and me are constituted with desire for God our creator. Yet we groan in bondage to desires malformed by our sin, malformed by our refusal to acknowledge that we are creatures seeking as we do to be our own creators, to be in control, to turn creation into 'nature.' All creation is subject to futility. Having drunk Abel's blood and being drunk by such drink we, Cain's descendants, continue to live by violence. Not the least violence is our refusal to acknowledge that we and all that is are God's creation. We prefer that which is not us to be dumb, dull, nature.

Creation is not just another name for 'something had to start it all.' Rather creation is the doctrine by which we Christians indicate that 'from nothing,' that is, *ex nihilo*, God desired all that is to exist. 'From nothing' means God was under no necessity to create, but God created out of love all that is, and all that is is constituted by that love. For God did not create because God was lonely without us. God the Father, God the Son, God the Holy Spirit, the Trinity, is the God that created and continues to create not out of lack but out of the fullness of the love between the Father, the Son, and the Holy Spirit. That is the 'freshness deep down things,' from which all that is, including us, is created from God's love to love God. Such a creation can never be dead, charged as it is with God's grandeur.

Trinity is the story that all that is, including us, is part of God's story. We arrogantly believe that the mountains and the valleys would have no story if we did not name them, climb them, or live on them.

[1] 'God's Grandeur,' *Modern American and British Poetry*, edited by Louis Untermeyer (New York: Harcourt Brace, 1955), p. 429.

But as we learn Sunday after Sunday through our reading of the Psalms, the mountains, the valleys, the rocks and trees, are storied by God. Listen to Psalm 24:

> The earth is the Lord's and all
> that is in it,
> the world, and those who live
> in it;
> for he has founded it on the seas,
> and established it on the
> rivers.

The seas and the rivers, the mountains and the valleys, the lions and the sheep praise God and through their praise we learn to be a people of praise acknowledging that we are not our own creators. We learn the joy of being creatures who have nothing to do but rest in, enjoy, God's good creation. We call that rest: worship.

It is in worship that we learn to tell the story of creation as part of God's Trinitarian life. Thus Paul rightly appeals to creation as a way to help the church at Rome understand their suffering. They need to know where they are. They feel lost and suffer accordingly. Some are beginning to fall away, returning to past habits which seemed so natural when they were children of nature (or even 'by nature children of wrath,' Ephesians 2:3). Paul acknowledges their suffering, but observes that such suffering will not be worth comparing to the glory to be revealed. For he says that from the beginning all creation has been waiting, in eager longing no less, for you. In other words, creation is part of a larger eschatological drama. Creation has an end and, lo and behold, Paul says, 'You are it.'

In the face of that claim, I, for one, would not have blamed the church in Rome if they had thought Paul had gone around the bend. Here you are a struggling group of people, not quite Jews, not quite pagan, not quite anything, trying to figure out who you are as followers of Jesus. From the point of view of the makers and shakers of Roman society you just do not matter. Yet this guy Paul says you have the first fruits of the Spirit – the same Spirit that presided over creation and made you part of God's very life through baptism into Jesus' death and resurrection. If I had been there I can hear myself saying, 'I don't think so.'

But, of course, the truth is that I am and you are in the same position as the church of Rome. Believe it or not, we – that is, this rather modest group of people called Aldersgate United Methodist Church – are that for which all creation has been waiting. You may well think, 'I am not ready for this. I just thought I would come to church this morning. I might even play softball with the church team this afternoon. I have no ambitions to be the revelation of the beginning and end of all that is. Let's go back to the Gospel text about the good seed and the weeds because given all this stuff about groaning I think I would just as soon be a weed. Being a weed at least seems to have a ring of humility to it.'

I am afraid, however, that we cannot get out of being God's people so easily. We do not get to resign. The God who has created out of love has promised to use even our unfaithfulness so that the world may know that God has made it possible for us to live at peace with God's creation. Jacob-like we must acknowledge that the Lord is in this place and it is the same Lord that brought into existence all that is. God's world is a storied world, a world with a beginning and an end. Our God is no absent deity that got it started and since then has not bothered to get involved again. Rather our God, the Triune One, remains present to us as only a lover can be present to the one they love.

That God is so present is why we, the first born of the new creation, are known as a people who have learned how to wait. We live by hope and so living can patiently tarry in a world that lives without hope, or worse, lives by a distorted hope in our ability to become our own creation. In such a hopeless world, a world that would turn God's creation into nature, we, Aldersgate United Methodist Church in Chapel Hill, North Carolina, become part of God's mighty company across time and space so that the world may know that we are creatures of a gracious and patient God. Is it any wonder that such a people, Sunday after Sunday, hopefully pray 'Christ has died, Christ is risen, Christ will come again?' knowing as we do that in Jesus' death and resurrection we have become the freshness of God's 'deep down?'

20

On Not Holding On
or
Witnessing the Resurrection

Acts 10:34–43 ✤ 1 Corinthians 15:1–11 ✤ John 20:1–18

They rush to the tomb. It is empty. Then we are told the disciples returned home. Returned home! How odd. They seem almost as stupid as those two in the Gospel of Luke who say they heard Jesus has risen from the dead yet they are out there on the Emmaus road leaving Jerusalem. Strange behavior to be sure. You have to wonder what the disciples talked about when they got home. How could people as dull as the disciples have ever come up with something like the resurrection?

I suspect we think it must have gone something like this. They begin to talk with one another about their time with Jesus. 'Was it not exciting? He was really something. Do you remember how he cleansed the temple? Strong stuff. And then there were all those miracles. Raised Lazarus no less. Moreover his teachings were so insightful. Really gave you something to chew on. Just thinking about it makes you feel like he is still among us. Yes, by God, it is like he is really here. Why I believe if we just remember hard enough he will still be here. My God, if we do not forget him it will be like he is still alive.'

I say we are tempted to think this kind of conversation happened because, like the disciples, we would like to think that resurrection does not mean our world has been turned upside down. We would like to celebrate Jesus' 'resurrection' and go on living within the presupposition and habits that sustain our lives. That is why we are tempted to try to 'explain' the resurrection. Our explanations are the way we, like Mary Magdalene, try to 'hold on' to Jesus.

But Jesus refuses to let us hold on. He just will not submit to our explanations of the resurrection. For as our Scriptures for today make clear, we cannot explain the resurrection. The resurrection explains us. For if God did not raise Jesus on the third day then our existence as church, the facts that we gathered here last night and this morning are unintelligible. This is about God. The reason we know that Jesus is very God and very man is that Jesus could not have raised himself

259

from the dead. God raised Jesus from the dead. This is not the resuscitation of a corpse. Jesus raised Lazarus from the dead, but Lazarus was still to die. Jesus lives with God.

Resurrection cannot, therefore, be a symbol for the renewal of life, even the renewal of life in the spring. Remember for many Christians Easter comes during winter or autumn. The resurrection is not butterflies breaking from their cocoons. No, the resurrection is God raising this man Jesus, God's very Son, from the dead. This is Jesus who after the resurrection eats and drinks with Peter and the disciples. You do not eat and drink with a symbol. Jesus, raised by God from the dead, is the same Jesus that called disciples, entered Jerusalem, and was crucified.

That Jesus is the one raised from the dead does not require explanation. Rather Jesus raised requires witnesses. But not just any witnesses. That is why in Acts Peter says that after God raised Jesus on the third day, 'God allowed him to appear, not to all the people but to us who were chosen by God as witnesses.' Paul is equally clear in 1 Corinthians that there was a definite order to Jesus' appearances. 'He appeared to Cephas, then to the twelve. Then he appeared to more than five hundred brothers and sisters at one time, most of whom are still alive, though some have died. Then he appeared to James, then to all the apostles. Last of all, as to one untimely born, he appeared also to me.'

Now I suppose what it means to be God is that you do not have to explain your guest list. But it is interesting to ask why these folks? Why Mary, Peter, the disciples, the five hundred, James and the apostles – and even Paul? I think quite simply it is these people that are able to recognize that the resurrected Christ is Jesus of Nazareth. Mary Magdalene, about whom we know very little in the Gospel of John except she was with Jesus' mother and the other Mary as witnesses to the crucifixion, thinks Jesus is the gardener until he says her name. She recognizes him instantly, becoming a witness who then witnesses to the disciples – 'I have seen the Lord.'

To witness the resurrection of Jesus it seems required that you are able to identify the one resurrected with the one, as Peter says in Acts, who came to the people of Israel preaching peace, who was baptized by John, anointed with the Holy Spirit, did good by healing all who are oppressed by the devil, and was put to death on a tree. He was, moreover, crucified because in his work, in his person, he was the Kingdom come. Resurrection does not mean that the crucifixion was some kind of misunderstanding that we can now leave behind because after all in the end everything came out all right. Crucifixion was not some kind of mistake, but rather the fearful result of Jesus' preaching, his miracles, his calling disciples, his very life. The resurrected Christ is the crucified Jesus.

But crucifixion names not failure, but triumph. That it is the crucified Messiah who is raised makes possible, as Peter says in Acts, that Jesus commanded that they 'preach to the people and to testify that he is the one ordained by God as judge of the living and the dead. All the prophets testify about him that every one who believes in him receives forgiveness of sins through his name.' Paul is equally insistent that 'Christ died for our sins in accordance with the scriptures,' thus making possible our faith in the one alone worthy of worship. Crucifixion is not some event in the past, but is now implanted in God's very heart.

Forgiveness, crucifixion, resurrection it seems are inseparably tied together, but it is important that we understand how they are so tied. I fear often that when we are told that through Jesus' resurrection we are offered forgiveness, we try to think of ourselves as particularly sinful in order to deserve such forgiveness. Ironically that is one of the ways we try to hold on to Jesus, making him submit to our understanding. No doubt we are sinners, but the forgiveness that God offers in the resurrection cannot be reduced to our pathetic sins. The forgiveness wrought through cross and resurrection is about the kingdom Jesus proclaimed and in proclaiming became. When we lose the vital connection between Jesus' life, crucifixion, and resurrection we are tempted to make Jesus' resurrection something less than the inauguration of God's kingdom of forgiveness.

God raised Jesus on the third day changing forever the way things are. No longer is it necessary to live as if there is no alternative to the powers that feed on our fears, our lusts, our hopelessness. There is an alternative kingdom to that rule of darkness – it is called forgiveness. To be forgiven is not to be told that no matter what we may have done or did not do, it is all right with God. No, to be forgiven is to be made part of a community, a history, that would not, could not exist if Jesus were not God's Christ, raised from the dead. To be forgiven means that we are now, through our baptism, given names, names that make it possible for Jesus to call us to recognition.

This is the miracle we celebrate today. This is the miracle we are today. Like Paul we were not followers of Jesus prior to the resurrection. Yet by God's grace we have been made witnesses to the resurrection. We know it is the resurrected Jesus, moreover, because we have been following him all year. We have waited for the birth, celebrated that birth, been baptized with him, heard him teach, marveled at his miracles, entered Jerusalem, and witnessed his crucifixion. We have been able to do this because through Jesus' resurrection we have been made witnesses, we have been made God's church.

We have been made such through this resurrection meal so that the world may know there is an alternative to the kingdoms built on death and destruction. In this meal we continue to eat and drink with our bodily Lord who came preaching peace. That Jesus is the resurrected Lord makes it possible for Paula to be our priest, representing Christ for us, offering Christ's invitation to enjoy this meal he alone could make possible. That Jesus is the resurrected Lord means in our eating and drinking we become for the world part of God's very life for the world. What a privilege. What a wonder. He is risen! He is risen indeed! Come let us eat and drink with our lively Lord who by resisting our grasp holds us fast in God's very life.

Index

Agency
  as naming 93–103
Allred, Susan xi, 161–63,
  168–73
Aquinas, Thomas 4n, 26–27,
  39–58, 95, 117n
Aristotle 23n, 27, 40–41, 50n,
  95, 116
Asad, Talal 213n
Augustine 11, 24–25, 47, 59,
  63–66
Ayers, Chris 157n

Bader-Saye, Scott 2n, 36n
Bailie, Gil 11n
Barron, Robert 41n
Barth, Karl 2–3, 4n, 19–23,
  30–35, 37–42, 64
Bauerschmidt, Frederick 53n
Bellarmine, Robert 64
Berry, Wendell 85–86n, 118n,
  150–51n
Berube, Michael 145–47,
  149–50
Biggar, Nigel 33n, 37
Body
  as sacrifice 21–22
  and Paul 80–84
  and illness 84–91
Bonhoeffer, Dietrich 35
Bottum, J. 191–92n
Bourdieu, Pierre 85n
Boyle, Leonard 26n

Bromiley, Geoffrey 140n
Brueggemann, Walter 57n
Buchan, John xii
Burrell, David 9, 39n, 42n,
  109, 111
Burtchaell, James 179–81
Bynum, Caroline Walker
  78–79n, 165n

Calvin, John 27–28, 51–52n
Cannon, William 124n
Cavanaugh, William 29n
Christ
  as God's dominion 45
  and the disunion of the
    Church 241–44
  and peace 245–48
  and the resurrection 259–62
Church
  as eschatological necessity 45
  as body chosen by God
    56–59
  as disciplined body of
    disciples 77–91
  local church as God's
    church 164–73
  as requiring enemies
    191–200
Cloutier, David xii
Creation
  Kant's account of 148–52
  Vanier's account of 152–56
  as God's desire 253–58

Day, Dorothy 35
Descartes, René 80–81, 98
Diggins, John Patrick 204n
Djerassi, Carl 9n
Donagan, Alan 46–47
Dunne, Joseph 7n, 98, 101n
Durkheim, Emile 37–38

Edwards, James 196–98, 243
Edwards, Jonathan and Sarah 35
Elshtain, Jean 9
Endo, Shusaku 72n
Ethics (Moral Theology)
  taught in liturgy 11
  Roman Catholic moral theology 11, 108–17
  and doctrine 19–20
  and Christian living 19–36
  as a problem of modernity 29–36
  against 'bottom up' ethics 37–43, 54–59
  and homosexuality 105–08
  as Christian fanaticism 177–78
  as inseparable from theology 201–05
  applied ethics 212–13

Farley, Edward 208n
Fergusson, David xii, 5n
Feuerbach, Ludwig 37–38
Fish, Stanley 100n, 229–30
Fodor, James xii, 9, 36n, 45n
Fodor, Janine 61n
Foucault, Michel 61, 96, 106, 145, 149
Fowl, Stephen 69, 71
Frank, Arthur 80, 84–90
Freedman, Sarah xii
Frei, Hans 31n
Freud, Sigmund 98

Friendship
  and the Gospel xi
  as a virtue and practice 117–21
  with the mentally handicapped 152–56
  as God's gift 249–52

Gallagher, John A. 25n
Gerrish, Brian 206n
Gilbert, Paula xi, 161–63
God
  as Trinity 2, 205
  Aquinas and Barth's account of 37–43
  in modernity and postmodernity 191–92
  as making a difference in theology 214–17
  and deism 254
Graham, Billy 157
Green, Garrett 4
Gustafson, James 32, 66, 93–96, 212–13

Habermas, Jürgen 145–46
Hadot, Pierre 23n
Hall, Pamela 48n, 55n, 74n
Hartle, Ann 97–98
Harvey, Van 206–08
Hays, Richard 21, 22n
Heilke, Thomas 188n
Hibbs, Thomas 41n
Hicks, Edward 246
History
  as ghostly presence 67
  as God's story 192
  Rauschenbusch's account of 209–12
  as 'slaughter-bench' 250
Hobbes, Thomas 98
Holiness
  sanctification in truth 4–5
  spiritualized in modernity 89–91

Holiness (*continued*)
  Wesley's account of
    stages 123–29
  Law's account of
    journey 130–42
Hopkins, Gerard Manley 231,
  247–48, 254–55
Huebner, Chris xii
Hunsinger, George 3n
Hütter, Reinhard 47n, 50n

Inchausti, Robert 157n
Israel
  as necessary part of Christian
    narrative 67
  terrorism and war 180
  and Protestant
    distortions 244
  and Jewish/Christian
    relations 246–48

Jameson, Frederick 197n
Janssens, Louis 110
Jenson, Robert 2n, 9, 192n,
  239n
Johnson, Kelly xii, 162n
Johnson, Samuel 132–33n,
  139n
Jones, Gregory xii, 9, 35n, 36n,
  45n, 73n, 103n

Kant, Immanuel 29–31, 148–51
Katongole, Emmanuel 188–89
Keane, Philip 107n
Kerr, Fergus 40n
Kitagawa, Joseph 211–12n
Kuklick, Bruce 208n

Lash, Nicholas 9
Law, William 10, 128–42
Lentricchia, Frank 194
Lindbeck, George 50, 51n, 239
Lindstrom, Harold 126n, 128n
Long, Steve 64
Luther, Martin 27–28, 43–45,
  49–59

Macaulay, Rose 71n
MacIntyre, Alasdair 27n, 53n,
  55–56, 66n, 95–96, 99n,
  101, 113–14, 126–27,
  151n, 183–90, 224–25,
  236–37
Macmurray, John 103
Mahoney, John 25n
Marsden, George 207n
Marshall, Bruce 2n, 5n
Martin, Dale 80–84
Marx, Karl 98
Matzko, David McCarthy 12n,
  99
McCabe, Herbert 48n, 54–56
McClendon, James 6n, 9, 22n,
  35–36, 46n, 70, 73
McCormack, Bruce 39n
McCormick, Richard 109–10
Meilaender, Gilbert 12n, 127
Milbank, John 9, 20n, 39–40,
  58–59, 68–69
Milton, John 61
Murphy, Nancey 9

Nature
  as graced 13
  intelligible without grace
    44–45
Neibuhr, H. Richard 32,
  93–94, 96, 158–160
Niebuhr, Reinhold 32, 57n, 64,
  66, 68, 194, 196, 202, 239
Nietzsche, Friedrich W. 96
Non-violence 179–90
  Christians at war with the
    world 194–200
  in God's peace 245–48
Nussbaum, Abraham xii
Nussbaum, Martha 66

Orsi, Robert 216–17
Outler, Albert 77

Pennington, Isaac xii
Pinches, Charles 56n

Practices
  and the Decalogue 46n
  and preaching 235–40

Quirk, Michael 119n

Rahner, Karl 64
Ramsey, Paul 32, 180–81
Rauschenbusch, Walter
  199–200, 209–12
Rawls, John 145–46
Rhonheimer, Martin 111–16
Ricœur, Paul 88
Rogers, Eugene 9, 13n, 39–42
Rorty, Richard 97
Rousseau, Jean-Jacques 97–98
Rubin, Miri 163n

Schleiermacher, Friedrich
  30–31, 33, 66, 208
Schweiker, William 101n
Scripture
  and ethics 21–23
  for Aquinas and Barth 41n
Self
  and the body 77–80
  modern, postmodern and
    Christian accounts of
    94–103
Selling, Joseph 109–10
Shuman, Joel xii
Sin
  and law and grace 27–28
  in recent theology 61–69
  and law 73–74
Soulen, R. Kendall 2n
Stackhouse, Max 181–83,
  187–90
Stubbs, David xii
Suhard, Cardinal 38

Tanner, Kathryn 65n, 159n
Taylor, Charles 99n
Tertullian 23
Theology 1–8
  as a curiosity 206–14

Theologians
  as speakers of the faith 6–7
  as bricklayers 9
  as church members 157–64
  in modernity and
    postmodernity 191–200
Tillich, Paul 57n, 194, 239
Torrance, Iain xii, 43n
Torrance, Morag xii
Torrance, Thomas F. 43n
Troeltsch, Ernst 22n, 208–11
Truth
  and sanctification 11
  and holiness 44
  and confession of sins 69–74

University
  constraints of 3
  and Christian theology
    31–32
  and the loss of theology
    201–18
  and academic freedom
    219–21
  determined by capitalism
    222–26
  and the study of beauty
    227–31

Vanier, Jean 10, 143–44, 148,
  152–56
Virtue
  and Aquinas 48n
  and character 236
von Balthasar, Hans Urs 4n

Wadell, Paul 116
Wainwright, Geoffrey 77n
Wannenwetsch, Berd 51n,
  56n
Weaver, Denny 196n
Webb-Mitchell, Brett 154n
Webster, John 33
Wesley, John 77–78, 123–29
Wilken, Robert 23n

Will, Frederick 189n
Williams, Raymond 159–60n
Williams, Robert 63–69, 73
Williams, Rowan 35–36
Willimon, Will 8n, 167
Wittgenstein, Ludwig 8
Woodward, Kenneth 235

Worship
   discovering God in 10–11
   as declaration of faith 48

Yeago, David 167n
Yoder, John Howard 9, 188n
Yordy, Laura xii